How To Protect
Your Creative Work

How To Protect Your Creative Work

All You Need To Know About Copyright

DAVID A. WEINSTEIN

Library of Congress Cataloging in Publication Data:

Weinstein, David A.
  How To Protect Your Creative Work: All You Need To Know About Copyright.

  Bibliography: p.
  Includes index.
  1. Copyright—United States—Popular works.

I. Title.
KF2995.W44 1987   346.7304′82   87-2101
ISBN 0-471-85270-8   347.306482
ISBN 0-471-85269-4 (pbk.)

Printed in the United States of America

10 9 8 7 6 5 4 3 2

To Gayle,
whose quest for learning inspires everyone

and to Lisa, Stacy, and Coby,
for their recognition of and willingness to support
the needs of others

Preface

Copyright law applies to a wide variety of things created and used by a very large segment of our society, ranging from consumers to business people. Yet my 17 years of experience in practicing copyright law have shown me that most people are unaware that what they create can be protected, have no idea how to gain protection, and rarely consider that copying someone else's material might be illegal.

Consequently, I concluded that there was a need for a book to help the general population easily recognize what can be protected, learn how to obtain the protection available under copyright law, and gain a fundamental understanding of this law. This book is the result, and it is my hope that it will prove valuable to those who create and use material in their pastime, as well as to those who do so professionally.

This book is not intended to be read in sequence. It is designed to be used as a source of information on copyright law which can be referred to when a specific question is raised regarding the application of this law to a given set of facts. The first few chapters contain basic information that will enable the reader to know what can be protected under copyright law, who is entitled to copyright protection, and what copyright protection means. Subsequent chapters discuss which uses of copyrighted material are and are not permissible, the registration process, transferring copyright ownership, licensing, and infringement.

David A. Weinstein

Denver, Colorado
April 1987

Contents

1 Everyone Can Protect Something   **1**

Protection Is Available to Everyone   1
Learn the Basics   2
Things that Can Be Protected   2
Chapter Summary   3

2 Copyright, Trademark, and Patent Rights Are not the Same   **4**

Copyright Denotes Specific Legal Rights for Literary, Musical,
and Audiovisual Material   5
A Patent Is a Grant of Rights by the Federal Government for
Inventions   6
A Trademark Is a Word, Name, or Symbol Used to Identify
Products and Services   7
The Right of Publicity Protects an Individual's Name and Image   9
Constitutional Basis for Copyright Protection   10
Chapter Summary   11

3 A Wide Range of Things Can Be Protected   **13**

Categories of Protectible Subject Matter   13
Original Creative Efforts Must Be Embodied in a Physical Object   16
Creator's Nationality and the Country of First Publication   18
Musical Works, Dramatic Works, Pantomimes, and Choreographic
Works   19
Literary Works   20
Pictorial, Graphic, and Sculptural Works   20
Audiovisual Works and Motion Pictures   22
Sound Recordings   23

Compilations and Derivative Works 24
Obscene Material 28
Chapter Summary 28

4 Some Things Cannot Be Protected 30

Public Domain Material 30
Works Lacking Sufficient Originality 31
U.S. Government Works 32
Ideas, Procedures, and Systems 33
Facts, Basic Plots, Thematic Concepts, and Scènes Á Faire 34
Chapter Summary 35

5 How to Determine Who Is a Copyright Owner 36

The First Owner 36
Collaborative Creations—Joint Ownership 37
"Works Made for Hire" 39
Chapter Summary 44

6 Five Exclusive Rights are Associated with a Work 46

Ownership of Rights Is Distinct from Ownership of Object 47
A Copyright Owner's Exclusive Rights 47
The Right To Reproduce 50
The Right To Prepare Derivative Works 53
The Right To Distribute Copies or Phonorecords Publicly 54
The Right To Perform Publicly 59
The Right To Display Publicly 62
Chapter Summary 64

7 Fair Use 66

Balancing Conflicting Interests 67
Guidelines for Determining Fair Use 67
Factors to Be Considered 68
Examples of Fair Uses and Uses that Are Not Fair 76
Chapter Summary 77

8 Limitations on Rights 78

Statutory Limitations 79
Limitations on Certain Performances and Displays 80
Limitations on the Exclusive Rights in Sound Recordings 88

Limitations on Rights in Pictorial, Graphic, and Sculptural Works   89
Reproduction by Libraries and Archives   90
Secondary Transmissions   92
Ephemeral Recordings   94
Noncommercial Educational Broadcasting   95
The Making of Copies or Adaptations of Computer Programs   96
Chapter Summary   97

9   **Protection Lasts for a Long Time**   **99**

Maximum Periods of Protection   100
Factors Affecting Applicable Maximum Period   101
Life of the Creator Plus 50 Years   103
Seventy-Five Years from the Year of Publication   106
One Hundred Years from the Year of Creation   111
Unpublished Works Not Registered as of January 1, 1978   114
Chapter Summary   115

10 **Copyright Notice**   **116**

Notice Requirements Prior to January 1, 1978   116
Misleading Effect of the Copyright Notice   117
Form of the Copyright Notice   118
Copies or Phonorecords Incorporating U.S. Government Works   124
Including Additional Information In or Around a Notice   125
Chapter Summary   125

11 **What Happens if Copyright Notice Is Incorrect or not Used**   **127**

Location and Position of Copyright Notice   127
Omission of Copyright Notice   132
Omission of the Owner's Name or Year of Publication   136
Errors in the Notice   136
Effect of Omission of Notice on Innocent Infringers   138
Removal of Notice Without Authorization   138
Penalties for Removal of Copyright Notice   139
Fraudulent Use of Copyright Notice   139
Chapter Summary   139

12 **What Is Copyright Registration?**   **141**

Registration Occurs After Rights Are Acquired   141
Mandatory Deposit of Copies   142
Registration May Be Required   142

When Registration Can Occur   142
Persons Entitled to Register an Ownership Claim   143
Only One Basic Registration Is Permitted   144
Registration in the Name of the Copyright Claimant   145
Compelling Reasons to Register   145
Investigating the Copyright Status of a Work   149
Chapter Summary   151

13 How To Register a Work   **152**

Choosing the Proper Form To Use   152
Coverage of Each Form   153
Information that Must Be Included in the Copyright Application   158
Copies or Phonorecords Must Accompany the Application   160
Return and Disposition of Copies Deposited   167
Reproductions of Deposited Copies and Phonorecords Can Be
Obtained   168
Filing Fees for Registration   169
Special Handling to Expedite Registration   170
Examination of the Application   170
Certificate of Registration   172
Chapter Summary   172

14 Depositing Copies with the Library of Congress   **173**

Number of Copies To Be Deposited and by Whom   174
Deposited Copies May Be Used for Registration   175
No Form To File or Fee To Pay   175
Nature of Copies Required To Be Deposited   176
Exempt Categories of Material   177
Unpublished Transmission Programs   178
Chapter Summary   179

15 Transferring Copyright Ownership   **180**

Ownership of Rights Distinct from Ownership of a Copy   181
Transfer of Rights Distinct from Transfer of Copies or
Phonorecords   182
Each Right Separately Transferable   182
What Constitutes a Transfer of Ownership   184
What Must Be Done To Transfer Rights Validly   186
Rights Acquired By Transferees and Licensees   188
Chapter Summary   190

16   Recording Transfers of Copyright Ownership   191

Prerequisite to Instituting an Infringement Suit   191
Recording Is a Condition of Giving Constructive Notice   192
Recordation May Defeat a Complete Defense To Infringement   193
Recordation Gives Priority to the Transfer that Occurs First   193
An Earlier Transfer May Defeat a Later One   195
A Nonexclusive License Can Prevail Over a Conflicting Transfer   196
What Should Be Submitted to the Copyright Office   196
Chapter Summary   198

17   How to Recover Ownership of Transferred Rights   199

Rights Recovery Prior to 1976 Act   200
Right To Terminate Grants Made After January 1, 1978   201
Exceptions to the Right of Termination   202
Persons Entitled To Exercise the Right   203
Works Created By Two or More Creators   204
The Procedure To Follow to Exercise the Right   205
When a Notice of Termination Can Be Served   205
When a Grant May Be Terminated   206
Actual Date of Termination   206
The Right of Termination Cannot Be Waived or Contracted Away   207
Failure To Give a Notice of Termination   207
The Right To Recover Rights for the Entire Renewal Term   208
The Right To Terminate Grants Made Before January 1, 1978
Covering the Extended Renewal Term   208
What Happens When Rights Are Recovered   211
Chapter Summary   215

18   Voluntary Copyright Licenses   217

Negotiated Copyright Licenses   218
A License Agreement Should Be Written   219
An Exclusive License Should Be Recorded   220
Exclusive Licensee May Be Able to Register Licensed Work   221
Licensee's Name Should Not Appear in the Copyright Notice   221
Exclusive Licensee Can Institute an Infringement Action   221
Licenses Are Subject to the Right of Termination   222
Representative Provisions for Negotiated Licenses   222
Chapter Summary   224

19 Compulsory Copyright Licenses   **226**

Background of Compulsory Licensing   227
Compulsory License for Making and Distributing Phonorecords
Embodying Nondramatic Musical Works   229
Compulsory License for the Public Performance of Nondramatic
Musical Works on Coin-Operated Phonorecord Players
(Jukeboxes)   233
Compulsory License for Secondary Transmission by Cable
Systems   235
Compulsory License for Noncommercial Educational
Broadcasting   238
Copyright Royalty Tribunal   240
Chapter Summary   241

20 What Constitutes Copyright Infringement   **242**

Who is Liable for Infringement?   242
Absence of Profit Motive, Making a Small Number of Copies, or
Copying Small Portions   244
Permitting or Causing Someone Else to Infringe   244
What Must Be Shown to Prove Infringement   247
Criminal Offenses   252
Defenses to Infringement   252
Chapter Summary   253

21 How to Institute an Infringement Action   **254**

Who Has a Right To Institute an Action   254
Infringed Work Must Be Registered   256
All Ownership Transfer Documents Must Be Recorded   257
Federal District Courts Have Exclusive Jurisdiction   258
Action Must Be Commenced Within a Specific Time Period   259
Giving Notice of an Infringement Action   260
Chapter Summary   260

22 Remedies for Infringement   **261**

Injunctive Relief   261
Impounding, Destruction, or Disposition of Infringing Copies or
Phonorecords   263
Money Damage Awards   264
Costs of the Action and Attorney's Fees   267

Criminal Penalties	268
Chapter Summary	269

23   Income Tax Considerations   **271**

Profit-Generating Activities	271
Capitalized Expenses	273
Deductible Expenses	273
Capital Gain Income	274
Ordinary Income	275
Chapter Summary	275

Appendix A   Agreements   **276**

Agreement for Commissioned Work	276
Agreement for Employee To Be Owner of Rights In a Work	278
Assignment of Copyright	278
Collaboration Agreement	279
Copyright License	283

Appendix B   Guidelines   **288**

Guidelines for Classroom Copying in Not-For-Profit Educational Institutions With Respect to Books and Periodicals	288
Guidelines for Educational Uses of Music	290
Photocopying—Interlibrary Arrangements	291
"Best Edition" of Published Copyrighted Works for the Collections of the Library of Congress	293

Appendix C   Copyright Forms   **298**

Glossary   **318**

Index   **336**

How To Protect
Your Creative Work

1

Everyone Can Protect Something

After reading this book, I hope the readers will better appreciate the scope and value of copyright protection. The copyright law offers the potential for everyone to reap greater benefits from things that are created and used. Individuals who are regularly engaged in activities involving the creation and use of material will see how important a role copyright law plays in their careers and business. The livelihoods of many people are dependent on the protection copyright law affords them to control the use of their material.

PROTECTION IS AVAILABLE TO EVERYONE

Everyone can take advantage of what copyright law has to offer. It provides benefits to a wide range of people and businesses that create tangible things. These benefits are available without regard to whether material is created on a professional basis, for profit or nonprofit, or soley for the sheer enjoyment of it.

Writers, poets, artists, composers, musicians, photographers, architects, software programmers, actors, actresses, entertainers, film directors and editors, camera technicians, as well as record producers and recording engineers represent the type of people who should be using copyright law to protect what they create. In addition, under this law individuals and businesses whose work is in the fields of advertising, television, radio, and the print media can protect what they create.

LEARN THE BASICS

It will take only a few hours or so to learn enough about copyright law to gain a good working knowledge of what it protects, how protection can be obtained, and how infringement of rights belonging to others may be avoided. There are some fundamental rules to learn and follow but none are complex nor difficult to apply and most are easy to remember. For example, to acquire valuable rights, all a person has to do is create material eligible for copyright protection.

Learning about copyright law and protection involves becoming familiar with a number of key words used in reference to copyright law, related areas of law, accepted procedures, legal relationships, and ownership rights. Most likely they have been heard or used at one time or another, but accuracy is required when referring to copyright law or the procedures, relationships, and rights discussed in this book.

The legal meanings of words like copyright, trademark, patent, registration, work, royalty, license, consent, release, and assignment are specific. The proper use of phrases such as work made for hire, Copyright Office, and Registered United States Patent & Trademark Office, and of symbols like ©, ™, and ® is critical to clear communication.

Failing to learn the basics can be costly. Potentially valuable rights may be lost and those belonging to others may be unknowingly violated.

THINGS THAT CAN BE PROTECTED

The variety of material that can be protected under copyright law is very broad. It includes materials that can be seen as well as materials that can be heard. It may be in the form of literary material such as poetry, books, plays, magazines, bulletins, newsletters, personal and business correspondence, speeches, scripts, research reports, computer programs, product packaging, promotional matter, and advertising copy. Or, it may be in the form of motion pictures, photographs, audiovisual programs, music, art, sculpture, cartoon strips, scientific and technical drawings such as architects' plans, maps, dolls, and sounds.

Individuals such as playwright Neil Simon, writer James Michener, artist Andy Warhol, columnist Andy Rooney, composer Burt Bacharach, performer Michael Jackson, designer Yves St. Laurent, and model Cheryl Tiegs use the copyright law skillfully to enhance the value of their various works. Companies like McDonald's Corp., General Foods, IBM, Doyle Dane Bernbach (Advertising), Warner Brothers, Universal Studios, and Walt Disney Productions also rely on copyright law to protect what they create.

For example, Neil Simon is able to exercise control over the performance of his plays. Cheryl Tiegs and Michael Jackson have a right to determine how pictures of them may be used. Walt Disney Productions has the authority to regulate reproduction of Mickey Mouse, Donald Duck, and other characters. Universal Studios can control the reproduction of the Star Wars characters as well as showings of that motion picture, and IBM can preclude others from reproducing its software programs.

Copyright law gives individuals and companies the exclusive rights to reproduce, alter, publicly perform, publicly display, and distribute material under their control. Individuals and companies can, therefore, demand to be paid by others who desire to use their copyrighted material. The monetary value of these rights is relative to the demand for the use of the protected works. It has been reported, for instance, that sales of products featuring Star Wars characters have exceeded $1.5 billion. CTW Products earns millions of dollars annually from reproduction by others of "Sesame Street" characters appearing on toys, clothes, linens, puzzles, and other merchandise. Yves St. Laurent is reputed to make over $35 million annually from licenses covering his creations. Franklin Computer agreed to pay Apple Computer $2.5 million in settlement of a copyright infringement lawsuit involving Franklin's unauthorized reproduction of Apple's software.

Although a good idea may have been the basis for individuals and companies (like those noted) to achieve success, *copyright law does not protect ideas*. It protects only the expression of an idea as it is manifested in a tangible work such as those discussed previously.

The concept that ideas can be protected by copyright law is a common fallacy and so is the concept that copyright law is the basis for protecting brand names, book titles, and the names of motion pictures. Therefore, before proceeding with a detailed discussion of copyright law, what it covers, and how protection can be obtained, other areas of law sometimes confused with it will be briefly described in Chapter 2.

CHAPTER SUMMARY

- Copyright law covers a wide variety of material.
- Personal and business correspondence, speeches, magazine articles, books, music, art, fabric and upholstery designs, architectural drawings, cartoons, motion pictures, photography, sounds, computer programs, advertising copy, and product labeling can be protected.
- Copyright protection differs from the kind of protection for other subject matter under trademark and patent law.

2
Copyright, Trademark, and Patent Rights Are Not the Same

The words copyright, trademark, and patent are frequently misused. A recent meeting with a new client typifies their misuse. The client wanted to know how he could protect the brand name of a line of greeting cards he had created and planned to market. He proposed using the picture of a well-known athlete on each. He asked how he could "patent" the cards as well as his idea for their content. He wanted to prevent others from producing similar cards and using his idea.

Although he did not know it, my client incorrectly used the word *patent* to describe the type of protection he wanted to secure. The terms "patent," "copyright," and "trademark" refer to a specific kind of legal protection; each is distinguishable from the other. In his case, patent protection was not applicable.

I explained that the protection for the *name* of his line of greeting cards would fall under trademark law. This area of law is applicable to brand names and designs used to distinguish products and services from each other. For example, the trademark Chevrolet is used to identify an automobile manufactured by General Motors Corp. and the trademark Plymouth is used to identify an automobile manufactured by the Chrysler Corp.

The *artwork* for my client's greeting cards would be protected by copyright law. This area of law protects works of art, photographs, books, music, and many other things.

Use of the picture of the athlete on the greeting cards would not be permissible without obtaining the athlete's permission. The right of publicity gives celebrities and others the authority to exercise control over who may use their names and pictures commercially.

My client's *idea*, however, could not be copyrighted, trademarked, or patented. Patent protection is available for inventions covering chemical compounds, electrical processes, mechanical articles, designs of mechanical articles, and horticultural plants.

At the conclusion of our meeting, my client understood that copyright, trademark, patent, and right of publicity denote specific but separate fields in the law. Each covers distinct legal rights and applies to subject matter peculiar to each just as classical, jazz, and folk are used to designate different kinds of music.

COPYRIGHT DENOTES SPECIFIC LEGAL RIGHTS FOR LITERARY, MUSICAL, AND AUDIOVISUAL MATERIAL

The word "copyright" is the name of a specific area of law and is a word used to indicate the rights in material that can be protected under this area of law. It is not used to designate a physical object. The phrases "copyright ownership" and "copyright owner" refer to ownership of rights recognized by this area of law. The phrase "copyright protection" as well as the word "copyright" itself generically refer to the type of legal protection available to a copyright owner by virtue of the Copyright Act of 1976 (the "1976 Act"). "Copyrightable works" generically describes the subject matter that can be protected by copyright law.

Copyright law provides for the protection of artistic, literary, musical, dramatic, and audiovisual creations as incorporated in such things as books, phonograph records, motion pictures, videocassettes, photographs, and paintings. It also regulates the use of such material by someone other than the copyright owner. The unauthorized use of copyrighted material may be an infringement of the copyright owner's rights.

Copyright protection is available as long as the creator of eligible subject matter has not copied material created by another person. That is, a person may protect material he or she creates if it is original in the sense of not being produced as a result of copying. It does not have to be unique or original in terms of being novel or brand new.

A copyright owner has five exclusive rights, which are the exclusive right to: (1) reproduce, (2) create variations of, (3) distribute publicly, (4) perform publicly, and (5) display the creative work publicly. These rights can last as long as the life of the creator plus 50 years following the creator's death.

The familiar copyright notice alerts us to claims to rights under copyright law. This notice consists of three components: (1) the symbol © (or word

Copyright, or abbreviation Copr.), followed by (2) a year date, and (3) a name. It is commonly used on the title page of a book, in the masthead of a magazine, and below the opening title at the beginning of a motion picture. Use of the notice is required by the 1976 Act to avoid losing protection for material distributed to the public.

Rights are automatically acquired by creating material eligible for copyright protection. There is no requirement that a governmental agency grant copyright protection. A claim of ownership of rights can be registered, if desired, with the U.S. Copyright Office, a federal agency within the Library of Congress, having offices only in Washington, DC. Registration involves paying a low fee and filing an application form obtainable from the U.S. Copyright Office.

A PATENT IS A GRANT OF RIGHTS BY THE FEDERAL GOVERNMENT FOR INVENTIONS

Patent serves as the name of a specific area of law. It is not used to designate a physical object. Rather, it is used to designate the rights in a physical object or industrial or technical process subject to protection under patent law. The phrases "patent ownership" and "patent owner" refer to ownership of those rights. The expression "patent protection" generically denotes the type of legal protection available to a patent owner by virtue of the Federal Patent Act. "Patented invention" describes an invention that is the subject of a patent grant by the federal government. A "patent grant" or "patent" is the limited monopoly applicable to an invention granted by the federal government.

Patent protection is available only for:

1. A new and useful industrial or technical process, machine, article of manufacture, or composition of matter (chemical compositions, mixtures of ingredients, or new chemical compounds), or any new and useful improvements for these items (35 U.S.C. 101).

2. A new, original, and ornamental design for an article of manufacture (35 U.S.C. 161)

3. Any distinct and new asexually reproduced variety of plant (35 U.S.C. 171).

To be eligible for a patent grant, the material must amount to an invention. That is, the person who devises the material must be the first to do so. Patent protection cannot be obtained for anything that is known or used by others in this country, protected by patent, or described in a printed publication in this or a foreign country. Patent protection cannot be obtained for small improvements that would be obvious to anyone with ordinary skill. Finally, patent protection cannot be obtained for anything that is first publicly used or on sale in this country one year or more prior to the date of filing of a patent application with the U.S. Patent & Trademark Office.

The owner of a patented invention has the exclusive right to preclude others from making, using, or selling the invention throughout the United States, its territories, and its possessions. This right can last for 17 years (for mechanical, electrical, chemical, and plant patents), or 3½, 7, or 14 years (for a design patent).

The word Patent (or abbreviation Pat.) followed by a series of numbers indicates that a patent grant is in effect. The improper use of this notice violates the law; offenders can be penalized. The notice "Patent Applied For" or "Patent Pending" simply means that a patent application has been filed; it carries no legal effect.

Patent protection is not available for an invention unless and until the U.S. Patent & Trademark Office issues a patent grant. Unlike copyright protection, only a governmental agency can grant patent rights.

Subject to a few exceptions, the first inventor is the only person entitled to apply for patent protection. The patent application must contain a detailed and precise description of the invention. While there is a prescribed format for the application, the government does not provide a form. The application is filed with the U.S. Patent & Trademark Office which is part of the Commerce Department and has offices only in Washington, DC.

The agency examines the application for compliance with certain legal requirements and reviews prior United States and foreign patents and literature to determine whether the invention is eligible for patent protection. If the invention is found to be allowable, the U.S. Patent & Trademark Office will grant patent rights (a patent) to the inventor, or his or her designee. Patent protection does not begin until the date the grant is given by the U.S. Patent & Trademark Office.

A TRADEMARK IS A WORD, NAME, OR SYMBOL USED TO IDENTIFY PRODUCTS AND SERVICES

The word "trademark" serves as the name of a specific area of law and is properly used to identify a particular thing. The phrases "trademark ownership" and "trademark owner" refer to ownership of a particular thing and the rights in it recognized by this area of law. The phrase "trademark protection" generically refers to the type of legal protection available to a trademark owner by virtue of a federal statute, a state law, common law, or all three.

A trademark is "any word, name, symbol, or device, or any combination of them used by a manufacturer or merchant to identify his products and distinguish them from those manufactured or sold by others (15 U.S.C. 1127)." A trademark may be referred to as a brand name. Service mark means any word, name, symbol, or device, or any combination of them "used in the sale or advertising of services to identify the services of one person and distinguish them from the services of others (15 U.S.C.)." Cheerios® is an example of a trademark used to identify a particular breakfast cereal marketed by General Mills, and McDonald's® is an example of a service mark used to identify restaurant services offered by McDonald's Corp.

To be eligible for trademark protection a word, name, or symbol should be distinctive. A word, name, or symbol that is generic with respect to a particular product or service cannot be protected as a trademark or service mark. For example, the word "table" cannot be protected as a trademark for tables.

A word, name, or symbol descriptive of a product or service, or of its ingredients, functions, or characteristics may be difficult to protect as a trademark. For example, "sticky" would be difficult to protect as a trademark for an adhesive tape product.

The owner of a trademark possesses the exclusive right to use it to identify particular products. This right includes the right to preclude others from using a confusingly similar mark to identify the same or similar products. This right lasts as long as a trademark is being used to identify a product or service.

The symbol ® is used to give notice that a trademark has been federally registered by the U.S. Patent & Trademark Office. Its use is required if a trademark has been registered. If it is not used many of the benefits of federal registration will be lost. This symbol should not be used in association with a trademark that is not registered with the U.S. Patent & Trademark Office.

The notice Registered United States Patent & Trademark Office or Reg. U.S. Pat. & Tm. Off. may be used in lieu of the ® symbol. If either of these phrases is used, it will usually be placed at a location somewhat remote from the trademark as it appears on labeling or in advertising material.

The symbol TM is used in close association with a trademark that has not been federally registered. There is no requirement to use it nor established rules prescribing the manner of its use. Nonetheless, this symbol is commonly used by many persons who wish to advise others of their claim of ownership rights to a trademark.

Rights in a trademark can be obtained by adopting and using it to identify a product or service. Accordingly, as a general rule, the person who first uses it is the person who acquires rights in it, at least in the geographic area where it is used. A person who creates a trademark but who does not use it to identify a product or service is not in a position to claim rights in it.

There is no need for the user of a trademark to obtain approval for its use by a government agency or to obtain a determination by such an agency that a word, name, or symbol is entitled to protection as a trademark. Further, it is not necessary to register a trademark to acquire rights in it or to protect it. However, in many instances federal registration of a trademark offers the owner many benefits, such as constructive notice of the owner's claim of exclusive rights.

No one governmental agency has exclusive jurisdiction over trademark subject matter, the rights associated with it, and the protection to which it is entitled. The federal government and the states can enact and enforce trademark laws. Presently, there are two systems in the United States under which trademark rights can be obtained and enforced. They are under (1) a federal statute and (2) law enunciated by court decisions (common law) and by virtue of state statutes.

The federal law, known as the Trademark Act of 1946 (Lanham Act), is administered by the U.S. Patent & Trademark Office. At the state level trademark matters are usually handled by the Office of the Secretary of State.

The existence of federal and state trademark protection does not seem to pose any significant problems since most state trademark laws are modeled on the federal law. As a result, there is a great deal of uniformity in trademark laws throughout this country including, among other things: what constitutes appropriate trademark subject matter, the rights attaching to it, and the available protection.

THE RIGHT OF PUBLICITY PROTECTS AN INDIVIDUAL'S NAME AND IMAGE

The phrase "right of publicity" refers to the kind of legal protection available to an individual with respect to his or her name as well as his or her physical features and characteristics. Most often, individuals who are entitled to rely on this right are those in the public spotlight, such as motion picture, television, and musical artists, models, sports figures, and other celebrities. These individuals acquire the right of publicity by virtue of their status as well-known persons and because they rely on and use their names, pictures, and/or talents as a means of earning a living.

The right of publicity gives an individual the right to preclude others from commercially using his or her name or picture without authorization. For example, Farrah Fawcett and Christie Brinkley have a right to determine who may feature their pictures on posters. And Johnny Carson has a right to object to the unauthorized use of his name to advertise and promote products.

Copyright protection is applicable to a picture of an individual possessing the right of publicity. And trademark protection can be obtained for the name of such an individual where his or her name is used to identify products and/or services. For example, a Farrah Fawcett poster can be protected by copyright law and the name Johnny Carson can be protected as a trademark when it is used to identify men's clothing.

There is no commonly used symbol or statutory notice to indicate that ownership of the right of publicity is claimed. Unlike claims to copyright, patent, and trademark rights, the failure to use a symbol or notice in connection with a claim of right of publicity ordinarily has no adverse effect on the rights of celebrities or their estates. However, if copyright protection is claimed for Elvis Presley statues, Christie Brinkley posters, or t-shirts featuring Bruce Springsteen's picture a copyright notice should be displayed. Similarly, if trademark rights are claimed to a picture or name and the trademark is federally registered, a trademark notice should be used on it.

The right of publicity is protected in a few states by specific statutes. In others protection has been developed through court decisions, also known as common law. Consequently, the protection given to this right varies from state to state, although the same theories for protecting it seem to be generally accepted.

CONSTITUTIONAL BASIS FOR COPYRIGHT PROTECTION

Currently, all rights and the kind of material that can be protected under the copyright and patent laws are governed exclusively by federal statutes. The 1976 Act and the Federal Patent Act provide that the federal government shall have the exclusive authority to designate the subject matter eligible for protection under them as well as the particular rights that can be acquired and how they can be protected. In addition, both provide that only the federal courts have the authority to interpret and enforce them.

The source of the federal government's authority with regard to the copyright and patent laws lies in Article 1, Section 8, Clause 8 of the Constitution:

> The Congress shall have the power to promote the Progress of Science and useful Arts by securing for limited Times to Authors and Inventors the exclusive Right to their respective Writings and Discoveries. . . .

Use of the words inventors and discoveries has been interpreted to mean that the federal government has authority to enact legislation to grant patent protection. Use of the words authors and writings is the basis for Congress's enactment of legislation granting copyright protection. These words have been construed by the courts broadly rather than literally.

For purposes of copyright law, the word "author" means a person who is an originator or creator of copyrightable material, whether literary or otherwise. It is used throughout the 1976 Act to designate the person who creates material eligible for protection and is the initial copyright owner. For the sake of clarity, I use the word "creator" throughout this book to refer to the originator of copyrightable material.

For purposes of copyright law the word "writings" means and includes any physical rendering of the fruits of creative, intellectual, or aesthetic labor. Accordingly, motion pictures, art, music, photographs, and literary material may be protected by copyright law. The word "works" is used, instead of "writings," throughout the 1976 Act and in this book as a generic term for material that possesses the potential for copyright protection.

CHAPTER SUMMARY

- The subject matter as well as the type of protection available under copyright, trademark, and patent laws are distinguishable.
- Specific symbols are used to indicate which area of law applies to a particular product.
- Copyright law protects literary material, music, art, motion pictures, and sounds.
- A copyright owner has the exclusive right to reproduce, create variations of, publicly perform and display, and distribute protected material.
- Copyright protection is a consequence of creating copyrightable material; it is not dependent on a governmental grant.
- Patent law protects inventions for new and useful industrial processes, machines, articles of manufacture, or compositions of matter, or any new and useful improvement of them. It also protects new, original, and ornamental designs for an article of manufacture and any distinct and new asexually reproduced variety of plant.
- A patent owner has the right to preclude others from making, using, or selling a patented invention.
- Patent protection is possible only by virtue of a U.S. Patent & Trademark Office grant.

- Trademark law protects a word, name, symbol, or combination of them used to identify and distinguish the products or services of one business from those of another.
- A trademark owner has the exclusive right to use the trademark to identify particular products or services.
- Trademark rights are a consequence of using a trademark; they are not based on a governmental grant.
- The right of publicity enables celebrities and individuals who are well-known to protect their names and images (pictures).
- A person who possesses the right of publicity can preclude others from commercially using his or her name or image.
- The right of publicity exists as a consequence of a person's status as a celebrity and, in some instances, is based on a state statute.

3
A Wide Range of Things Can be Protected

Copyright protection has not always been available for the kinds of things that are now covered by the 1976 Act. When Congress enacted the first federal copyright statute in 1790, it elected to grant protection only for three types of "writings," namely maps, charts, and books. At the time, Congress did not feel that other creative materials such as music, art, and plays were worthy of protection and, therefore, made no provision for their protection. However, slowly, over many years, the copyright law was amended and revised, resulting in additional material receiving statutory protection.

CATEGORIES OF PROTECTIBLE SUBJECT MATTER

Subject Matter Protected Under the 1909 Act

In 1802 prints were added as a new category of material eligible for protection, and in 1831 the law was again revised to cover musical compositions. Photographs and photographic negatives were added as a category in 1865 when Matthew Brady's pictures of the Civil War became widely known. In 1870, paintings, drawings, lithographs, statuary, and models or designs of fine art were included.

By 1909, eleven categories of material were protected:

1. Books
2. Periodicals
3. Lectures
4. Dramatic or dramatico-musical compositions
5. Musical compositions
6. Maps
7. Works of art and modes or designs for works of art
8. Reproductions of works of art
9. Drawings of a scientific or technical character
10. Photographs
11. Prints

In 1912 this number grew to thirteen with the addition of a category covering motion pictures. In 1917 another category was added covering sound recordings.

Subject Matter Protected Under the 1976 Act

In 1976 the copyright law was comprehensively revised, resulting in a reduction of the total number of categories of protectible material from thirteen to nine and the development of new criteria for properly classifying that material. This reduction was done to arrange related kinds of material together in broad groups to illustrate the types of material that may be protected.

Six broad categories were developed from the original thirteen and three additional ones were created, resulting in the following categories of protectible material under the 1976 Act:

1. Literary works
2. Musical works, including any accompanying words
3. Dramatic works, including any accompanying music
4. Pantomimes and choreographic works
5. Pictorial, graphic, and sculptural works
6. Motion pictures and other audiovisual works
7. Sound recordings

8. Compilations
9. Derivative works

Of the three new categories, pantomimes and choreography cover subject matter not protected previously. Material falling within the other two categories, namely, compilations and derivative works, consists of material assembled together in collections and/or variations of material found in the first seven categories. All of this material was protected under the 1909 Act but separate categories had not been established.

Criteria for Classifying Subject Matter. Under the 1976 Act material is classified on the basis of what it consists of—words, numbers, symbols, images, or sounds—rather than by the name commonly used to identify it: book, map, print, for instance. No longer does the physical form of creative material necessarily determine the category in which it is classified.

For example, a book consisting of text in the nature of words or numbers, or a combination of them, is a literary work, but a book consisting predominantly of photographs or illustrations is a pictorial work. Similarly, a cassette tape or phonograph record featuring spoken words is also a literary work, but a tape or record that features the performance of music is a musical work.

Copyrightable "Works" Are Specific Things. In addition to making a change in the categories of protectible materials and the way of classifying them, the 1976 Act adopted the word "work" as a generic term for anything that possesses the potential for copyright protection. It is used throughout the 1976 Act alone and in combination with other words, such as original, for hire, joint, collective, published, unpublished, pseudonymous, and anonymous. However, there is no definition for work anywhere in the Act.

In effect, a work is the product of an individual's creative effort manifested in a material object by means of sounds and/or images. Or, in other words, a work is something that originates in thought and is then rendered in tangible form as a literary work, a pictorial work, or a sound recording.

"Copies" and "Phonorecords" Are Defined Terms. The words "copies" and "phonorecords" take on generic meanings in the 1976 Act. This approach was taken so as not to limit copyright protection to a narrowly defined medium such as paper, videotape, canvas, or clay.

For purposes of the 1976 Act, "copies" are defined as "material objects, other than phonorecords, in which a work is fixed by any method now known or later developed, and from which the work can be perceived, reproduced, or otherwise communicated, either directly or indirectly or with the aid of a machine or device." The material object, other than a phonorecord, in which a work is first embodied is a "copy."

"Phonorecords" are "material objects in which sounds, other than those accompanying a motion picture or other audiovisual work, are fixed by any method now known or later developed, and from which the sounds can be perceived, reproduced, or otherwise communicated, either directly or with the aid of a machine or device." The material object in which sounds are first embodied is a "phonorecord."

ORIGINAL CREATIVE EFFORTS MUST BE EMBODIED IN A PHYSICAL OBJECT

Determining Sufficient Creative Effort

The 1976 Act, in addition to the requirement discussed under "creator's Nationality and the Country of First Publication," following, makes protection for an individual's creative effort dependent on whether it:

1. Falls within one or more of the nine categories established by the Act (i.e., is copyrightable subject matter)
2. Is "fixed in a tangible medium of expression"
3. Is "an original work of authorship"

All three requirements must be satisfied. If one or more is not met, protection is not available under copyright law.

It is not difficult to ascertain whether a creative effort is protectible. A quick scan of the nine category headings or a closer look at their definitions reveals what type of material is covered by the law.

"Fixation in a Tangible Medium of Expression"

If an individual's creative effort (e.g., words, numbers, images, sounds, or combinations of them) is embodied on paper, canvas, in phonograph records, or in any other physical object by that individual or by another person with that individual's permission, it has been "fixed in a tangible medium of expression." Nothing more is required as long as the embodiment of it is sufficiently permanent or stable to permit it to be perceived, reproduced, or otherwise communicated for a period of more than a moment.

In many cases, creative efforts suitable for copyright protection are produced, but for one reason or another they are not "fixed" at the time they are first communicated to others. For example, improvisations, live news reports, sporting events, concerts, and other live performances of material not previously recorded or rendered in physical form (e.g., scripts, phonograph records, etc.) will not be protected by copyright law because the "fixation" requirement is not met. However, if a creative effort is recorded simultaneously with the production of it (as is done with most live radio and television broadcasts of football, baseball, and basketball games) this requirement is satisfied and copyright protection is available for it from the moment it is produced.

"An Original Work of Authorship"

To qualify for copyright protection, a work is considered to be "original" if it:

1. Exhibits a minimal degree of creativity
2. Was created without copying another work

Sufficient creativity will be found if there is some portion or feature of it that is recognizably the result of the creator's own efforts. That is, something in or about it which is attributable to independent creation. There is no independent creation when the material of one person is slavishly or mechanically copied by another. To support independent creation more must be done than making an insignificant or trivial variation of what has been created before by someone else.

For example, a court concluded that plastic reproductions of a cast iron bank in the shape of "Uncle Sam" (which is in the public domain and not protected under copyright law) did not exhibit a minimal degree of creativity to satisfy the originality requirement even though the medium is not the same and the dimensions of the plastic reproductions are different. The court stated that changing the medium and altering the dimensions of an earlier work would be viewed as nothing more than an insignificant or trivial variation of it. Likewise, merely listing the ingredients of a food product on a label or arranging a few words to produce a short phrase or slogan, such as "This Bud's for you," does not reflect sufficient creativity.

The artistic quality of the creator's efforts, no matter how poor, is not a factor in determining whether the resulting work contains enough creativity to be original. Similarly, a work may exhibit the minimal creativity required even though it does not possess aesthetic or intellectual merit.

The test of originality is one with a low threshold. All a person needs to do to pass is produce a work that is a distinguishable variation of a prior work. That is, a person must produce a work without copying the work of another. There is no requirement that a work be inventive, unique, or novel, meaning that something like it has never been created before by anyone else. And it is not necessary that a work be clever, unusual, or radically different from what others have created.

A work will be considered original if it has been produced as the result of a person's independent efforts even if it is completely identical to a prior work created by another person. As long as one work is not copied from the other both are entitled to copyright protection. For example, if two individuals independently create the exact same picture, musical composition, or text for a publication without copying what has been done by the other, the resulting work of each will be considered original and eligible for copyright protection.

CREATOR'S NATIONALITY AND THE COUNTRY OF FIRST PUBLICATION

If a work has been made available to the public (see Chapter 9) and satisfies the criteria discussed previously, the ability to obtain copyright protection for it in the United States under the 1976 Act is dependent on compliance with one or more of the following requirements:

(1) on the date of first publication, one or more of the authors is a national or resides in the United States, or is a national, domiciliary, or sovereign authority of a foreign nation that is a party to a copyright treaty to which the United States is also a party, or is a stateless person, wherever that person may be domiciled; or

(2) the work is first published in the United States or in a foreign nation that, on the date of first publication, is a party to the Universal Copyright Convention; or

(3) the work is first published by the United Nations or any of its specialized agencies, or by the Organization of American States; or

(4) the work comes within the scope of a Presidential proclamation.

An exception to these requirements exists with respect to an unpublished work. Unpublished works are subject to protection under the 1976 Act without regard to the nationality or domicile of the creator.

MUSICAL WORKS, DRAMATIC WORKS, PANTOMIMES, AND CHOREOGRAPHIC WORKS

There are no definitions or descriptions in the 1976 Act (beyond the category headings) for musical, dramatic, or choreographic works or for pantomimes. Congress did not feel it necessary to expressly provide definitions for these works because it believed that the composition of each is readily apparent and that the words used to denote them have fairly settled meanings.

Musical works are generally deemed to be those which consist of a combination of varying melody, harmony, rhythm, and timbre regardless of the material objects in which they are embodied. They can be manifested in terms of notation (musical notes on a staff with or without accompanying words) as found on sheet music and lead sheets. Or they can be manifested in other visually perceptible forms like player piano rolls, for instance. Further, they may be expressed in formats you cannot see (e.g., sounds) when they are embodied in phonograph records, cassette tapes, or disks.

Some musical works are expressed solely in terms of notation (e.g., a symphonic score) while others are expressed in terms of words integrally associated with notation (e.g., an opera or popular song). The fact that words compose part of a musical work will not make any difference insofar as classification is concerned. The combination is still treated as a musical work. This is one exception to the classification of works comprised of words as literary works. However, when words are created independent of musical notation with no intention at the time of creation to combine them with music (e.g., poetry), and subsequently they are so combined, the words will be classified as a literary work.

Dramatic works are distinct from literary works, from a copyright standpoint, and therefore merit a separate category. However, because dramatic works also consist of words, the categories overlap to a certain extent and it is possible to classify a dramatic work as a literary work. This is another exception to the classification of works comprised of words as literary works.

Generally, dramatic works are literary compositions that tell a story through action with dialogue (e.g., *A Streetcar Named Desire*). They may be accompanied by music (e.g., *West Side Story*).

Choreographic works consist of the recorded or notated movements of a dancer before an audience. Social dance steps and simple routines are not choreographic works.

Pantomimes comprise a drama presented by gestures and action without words.

LITERARY WORKS

Literary works are defined by the 1976 Act as

> works, other than audiovisual works, expressed in words, numbers, or other verbal or numerical symbols or indicia, regardless of the nature of the material objects, such as books, periodicals, manuscripts, phonorecords, film, tapes, disks, or cards, in which they are embodied.

They are defined in terms of their structural elements (namely words and numbers), not on the basis of their intellectual content (e.g., prose or verse) or physical form (e.g., books or magazines). Neither intellectual qualities nor cultural values are essential attributes of a literary work, from a copyright standpoint. Consequently, a wide variety of material is included within this category. For example, in addition to the kinds of things specifically noted in the definition, the following items, among others, fall within this category:

Computer data bases	Directories
Software programs	Catalogs
Advertising text	Indexes
Bibliographies	Answer material for tests
Scripts	Research reports
Written speeches	Written jokes
Newspapers	Poems
Personal letters	Diaries
Phonograph records featuring stories	Audio cassette tapes featuring lectures

PICTORIAL, GRAPHIC, AND SCULPTURAL WORKS

Pictorial, graphic, and sculptural works are defined by the 1976 Act as:

> Two-dimensional and three dimensional works of fine, graphic, and applied art, photographs, prints and art reproductions, maps, globes, charts, technical drawings, diagrams, and models. Such works shall include works of artistic craftsmanship insofar as their form but not their mechanical or utilitarian aspects are concerned; the design of a useful article . . . shall be considered a pictorial, graphic, or sculptural work only if, and only to the extent that, such design incorporates pictorial, graphic, or sculptural features that can be iden-

tified separately from, and are capable of existing independently of, the utilitarian aspects of the article.

The first part of this definition describes the kinds of works falling within this category. The second part attempts to distinguish them from those designs or shapes of useful articles not protected by copyright even though they may be aesthetically appealing. If such designs and shapes cannot be physically or conceptually separated from the utilitarian aspects of that article they cannot be protected under copyright law. For example, when the shape of an automobile or a television set cabinet or the configuration of a street lamp or the design features of a chair cannot be separated from those objects, they are not eligible for copyright protection.

A "useful article" is considered to be one having an intrinsic utilitarian function. If the function served by an article is more than merely to portray its appearance or to convey information, the article is considered to have an intrinsic utilitarian function and cannot be protected under copyright law. For example, a light fixture possessing an artistic shape will not justify copyright protection for that shape because the fixture itself has an intrinsic utilitarian function. The principal function of the fixture is to provide light.

The phrase "works of fine, graphic, and applied art," as used in the definition, is intended to include the types of art traditionally thought of as fine and graphic art. In addition, this phrase is intended to include all original creations that constitute applied art.

Applied art comprises original pictorial, graphic, and sculptural creations intended to be embodied in useful articles and capable of being identified separate from such articles. For example, drawings, paintings, and graphic designs printed or applied to textile fabric, gift-wrapping paper, china, and the like are considered to be applied art. And so are carvings on the backs of chairs and floral relief patterns on silverware.

In addition to those particular items described in the definition, this category includes the following:

Advertising artwork	Cartoons
Comic strips	Blueprints
Scientific drawings	Schematics
Original color combinations	Dolls
Scale models	Logos
Product labels featuring designs	Architect's drawings
Three-dimensional models	Etchings
Sculpture	Engravings
Lithographs	Woodcuts
Silk screens	Art posters

The "useful article" limitation affects the extent to which copyright protection may be available for all of the items. For example, an architect's drawings and plans may be protected as graphic works but the functional structures constructed from them cannot be protected as of July 1, 1986.

It is important to keep in mind that copyright protection will not be available for a pictorial, graphic, or sculptural work if it is not an original work. However, just as they are not factors in determining whether a work is original, ingenuity, visual appeal, and artistic taste are not controlling factors with respect to whether a work is a pictorial, graphic, or sculptural work.

AUDIOVISUAL WORKS AND MOTION PICTURES

Audiovisual works are defined by the 1976 Act as works:

> that consist of a series of related images which are intrinsically intended to be shown by the use of machines or devices such as projectors, viewers, or electronic equipment, together with accompanying sounds, if any, regardless of the nature of the material objects, such as films or tapes, in which the works are embodied.

Motion pictures are defined as:

> audiovisual works consisting of a series of related images which, when shown in succession, impart an impression of motion, together with accompanying sounds, if any.

As indicated by the category description and the definitions, motion pictures are a type of audiovisual work. Like an audiovisual work, motion pictures are comprised of a series of related images. However, they are distinguishable in that the series of related images must be shown in succession and be capable of giving the impression of motion.

The category of audiovisual works includes such things as:

Multiimage slide shows
Projected charts, diagrams, or drawings
A series of still photographs

The following things, among others, may be classified as motion pictures:

Videodisks
Dramatic and nondramatic films

Television programs
Educational as well as entertaining videotapes

SOUND RECORDINGS

Sound recordings are defined as:

> works that result from the fixation of a series of musical, spoken, or other sounds, but not including the sounds accompanying a motion picture or other audiovisual work, regardless of the nature of the material objects, such as disks, tapes, or other phonorecords, in which they are embodied.

In 1972 sound recordings were added as a new category of works eligible for copyright protection. Federal copyright protection was extended to such works through amendment of the 1909 Act by the Sound Recording Amendment of 1971. As a result, sound recordings fixed in a tangible medium of expression on or after February 15, 1972 were protected by federal copyright law. Sound recordings fixed prior to that date were and remained subject to protection by the common law or by state statute regardless of their publication status.

The 1976 Act continued federal copyright protection for sound recordings and is the exclusive basis for such protection, but only for sound recordings fixed on or after February 15, 1972. Sound recordings fixed prior to that date can be protected under state or common law. The 1976 Act expressly states, that protection for such recordings is not preempted by the Act until February 15, 2047:

> With respect to sound recordings fixed before February 15, 1972, any rights or remedies under the common law or statutes of any State shall not be annulled or limited by this title until February 15, 2047. (17 U.S.C. 301(C))

This category protects sounds, but only if they are embodied in a physical object, such as cassette and reel-to-reel tapes, phonograph records, wire, disks, electronic piano rolls, and the like.

For example, a vocalist's and musician's rendition of the words and melody comprising a musical work (e.g., a recording of Randy Goodrum's song "He Needed Me" by Ann Murray) is a copyrightable work (sound recording) distinct from those words and melody. It is possible for the vocalist and musicians (Ann Murray) to acquire copyright ownership for the sounds only, even though the copyright for the words and music may be owned by someone else (Randy Goodrum).

Sounds may be protected if they are original with the creator and regardless of whether the underlying work is or is not protected by copyright. Thus, a rendition of the "Star Spangled Banner" can be the subject of a sound recording copyright although the words and music may be freely used by everyone.

To a certain extent this category overlaps with those for musical and literary works. Recorded sounds can and often do consist of musical works performed as well as words and numbers spoken.

The kinds of sounds that may be protected include those noted in the definition and the following, among others:

Synthesized sounds
Sounds of mechanical devices
Thunder and other sounds of nature
Birdcalls
Animal sounds

COMPILATIONS AND DERIVATIVE WORKS

Compilations And Derivative Works Containing Preexisting Material

A compilation is defined as:

> a work formed by the collection and assembling of preexisting materials or of data that are selected, coordinated, or arranged in such a way that the resulting work as a whole constitutes an original work of authorship. The term "compilation" includes collective works.

> A "collective work" is a work, such as a periodical issue, anthology, or encyclopedia, in which a number of contributions, constituting separate and independent works in themselves, are assembled into a collective whole.

A derivative work is defined as:

> a work based upon one or more preexisting works, such as a translation, musical arrangement, dramatization, fictionalization, motion picture version, sound recording, art reproduction, abridgment, condensation, or any other form in which a work may be recast, transformed, or adapted. A work consisting of editorial revisions, annotations, elaborations, or other modifications which, as a whole, represent an original work of authorship, is a "derivative work."

In other words, a compilation is a work consisting of preexisting material collected together. A derivative work is one based on or derived from preexisting material.

The works covered by these categories are the transformations of, changes in, and efforts involved in rearranging preexisting material which result in a new version of it. More particularly, it is the transformations, changes, and efforts themselves that constitute the work and they must meet the originality requirement.

Each new version of preexisting material, whether it be a derivative work or a compilation, will also be classified as a literary work, a musical work, a dramatic work, and the like. The specific classification will depend on the composition of the derivative work and compilation (the new version).

For example, if a novel (a literary work) is used to create a motion picture, the resulting derivative work will also be classified as a motion picture. And if a two-dimensional cartoon character (a pictorial work) is reproduced in a three-dimensional format, the resulting derivative work will also be a sculptural work. Similarly, if a group of short stories (literary works) are collected together to form a compilation, the compilation will also be a literary work.

Protection for a compilation or a derivative work employing preexisting material that is protected by copyright does not extend to any part of the compilation or derivative work in which such copyrighted material has been used unlawfully (see "Derivative Works"). Further, protection for a compilation or derivative work extends only to the original contribution of the creator of it, as distinguished from the preexisting material employed in the compilation or derivative work, and does not imply any exclusive right in the preexisting material. Rights in the compilation or derivative work are independent of, and do not affect or enlarge the scope, duration, ownership, or subsistence of, any rights in the preexisting material.

Derivative Works

The preexisting material found in a derivative work must be the kind that is capable of copyright protection, regardless of whether it is or was ever protected by copyright. That is, it must consist of the kind of material that may be classified within one or more of the first seven categories.

For example, a work by Homer, Beethoven, or Van Gogh (works in the public domain) would qualify as preexisting material for the creation of a derivative work because such works fall within the aforementioned categories. Additions to and changes in such works can be made without any need to obtain permission to do so in order to create a derivative work that can be separately protected.

Similarly, a copyrighted work by John Steinbeck, Leonard Bernstein, or Andy Warhol would qualify as preexisting material for the creation of a derivative work. However, because such works are currently protected by copyright law, someone who wants to create a derivative work based on them (by making additions to or changes in them) must obtain permission to do so from the copyright owner. The copyright owner of a work has the exclusive right to create a derivative work based on it. (See Chapter 6.)

A derivative work borrows heavily from preexisting material to the extent of substantially incorporating it. Accordingly, the transforming, recasting, or adapting of that material, which results in a new version of it (as mentioned earlier), must satisfy the originality requirement. If a distinguishable variation of the earlier material is produced it is likely that this requirement will be satisfied and it is the transformation, recasting, or adaptation that represents the "work" insofar as this category is concerned.

In some instances changes in preexisting material are the only aspect of the new version that can be protected. Consequently, there can be no protection for the preexisting material itself. This is the case where the preexisting material is in the public domain or cannot be protected for other reasons (see Chapter 4). Accordingly, if preexisting material is transformed or changed by one person and another person subsequently copies that preexisting material without including the transformation or changes, the person who made the transformation or changes has no basis to object.

For example, if Othello (a preexisting public domain work by Shakespeare) is translated into the French language, the translation can be protected under copyright law as a derivative work. However, another translator can create a Greek language translation of Othello (and protect it as a derivative work) without infringing the rights of the person who produced the French translation. Similarly, one person can create an arrangement of a musical composition by Mozart (a preexisting public domain work) and obtain protection for that arrangement as a derivative work. If the same Mozart composition is arranged by another person, without copying the first arrangement, that person can also obtain protection for the second arrangement as a derivative work.

On the other hand, a person who makes a contribution to preexisting material which is protected by copyright cannot acquire any rights in the contribution without permission from the copyright owner of the preexisting material. Only the owner of a copyrighted work has the right to create derivative works based on it (see Chapter 6). This means that the owner has (1) the ability to preclude others from creating derivative works based on it as well as (2) the authority to allow others to acquire separate rights to contributions made to it. Therefore, no other person can create a derivative work or acquire any rights to the contribution made to a preexisting copyrighted work without the owner's authorization.

Permission to create a derivative work does not necessarily include permission to acquire separate rights to the contribution made to it. However, permission to acquire rights to the contribution would seem to include permission to create a derivative work.

For example, a person who wishes to make a new arrangement of a musical work protected by copyright, and to acquire rights to that arrangement, must obtain permission from the owner of the musical work to make the arrangement and to acquire rights to it. Similarly, a motion picture production company that wishes to make a motion picture based on a bestselling novel, and to obtain rights for itself to the motion picture, must obtain the same kinds of permissions from the author. Reproduction of a two-dimensional cartoon character (Mickey Mouse) or motion picture character (E.T.) in the form of three-dimensional toys requires the same type of permissions.

The following items among others, including those indicated in the definition of a derivative work, can be protected as derivative works:

A three-dimensional object based on a two-dimensional object or vice versa

A play based on a short story

A portrait or sculpture based on a photograph or vice versa

A play or book based on a motion picture or vice versa

A popular song based on a classical piece

The edited, condensed, or annotated version of a book or article

Compilations

There is no requirement that the preexisting material incorporated in a compilation be the kind that is capable of copyright protection. Both preexisting material that is capable of protection, and that which is not, are suitable subject matter.

For example, names and addresses of people and businesses, names of manufactured articles, part numbers, and general facts, among other things, are the kinds of preexisting material that are not ordinarily capable of copyright protection. In and of themselves they do not constitute original material from a copyright standpoint. However, this kind of material can be the subject matter of a compilation and the creative effort involved in the selection, coordination, or arrangement of it can be protected.

Similarly, although poems, short stories, photographs, and songs among other things are capable of copyright protection, they too are the kinds of preexisting material that can be selected, coordinated, or arranged to create a compilation, and the creative effort involved in compiling them is subject to protection.

Creation of a compilation does not involve making any internal changes in the preexisting material as typically happens when a derivative work is created. Rather, the creative contribution is made through the process of selecting, bringing together, organizing, and arranging such material without significantly altering it. Such efforts constitute the *work* and are all that may be protected, if they satisfy the originality requirement by amounting to more than a trivial contribution to the preexisting material.

If preexisting material is selected or arranged by one person and another subsequently does the same thing without copying the first efforts, the first selector or arranger has no basis for objection.

For example, one person can compile and list in a directory all of the names and addresses of the residents of a particular neighborhood, or those of all the restaurants in a city, and obtain protection for the directory as a compilation. At the same time, someone else can use this same information and produce a competitive directory eligible for protection as a compilation, as long as the second directory was not copied from the first.

The following items represent what can be protected as a compilation:

Catalogs
Collections of photographs, songs, and the like
Directories
Anthologies

OBSCENE MATERIAL

There are no content-based restrictions on works entitled to copyright protection. Accordingly, obscenity laws are not used as a means of ascertaining whether creative works may be protected. If obscene material otherwise meets the requirements for copyrightable subject matter, it is entitled to protection under the copyright law.

CHAPTER SUMMARY

• Copyright protection is available for a wide variety of things generically referred to as "works"; they must be original and embodied in a tangible medium of expression.

- "Copies" are material objects, other than phonorecords, in which a work is embodied; "phonorecords" are material objects in which sounds, other than those accompanying a motion picture or audiovisual work, are embodied.
- There are nine broad categories of works based on their composition (e.g., words, images, sounds) instead of their physical form (e.g., book, photograph, cassette tape).

4

Some Things Cannot
Be Protected

A significant amount of material is not protected under copyright law. Consequently, material not protected under trademark or patent law can be used by anyone without any obligation or requirement to obtain permission and without violating the rights of anyone. At the same time, the creator's position is no different from anyone else's with regard to claiming rights to it. Material, of the type noted below, cannot be protected unless an original contribution is made to it that results in a distinguishable variation of the preexisting material. If this is done, it is likely that all that can be protected is the original contribution made (see Chapter 3).

There are a number of reasons why the material discussed in this chapter is classified as "public domain" and cannot be protected. It may lack the requisite amount of originality, or may have been created by an employee of the U.S. government, or it may consist of facts, basic plots, or thematic concepts.

PUBLIC DOMAIN MATERIAL

Public domain material is that which belongs to the general public and cannot be appropriated by anyone. Therefore, none of the exclusive rights of a copyright owner (see Chapter 6) can be acquired for it and no person has the right to prohibit anyone else from using it. Public domain material is available for use by anyone free and clear of all ownership claims and limitations on its use whatsoever.

Some material can be used without restriction as soon as it is created because it immediately goes into the public domain. This is the case for material that does not satisfy all three requirements for copyright protection (see Chapter 3) and for material which cannot be protected because of a statutory prohibition.

On the other hand, some material goes into the public domain after a specific period of time passes or an event occurs that causes it to lose the status of protectible material. Since copyright protection lasts for only a limited time (see Chapter 9), the term of protection may have expired. Or for one reason or another, the creator may have allowed it to go into the public domain by deciding not to obtain protection for it at the time of creation, or by neglecting to take the action required to avoid losing protection (see Chapters 10 and 11).

Once material is in or becomes part of the public domain, it can never be protected by copyright. If it is combined with material that can be protected, only the added material can be copyrighted.

WORKS LACKING SUFFICIENT ORIGINALITY

Material that does not contain the minimum amount of creative authorship ("originality") required for a copyrightable work can never achieve the status of copyright protection. Such material is public domain material from the moment it comes into existence. Examples of material that the government and courts have found to lack sufficient originality are:

Names, titles, and short phrases or expressions, such as:

Names of products or services

Names of business organizations or groups, including the name of a group of performers

Names of pseudonyms of individuals, including a professional name or stage name

Titles of books, motion pictures, and the like

Catchwords, catchphrases, mottoes, slogans, or short advertising expressions

Familiar symbols or designs:

Mere variations of typographic ornamentation

Lettering or coloring

Mere listings of ingredients or contents

Blank forms designed for recording information which do not in themselves convey information, such as:

  Time cards
  Graph paper
  Account books
  Diaries
  Blank checks
  Scorecards
  Address books
  Report forms
  Order forms

Material consisting entirely of information that is common property containing no original authorship, such as:

  Standard calendars
  Height and weight charts
  Schedules of sporting events
  Lists or tables taken from public documents or other common sources

Devices for measuring and computing, such as:

  Tape measures
  Rulers
  Slide rules
  Wheel dials
  Nomograms

U.S. GOVERNMENT WORKS

The 1976 Act expressly denies protection to material created by an officer or employee of the U.S. government as part of that person's official duties. This is so even though the material may be of the type that otherwise would be protectible. Accordingly, this material is in the public domain immediately upon creation and can never be protected by copyright. This means that a high percentage of government publications are available for use by anyone, such as the consumer and business pamphlets prepared by the Consumer Product Safety Commission, the U.S. Patent & Trademark Office, the Copyright Office, the Small Business Administration, and the U.S. Department of Agriculture.

The statutory prohibition in the 1976 Act applies only to material created by individuals employed by the U.S. government. It does not prohibit the federal government from claiming rights to material created under a federal contract or grant by individuals who are not government officials or employees. If such material is eligible for copyright protection, the federal government may acquire rights to it by virtue of language in a contract or grant. The federal government can also acquire copyrightable works from citizens by gift or purchase and assert the rights of an owner the same as any citizen.

The 1976 Act does not prevent a federal employee from obtaining copyright protection for works created outside official duty. For example, an employee of the Federal Trade Commission responsible only for the writing of trade regulation rules has a right to obtain copyright protection for a creative work such as a novel or photograph since the creation of such works is not part of that person's official duties.

Finally, this prohibition does not affect works created by state or local officials and employees. It covers only works created by U.S. government employees in an official capacity. Consequently, the works created by employees of state and local governments can be protected by such governments and are not automatically in the public domain.

IDEAS, PROCEDURES, AND SYSTEMS

People with some understanding of copyright law are often under the impression that their ideas, as expressed in their creative work, cannot be used or copied by others without permission. However, this is not the case. To use an example from my own practice, one client was disappointed to learn that copyright law would not protect his idea of creating music, with a specific tempo and style, to be sold on cassette tapes for use by individuals who listen to music on "Walkman" type portable stereos while jogging.

While the composer of music for joggers may protect the music itself as a musical work, it is not possible to protect the idea of creating music especially for joggers, or the specific tempo and style of that music.

The 1976 Act specifically denies copyright protection to ideas, procedures, processes, systems, methods of operation, concepts, principles, or discoveries that are described, explained, illustrated, or otherwise revealed in a copyrightable work.

This particular prohibition attempts to reconcile two competing interests of society. One allows society to benefit from further improvements and progress that may be derived from ideas by generally making them available for use by everyone. If an individual could protect and obtain exclusive rights under copyright law to every idea by merely expressing it in some physical form, soon there would be few, if any, ideas freely available for use by society as a whole.

The other interest of society is to reward an individual's ingenuity and effort by granting a certain degree of protection to his or her ideas. By granting exclusive rights to the expression of an individual's ideas as manifested in a tangible work, this objective is accomplished in a somewhat limited way, under the copyright law. The 1976 Act does not preclude anyone from protecting the particular expression of the idea, process, or principle.

In effect what the copyright law says is that the only way an idea can be protected, if at all, is the specific manner in which it is expressed such as the exact arrangement of words, designs, or objects in the sequence they are combined with each other. In fact, one idea may be expressed in a number of different ways and each way it is expressed may be protected.

The demarcation between the idea and the expression of it is difficult to define. Accordingly, where two works are the same or substantially similar, a question frequently asked is, "Was the expression of the idea copied or merely the idea?" If the expression was copied, there may be copyright infringement.

For instance, if a detailed written description of an idea, or a picture representing the idea, is created, the expression of the idea, that is, the written description or the picture, can be protected, but only to the extent that copyright law allows. The written description or picture of the idea cannot be copied or publicly performed. However, someone can read the description, look at the picture, or otherwise learn about the idea and then copy or use it without violating rights under copyright law, as long as the expression is not copied or publicly performed. Referring back to the music tape for joggers, anyone can make a competitive product by using the "music for joggers" concept, as long as the music is not copied.

FACTS, BASIC PLOTS, THEMATIC CONCEPTS, AND SCÈNES À FAIRE

From a copyright protection standpoint, historic and contemporary facts cannot be protected as such. Facts must be available for use by everyone free to copyright ownership claims, to further the cause of knowledge. Accordingly, any protection that may be associated with facts is narrow and limited to no more than the expression of them, as is the case with ideas.

For example, a number of years ago Margaret Walker Alexander wrote a book entitled *Jubilee*, which was an amalgam of fact and fiction derived from the history of black slavery in the United States. Later, Alex Haley wrote the well-known book *Roots*, which also was a mixture of fact and fiction derived from the same history of slavery. Copyright protection was obtained for both of these works, but was limited to each author's expression of facts.

Basic plots, thematic concepts, and scenes that must necessarily follow from certain plot situations are also treated the same as ideas. They are denied protection as are incidents, characters, and settings that are indispensable or at least standard in the treatment of a given theme. As a matter of law, these things are not copyrightable. It is virtually impossible to write about a particular historical era or fictional theme without employing certain stock or standard literary devices. Therefore, anyone has the right to use them free of claims by others.

For example, the Romeo and Juliet romance theme cannot be protected. It has been repeated in a number of works including, among others, the book *Abie's Irish Rose*, the motion picture *The Cohens and The Kelleys*, and the musical play *West Side Story*. Copyright protection for each of these works is available, but only with respect to the particular expression of the theme.

CHAPTER SUMMARY

- Public domain material, works lacking sufficient originality, and U.S. government works are not eligible for copyright protection.
- Names, titles, slogans, listings of ingredients or contents, blank forms, material consisting of common property (such as calendars, schedules of events, etc.), and devices for measuring and computing are examples of things that do not meet the originality requirement.
- Copyright protection does not extend to any idea, procedure, process, system, method of operation, concept, principle, or discovery that is explained, illustrated, or embodied in a work.
- Facts, basic plots, and thematic concepts cannot be protected by copyright law.

5

How to Determine Who Is a Copyright Owner

Ownership of rights can be acquired in a work in a number of ways. It may occur by creating the work or through the transfer of ownership of rights from someone who possesses them.

Contrary to popular belief, copyright registration is not equivalent to acquiring rights in a work. Rights in a work do not arise from and are not obtained solely by registering it with the U.S. Copyright Office. Registering a work does not protect an individual who is not a rightful owner.

Registration of a work records a claim of rights, and results in some procedural as well as substantive benefits (see Chapter 12), but it does not establish ownership of rights.

THE FIRST OWNER

As a general rule, the creator of a work ("author" is the term used in the 1976 Act) is the initial owner of the work as well as all the exclusive rights (see Chapter 6) to it. That person is the sole and exclusive owner, subject to some exceptions, and possesses the authority to determine how and under what circumstances the work can be used by others. Ownership will remain with the creator until the time it is transferred. When two or more individuals create a work through a collaborative effort, they will be the initial co-owners of it.

In order to obtain copyright ownership, the creator only has to satisfy the criteria for a copyrightable work discussed in Chapter 3. Ownership of as well as protection for a work arises at the instant that pen is put to paper, music is recorded, or a photograph taken.

COLLABORATIVE CREATIONS—JOINT OWNERSHIP

Joint Works

If a work is created by two or more individuals, it is possible that everyone who participates in creating it will share copyright ownership. This type of work is referred to as a "joint work."

Co-ownership of a work will result if, at the time it is created, the creative individuals intend their contributions to be merged into inseparable or interdependent parts of a whole. If so, each will possess an undivided ownership interest in the copyright for that work.

Co-ownership of a work is also possible under circumstances when two or more individuals, who do not know each other, create portions of a work at different times independent of each other. However, this is possible only if, at the time each creates his or her part, that individual has an intention that it will be combined with another part created by someone else, in the near or distant future, to form one work.

For example, when a lyricist creates words for a song with the intention that they will later be combined with a melody written by a composer, regardless of whether the identity of the composer is or is not known at the time, co-ownership of the resulting musical composition is possible. Likewise, where chapters of a book are written by various authors knowing that each author's contribution will be combined with those of others to comprise the book, all contributors will possess an ownership interest in the resulting literary work.

Intention To Create a Joint Work

The controlling factor that determines co-ownership of a work at the time of creation is the intention of the persons who create it at that time, not at a later time. Their intention must be that their respective contributions will be combined into one work. It does not matter if the combination of the parts occurs shortly after their creation or weeks, months, or years later.

In the absence of such an intention, co-ownership of a work is not possible through the process of creating it. However, this does not mean that co-ownership of a work is not possible. It can occur, but not through the process of creating a work. Two or more persons can acquire co-ownership of a work by means of a transfer of rights from someone else (see Chapter 16).

Extent of Each Contributor's Ownership

If there is no agreement between collaborators providing otherwise, each possesses an undivided ownership interest in the joint work as a "tenant in common" with the other creators. The essence of a "tenancy in common" is that the whole is not capable of separation into identifiable parts.

Where there are two or more owners of a work, each has the right to use it and to allow others to use it without any obligation to seek authorization from the other owners. However, each co-owner must account to the others for any moneys or other tangible benefits received from third parties who have been authorized to use it. All co-owners are entitled to receive their proportionate shares of such moneys or benefits.

For example, if a musical work is owned by two songwriters, each can grant permission to a third party to record a performance of the work in return for the payment of a royalty. Neither songwriter is required to obtain the approval of the other as long as the work is not transferred and no exclusive license is granted to record it. If and when income is earned from the records, each songwriter is entitled to one-half of those moneys even though only one was responsible for negotiating the transaction.

However, one co-owner cannot transfer all rights in the work, or grant an exclusive license, to a third party without the consent of the other owners. To do so would preclude the other co-owners from exercising their rights. The consent of all co-owners is required to transfer rights or to grant exclusive licenses for any of them.

The law presumes that the percentage of each co-owner's undivided interest in a work is proportionate to the total number of collaborators. For example, if two collaborators create a work, the law presumes that each owns a 50 percent interest in it. If there are three collaborators, each would own a 33⅓ percent interest in it, and so on. However, the co-owners of a joint work can agree otherwise.

There is not set rule to follow with respect to how and to what degree ownership percentages may vary. Co-owners are not required to base each contributor's share of ownership on the number of individuals involved in creating the work, nor on the amount of effort involved in making each contribution, nor on the value of a contribution. Similarly, there is no rule for allocating the revenues derived from a work nor rules that state that the division of such revenues must be equal to or based on ownership percentages in the work. Consequently, it is possible for co-owners to agree on one set of percentages for ownership interests and another for shares in the revenues derived from the joint work.

For example, one co-owner may be entitled to a 75 percent ownership interest in a work although that individual contributed what might be viewed as only 10 percent of the effort in creating it, or vice versa. Or, one co-owner may be given a 30 percent ownership interest in the work and a 90 percent share of revenues derived from it.

The allocation of percentages, both as to ownership and to revenues, is subject to negotiation by and between the creators of the joint work (a copy of a collaboration agreement is included in Appendix A). But if it is not negotiated or otherwise agreed on, the law sets percentages in accordance with its stated presumption.

"WORKS MADE FOR HIRE"

An Exception to the General Rule

There are two exceptions to the general rule that the creator of a work is the initial owner of rights in it.

A work initially owned by someone other than the individual who creates it is known as a "work made for hire." This means that the work has been created either by an individual who has been hired as an employee of someone considered the first owner, or an individual whose services have been engaged, as an independent contractor, by someone considered the first owner.

The work-made-for-hire rule acknowledges that an employer is entitled to the proceeds of an employee's efforts within the scope of his or her employment. The underlying reasoning is that works are created under the employer's direction and at the employer's expense. If there are benefits to be gained from the employee's activities, the employer should receive them just as risks associated with the employee's activities are borne by the employer. This same rationale applies to works created by an independent contractor.

Designation as a work made for hire has significance in many respects. For example, it determines the life of copyright protection for rights in it and whether the initial owner of rights in it can recover ownership after they have been transferred to another party (see Chapter 17).

Employer–Employee Relationship

Unless an employee and employer agree otherwise, in writing, all rights of a copyright owner, in works prepared by an employee within the scope of his or her employment, will belong to the employer on the date of creation. Accordingly, the employee has no rights to the work at all. Under the work-made-for-hire rule, upon creation of a work, the employer is automatically the owner of all rights in it. As a consequence, the employer is considered the "author" and first owner of copyright.

For example, all the works created by a graphic artist employee of an advertising agency within the scope of that individual's employment, belongs to the agency not the artist. And all of the works created within the scope of employment of a landscape architect, who is an employee of the state of Colorado, belong to the state not the landscape architect.

What Constitutes an Employer–Employee Relationship. For purposes of determining whether an employee–employer relationship exists the status of an individual as an employee is not necessarily based on the payment of a regular salary, or the withholding of taxes, or the performance of services at the employer's facilities, or continuous periods of employment.

While these factors may be considered in determining whether an employee–employer relationship exists, what counts most is the right of one party to control, direct, and supervise the way in which the other party performs the services and creates the work.

For example, when a photographer, who is an independent contractor, is retained to create photographs for an advertising brochure, the photographer may not be a copyright owner of the resulting pictorial works. If a representative of the hiring company directs the arrangement of the scenes for the photographs and instructs the photographer with regard to composition, a valid argument can be made that copyright ownership belongs to the company, not the photographer. The fact that the photographer is closely supervised and follows the instructions of the company representative is enough to treat the relationship as employee–employer for purposes of copyright law. A federal district court made such a finding in 1985.

The same determination can be made even when an individual volunteers his or her time and efforts without pay, to an organization, a local or state government, or another person. If the organization, for instance, has the right to control that individual's activities, and to direct as well as to supervise the creation of any works associated with those activities, it is arguable that an employer–employee relationship exists for purposes of copyright law. When facts similar to these were presented to a federal court in 1983, it concluded that the organization, not the unpaid volunteer, was the initial owner of rights.

Furthermore, employers are not required to advise employees that what they create at work will be automatically owned by the employer. It is not necessary that an employee consent to ownership by the employer. The employer's ownership of works under such circumstances is a natural consequence of the employment relationship.

Employees Can Own Works. It is possible for an employee to own all or some of the rights to a work created by the employee within the scope of employment if the employer expressly agrees to such ownership. This agreement must be set forth in a document, signed by the employee and the employer, providing that all or specific rights to the work, for all or certain works created by the employee, will be owned by the employee.

An agreement of this type will not affect the status of the employer as the initial owner of such works. It simply means the owner has transferred all or part of his or her rights in the work to the employee. (A copy of the type of agreement that can be used for this purpose is included in Appendix A.)

The requirement that both the employee and employer sign the agreement must be satisfied otherwise the employee will not acquire the desired rights. The 1976 Act provides that a transfer of copyright ownership is not valid unless stated in writing and signed by the owner of the rights transferred (see Chapter 16). For example, an employee cannot obtain ownership by merely writing a letter to the employer setting forth the agreement reached, or vice versa. Until both parties acknowledge their agreement by placing their signatures on a document, all rights to the work will remain with the employer.

What Constitutes "Scope of Employment." Although a written agreement with the employer is necessary if the employee desires to possess the rights to works created within the scope of employment, this is not so with respect to works created outside the scope of employment. The employee is automatically the initial copyright owner of such works and the employer will possess no rights to them whatsoever, in the absence of a transfer or license from the employee.

A determination of whether a work is created within or outside the scope of employment is made by referring to the work itself. In addition, reference must be made to the duties actually performed by the employee and to the employee's written job description, if any. Other factors to be considered are the location where a work is created and the time of day or day of the week when it is created. However, these factors do not always determine whether a work is created within or outside the scope of employment. An employee's creation of a work at home or off the premises of the employer does not necessarily mean it was created outside the scope of employment. Nor does creation of it while on vacation, during weekends, or during times other than the usual hours of employment.

If a work created by an employee is of the kind that reasonably would be expected to fall within the employee's duties, as may be defined by a job description, by custom and practice in the industry, or otherwise, it is arguable that initial ownership belongs to the employer. This may be the case, regardless of where and when it was created, as long as this was done during the term of employment.

On the other hand, if a work created by an employee refers to or in some way is based on the experiences of an employee's employment activities, but it is not within the employee's scope of employment to create such a work, ownership of it will belong to the employee.

For example, initial copyright ownership to an article about the automobile industry written by a car salesperson belongs to the salesperson, not to the automobile dealer-employer. Copyright ownership of a song composed by a manager of a record store will belong to the manager if his or her responsibilities as a store manager do not include or anticipate songwriting.

Works Created by Teachers and Professors. The creation of works by teachers and professors is an exception to the work-made-for-hire relationship. The employer (the educational institution) will not automatically be the initial copyright owner of such works, even though they might otherwise be thought to fall within the scope of employment. Here, as a result of generally accepted practices, teachers and professors are entitled to possess initial copyright ownership.

Works Created Prior to and After Employment. Initial copyright ownership to works created by an individual before the term of employment with a particular employer do not belong to the employer even if they are of the type the individual would be expected to create during the employment term. Similarly, initial ownership of rights in works prepared after the employment relationship ends do not belong to the former employer on the basis they are of the kind of works that would have been within the scope of employment, or because they were prepared as a result of knowledge and skills gained by the former employee.

Commissioned Works

Ordinarily, initial ownership of a work created by an independent contractor will belong to the independent contractor. This is in accordance with the general rule that the creator of a work is the initial owner of it. However, there are exceptions to this rule. One was discussed in the preceding section; another arises when the independent contractor signs a document agreeing to create the work as a work made for hire and the hiring party also signs it. Such a work may also be referred to as a "specially ordered" or "commissioned" work and the person or organization for whom the independent contractor creates the work may be referred to as the "commissioning party."

A Signed Agreement Is Required. Unlike its applicability to the employee–employer relationship, the work-made-for-hire rule is not automatically effective when an independent contractor and commissioning party establish a relationship. And it does not cover every kind of work that may be created by an independent contractor.

Establishment of the employee–employer relationship is enough to make this rule applicable to all works created by an employee within the scope of employment. This is not the case with respect to an independent contractor–commissioning party relationship. As mentioned earlier, those parties must enter into a signed written agreement providing that the work created by the independent contractor will be a work made for hire.

There is no limitation on the kind of works that will be initially owned by the employer. All works created by an employee within the scope of employment, regardless of category, may be initially owned by an employer. To the contrary, a commissioning party can be the initial owner of only certain works which are specified in the 1976 Act.

Only Certain Works Qualify. If an employer–employee relationship does not exist, a person other than the creator of a work cannot be the initial owner of it merely by asking another party to create it. If a person, other than the creator of a work, desires to be the initial owner, the following requirements must be satisfied (they are set forth in the 1976 Act definition of work made for hire):

1. The work must be specially ordered or commissioned
2. There must be a written agreement signed by the creator of the work and the party who desires to be the initial owner to the effect that the work shall be considered a work made for hire
3. The work can only be used by the person who desires to be the initial owner of it as:
   a. A contribution to a collective work (a "collective work" is a work, such as a periodical issue, anthology, or encyclopedia, in which a number of contributions, constituting separate and independent works in themselves, are assembled into a collective work, for example, a contributing article to a magazine)
   b. Part of a motion picture or other audiovisual work

    c. A translation

    d. A supplementary work (a "supplementary work" is a work prepared for publication as a secondary adjunct to a work by another author for the purpose of introducing, concluding, illustrating, explaining, revising, commenting on, or assisting in the use of the other work, such as forewards, afterwords, pictorial illustrations, maps, charts, tables, editorial notes, musical arrangements, answer material for tests, bibliographies, appendixes, and indexes)

    e. A compilation

    f. An instructional text

    g. A test

    h. Answer material for a test

    i. An atlas

These are the only uses that qualify a work created by an independent contractor as a commissioned work and make it eligible for treatment as a work made for hire. Accordingly, if an independent contractor's work is specially ordered or commissioned for any other purpose, it cannot be a work made for hire and initial ownership of it will not belong to the commissioning party. A written and co-signed work-made-for-hire agreement has no bearing on this point. If a work does not qualify as a work made for hire, as defined in the 1976 Act, the commissioning party will not be the initial owner of it.

For example, if a portrait artist is commissioned to create a portrait of the commissioning party or someone else, the resulting pictorial work cannot be a work made for hire because it does not fall within any of the previously mentioned uses. On the other hand, if a photographer is commissioned to take a picture for a corporation's annual report or a promotional brochure, that photograph is subject to the work-made-for-hire rule. Initial ownership will be in the corporation, but only if there is a written agreement, signed by both parties, to the effect the photograph will be a work made for hire. (A copy of an agreement for a commissioned work made for hire is included in Appendix A.)

CHAPTER SUMMARY

• Copyright protection for a work occurs in two ways, neither of which requires registering the work with the U.S. Copyright Office.

- Ownership can be obtained by creating the work, or from someone who possesses rights in it.
- A work created by two or more individuals through a collaborative effort is owned by everyone who participated in the creation of it and each owns a proportionate share unless otherwise agreed.
- An individual who creates a work is the initial owner of it unless the work-made-for-hire rule applies.
- A work created within an individual's scope of employment is a work made for hire and is owned by the employer.
- A work created by an individual who is an independent contractor may also be a work-made-for-hire and owned by someone else if that individual's activities are closely supervised and directed.
- A work created on commission may be a work made for hire and owned by the commissioning party if there is a written agreement referring to its creation and it is a qualifying work.

6

Five Exclusive Rights Are Associated with a Work

Copyright ownership and the legal protection available for a work are expressed in terms of five exclusive rights that are provided for by and enforceable only under the 1976 Act. These rights are exclusive rights in the sense that they may be exercised only by the owner of them. Consequently, that person has the sole power to exert control over a given work. However, this power is not absolute in all instances because of a number of limitations on them provided for by the 1976 Act.

The word "copyright" generically refers to these rights. A person who owns one or more of these rights (or any subdivision of a right) is a "copyright owner"; the legal protection provided by these rights is known as "copyright protection"; and a work eligible for copyright protection is a "copyrighted work."

The 1976 Act preempts all federal, state, and local laws that might otherwise grant rights that are the same as or equivalent to those governed by it. The Act is the only basis for acquisition and enforcement of rights for the kinds of works discussed in Chapter 3. Consequently, no other federal law and no state or local law can grant rights equivalent to those covered by the 1976 Act, and no state or local court can enforce rights that are available under the Act. Infringement actions can only be litigated in federal courts.

OWNERSHIP OF RIGHTS IS DISTINCT FROM OWNERSHIP OF OBJECT

Initially, the five exclusive rights belong to the creator(s) of a work or, in the case of a "work made for hire," to the creator's employer or to the party who commissioned creation of it (see Chapter 5). They remain with the initial owner until they are transferred (either individually, in groups, or collectively) to someone else by means of a written agreement, or by a last will and testament, or by operation of law (see Chapter 15). These are the only ways in which these rights can be conveyed.

It is desirable for the initial copyright owner to retain ownership of all five rights because of the control they give that person over how, when, and where a work can be used and who can do so. For this reason, a high percentage of copyright owners allow others to exercise one or more of these rights by giving permission to do so rather than by transferring ownership of them. This can be accomplished by licensing the exercise of rights as discussed in Chapter 19. However, under certain circumstances it may be preferable to transfer ownership of one or more rights, or subdivisions of them, to a third party and to retain all others as discussed in Chapter 15.

Transferring ownership of a physical object that embodies a work does not automatically include transfer of all the exclusive rights in the work. Accordingly, the owner of a particular copy or phonorecord is not entitled to reproduce it, prepare derivative works based on it, or publicly perform it. This is so, regardless of the fact that payment was made for the copy or phonorecord. However, the owner of a copy may further distribute it and, under certain circumstances, publicly display it.

For example, a person who purchases or obtains ownership of a book cannot make copies of it, create a screenplay based upon it, or read it before an audience in public. To do any of these things requires permission from the owner of the rights that are applicable to them.

The 1976 Act expressly provides that ownership of the five rights is distinct from ownership of any object in which a work is embodied.

A COPYRIGHT OWNER'S EXCLUSIVE RIGHTS

The 1976 Act expressly states that the owner of a work automatically acquires the exclusive rights to do and to authorize any of the following with respect to it (subject to a number of limitations discussed in Chapters 7 and 8):

1. To reproduce the copyrighted work in copies or phonorecords
2. To prepare derivative works (adaptations or variations) based on the copyrighted work
3. To distribute copies or phonorecords of the copyrighted work to the public by sale or other transfer of ownership, or by rental, lease, or lending
4. In the case of literary, musical, dramatic, and choreographic works, pantomimes, and motion pictures and other audiovisual works, to perform the copyrighted work publicly
5. In the case of literary, musical, dramatic, and choreographic works, pantomimes, and pictorial, graphic, or sculptural works, including the individual images of a motion picture or other audiovisual work, to display the copyrighted work publicly

The words "copies" and "phonorecords" are defined in Chapter 3.

Some Rights Are not Available for Certain Works

The exclusive rights listed in the previous section are not available for all works. More particularly, the exclusive right to perform publicly is not applicable for sound recordings or for pictorial, graphic, and sculptural works. And the exclusive right to display publicly is not applicable for sound recordings.

For example, the owner of copyright for a sound recording cannot prohibit others from publicly performing it. Likewise, the owner of copyright for a pictorial work does not have the ability under copyright law to preclude someone else from publicly performing it, if this were possible for such a work.

Rights Are Divisible and Independent of Each Other

The 1976 Act establishes the principle of divisibility with respect to copyright ownership. This means that the five exclusive rights in a work can be divided as well as subdivided in terms of their ownership. As a consequence, each right including its subdivisions can be separately owned, exercised, transferred, and enforced independent of the others. Thus, a particular right may be owned by one person, and another by someone else.

For example, the exclusive right to reproduce a book can be owned by a publishing company while the exclusive right to create a screenplay derived from the book can be owned by a motion picture production company.

Generally, a right can be subdivided in an endless number of ways. The extent of subdivision is dependent on the imagination and creativeness of the owner (see Chapter 16 for a discussion on transferring and subdividing rights).

For example, the exclusive right to reproduce a musical work can be subdivided as follows. One person can own the right to reproduce it only in phonograph records, another can own the right to reproduce it only in cassette tapes, and a third can own the right to reproduce it only in sheet music. Or, one person can own the right to perform it publicly in Denver, Colorado, only on the second Monday of each month, another can own the right to do the same only on the first Monday of each month, and a third can do so only on every Wednesday of each month but only in Boulder, Colorado, at a particular nightclub.

Scope of Protection for Each Right

The owner of a particular right (or subdivision of it) in a work, though not the owner of all exclusive rights in the work, is entitled to all of the protection and remedies for that right (or subdivision) available to a copyright owner under the 1976 Act. Thus, the owner of one right can preclude others from exercising it, can license the right or transfer ownership of it, and can seek damages from an infringer.

For example, the legal protection and remedies available to the owner of the exclusive right to perform a musical work publicly are substantially the same as those available to the owner of the exclusive right to reproduce it. Each is entitled to transfer ownership to another person, or to license the exercise of it by someone else, and to preclude others from exercising the right as well as to obtain an injunction for infringement and to seek money damages for the injury suffered or the profits made by the infringer.

On the other hand, there are some inherent limitations on the protection and remedies associated with each right. The scope of protection and remedies available to the owner of a particular right (or subdivision of it) are dependent on the nature of that right.

For example, the owner of the exclusive right to perform a musical work publicly has the power to preclude others from publicly performing it, but not the power to prohibit others from reproducing it in phonograph records or tapes. And the owner of the right to reproduce a literary work in hardcover book form does not have the right to reproduce it in the form of a motion picture.

Authority To Allow Others To Exercise Rights

As noted in the preceding section, there are two things that the owner of rights can do with them on an exclusive basis. The owner has the power to exercise them as well as the power to authorize others to exercise them. The latter is the owner's basis for licensing the exercise of rights by others.

Ownership of the exclusive right to authorize others to do any of the five things enumerated means that the owner of rights is the only person who can grant permission to others to exercise those rights. Consequently, the owner of rights is in the position of being able to exert control over who can exercise those rights.

For example, in the absence of an agreement providing otherwise, the author of a book who has given a publisher the right to reproduce it in hard-cover only, can prevent the publisher from granting permission to reproduce the work in paperback or to create a screenplay based on it. The author has the power to do this by ownership of the exclusive authorization right. Similarly, an advertising agency that acquires from an independent photographer only the right to reproduce a photograph in an ad, does not have the right to give its client permission to print the picture in its annual report.

THE RIGHT TO REPRODUCE

Control Over Making Copies and Phonorecords

The exclusive right to reproduce a work in copies or phonorecords is a very valuable and powerful right. It enables the owner to determine and control how, when, and where a work can be reproduced as well as who can reproduce it, the medium of reproduction, and the number of copies or phonorecords made.

For example, the owner of this right for a pictorial work can reproduce it in any medium desired ranging from photographs to oil paintings to posters, and is the only one who can do so. At the same time the owner is the only one who can authorize someone else to reproduce the work and determine how it can be reproduced in terms of medium, location, or number of copies.

What Constitutes Reproduction of a Work

From a copyright law standpoint, "reproduction" of a work occurs only when it is embodied in a physical object ("copies" or "phonorecords") that is sufficiently permanent or stable to permit the work to be perceived, reproduced, or otherwise communicated, either directly or with the aid of a machine or device. In other words, the creative effort of an individual must be manifested in the form of a lasting physical object, not one that has only a momentary existence.

Keeping this in mind, the exclusive right to reproduce a work would not be violated if it is shown on a screen or television set for a few seconds or minute portion of time without being simultaneously recorded. For example, the television broadcast of a program, which is not being simultaneously recorded by the broadcaster, does not constitute a reproduction of the program. In such situations, if the work is embodied in anything, it is in the form of electronic signals that last only for a moment.

Ordinarily a television broadcast of the type just noted will not constitute a reproduction of the work. However, it may violate one or more of the other exclusive rights. Generally, the broadcast of a work to the public will be a public performance of it and may also constitute a public display of it under certain circumstances.

The Right To Reproduce in All Mediums

Although showing a work for a very brief period would not be a violation of this exclusive right, reproduction of it in a medium other than the one used by the owner of the right would be an exercise of this right and would constitute an infringement of it. For example, if the owner of this right reproduces a musical work only in the form of phonograph records, reproduction of it by someone else in a different medium or different kind of object, such as sheet music or a cassette tape, would nonetheless be a violation of it.

The 1976 Act does not impose any restrictions on the owner of this right with respect to the kinds of physical objects in which a work may be embodied. Consequently, the owner of it can reproduce a work in any medium and is the sole owner of the right to do so.

Others Can Copy From the Same Source

The right to reproduce protects against copying only from a copyrighted work. It is not so broad as to entitle the owner of that right to prevent another person from copying from public domain source material, even if that source material was used to create a copyrighted work.

For example, a fine artist who creates an oil painting reproduction of the *Mona Lisa* and adds original material to it to produce a pictorial work entitled to copyright protection, cannot rely on this right to prevent another artist from creating a pictorial work that is also a reproduction of the *Mona Lisa*. The painter can protect only the original portion of the work. And the writer of a copyrighted article based on historical fact cannot prevent another writer from using the same facts to create a different article.

No Control Over Using Copies or Phonorecords

This right only provides a basis for controlling reproduction of a work, not the use of it. Accordingly, use of a work that does not involve reproduction of it in the form of copies or phonorecords cannot be prevented by virtue of ownership of this particular right.

For example, a third party's performance of a literary work by reading it, or of a motion picture by exhibiting it, constitutes use of the work, but not an exercise of the reproduction right. Likewise, displaying a copy of a pictorial work, broadcasting a musical work, or distributing copies of a dramatic work all constitute use of a work but they are not exercises of the reproduction right.

That use of a work cannot be controlled under the reproduction right does not mean that use of a work is not subject to any control under copyright law. It may be subject to control under the public performance and public display rights.

Reproduction for Private Purposes Infringes

A third party's reproduction of a work by making one or more copies of it for private purposes only (whether for personal use of them or for other uses) is an exercise of this right. This is no less an exercise of this right than when a third party reproduces numerous copies of a work for commercial purposes (i.e., when the copies are produced for sale or distribution to the public).

In this regard, the reproduction right is broader than the exclusive performance and display rights discussed in the following section. They are exclusive only with respect to public performances or displays of a work. Private performances or displays do not constitute an exercise of those rights.

For example, reproducing a few copies of a newsletter for private use constitutes an exercise of this right just as reproducing numerous copies for purposes of selling them to the public. However, performing a musical work in your home hundreds of times, by playing a phonograph record which embodies it, would not be an exercise of the public performance right. Home use does not ordinarily constitute a public performance.

THE RIGHT TO PREPARE DERIVATIVE WORKS

Varying, Altering, Modifying, and Adapting

An owner of the exclusive right to prepare derivative works is the only person who is entitled to vary, alter, modify, adapt, or prepare another version of a preexisting work, and the only one entitled to authorize others to do so. However, someone who is given permission to create a derivative work does not necessarily acquire permission to acquire separate rights in it. This can be done only if the owner of the right to prepare derivative works grants permission to acquire separate rights in the derivative work. (For a review of what constitutes a derivative work and the rights in it, refer to Chapter 3).

As is possible under the reproduction right, possession of the right to prepare derivative works enables the owner to determine and control how, when, and where any one of the aforementioned things can be done to a preexisting work and who will be given permission to do them. Consequently, this is a very valuable and powerful right.

For example, the owner of this right for a musical work is the only person entitled to change its lyrics or melody, or to permit the adaptation of it for use as an advertising jingle (e.g., as was done with "Beat It," written by Michael Jackson and used by Pepsi Cola to promote its products). Similarly, the owner of this right for a literary work written in the English language can control when and who will prepare a foreign language version. The owner of this right for a cartoon character can determine whether someone else will be given permission to create a toy of it.

Right To Create Derivative Works in All Mediums

A derivative work is made by recasting, transforming, or adapting a preexisting work. Consequently, creation of a derivative work necessarily involves incorporating a considerable portion of a preexisting work. This does not mean that the derivative work must be embodied in the same medium or in the same kind of physical object as the preexisting work is embodied.

The exercise of this right, therefore, is not limited with respect to the medium or types of physical objects in which a derivative work may be embodied. The owner of this right can create a derivative work in any medium suitable to it, and is the only person who is entitled to do so.

For example, the owner of this right for a hardcover book can write a screenplay based on it which may then also be printed in book form, or stored on a computer diskette. And the owner of this right for a sculpted porcelain figurine can draw a cartoon character based on it, thus creating the figure in porcelain and on paper.

THE RIGHT TO DISTRIBUTE COPIES OR PHONORECORDS PUBLICLY

The Right To Sell, Give Away, or Loan Each Copy or Phonorecord

Subject to the limitations discussed in this section, this right gives the owner the ability to prevent the unauthorized distribution of copies or phonorecords of a work to the public. This right entitles the owner to exercise control over the selling, giving away, renting, leasing, and lending of each and every copy or phonorecord of a work. And, as is the case with the other exclusive rights, it also entitles the owner to authorize others to do these things.

By virtue of this right the owner can decide how and under what conditions copies or phonorecords of a work will be first made available to the public, whether by sale or gift. In addition, the owner is entitled to determine who will first make them available.

For example, the owner of this right for a software program encoded on diskettes has the sole discretion to decide whether each diskette should be sold, given away, or rented, or whether some should be sold and others rented. Until such time that the owner makes these decisions with respect to each and every diskette, no one else can sell, give away, or rent that particular diskette.

The Effect of a "First Sale" on the Distribution Right

No one can distribute a copy or phonorecord to the public until it has first been sold or given away by the owner of this right or with the permission of the owner. The first sale or gift of each copy or phonorecord by the owner of this right, or under that person's authority, is referred to as a "first sale".

Once a first sale has occurred with respect to a particular copy or phonorecord, the owner of this right loses all physical control over that copy or phonorecord (but not phonorecords embodying musical works and sound recordings—see "Limitations on Commercial Rental, Leasing, or Lending Phonorecords—Embodying Musical Works", later in this chapter). Thereafter, each subsequent owner of that copy or phonorecord can resell it, give it away, rent it, lease it, or loan it without any legal requirement to seek approval to do so from the owner of this right.

Loss of control over distribution by the owner of this right does not necessarily mean that the copy or phonorecord can be used without restriction.

The public performance and/or display of the work continues to be subject to the control of the owner of the public performance and/or public display right. Those rights, as well as the right to reproduce and to prepare a derivative work, remain with the owner of them and are not affected by a transfer of ownership of a copy or phonorecord (see Chapter 16).

It is important to recognize that distribution of a copy or phonorecord by or with the permission of the owner of this right is a determining factor as to whether a first sale has taken place. An initial transfer of ownership not made by or with the permission of such owner will not constitute a first sale of it. Similarly, the rental, lease, or loan of a copy or phonorecord by the owner of this right, without ever transferring ownership of it, does not constitute a "first sale" (see "Renting, Leasing, or Loaning Is Not A First Sale," this Chapter). In both cases, the owner of this right will not lose the right to control physically that copy or phonorecord. Consequently, anyone who has possession but not ownership of it, who resells, gives away, rents, leases, or loans it will violate the distribution right.

The following example illustrates how this exclusive right ceases to be applicable to a copy or phonorecord once there has been a first sale of it.

The owner of the distribution right for a book is the only person entitled to sell, give away, rent, loan, or lease each of the copies in a printed run of 100 copies. If that owner sells or gives away a copy of the book to another person, the purchaser or recipient becomes the owner of the book, but not of any exclusive rights in it. Thereafter that person can resell it, give it away, rent, loan, or lease it to someone else without any legal obligation to obtain permission to do so from the owner of the distribution right. However, although the purchaser or recipient of the book and all subsequent owners of it can deal with it as they please, they cannot reproduce it or otherwise exercise any of the rights of a copyright owner with respect to the literary work embodied in it.

That the owner of the distribution right sells or gives away one book does not affect that person's right to distribute the remaining 99 copies of the book. The right to sell or give away each of the remaining 99 copies remains with the owner and ceases to exist with respect to each of those copies once it is the subject of a first sale.

Distribution of a "Lawfully Made" Copy or Phonorecord

This exclusive right cannot be used to prohibit distribution of a lawfully made copy or phonorecord by the owner of that copy or phonorecord even though there has been no first sale of it. The 1976 Act expressly provides that the owner of a lawfully made copy or phonorecord has the right to sell or otherwise dispose of the possession of it without obtaining permission to do so from the owner of the distribution right.

A lawfully made copy or phonorecord is one made by or under the authority of the owner of the reproduction right or under the authority of a compulsory license for making phonorecords provided for by the 1976 Act.

There are a number of ways in which a person can obtain a lawfully made copy or phonorecord without a first sale taking place.

If the reproduction right is owned by one person and the distribution right is owned by another, anyone who obtains copies or phonorecords made by the owner of the reproduction right will acquire lawfully made copies or phonorecords. A first sale will not occur because the copies are not acquired from the owner of the distribution right. The owner of the distribution right is not able to prevent further distribution by the purchaser.

For example, if a sculptor, who owns all rights to a sculptural work, transfers ownership of the right to reproduce it in bronze castings to a foundry and the right to distribute those castings to an art gallery, anyone who purchases a casting from the foundry has a right to further distribute it. The gallery cannot prevent a purchaser from the foundry from selling a casting because that person obtained a lawfully made copy.

If the owner of the distribution right also owns the reproduction right and permits someone else to make copies or phonorecords, anyone who acquires ownership of them from that party will acquire lawfully made copies or phonorecords. This is the case although there was no first sale of them. There is no basis to prevent further distribution by the purchaser because that person obtained a lawfully made copy.

It would, therefore, be prudent for the owner of the distribution right to prohibit contractually the unauthorized sale and gift of copies or phonorecords made by another party who is given permission to reproduce.

For example, an advertising agency owns all rights to artwork and authorizes reproduction of it by a printer. Rather than transferring reproduction rights to the printer, the agency should draw up an agreement prohibiting unauthorized distribution of the artwork and imposing monetary penalties on the printer if this is done.

Renting, Leasing, or Loaning Is not a First Sale

If the owner of the distribution right rents, leases, or loans a copy or phonorecord instead of selling it or giving it away, there is no first sale of it. Consequently, the person who obtains possession (as contrasted with ownership) does not have a right to make any further distribution of it.

For example, if a computer software company that owns all rights to a software program leases a copy of it to a customer, the customer cannot sell, give away, rent, lease, or loan it to anyone else without permission from the software company. However, if instead the customer buys a copy of the program, the customer would be able to do any of these things without the approval of the software company.

Limitations on Commercial Rental, Leasing, or Lending Phonorecords Embodying Musical Works

The rental, lease, or loan of phonorecords embodying a musical work can also be prevented by the owner of the distribution right, but only under certain circumstances. The 1976 Act expressly prohibits an owner of a phonorecord embodying a musical work from renting, leasing, or loaning it when this is done for purposes of direct or indirect commercial advantage. This is so even if the phonorecord was lawfully made and there has been a first sale.

For example, a record store has no right to rent phonograph records it purchases from a record company.

The 1976 Act sets forth two exceptions to this prohibition and a time limited on it:

(a) A nonprofit library or nonprofit education institution can rent, lease, or loan such a phonorecord if it is done for nonprofit purposes.

(b) The owner of a phonorecord who acquired ownership of it prior to October 4, 1984 is entitled to rent, lease, or loan it.

(c) This prohibition will not be effective after October 4, 1989.

Distribution of Infringing Copies or Phonorecords

The owner of this right can prevent the distribution of infringing copies or phonorecords. An infringing copy or phonorecord is one made without the permission of the owner of the reproduction right. Therefore, an infringing copy or phonorecord is not a lawfully made one and, therefore, is not covered by a first sale.

For these reasons, the owner of an infringing copy or phonorecord cannot distribute it without violating the distribution right.

Distribution of Stolen Copies and Phonorecords

The owner of this right can prevent the distribution of stolen copies or phonorecords regardless that they have been lawfully made, if they have not been the subject of a first sale. A thief does not acquire ownership of stolen property by stealing it because ownership of property cannot be acquired by an unlawful taking of it.

Only the *owner* of a lawfully made copy or phonorecord can distribute it. However, since a thief is not an owner of the copy or phonorecord, this exception to the distribution right is not applicable. Consequently, distribution by a thief as well as by everyone who thereafter possesses the stolen copies or phonorecords will constitute a violation of this right.

For example, if an artist, who owns all rights to a painting, authorizes a printing of it and copies of the print are stolen from the printer, the artist can prevent distribution of the stolen prints. However, if the theft of the print occurs after there has been a first sale of it, this right is no longer in effect. As noted earlier, the owner of this right can no longer control distribution of a copy or phonorecord after a first sale.

Unauthorized Importation of Copies or Phonorecords Into the United States

There is a provision in the 1976 Act that expressly provides that the unauthorized importation of copies or phonorecords acquired outside the United States infringes the distribution right. Accordingly, the owner of this right can prevent such importation. The Act states that this prohibition does not apply to:

1. Importation of copies or phonorecords under the authority or for the use of the Government of the United States or of any State or political subdivision of a State, but not including copies or phonorecords for use in schools, or copies of any audiovisual work imported for purposes other than archival use

2. Importation, for the private use of the importer and not for distribution:
   a. By any person with respect to no more than one copy or phonorecord of any one work at any one time, or
   b. By any person arriving from outside the United States with respect to copies or phonorecords forming part of such person's personal baggage

3. Importation by or for an organization operated for scholarly, educational, or religious purposes and not for private gain, with respect to:
   a. No more than one copy of an audiovisual work solely for its archival purposes, and
   b. No more than five copies or phonorecords of any other work for its library lending or archival purposes unless the importation of such

copies or phonorecords is part of an activity engaged in by such organization consisting of the systematic reproduction or distribution of copies or phonorecords

THE RIGHT TO PERFORM PUBLICLY

Live Performances as Well as Performance by Broadcasting

The owner of the performance right is entitled to exercise a significant amount of control over the use of a work. However, this right is subject to many limitations that allow others to exercise this right if they meet the conditions expressly set forth in the 1976 Act (see Chapters 7 and 8).

Except as otherwise provided by the statutory limitations, the owner of this right is the only person who is entitled to perform "publicly" a work. Furthermore, the owner is the only person entitled to authorize someone else to permit others to perform a work publicly. Third parties may be able to obtain permission to perform publicly a work directly from the owner of this right under voluntary licensing agreements (see Chapter 19.)

This right covers the broadcast of music by radio and television as well as the performance of it at nightclubs, concerts, and in other places open to the public including department stores or dentists' offices. This right also gives the owner the power to determine and control how, when, and where the presentation of stage plays, operas, choreographed works, videotapes, motion pictures, and slide shows can take place as well as who can make them. The owner's control includes readings of poetry, recitations of passages from books, and the giving of lectures, among other activities.

What Constitutes a Performance?

A work is performed if it is recited, rendered, presented, played, danced, or acted. This is true whether it is performed live or by a mechanical device or process. A motion picture or other audiovisual work is performed by showing its images in any sequence or by making sounds accompanying it audible. Thus, playing a movie sound-track constitutes a performance of the film even if its visual images are not seen.

The initial act of reciting, playing, or dancing constitutes a performance of a work and so does any other act that transmits or otherwise communicates those actions by a mechanical device or by a process. Thus, any act by which an initial performance is transmitted, repeated, or made to recur is itself a performance.

To transmit a performance is to communicate it by any device or process whereby images or sounds are received beyond the place from which they are sent. Thus, television and radio broadcasts constitute transmissions of a performance of a work and so do all conceivable forms and combinations of wired or wireless communications media. Each method by which the images and sounds comprising a performance are picked up and conveyed is a transmission.

For instance, a musician performs a song when he or she plays it live. If this performance is transmitted by a television broadcasting network, the transmission constitutes a performance of the song. And if a local television station transmits the network broadcast, the local television station's transmission is also a performance. Similarly, if the musician's performance is recorded on a videotape and that tape is used by a television station in a broadcast, the transmission constitutes a performance. And if the performance is recorded on a phonograph record or cassette tape, playing that record or tape also constitutes a performance.

The kinds of mechanical devices that perform works are those that reproduce or modify sounds or visual images (motion picture projectors, radios, television sets, videocassette and videodisk players, as well as record, tape, and compact disk players). They also include any sort of transmitting apparatus (television and radio broadcasting equipment), any type of electronic retrieval system, and, as indicated in the Act, any other techniques and systems not yet in use or invented. A television or radio broadcast is a process that performs works.

Although the owner is entitled to control performances of a work, this right is not so broad as to allow the owner to control all performances of a work. This right is applicable only to public performances. Therefore, a private performance of a work can be made by everyone without violating this right.

What Constitutes a "Public" Performance

The Act provides that a work is publicly performed when it is performed at a place open to the public or at any place where a substantial number of persons outside of a normal circle of a family and its social acquaintances is gathered.

For example, a public performance of a motion picture is made when it is shown by means of a videocassette player in a bar, restaurant, or department store. The same is true when a record is played on a stereo in a hotel lobby.

In addition, a public performance occurs when a live or recorded performance is transmitted or otherwise communicated to a place open to the public or a location where a substantial number of unrelated people are gathered. A public performance is also made when it is viewed by people located at different places even if they view it at different times.

For example, a public performance of *Fiddler On The Roof* takes place not only at the time the actors present it live before an audience in a theater, but also when a network broadcasts the live or taped performance to the public in their homes. A local broadcaster also performs the play publicly by transmitting the network broadcast to its viewers.

A public performance of a work also occurs when a work is performed in "semipublic" places such as clubs, lodges, factories, summer camps, and schools. On the other hand, it is arguable that routine meetings of businesses and governmental personnel would not be a "public" performance. Ordinarily, they do not represent the gathering of a "substantial number of persons."

Sound Recordings and Pictorial, Graphic, and Sculptural Works

The 1976 Act expressly provides that this right does not extend to sound recordings. In addition, it is not available for pictorial, graphic, and sculptural works since they are not included in the listing of works to which this right applies.

The nonapplicability of this right to pictorial, graphic, and sculptural works does not preclude an equivalent type of protection for them. This is possible under the right to display publicly.

The inability of the owner of a sound recording to prevent its public performance does not necessarily mean that the underlying work, which has been recorded and is being expressed aurally by means of the sound recording, is not entitled to the protection of this right. It only means that the persons who created the sounds and own the sound recording cannot prevent others from publicly performing those sounds. If the underlying work is a copyrighted work, the public performance right would be applicable to it and the owner of this right for that work would be entitled to prevent the public performance of it.

For example, a record company that releases a record featuring the song "Moon River" sung by Andy Williams (who created the sound recording as a work made for hire) has no right to prevent the broadcast of that sound recording by a radio station. However, the music publisher that owns "Moon River" can do so because it controls the public performance right to the song.

On the other hand, if the underlying work is not protected under copyright law, a sound recording of it can be publicly performed wihout restriction. For example, a record featuring the "Star Spangled Banner" or a musical work by Mozart can be played in public and broadcast by a radio station without violating the public performance right.

THE RIGHT TO DISPLAY PUBLICLY

Phonorecords Are not Subject to this Right

This exclusive right applies only to copies of a work. Subject to a number of limitations, it gives the owner the ability to determine how, when, and where copies of a work can be publicly displayed and who can publicly display them. It also gives the owner the power to prevent the unauthorized public display of a copy of a work. In addition, this right is the basis for the owner's ability to determine whether someone else can give permission to others to display publicly copies of a work.

What Constitutes a Display

A work is displayed by means of showing a copy of it, either directly or by means of a film, slide, television image, or any other device or process. Thus, a work is displayed by direct live showings of the copy itself as well as by indirect showings. Indirect showings are made by projecting an image of the copy on a screen or other surface, by transmitting an image of it by electronic or other means, by showing an image of it on a cathode ray tube (e.g., a television monitor) or similar viewing apparatus connected with any sort of information storage and retrieval system.

A motion picture or other audiovisual work is displayed by showing individual images nonsequentially. If the images are shown in sequence they would be performed, not displayed.

As is the case with the performance of a work, the initial act of showing a copy of a work constitutes a display of it and so does any other act that transmits or otherwise communicates those actions by a mechanical device or by a process. Accordingly, any act by which the initial display is transmitted, repeated, or made to recur also constitutes a display. A display is transmitted in the same way that a performance can be transmitted. That is, by communicating it by any device or process whereby images are received beyond the place from which they are sent.

For example, the showing of photographs, art prints, and bronze sculpture at an exhibition will constitute a live display of copies of pictorial as well as sculptural works and a showing of pages from a book at an exhibition will also constitute a live display of a copy of a literary work. If the exhibition is videotaped and the videotape is shown, the act of showing it will also constitute an indirect display of these copies. Similarly, if the exhibition is being televised, a transmission of the display will be an indirect display of the copies.

This right does not extend to the private display of a copy of a work and it ceases to be applicable to a copy once there has been an initial transfer of ownership of it (first sale). The owner of this right can only enforce it where a copy is publicly displayed but not if the public display is made by the owner of the copy under certain conditions.

What Constitutes a "Public" Display?

The same criterion used to determine whether a work is publicly performed is used to determine whether there is a public display of it. Thus, a work is publicly displayed when it is shown at a place open to the public or at any place where a substantial number of persons outside of a normal circle of a family and its social acquaintances is gathered.

A copy of a work is also publicly displayed where a live or recorded display of it is transmitted or otherwise communicated to a place open to the public, a location where a substantial number of unrelated people are gathered, or to the homes of the recipients in those cases where the transmission or communication can be received by members of the general public. In addition, the live display of a copy of a work in a semipublic place, or the transmission of a live or recorded display of it to such a place, constitutes a public display.

A "Lawfully Made" Copy Can Be Publicly Displayed

The 1976 Act expressly provides that the owner of a lawfully made copy is entitled to display it publicly if certain conditions are met. Accordingly, the owner of such a copy can publicly display it without any requirement to obtain permission from the owner of this right.

The owner of a lawfully made copy can display it directly or indirectly. In both cases, the display must be at the place where the copy is located. The "place where the copy is located" is a location where the viewers are present in the same physical surroundings as the copy, even though they may not be able to see the copy directly.

A direct display can be made by showing the copy to viewers who are present at the place where the copy is located. If an indirect display is made to such individuals it can be done by the projection of no more than one image of the copy at a time.

For example, a purchaser of an art print has the right to display it publicly on a wall at a gallery, or any other location where the print is located, but only to viewers who are present at the gallery. The purchaser can also display the print at the same place where it is located by using a projector to show a photographic slide that features an image of the print. However, only one image at a time can be shown. The simultaneous projection of multiple images is not permitted and the owner is not entitled to transmit the image of the print to another place. Over-the-air or cable television, or other means of transmitting an image, is not permitted.

Renting, Leasing, or Loaning a Copy Is not an Ownership Transfer

A person who obtains possession of a copy by rental, lease, or loan from the owner of this right is not entitled to display it publicly. That person is not the owner of the copy and, therefore, the statutory limitation on the public display right is not applicable.

For example, a gallery that obtains possession of an oil painting on consignment from an artist who retains ownership of all rights in it does not have any right to display publicly the painting without permission by the artist. Furthermore, from the standpoint of copyright law, unless the artist gives permission, the gallery is not entitled to reproduce the painting in the form of posters for public display to promote the artist's painting.

The Public Display of Infringing Stolen Copies

The owner of this right can prevent the public display of infringing and stolen copies for the same reasons and under the same circumstances that the owner of the distribution right can do so. (see "Distribution of Infringing Copies or Phonorecords" and "Distribution of Stolen Copies or Phonorecords," this Chapter.)

Phonorecords Are not Covered

The only category of works not covered by the public display right is sound recordings. They are not included in the listing of works to which this right applies.

Although the material objects in which sounds are embodied are visually perceptible, namely phonorecords, sounds are not. Thus, they cannot be displayed.

CHAPTER SUMMARY

• The legal protection for a work under copyright law is in the form of five exclusive rights.

- A copyright owner possesses the exclusive right to reproduce a work, prepare derivative works based on it, publicly distribute copies or phonorecords of it, publicly perform it, and publicly display it.
- A person who acquires ownership of a copy or phonorecord embodying a work is not necessarily the owner of exclusive rights in it; ownership of rights is distinct from ownership of a material object in which a work is embodied.
- Each right is independent of the others and is divisible.

7

Fair Use

As mentioned in Chapter 6, the 1976 Act imposes a number of limitations on the exclusive rights in a work. These limitations are referred to as "limitations on exclusive rights" because they impose limits on the ability of a copyright owner to exercise rights exclusively. In other words, they permit the exercise of certain rights by persons other than the copyright owner, but only in particular situations. The "fair use" limitation is one of these limitations and is discussed here. The other limitations are briefly discussed in Chapter 8.

All of the limitations provided for by the Act are based on the principle that there should be a balancing of the interest of copyright owners to maintain maximum control over their rights against the public's genuine needs to use protected material. This balancing occurs by subordinating the exclusive rights of copyright owners and by imposing restrictions on the uses made of copyrighted works by the public.

The circumstances under and the extent to which these rights can be exercised are dictated by the Act. This is done in the form of guidelines for the "fair use" limitation and rules for the other limitations. If there is compliance with the guidelines and rules, the person who desires to exercise these rights is not obligated to obtain the copyright owner's consent. Failure to comply fully with the guidelines and rules may result in a copyright infringement lawsuit.

Some limitations are applicable to a number of rights and available for the benefit of specific persons, groups, and businesses. Other limitations are applicable to a particular right but are available to everyone.

BALANCING CONFLICTING INTERESTS

The fair use limitation permits the exercise of any one or more of the exclusive rights to a work and is applicable to all categories of works. There is no particular class of persons for whose benefit it was created. Consequently, it has the broadest application of all the limitations under the Act and is the one most likely to be relied on by everyone as justification for exercising a right with respect to a work. In addition, it is probably the one most often raised as a defense in copyright infringement actions.

The phrase "fair use" accurately describes this limitation because it attempts to achieve a proper balance of the conflicting interests discussed earlier in this chapter. However, there is no definition of fair use in the 1976 Act and there has never been a specific provision covering this limitation in any statute prior to the Act.

The principle of law on which this limitation is based was established through court decisions rendered over many years and was codified for the first time in the 1976 Act. The criteria for determining fair use, which evolved from these decisions, are now stated in terms of guidelines in the Act rather than as strict rules. Thus, there is room for flexibility in every case to determine the effect a particular use may have on the rights of a copyright owner.

Refer to these guidelines, just as the courts must do, to evaluate a particular use of a work for permissibility under this limitation.

GUIDELINES FOR DETERMINING FAIR USE

The guidelines for application of the fair use limitation give examples of the types of uses that can be made of a work and indicate that a number of factors must be considered in evaluating whether the use in a particular case is fair. The listing of the types of uses that can be made is not meant to be exhaustive. Furthermore, there is nothing in the Act that indicates that any one factor is more important than the others.

The fair use limitation is set forth in the Act as follows:

> The fair use of a copyrighted work, including such use by reproduction in copies or phonorecords or by any of the other exclusive rights of a copyright owner, for purposes such as criticism, comment, news reporting, teaching (including multiple copies for classroom use), scholarship, or research, is not an infringement of copyright.

> In determining whether the use made of a work in any particular case is a fair use the factors to be considered shall include—

(1) the purpose and character of the use, including whether such use is of a commercial nature or is for nonprofit educational purposes;

(2) the nature of the copyrighted work;

(3) the amount and substantiality of the portion used in relation to the copyrighted work as a whole; and

(4) the effect of the use upon the potential market for or value of the copyrighted work.

FACTORS TO BE CONSIDERED

Every exercise of a right claimed under this limitation is evaluated with the four enumerated factors in mind. A finding with respect to each factor is taken into consideration and weighed against the findings for the others, keeping in mind the particular right being exercised. If one finding or more is unfavorable it is not necessarily conclusive that a fair use has not been made with respect to the right being exercised. In each case, it is the net effect of all the findings that controls the decision since the Act does not require that any one factor be given more weight than the others.

Although the limitation lists only four factors to be considered, these are only guidelines and other factors can also be considered. Courts are given a significant amount of discretion under this limitation with respect to the factors they can consider in determining whether a specific use is fair or not. Where strict enforcement of the rights of a copyright owner conflict with the purpose of the copyright law or with some other important societal value, a court may fashion an appropriate fair use limitation. Therefore, any factor that may have a bearing on whether a fair use has been made can be considered as long as the four set forth in the Act are also considered. If a factor other than one set forth in the Act justifies a fair use finding, a decision can be rendered based solely on that factor.

The Purpose and Character of Use Factor

The kinds of uses specified in the guidelines give some idea of those generally regarded as fair. However, they may not be fair under all circumstances and, as mentioned earlier, they are not the only uses that qualify under this limitation. In all cases, the purpose and character of the use must be considered.

In considering whether a fair use has been made, the commercial or nonprofit educational character of a use must be weighed. This does not mean fair use will be found *only* for nonprofit purposes or that fair use will be found in *every case* when there are nonprofit purposes.

For example, copying substantial portions of a copyrighted book in another book by a different author would not necessarily be a fair use, even though the copying is done for nonprofit educational purposes. Similarly, the large scale videotaping of copyrighted motion pictures by a nonprofit educational cooperative, and distribution of the videtape copies to schools for education purposes, would not necessarily be a fair use. On the other hand, the use of verbatim quotations from a copyrighted magazine article on vacuum cleaners in a television commercial promoting a particular vacuum cleaner may be a fair use even though it is done for commercial purposes.

The kinds of uses specified in the guidelines suggest that those that are for the benefit of society in general are more likely to be fair than those that are purely commercial. Arguably, society benefits from uses that serve to disseminate information to the public (e.g., criticism, comment, and news reporting) as well as from those that tend to promote the development of education, the arts, science, and industry (e.g., teaching, scholarship, and research). However, that society may benefit from a particular use does not mean it is a fair use.

For example, reproducing frames of a copyrighted home movie of the assassination of President Kennedy in a nonfiction book analyzing the evidence on the assassination was held to be a fair use because of the public interest in having as much information as possible about that event. At the other extreme, the television broadcast of copyrighted motion picture clips from Charlie Chaplin films, as part of a news story on Charlie Chaplin, was found not to be a fair use because the public interest did not outweigh the rights of the copyright owners to the motion pictures.

For-profit uses can qualify for this limitation, as suggested by the language of this factor, but they are presumed to be unfair. As a result, commercial uses of copyrighted works are less favored than nonprofit uses. Courts are generally reluctant to subordinate a copyright owner's exclusive rights to accommodate the commercial motivation of a user, especially where the for-profit use is primarily for the benefit of the user rather than society in general.

For example, the fair use limitation was not available when a substantial number of copyrighted questions from a medical college admission test were copied in a practice test booklet. The practice test booklet was prepared by the operator of a for-profit course to teach medical school applicants how to take the copyrighted test. The for-profit purpose in that case was enough to outweigh the educational use claimed.

Guidelines for Educational Copying and for Educational Uses of Music. During the time that Congress was conducting hearings on the 1976 Act, and prior to its enactment, guidelines were developed covering copying from books and periodicals for educational purposes and for the educational uses of music. Each set of guidelines was developed independently of Congress through the joint effort of citizens representing educational institutions, author organizations, publishers, and music educators. However, the guidelines were not officially adopted by Congress. Consequently, they have no legal impact on any fair use determination by the courts, but it is likely that courts will refer to them and give them some weight when the facts of a given case are within their scope.

These guidelines are not intended to apply to and do not cover the educational use of audiovisual works.

The stated purpose of the guidelines is to set forth minimum standards of educational fair use, but they are not intended to limit the types of copying permitted under the statutory guidelines. There may be instances in which copying that does not fall within the guidelines may, nonetheless, be permitted.

The educational use guidelines are known as "Guidelines for Classroom Copying in Not-For-Profit Educational Institutions with Respect to Books and Periodicals" and "Guidelines for Educational Uses of Music." The text of each is included in Appendix B.

Parody. The copying of portions of a copyrighted work may be a fair use of it where the purpose and nature of the copying are to create a parody or satire. Courts have held that parody and satire are deserving of substantial freedom in this regard because they entertain, inform, stir public consciousness, and foster creativity. However, as a general proposition the amount that can be taken for such purposes is no more than is necessary to recall or conjure up the object of the parody or satire. It is not permissible to make a verbatim copy or to paraphrase a copyrighted work substantially to create a parody or satire.

For example, a court found fair use when four notes and two words were copied from a copyrighted song that was composed of a 45-word lyric and 100 measures. But there was no fair use when the essence of a copyrighted television commercial and accompanying jingle were copied.

Incidental Use. In some instances fair use may occur where a copyrighted work, or a portion of it, is used incidentally and as background in an entirely different class of work. The incidental nature of such a use and its noncompetition with the copyrighted work would be a basis for a fair use finding.

For example, a television broadcast of a filmed parade that included a float on which a band was playing a copyrighted song was found to be a fair use of that song. If the broadcast also showed a copyrighted sign, sculpture, and the like, in the background it is likely that such a showing would likewise be a fair use. The use of 15 seconds of a copyrighted song, which was part of an incumbent state governor's recorded political advertisement, was found to be fair use when such use was in the background of an opposing politician's radio commercial.

Copies for the Use of the Blind. The making of a single copy or phonorecord of a work as a free service for the blind is a fair use. However, making multiple copies for general circulation requires the permission of the copyright owner. Copies made by the Library of Congress's Division for the Blind and Physically Handicapped have such permission.

Off-the-Air Videotaping for Private Use. A 1984 U.S. Supreme Court decision expressly provides that off-the-air home videotaping of copyrighted television broadcasts is permissible under the fair use limitation. That is, if the taping is done by an individual for his or her own private home use and not for commercial purposes.

Off-the-air audiotaping of television or radio broadcasts for private use is not covered by that decision and neither is off-the-air audio or videotaping of television and radio broadcasts for nonprofit purposes. However, off-the-air videotaping of televised newscasts by libraries and archives is permissible under the libraries and archives limitation if it is done without any purpose of direct or indirect commercial advantage. Similarly, off-the-air audio- or videotaping of a noncommercial educational broadcast station transmission is permissible if:

1. It is done by a governmental body or a nonprofit institution simultaneously with the transmission, and

2. The tape is played in the course of face-to-face teaching activities of a nonprofit educational institution in a classroom or similar place devoted to instruction, but only if

3. The transmission is of a published nondramatic musical work or a published pictorial, graphic, and sculptural work, and

4. The tape is destroyed no later than seven days from the date of the transmission

Nature of the Work Factor

Works that are compilations or of an informational nature appear to be subject to a fair use finding more so than those that are of an entertaining nature, if the use is for noncommercial purposes. As mentioned before, the nonprofit or commercial nature of a use is a factor that must be considered.

Informational Nature. Works that may be classified as informational include those that are scholarly, technical, or scientific. Depending on the facts of a particular case, portions of such works may be fairly used on the premise that the creation of many new works necessarily involves borrowing from informational resources. For similar reasons, portions of compilations of fact may be fairly used. Such works include directories, indexes, and catalogs usually produced by diligently gathering facts rather than by any creative effort. It has been held by a court that there is greater freedom to use portions of works created through sheer diligence than to use those produced through creativity and imagination.

For example, it is likely that the copying, in a college research paper, of portions of an encyclopedia or other resource would be a fair use. A court found that the copying of names from a copyrighted index which included other information and was produced through fact-gathering was a fair use where the names were used to produce a different index.

Limited Circulation, Unpublished, and Consumable Material. If a work such as a limited circulation newsletter is not generally available to the public, the fair use limitation may be more narrowly construed by the courts than with respect to mass-circulation works like newspapers. Congress suggested that the fair use limitation should not be loosely applied to limited circulation newsletters because they are particularly vulnerable to mass photocopying. If fair use were broadly applied, the demand for the original newsletter might be significantly decreased. Arguably, in the case of an unpublished work, the owner may have deliberately chosen not to make it generally available. Accordingly, to allow a broad fair use of such a work would defeat the owner's right to make it available if and when he or she chooses to do so.

For similar reasons it has been stated that the scope of fair use should not be broadly applied with respect to a work intended to be consumable in the course of using it such as a workbook, standardized test, or answer sheet. If such works can be freely copied under the fair limitation, the market for them would be substantially reduced.

Material of an Entertaining Nature. The fair use limitation is also narrowly construed with respect to works whose creation involves a reasonable amount of originality and imagination. Many literary, musical, and artistic works fall within this category, as do other works that are generally entertaining in nature. Two examples are motion pictures and works in the performing arts area such as plays. Often, the use made of these kind of works is for commercial purposes rather than for nonprofit and educational purposes.

For example, taking excerpts from a novel to produce a condensed version of it would not ordinarily be justifiable under the fair use limitation, although the use of excerpts for purposes of a book review would be acceptable. Also, it is unlikely that a fair use of a popular song can be made by taking the melody and substituting the original lyrics with an advertising message.

The Amount and Substantiality Factor

Some people believe it is permissible to use one paragraph or so from a literary work, two measures or eight notes from a musical composition, four frames from a motion picture, and so on, without incurring liability for copyright infringement. While this may be true in specific situations, there is no general rule in this regard. However, there is one with respect to the use or copying of an entire work or the excessive use or copying of it. Ordinarily, such use precludes application of this limitation. On the other hand, if the copying or use involves an amount less than all of a work, a determination of whether such a use is fair (insofar as this factor is concerned) requires a consideration of the substantiality of the portion used.

Quality of the Amount Used Must Be Considered. An evaluation of the substantiality of the portion of a work used involves consideration of the relationship of that portion to the work as whole in terms of quality and substance. The use of an essential part of a work, or portion that constitutes the substance of it, weighs heavily against a fair use finding even though the amount used is relatively small.

For example, there was no fair use when 50 percent of a book was copied verbatim and that percentage contained virtually all of the substance of the book copied.

Giving Credit Does not Justify Copying. Many people are under the mistaken impression that it is okay to use an entire work, or significant portions of it, as long as the copyright owner is given credit or the work itself is acknowledged as a source. Although the citation may be an element considered by a court in determining whether a fair use has been made, it is unlikely to be given much weight and certainly will not be persuasive if findings with respect to this factor and the others do not support a fair use.

The Effect of the Use

As indicated earlier, the Act does not provide that one factor should be given more weight than the others with respect to determining fair use. However, at the present time, decisions by the courts appear to do so. These decisions indicate that the fourth factor is widely accepted to be the most important. That is, the effect of the use on the potential market for or value of the work used or copied.

The Market Must Be Considered. It has been held that a balance must sometimes be struck between the benefit the public will derive if the use of a work is permitted and the personal gain a copyright owner will receive if such use is denied. The less adverse effect the use has on a copyright owner's expectation of gain, the less public benefit need be shown to justify use of the work.

It should be noted that the presence or absence of measurable pecuniary damages by the owner of the work copied or used is not necessarily determinative of whether there has been or will be such an adverse effect. There can be a finding of an adverse effect on the market where the sale of only one copy of the work has been lost.

Keeping the foregoing in mind, if the effect of copying portions of a copyrighted work is the creation of another work that competes with or takes away the potential market for the copyrighted work, it is likely that there will be an adverse effect on that work and that a court will find that the copying is not fair. Similarly, if the use of a copyrighted work (e.g., publicly performing or publicly displaying it) is the same kind of use that would be made by the owner of that work, it is likely that such use will have an adverse effect on the market for the work and that a court will find that a fair use has not been made.

For example, a television network's use of excerpts from a copyrighted film, as part of its coverage of the Olympics, was found to have a meaningful adverse effect on the market for the film and, therefore, such use was not fair. The court stated that the telecast foreclosed a significant potential market to the copyright owner, namely the sale of the film for use on television in connection with the Olympics. Similarly, a court found that a stage play featuring a number of scenes and portions of its script based on the copyrighted novel *Gone With The Wind* was not a fair use. The court stated that the play is likely to harm the potential market for or value of a stage version of *Gone With The Wind*. On the other hand, copying five or six frames together with words and dialogue from television commercials (which were videotaped off-the-air) on photo boards that are sold to advertisers as part of a report evaluating the commercials, was found to be a fair use. This finding was based on a court's conclusion that the reports did not measurably diminish any demand for the commercials.

Fulfilling the Same Need. In many cases the market demand for a particular work can be fulfilled by a separate but similar work even though the format or medium of each differs from the other. For example, it is possible that the market demand for a book can be met by a motion picture that has used portions of the literary work. In addition, production of one motion picture using portions of the literary work may reduce the value of that work for a later movie based on it by, or authorized by, the owner of that work.

In summary, if the use of a work (by copying portions of it or otherwise) results in another work that performs the same function or fulfills the same need as the copied work, it is likely that a court will find that the use is not fair. The fact that the two works may differ in format, medium of expression, or otherwise, would not necessarily be a basis to justify the use under this limitation.

In the case of *Gone With The Wind*, the court held that the overall function of both the novel and the stage play is to entertain. Consequently, it concluded that the stage play was likely to harm the potential market for or value of the novel by destroying a demand for an authorized stage version of it. For similar reasons, a court held that the videotaping and sale of portions of television news programs by an independent service was not a fair use because the effect of such activities could adversely impact on the potential market for the television station to market copies of its news programs.

On the other hand, where the use of a work results in another work that does not compete in any way with it, and the potential market for or value of the work used is not adversely impacted, the chances are good that a fair use finding will be made. For example, in a case where the cover of a copyrighted television guide was reproduced in a television commercial for a competitive guide, the court found that a fair use had been made. It stated that it was unable to find any effect, other than possible *de minimus*, on the use of the guide cover in the commercial.

EXAMPLES OF FAIR USES AND USES THAT ARE NOT FAIR

Some additional examples of the kind of activities that may or may not constitute fair use are:

FAIR

Quotation of excerpts from a book in a review or criticism for purposes of illustration or comment

Quotation of short phrases in a scholarly or technical work, for illustration or clarification of the author's observations

Use in a magazine of parody lyrics designed to be sung to the tunes of various popular songs which had neither the intent nor the effect of fulfilling the demand for the original songs

Summary of a written speech or an article, with brief quotations, in a news report

Reproduction by a teacher or student of a small part of a work to illustrate a lesson

Casual display of a copyrighted hand puppet in a television program

Use of excerpts from copyrighted magazine articles in a biography of a public figure

Reprinting portions of a letter to the editor of a publication even though permission to reproduce the letter was conditioned upon printing it in its entirety or not at all

NOT FAIR

Large-scale videotaping of copyrighted motion pictures by a nonprofit educational group even though the copies were used for educational purposes

Substantial quoting from copyrighted speeches in advertising pamphlets used to induce consumers to purchase plastic busts of a public figure

Incorporating substantially all of a copyrighted piano and solo voice composition into an arrangement for choirs

Using three sentences from a scientific treatise in an advertising pamphlet to enhance the sale of a tobacco product

Use of a substantial amount of a motion picture to create a television program that was a parody of the motion picture

Use of one-third of a musical composition by a nonprofit organization engaged in commercial activities to raise funds for its expenses

CHAPTER SUMMARY

- The exclusive rights and legal protection available for a work are not absolute in all respects.
- Under certain conditions specified in the 1976 Act the ability of a copyright owner to prevent others from exercising one or more rights is limited.
- Under the fair use limitation everyone is entitled to reproduce, publicly perform, and/or display a work for purposes of criticism, comment, news reporting, teaching, scholarship, research, or parody.
- Four factors are considered in determining whether a use is "fair," namely the character of the use, the nature of the work, the amount of the work used, and the effect of the use on the potential market for or value of the work.

8
Limitations on Rights

$\mathbf{T}$he limitations on the exclusive rights of a copyright owner discussed in this chapter permit a variety of uses of works. Generally, they permit the public performance and display of works as part of nonprofit educational teaching activities, in the course of religious services, before a live audience when there is no purpose of direct or indirect commercial advantage, and by showing them on television and radio sets, among other types of performances and displays. Furthermore, they allow the reproduction of pictorial, graphic, and sculptural works in advertising under certain circumstances, the reproduction and adaptation of works embodied in computer programs, and the reproduction of works by libraries and archives.

These limitations are of interest to copyright owners and to persons who wish to exercise a right in a work. They establish the circumstances under which it is permissible to perform, display, copy, and adapt a work without the necessity of obtaining permission from the copyright owner. For instance, individuals who are employed by noncommercial libraries or archives, and researchers who use them, can determine when it is permissible to reproduce copies of works. Similarly, these limitations indicate when and what works can be publicly performed and displayed by individuals engaged in commercial and noncommercial radio and television broadcasting activities and those who are involved in the management of hotels, apartment houses, nightclubs, and similar establishments.

The circumstances under which each of these limitations is applicable are defined in the 1976 Act and are set forth as specific rules. They are not complex, although the headings used to describe each of them may make them seem dry and incomprehensible.

In the event the facts of a given case do not justify use of a work under one of the limitations referred to in this chapter, it is nonetheless possible that the use may be permissible. The fair use limitation may be applicable.

STATUTORY LIMITATIONS

The limitations on a copyright owner's rights discussed in this chapter are generally identified by the following headings:

1. Certain performances and displays
   a. Face-to-face teaching activities of a nonprofit educational institution
   b. Instructional broadcasting to nonprofit educational institutions
   c. Religious services
   d. Certain nonprofit performances
   e. Reception of broadcasts in a public place
   f. Agricultural and horticultural fairs
   g. Retail sale of records and tapes
   h. Noncommercial broadcasts of nondramatic literary works to the blind or deaf
   i. Nonprofit performances of dramatic works broadcast to the blind or other visually handicapped persons
   j. Nonprofit veterans' or fraternal organizations
2. Limitations on the rights in sound recordings
3. Limitations on rights in pictorial, graphic, and sculptural works
4. Reproduction by libraries and archives
5. Secondary transmissions
6. Ephemeral recordings
7. Noncommercial educational broadcasting
8. Making copies or adaptations of computer programs

LIMITATIONS ON CERTAIN PERFORMANCES AND DISPLAYS

The limitations on performances and displays do not permit reproduction or the creation of variations of a work, or the distribution of copies or phono-records to the public. They are applicable only to the public performance and display of a work in 10 separate fact situations, each of which is precisely defined in the Act.

Generally, literary and musical works are the kind that can be publicly performed under these limitations. All categories of works can be publicly displayed under them.

Whereas the fair use limitation involves a subjective consideration of the facts in each case, according to the guidelines, these limitations prescribe strict rules be applied to the facts in each case. The merits of each use is not evaluated. If a use falls within the boundaries of one of the 10 rules, it will be permissible under these limitations.

The fair use factors were taken into consideration by Congress in defining the permissible uses under these limitations. However, unlike the fair use limitation, it is permissible to perform publicly or to display publicly an entire work.

As noted in the following section, all but one of the permissible uses that can be made of a work are for the benefit of designated classes of users or for specific purposes. For example, in one instance a permissible use can be made only by nonprofit educational institutions; in another, it can be made only in the course of services at a place of worship.

Face-to-Face Systematic Teaching Activities

It is permissible to perform publicly and to display publicly works in all categories under this rule, but only in connection with face-to-face systematic teaching activities as described below. However, it is not permissible to perform or display an unlawfully made copy of a motion picture or other audiovisual work if the person responsible for the performance knew or had reason to believe the copy was made without permission of the owner. For example, it would not be permissible to play a videotape of a network television program made from an over-the-air broadcast.

The public performance or display of a work is permissible if it is done by instructors or pupils in the course of face-to-face systematic teaching activities of a nonprofit educational institution, in a classroom or similar place devoted to instruction.

Instructors or Pupils. Ordinarily, actors, singers, or instrumentalists invited to perform at a nonprofit educational institution are not considered instructors. Accordingly, their performances would not be permissible even though they might be made in the course of face-to-face teaching activities. "Pupils" refers to enrolled members of a class.

Performances and displays in such places as a school gymnasium, training field, studio, workshop, library, or auditorium are as permissible under this rule as when they are done in a classroom. However, they are permissible in such locations only if the audience is confined to members of a particular class. If the audience is composed of more than the members of a class, such as members attending a school assembly, graduation ceremony, class play, or sporting event, the performance or display would not be permissible under this rule, although a nonprofit performance in those situations may be permissible under the rule discussed in the next section of this chapter.

Classroom or Similar Place. Congress indicated that the concept of "face-to-face teaching activities" does not require that an instructor and pupils be able to see each other during the course of such activities. However, it does require that they be present at the same time in the same general place. Thus, a permissible performance or display can be made by using intercom, loudspeaker, and closed-circuit television or other amplifying or projecting systems to communicate it from one classroom or building to another for reception as long as the classrooms and buildings are in the same general area. However, the communication of the performance or display is not permissible if it goes beyond the place where the copy of the work is located, such as to the community at large. Similarly, it would not be permissible to broadcast or otherwise transmit a performance or display to a classroom from a place outside the general area where an instructor and pupils are located, such as from a television station in the same city.

Performances and displays made for purposes of recreation or entertainment would not be permissible, regardless of their cultural value or intellectual appeal.

Instructional Broadcasting

Nondramatic literary and musical works are the only categories of works that can be publicly performed under this rule, by or in the course of a transmission, subject to the conditions noted below. Consequently, works such as motion pictures, musical comedies, plays, and other works that do not fall within those two categories are not covered under this rule. On the other hand, all categories of works can be publicly displayed by or in the course of a transmission.

The 1976 Act expressly provides that three conditions must be satisfied to make the performance or display, by or in the course of a transmission, permissible. The performance or display must:

1. Be a regular part of the systematic instructional activities of a governmental body or nonprofit educational institution,
2. Be directly related and of material assistance to the teaching content of the transmission,
3. Be made primarily for reception
   a. In classrooms or similar places normally devoted to instruction
   b. By persons to whom the transmission is directed because their disabilities or other special circumstances prevent their attendance in classrooms or similar places normally devoted to instruction
   c. By officers or employees of governmental bodies as part of their official duties or employment

Commercial facilities, such as a for-profit cable television system, can be used to make qualifying transmissions if the performance or display would be permissible even though it may be received by the public at large as long as the transmission is made "primarily" for reception by any one of the three groups noted.

Generally, it would be permissible to make radio and television broadcasts of music performances as well as the reading and/or display of the text of literary works. Congress indicated that broadcasts that are directed to enrolled students regularly and are made by recognized higher educational institutions would be permissible, such as televised college credit courses.

Religious Services

Nondramatic literary and musical works are the only categories of works that can be publicly performed, but only if this is done in the course of services at a place of worship or other religious assembly. There is no restriction that they be religious in nature, so all kinds of such works can be performed. However, this is not the case with respect to dramatico-musical works. They can be performed, but only if they are of a religious nature. All categories of works can be publicly displayed.

Dramatico-musical works of a religious nature would include oratorios, cantatas, musical settings of the Mass, and choral services. But they would not include such things as secular operas, musical plays, and motion pictures even though they may have an underlying religious or philosophical theme.

Performances or displays that are for social, educational, fund-raising, or entertaining purposes would not be permissible under this rule, although they are made at a place of worship. However, if certain conditions are satisfied, it is possible that such performances may be permissible under the nonprofit performance rule, which is discussed next.

Broadcasts or other transmissions of religious programs to the public at large from a place of worship are not permissible under this rule.

Certain Nonprofit Performances

Nondramatic literary and musical works are the only categories of works that can be publicly performed under this rule, but only if this is done before a live audience and the conditions described in the following list are satisfied. There is no right to display works publicly under this rule.

The 1976 Act states that a public performance is permissible if:

1. It is without any purpose of direct or indirect commercial advantage
2. It is without payment of any fee or other compensation to any of its performers, promoters, or organizers
3. There is no direct or indirect admission charge
4. The proceeds, after deducting the reasonable costs of producing the performance, are used exclusively for educational, religious, or charitable purposes and not for private financial gain
5. The copyright owner of the work to be performed does not object to the performance

Before a Live Audience. The performance can be made by live performers or by means of the playing of tape, record, disk players, or videotape players or by the reception of radio and television broadcast signals. However, it is not permissible under this rule to transmit the performance to another location.

No Profit Motive. If there is any direct or indirect commercial advantage to anyone as a result of the performance, it will not be permissible under this rule. That the audience is not charged for seeing or hearing it will not make the performance permissible if anyone profits from it, directly or indirectly. On the other hand, Congress has indicated that the payment of performers, directors, or producers will not disqualify the performance under this rule if such individuals are paid a salary for duties encompassing it rather than being paid directly for the performance itself. For example, if an annual salary is paid to the conductor of a school orchestra that performs music before a live audience, the payment will not disqualify a performance that otherwise meets the conditions noted previously.

Reception of Broadcasts in a Public Place

All categories and types of works may be publicly performed and displayed under this rule, but only by the reception of radio and television broadcasts in a public place and only on a single radio or television set of the kind commonly sold to members of the public for use in their homes. The act of simply turning on a radio or television set to receive the broadcast of a performance or display of a work in a place open to the public is treated as a public performance of the work under the broad definition of "to perform or display a work publicly" as found in the 1976 Act.

A number of things will disqualify a performance under the rule.

No Direct Charge To See or Hear. If there is a direct charge made to see or hear the broadcast, the reception of it is not permissible. For example, the reception of television broadcasts by a restaurant or lounge would not be permissible under this rule if it requires patrons to pay a cover charge to watch a televised sporting event, or other program, on television sets located throughout its facilities.

No Use of Commercial Receiving Equipment. If commercial receiving apparatus is used in a place open to the public, or if a standard home receiving system is used in such locations, but it is altered or augmented for the purpose of improving the aural or visual quality of a broadcast, it is likely that the reception of the broadcast would not be permissible. For example, it has been held that a retail store's use of an elaborate sound system to receive and play radio broadcasts was not permissible under this rule. The court considered a number of factors suggested by Congress to determine whether the use of the sound system was appropriate and concluded that it was beyond what is allowable under this rule. Congress indicated that consideration should be given to such factors as the size, physical arrangement, and noise level of the areas in an establishment where the broadcasts are made audible or visible. In addition, consideration should be given to the extent to which the receiving equipment is altered for the purpose of improving the aural or visual quality of the broadcast for individual members of the public using those areas.

Similarly, it would not appear to be permissible to use more than one radio or television set in a place open to the public to receive broadcasts or to use a satellite signal receiving antenna for the reception of broadcasts.

The Act expressly provides that a performance is permissible on a single receiving apparatus. And one court has held that a satellite dish system is not the kind of a receiving apparatus commonly used in private homes. In that case the court concluded that the use of such a system by a bar and restaurant to receive a satellite transmission of a sporting event was not permissible under this rule.

No Further Transmission of a Broadcast. Finally, if a broadcast is received and then further transmitted to the public, the reception of it would not be permissible under this rule. In the case noted, referring to the retail store, the court found that the use of the particular loudspeaker system in question constituted a further transmission of the broadcast to the public.

In summary, if a broadcast is not further transmitted, a retail store, bar, or other facility open to the public may turn on a standard radio or television set and receive it for the entertainment of customers without liability for copyright infringement. But such establishments would not be entitled to play a videotape on a television set or a cassette tape on a tape player under this rule because it permits only the public performance of works by the reception of broadcasts.

Agricultural and Horticultural Fairs and Exhibitions

Nondramatic musical works are the only category of works that can be publicly performed under this rule. It does not cover the display of works.

The right to perform eligible works publicly is permissible only if it is done by a governmental body or a nonprofit agricultural or horticultural organization in the course of an annual agricultural or horticultural fair or exhibition conducted by such a body or organization.

For example, a state or county extension service would be entitled to play music from a booth at a state fair assuming the fair is conducted by the state department of agriculture.

This rule does not permit a concessionaire, business establishment, or other person at such a fair or exhibition to perform a nondramatic musical work without obtaining a license to do so from the owner of the work. Consequently, a performance by such a group would constitute copyright infringement. But the infringing performance would not impose liability on the fair or exhibition sponsor.

Retail Sale of Records and Tapes

Nondramatic musical works are the only category of works that can be publicly performed under this rule. It does not cover the public display of works.

Businesses that sell and promote the retail sale of copies or phonorecords of musical works are the only kind that can publicly perform an eligible work under this rule. Accordingly, this limitation can be relied on only by retail stores of the kind that sell sheet music, phonograph records, cassette tapes, compact disks, and similar media for nondramatic musical works.

To be entitled to rely upon this limitation on rights, a qualifying vending establishment must be open to the public at large. It cannot make any direct or indirect charge for admission and the sole purpose of playing a record or tape must be for the promotion of the retail sale of records, tapes, and the like. The performance of the musical work cannot be transmitted beyond the place where the store is located and can only be made within the immediate area where the sale is occurring.

Noncommercial Broadcasts of Nondramatic Literary Works to the Blind or Deaf

Nondramatic literary works are the only works that can be publicly performed under this rule. It does not cover the public display of works.

A performance can be made by anyone but only if it is made without any purpose of direct or indirect commercial advantage, and by or in the course of a transmission through the facilities of:

1. A governmental body
2. A noncommercial educational broadcast station
3. A radio subcarrier authorization (a point-to-point nonbroadcast radio channel)
4. A cable system which is specifically designed for and primarily directed to:
   a. Blind or other handicapped persons who are unable to read normal printed material as a result of their handicap
   b. Deaf or other handicapped persons who are unable to hear the aural signals accompanying a transmission of visual signals

For example, the reading of a book or other kind of literary work is permissible under this rule when the reading is broadcast to handicapped persons, using the appropriate transmitting facilities. A transmission that features subtitles is an example of one specifically designed for handicapped persons. Reception of such a transmission by the public at large will not disqualify it as long as it is primarily for handicapped persons.

Noncommercial Broadcasts of Dramatic Literary Works to the Blind or Other Visually Handicapped Persons

Dramatic literary works are the only works that may be publicly performed under this rule. It does not cover the public display of works.

A performance can be made only on a single occasion and only for a dramatic literary work (e.g., a play) which was published at least 10 years before the date of the performance. More particularly, there can be only one performance of the same work by the same performers or under the auspices of the same organization.

In addition to the foregoing requirements, the performance can be made only if it is made without any purpose of direct or indirect commercial advantage, and by or in the course of a transmission through the facilities of a radio subcarrier authorization. The transmission must be specifically designed for and primarily directed to blind or other handicapped persons unable to read normal printed material as a result of their handicap.

For example, a play can be performed by the reading of it during the course of a transmission by a radio subcarrier authorization, but the play must have been published at least 10 years before the transmission. However, this can be done only once by the same group of performers with respect to a particular play, or under the auspices of a particular organization.

Nonprofit Veterans' or Nonprofit Fraternal Organizations

Nondramatic literary and musical works are the works that can be publicly performed under this rule. It does not cover the public display of works.

The public performance of eligible works can be made only in the course of a social function organized and promoted by a nonprofit veterans' organization or a nonprofit fraternal organization. But the social function must be one to which the general public is not invited and the proceeds of the performance, after deducting the reasonable costs of producing it, must be used exclusively for charitable purposes and not for financial gain.

The performance of an eligible work at a social function conducted by a college or university fraternity or sorority would be permissible only if the function is held solely to raise funds for a specific charitable purpose.

For example, the performance of music by a band at a dance sponsored by an American Legion Post for its members and invited guests would be permissible as long as any moneys raised from the dance, after paying for the band, refreshments, and the like, are used exclusively for charitable purposes.

LIMITATIONS ON THE EXCLUSIVE RIGHTS IN SOUND RECORDINGS

Public Performance and Display

Unlike other categories of works, all five exclusive rights are not available for sound recordings, and in certain circumstances, there are limitations on those that are available. The owner of copyright in a sound recording has only the exclusive right to reproduce, prepare variations, and distribute copies or phonorecords.

Sounds are not visually perceptible. Thus, there is no exclusive right to display them publicly. In addition, the 1976 Act expressly states that there is no public performance right with respect to sound recordings. Consequently, copyright owners of sound recordings have no basis to control or prohibit the public performance of such works. This is the case regardless of the fact that the public performance right may be applicable to an underlying work communicated by the playing of a sound recording. However, the copyright owner of the underlying work is entitled to control or prohibit the public performance of that work and, thereby, has the ability to control the public performance of the sound recording.

Limitation on the Right To Reproduce

The exclusive right to reproduce a sound recording is limited to the right to duplicate only the particular sounds in a record. This right is limited to the making of *exact* reproductions of those sounds.

The owner of sound recording cannot prevent a recording of another performance of the same work by someone else which features sounds that imitate those in the owner's sound recordings. This would be the case even when the imitation is substantially similar to the sound recording and was deliberately made with the intention that it simulate the sounds in the sound recording as exactly as possible.

For example, the owner of a recording of an orchestral performance of Beethoven's Fifth Symphony does not have a right to preclude another party from recording the performance of the same musical composition by a different orchestra. Similarly, a record company that owns a sound recording featuring the performance of "White Christmas" by Bing Crosby would not have a basis (relying only on copyright ownership of the sound recording) to challenge the recording of a performance of the same song by another vocalist who imitates Bing Crosby.

The exclusive right to prepare variations of a sound recording (derivative works) is limited to the right to prepare only a variation in which the particular sounds embodied in a phonorecord are rearranged, remixed, or otherwise altered in sequence or quality. This limitation is similar to that on the reproduction right for sound recordings. Only the actual sounds in the sound recording are protected against the creation of a derivative work by someone other than the owner of the copyrighted sound recording. Consequently, an independent fixation of rearranged, remixed, or otherwise altered sounds by a third party is permissible even though they imitate or simulate those in the copyrighted sound recording.

Use of Sound Recordings in Educational Television and Radio Programs

Anyone who produces an educational television and/or radio program distributed or transmitted by or through a "public broadcasting entity" is permitted to reproduce and prepare variations of sound recordings under this limitation as well as to distribute them as part of the program. This right exists as long as copies or phonorecords of such programs are not commercially distributed by or through public broadcasting entities to the public.

LIMITATIONS ON RIGHTS IN PICTORIAL, GRAPHIC, AND SCULPTURAL WORKS

The owner of the right to reproduce a pictorial, graphic, or sculptural work can do so by reproducing it in or on any kind of article, whether useful or otherwise. However, the 1976 Act imposes a limitation on the reproduction right if such a work is lawfully reproduced in useful articles and they are offered for sale or other distribution to the public. The Act provides that the owner does not have any power under this right

> to prevent the making, distribution, or display of pictures or photographs of such articles in connection with advertisements or commentaries related to the distribution or display of such articles, or in connection with news reports.

For example, the owner of the right to reproduce a floral design may authorize its reproduction on dinnerware produced by another person. By virtue of the reproduction right the owner can prevent others from reproducing the design on the same or different products. But, because of the statutory

limitation on this right noted previously, the owner cannot prevent the dinnerware manufacturer from using pictures of dinnerware featuring the floral
design in advertising for it even though those pictures reproduce the floral
design.

REPRODUCTION BY LIBRARIES AND ARCHIVES

Permissible Reproduction

This limitation permits the reproduction and public distribution of copies
or phonorecords of all categories of works by a library or archives and its
employees acting within the scope of their employment. The reproduction
and distribution can be made for its own use, for other libraries or archives,
and, under certain circumstances, for library users.

Musical works, pictorial, graphic, or sculptural works, motion pictures,
and audiovisual works (other than audiovisual works dealing with news)
can be reproduced and distributed, but only for purposes of archival reproduction and research, and for purposes of replacing a damaged copy.

By virtue of this limitation, a library or archive is entitled to make an
isolated and unrelated reproduction or distribution of a single copy or phonorecord of the same work on separate occasions, but only if

1. The reproduction or distribution is made without any purpose of direct
   or indirect commercial advantage
2. The collections of the library or archives are:
   a. Open to the public
   b. Available not only to researchers affiliated with the library or ar-
      chives or with the institution of which it is a part, but also to other
      persons doing research in a specialized field
3. The reproduction or distribution of the work includes a copyright notice

A library or archive is also entitled to reproduce systematically and distribute copies or phonorecords in connection with its participation in interlibrary networks and other arrangements involving the exchange of copyrighted works or phonorecords. However, this can be done only if the effect
of such reproduction and distribution is not to provide a receiving library or
archive with such aggregate quantities as to allow it to substitute the copies
received for a subscription to or purchase of the work copied.

If requested by a library user, a library may make a copy of no more than one article or other contribution to a copyrighted collection or periodical, or a small part of any other copyrighted work. This is permissible only if:

1. The copy or phonorecord becomes the property of the user, and the library or archives has had no notice that the copy or phonorecord would be used for any purpose other than private study, scholarship, or research
2. The library or archives displays prominently, at the place where orders are accepted, and includes on its order form, a "warning of copyright"

In addition, an entire work, or a substantial portion of it, can be reproduced and distributed if a user makes a request for it, the library or archives first determines (on the basis of a reasonable investigation) that a copy or phonorecord of it cannot be obtained at a fair price, and the previously discussed two conditions are satisfied.

The prescribed language for a "warning of copyright" is:

The copyright law of the United States (Title 17, United States Code) governs the making of potocopies or other reproductions of copyrighted material.

Under certain conditions specified in the law, libraries and archives are authorized to furnish a photocopy or other reproduction. One of these specified conditions is that the photocopy or reproduction is not to be "used for any purpose other than private study, scholarship, or research." If a user makes a request for, or later uses, a photocopy or reproduction for purposes in excess of "fair use," that user may be liable for copyright infringement.

This institution reserves the right to refuse to accept a copying order if, in its judgment, fulfillment of the order would involve violation of copyright law.

Qualifying Libraries and Archives

A library or archives engaged in the for-profit reproduction or distribution of copies or phonorecords of a work may not rely on this limitation. Similarly, this limitation does not apply to the for-profit reproduction or distribution activities of a commercial enterprise that has assembled a collection of books, manuscripts, musical scores, or other literary and artistic materials. And it is not applicable when a nonprofit library or archive authorizes the for-profit reproduction and distribution of copies or phonorecords in its collections by a third party, or if the library hires a commercial copying business to carry out its own, otherwise permissible copying and distribution functions.

Nonprofit libraries or archives can rely upon this limitation as long as there is no immediate commercial motivation behind the reproduction and distribution activities themselves. This limitation can also be relied on by a library or archives that is part of a profitmaking organization, such as a law firm, medical group or proprietary hospital, or a chemical, pharmaceutical, automobile manufacturer, or oil corporation. This is the case only if there is no commercial motivation behind the reproduction and distribution activities of such a library or archives. That there may be a profitmaking motivation of such an organization with respect to its other activities does not in and of itself make this limitation inapplicable.

As indicated earlier, in addition to the requirement that there be no commercial motivation behind the reproduction and distribution activities of a library or archives, the collections of a qualifying library or archives must be open to the public or they must be available to any researcher, whether affiliated with it or not. If its collections are not open or available in this regard, a library or archives cannot reproduce or distribute copies or phonorecords nor can they avoid infringement for doing so.

SECONDARY TRANSMISSIONS

This limitation permits qualifying organizations to make "secondary transmissions" of performances or displays of copyrighted works to the public. It is applicable to all categories of works, but can be relied on only by the kind of organizations specified in the Act. The conditions under which permissible secondary transmissions may be made are spelled out in terms of objective criteria.

The transmission of a performance or display occurs when it is communicated in the form of images or sounds by any device or process from one place to another. For example, a radio station transmits the performance of a musical work by broadcasting it and a television station transmits an audiovisual work by telecasting it.

The secondary transmission of a performance or display of a work is defined as the further transmitting of a "primary transmission" of the performance or display simultaneous with its primary transmission. A "primary transmission" is defined as a transmission made to the public by the transmitting facility whose signals are being received and further transmitted by the secondary transmission service.

An example of a secondary transmission is a cable television system's simultaneous and further transmission of a network television broadcast to its subscribers.

Hotels, apartment houses, and similar establishments, which relay broadcast signals to the private lodgings of guests or residents at no charge, are entitled to do so under this limitation. In addition, it can be relied on by instructional broadcasters in specified situations. For example, a university is entitled to make a secondary transmission to music students in classrooms at branch sites if the subject matter of the signal being further transmitted consists of the performance by a symphony orchestra of a musical work and the performance of such works is a regular part of the university's instructional activities.

Secondary transmissions by broadcast signal common carriers qualify under this limitation if they are the kind who provide wires, cables, or other communications channels for the use of others and have no direct or indirect control over the content or selection of the signal. Furthermore, this limitation can be relied on by governmental bodies or other nonprofit organizations (e.g., translators or boosters) that transmit broadcast signals without any direct or indirect commercial advantage. For example, the operation of nonprofit translators or boosters is permissible if they involve nothing more than amplifying broadcast signals and retransmitting them to everyone in an area free for reception. Representative operations would be those that amplify broadcast signals for reception by the residents of a mountain town who are not able to receive unamplified broadcast signals from a distant source.

Cable systems, which transmit broadcast signals to their customers, are also covered by this limitation. However, its applicability differs substantially from its applicability to the qualifying secondary transmitters. Cable systems are required to pay royalties and comply with certain requirements under a compulsory licensing system, whereas other qualifying secondary transmitters are not.

A "cable system" is defined in the Act as

A facility, located in any State, Territory, Trust Territory, or Possession, that in whole or in part receives signals transmitted or programs broadcast by one or more television broadcast stations licensed by the Federal Communications Commission, and makes secondary transmissions of such signals or programs by wires, cables, or other communications channels to subscribing members of the public who pay for such service.

Under this licensing mechanism, cable systems do not directly deal or negotiate with copyright owners. The U.S. Copyright Office administers the licensing system and handles all transactions with cable systems under it. Among other things, compulsory licensing for cable systems obligates them to comply with prescribed reporting requirements and to pay royalties in accordance with established fee schedules. These fees are based upon gross receipts for the basic secondary transmission services they provide to subscribers.

EPHEMERAL RECORDINGS

The limitation applicable to "ephemeral recordings" permits the making of a copy or phonorecord of the performance or display of a work in a "transmission program" by an organization entitled to make the transmission. The resulting copy or phonorecord is known as an ephemeral recording.

A recording of this type is referred to as "ephemeral" because it is generally made for purposes of later transmission and then destroyed within a specified time period. A "transmission program" is a body of material that, as an aggregate, has been produced for the sole purpose of transmission to the public in sequence and as a unit. For example, a television program featuring the live performance of a play will constitute a transmission program and so will a radio program of a concert.

The phrase "transmitting organization" is not defined in the Act. However, it is generally understood to include network and local radio and television broadcasters, operators of cable television systems, operators of background music services, and other transmitters. Governmental bodies and other nonprofit organizations as well as commercial broadcasters fall within this group.

A transmitting organization is entitled to transmit a performance or display if it is a transferee or a licensee of the public performing right in a work. For example, a broadcaster that acquires ownership of the right to perform publicly a play seen in a transmission program (or has obtained a performance license from the owner of the work) is entitled to transmit the program. A cable television system that complies with the compulsory licensing provisions of the Act is entitled to transmit any work covered by such a license.

If an organization does not have the right to transmit a performance or display, it is not permitted to make an ephemeral recording, even though it may be able to transmit a performance or display by receiving it over-the-air or by other means. For example, it is not permissible for a local broadcaster to make an ephemeral recording of a network broadcast which it receives but does not have the right to broadcast.

The intended use of an ephemeral recording, the nature of the principal activity of a transmitting organization, and the category work performed or displayed in a program determine the number of permissible ephemeral recordings that can be made and the period of time each can be used before destruction is required. For instance, a local commercial television station affiliated with a network is entitled to make one recording of a network broadcast of a copyrighted work except a motion picture or other audiovisual work, and keep it up to six months, as long as the recording is used solely for broadcast within the station's local service area.

In most cases, there are not restrictions with regard to the number of times a recording can be transmitted before it must be destroyed.

The commercial or noncommercial nature of the transmission made does not affect the availability of this limitation. However, the kind of work transmitted will determine whether a transmitting organization can rely on this limitation and under what circumstances. For example, the making of ephemeral recordings of motion pictures or other audiovisual works is not permitted.

NONCOMMERCIAL EDUCATIONAL BROADCASTING

A public broadcasting entity is permitted to engage in the following activities:

1. The performance or display of published nondramatic musical works and published pictorial, graphic, and sculptural works by or in the course of a transmission

2. The use of such works in the production of a transmission program where the program is produced by a nonprofit institution or organization solely for the purpose of a transmission made by a noncommercial educational broadcast station

3. The reproduction of copies or phonorecords of such a transmission program where the reproduction is made by a nonprofit institution or organization solely for the purpose of a transmission made by a noncommercial educational broadcast station

4. The distribution of copies or phonorecords of such a transmission program where the distribution is made by a nonprofit institution or organization solely for the purpose of a transmission made by a noncommercial educational broadcast station

In other words, this limitation permits the performance or display of published nondramatic musical works, and of published pictorial, graphic, and sculptural works in the course of a transmission by a public broadcasting entity. Incidental to this is the right to reproduce one or more of these kind of works in connection with the production and as part of a transmission program as well as the right to distribute copies or phonorecords of such programs.

A "public broadcasting entity" is defined as:

A noncommercial educational broadcast station" as defined in section 397 of title 47 of the United States Code, and any nonprofit institution or organization engaged in . . . production of a transmission program, reproduction of copies or phonorecords of such a transmission program and distribution of such copies or phonorecords, where such production, reproduction, or distribution is made solely for the purpose of transmission. . . ." by a noncommercial educational broadcast station.

Section 397 of title 47 defines a "noncommercial educational broadcast station" as:

A television or radio broadcast station which

(A) under the rules and regulations of the Federal Communications Commission in effect on November 7, 1967, is eligible to be licensed or is licensed by the Commission as a noncommercial educational radio or television broadcast station and which is owned and operated by a public agency or nonprofit private foundation, corporation, or association, or

(B) one which is owned and operated by a municipality and which transmits only noncommercial programs for educational purposes.

As suggested by the definitions, this limitation can be relied on by a broad range of public broadcasters. For example, radio and television stations licensed to and operated by colleges and universities as well as those licensed to and operated by other nonprofit educational institutions are public broadcasting entities. In addition, radio and television stations that are part of the Public Broadcasting Service (PBS) and National Public Radio (NPR) fall within this category of broadcasters.

THE MAKING OF COPIES OR ADAPTATIONS OF COMPUTER PROGRAMS

The use of a computer program often involves the making of a copy and/or an adaptation of it as a necessary part of operating it. Loading a program into a computer constitutes a reproduction of it and the adaptation of a program (to make it possible for it to perform the function for which it was acquired) constitutes the creation of a derivative work.

A computer program is defined in the 1976 Act as "a set of statements or instructions to be used directly or indirectly in a computer to bring about a certain result."

This limitation permits the making of copies and or adaptations of copyrighted computer programs under certain circumstances. The Act provides that the owner of a computer program can make or authorize the making of another copy or adaptation of it if:

1. The new copy or adaptation is created as an essential step in the utilization of the program in conjunction with a machine and it is used in no other manner

2. The new copy or adaptation is for archival purposes only and all archival copies are destroyed in the event that continued possession of the program should cease to be rightful

It has been held that permissible reproduction of a computer program covered under (1) in the list can be made only by the owner of the program and is strictly limited to inputting it into the program owner's computer in connection with utilizing the program.

Exact copies of programs (but not adaptations of them) prepared under (1) or (2) in the list may be leased, sold, or otherwise transferred along with the program from which such copies were prepared. However, this is permissible only if done as part of the lease, sale, or other transfer of all rights in the program.

Adaptations that are prepared may be transferred but only with the authorization of the copyright owner.

CHAPTER SUMMARY

• The public performance and display of certain categories of works by a person other than the copyright owner is permitted in 10 separate fact situations, each of which is covered by a specific limitation set forth in the Act.

• There is no public performance or display right applicable to sound recordings.

• The right to reproduce a pictorial, graphic, or sculptural work does not prevent the making or display of pictures of it as it appears on a useful article if it was lawfully reproduced on such an article and the picture is used in connection with advertising the article.

- The right to reproduce does not prevent a noncommercial library or archives from reproducing works for archival reproduction and research and for purposes of replacing a damaged copy.

- Secondary transmissions of performances or displays of works can be made by qualifying organizations such as hotels, apartment houses and similar establishments, broadcast signal common carriers, and governmental bodies or other nonprofit organizations.

- Cable systems are permitted to make secondary transmissions under a compulsory license which requires royalty payments to copyright owners.

- A qualifying transmitting organization is entitled to make ephemeral recordings of the performance or display of a work in a transmission program.

- Public broadcasting entities may make transmissions of the performance or display of published nondramatic musical works and of published pictorial, graphic, and sculptural works under certain circumstances.

- The owner of a computer program is entitled to make a copy and/or adaptation of it as a necessary part of operating it and for archival purposes.

9

Protection Lasts for a Long Time

$\mathbf{P}$rior to January 1, 1978 it was not possible under federal law to protect a work for as long a period as is now available. The prior federal copyright statute, namely the 1909 Act, provided that the maximum period of protection available for a registered published or unpublished work was 56 years. This period was comprised of an initial 28-year term plus a renewal term of 28 years.

Under the common law system of copyright protection, which was in effect prior to the 1976 Act, it was possible to protect an unregistered unpublished work for a period of time longer than is now available. Before January 1, 1978, this kind of work could be protected for an unlimited period of time as long as it remained unpublished and unregistered.

All of the periods of protection available for works prior to January 1, 1978 were changed by the 1976 Act. Congress felt that the 56-year term was not long enough to enable creators and their dependents to obtain the fair economic benefits from their copyrighted works. The life expectancy of individuals had increased since 1909 and so did the commercial life of many works as a result of growth in the area of communication and media.

Currently, everyone who creates a copyrightable work and lives a long time may be able to protect it up to 100 years or more. Assuming everything goes well, as it usually does, protection for a work can usually be expected to last for the maximum period applicable to it under the 1976 Act. This period ranges from 28 years to over 100 years depending on a number of factors discussed in this chapter. If protection does not last for the full term applicable to a given work, it is likely that an act of the copyright owner has shortened it.

When the 1976 Act became effective it did not disregard federal protection available for works created before January 1, 1978, which were protected under the 1909 Act on September 19, 1962 or under the common law on January 1, 1978. The ability of a copyright owner to protect such works was preserved by the 1976 Act as discussed in this chapter. Accordingly, that a work may have been created prior to January 1, 1978 does not necessarily mean it is not currently subject to copyright protection. Keeping this in mind, individuals who create works at this time and wish to incorporate in them material created by others years ago should investigate the copyright status of such material. For instance, if protection continues for a work created in 1918, the use of all or portions of it without permission of the owner may result in copyright infringement.

The 1976 Act did not change the status of works covered by registrations which were not renewed under the 1909 Act or whose maximum period of protection expired. Those works are in the public domain and remain in the public domain.

MAXIMUM PERIODS OF PROTECTION

There are four possibilities with respect to the maximum period of protection available for a particular work under the 1976 Act. If the work qualifies for one period, the other time periods do not apply. The four periods are:

1. The life of the creator plus 50 years after the date of the creator's death
2. Seventy-five years from the year a copy or phonorecord embodying the work is first published
3. One hundred years from the year of creation of a work
4. Twenty-eight years from the date a copy or phonorecord embodying a work is first published or from the date a claim of copyright ownership for an unpublished work is registered with the U.S. Copyright Office, if either event occurred prior to January 1, 1978; plus an additional 47 years if a registration secured from the U.S. Copyright Office for the work is timely

All of these periods run to the end of the calendar year in which they would otherwise expire. For example, a 75-year term of protection that begins on July 1, 1986 will end on December 31, 2061 and a life-plus-50-year term will end on December 31 of the fiftieth year after the date of the creator's death.

FACTORS AFFECTING APPLICABLE MAXIMUM PERIOD

Questions to Ask

A number of things determine which of the periods of protection previously discussed is available for a particular work. For example, the circumstances under which the work is created, the year in which it is created, the year it is first published, and acts by a copyright owner after it is created all have an impact on how long a work can be protected. But, the kind of work or category within which it is classified does not ordinarily have such an impact. There is nothing inherent in a literary work, audiovisual work, or any other type of work that makes one entitled to a longer or shorter period of protection.

In order to determine the applicable protection period for a specific work, it may be helpful to ask the following questions:

1. What is the employment status and scope of employment of the creator at the time of creation?
2. Was creation of the work specially ordered or commissioned?
3. Did more than one individual participate in creation of the work?
4. Did creation of the work occur before or after January 1, 1978.
5. If a work was created before January 1, 1978, was it published before or after that date?
6. Was a copyright notice featured on copies of a work at the time it was first "published"?
7. Is a natural person identified as the creator of the work in the copyright notice?
8. Is the creator of the work identified under a fictitious name in the copyright notice?
9. Do the records of the U.S. Copyright Office reveal the identity of the creator of (a) an "anonymous work" or (b) a "pseudonymous work"?

Creator's Employment Status

The employment status and scope of employment of the creator of a work at the time it is created, as well as whether the work was created on a commission basis, determines whether it can be protected for that individual's life plus 50 years. If a work is created by an individual on commission or within the scope of his or her employment, the maximum period of protection for it will not be measured by that individual's life.

Number of Individuals Involved in Creating

When the creators of a work are not employees and not commissioned to create it, the number of individuals involved in creating it has an effect on the total number of years the work can be protected. The life of the creator, which is used to measure the maximum period of protection, will be the life of the last surviving creator. (See "Two or More Creators" in this chapter for a discussion of how the period of protection for a work created by more than one individual is calculated.)

Works Created Before January 1, 1978

A work created prior to January 1, 1978 will qualify for the maximum period measured by the life of the creator, or for one of the other maximum periods. The applicable period depends on whether the work was published or unpublished prior to that date and whether it was created by an employee or on commission.

Use of a Proper Copyright Notice

If a proper copyright notice is not placed on copies or phonorecords of a work at the time they are first published, the maximum period of protection may be for a period as short as five years from the date copies or phonorecords are first published without the notice. The period of protection is affected by the absence of a proper copyright notice on published copies or phonorecords.

The word "published," as used in reference to copyrightable works, has a specific meaning. The date a work is first published is significant because that is when a copyright owner must start using a copyright notice on copies or phonorecords to avoid losing copyright protection, and it is used to measure the 28- and 100-year periods of protection for certain works.

The act of publishing a work, from a copyright standpoint, does not mean that a copy or phonorecord of it must be produced and distributed by an art, book, music, or other type of publisher. Although such activities constitute publication of a work under the 1976 Act, the sale, giving away, or other transfer of ownership of a copy or phonorecord by an individual is also considered "publication."

The 1976 Act provides that publication of a work occurs when copies or phonorecords of it are distributed to the public by:

1. Sale or other transfer of ownership (i.e., gifts, barter)
2. Rental, lease, or lending
3. The act of offering to distribute such copies or phonorecords to a group of persons for purposes of further distribution, public performance, or public display

A public performance or display of a work does not of itself constitute publication of the work performed or displayed. But the act of offering to distribute a copy or phonorecord of it, for purposes of public performance, will be treated as an act of publication.

The Name of the Owner in a Copyright Notice

When the name that appears in a copyright notice is not the true name of the creator of a work, or it is not the name of a natural person, the maximum period of protection for the work will be either 75 or 100 years. But, if the records of the U.S. Copyright Office reveal the identity of the creator it is possible that the maximum period of protection will be for the life of the creator, plus 50 years.

A "pseudonymous work" is defined in the 1976 Act as "a work on the copies or phonorecords of which the creator is identified under a fictitious name." For example, a literary work, in the form of a book that features the writer's pen name in the copyright notice rather than the writer's real name, is a pseudonymous work.

An "anonymous work" is defined as "a work on the copies or phonorecords of which no natural person is identified as the creator." For example, an anonymous work is one that features the name of a corporation in the copyright notice on copies or phonorecords.

LIFE OF THE CREATOR PLUS 50 YEARS

One Creator

Protection for a work created on or after January 1, 1978 will last for the life of the creator plus 50 years after the date of the creator's death (regardless of whether it is published or unpublished), if it is not an anonymous work and it is created by an individual outside of a work-made-for-hire relationship.

This period is also available for a work created before January 1, 1978, if it was created outside a work-made-for-hire relationship, but only if the work

1. Was not published
2. A claim of copyright ownership for it was not registered with the U.S. Copyright Office prior to that date

Accordingly, the life of an individual who creates a work, under either of the two in the list of circumstances, without the assistance or involvement of other persons, will be the measure for determining the maximum period of protection available for the work. This maximum period will not change even if the creator transfers copyright ownership for the work to another party. The life of the creator determines the maximum period of protection, not the life of the copyright owner at the time of the creator's death, if that is someone other than the creator.

Two or More Creators

If two or more individuals collaborate to create a work that is not an anonymous work and (1) none of the creators does so as an employee within the scope of employment, and (2) the work is not a "commissioned" work, the maximum period of protection for the work will also be equal to the life of the creator plus 50 years. However, the life used to measure the maximum period will be the life of the creator who lives the longest.

The life of the surviving creator will be used only with respect to joint works. A joint work is one that is or was created by two or more creators with the intention of all of them to merge their respective contributions into inseparable or interdependent parts of a unitary whole.

That the surviving creator held only a small percentage of copyright ownership in the work will not have any impact on the use of that individual's life as the measuring life. Similarly, the number of creators of a work will not have any impact on how long protection will last. Only the life of the one who lives longest is used to determine the total period of protection available.

Determining When Protection Ends

The calendar year in which the creator or surviving creator of work dies is a controlling date with respect to how long protection lasts (for this maximum period) because the 50-year portion begins to run from that date. Accordingly, the year that a creator dies must be known to determine when protection ends (for a work covered by this maximum period).

In some cases, it is relatively easy to find when a creator died because the news of that person's death is or has been widely circulated or this information is readily accessible. However, in the majority of cases this information is often difficult to obtain.

Congress recognized that if the year of death of a creator cannot be discovered, there would be no way to determine when this maximum period of protection ends for a particular work. Consequently, it made provision for situations where this date cannot be ascertained by establishing a procedure under the 1976 Act. If followed, this provision makes available a complete defense to any action for infringement of a work whose maximum period of protection has not ended at the time the action is instituted.

Any person who has an interest in a copyright, such as the copyright owner or a licensee or anyone else, may record a statement with the U.S. Copyright Office at any time indicating the date of death of the creator of a copyright work, or that the creator is still living on a particular date. This statement must identify the person filing it, the nature of that person's interest, and the source of the information in the statement. The statement must comply in form and content with any requirements prescribed by regulation by the Copyright Office.

The Copyright Office must maintain current records, based on such statements, relating to the death of creators. It also must maintain, to the extent it considers practicable, information of this kind based on data contained in any of its records or in other reference sources, such as newspapers or obituary notices.

The information in these records is used by the U.S. Copyright Office to issue a certified report to anyone requesting it for a particular work. This report certifies that its records disclose nothing to indicate that the creator of a particular work is living, or died less than 50 years before the date of the report. In other words, it certifies that no one has previously filed a statement with the U.S. Copyright Office that the creator of a work is alive — or that no one has filed a statement of the date of death of the creator. The effect of this report is to create a statutory presumption that the creator has been dead for at least 50 years. Reliance in good faith on this presumption, by the person obtaining it, will be a complete defense to an infringement action.

A specific period of time must elapse before reliance can be placed on this kind of report with respect to a particular work. This period is 75 years from the year a work is first published, or a period of 100 years from the year of its creation, whichever date expires first.

Ways To Obtain Protection for a Longer Time

The maximum period of protection for all works created by individuals under the circumstances noted in the preceding paragraphs is the same, namely the life of the creator plus 50 years. However, the total period of time a particular work can be protected will vary depending on how long the creator of it lives.

This fact can be used to prolong the total time of protection for a work created by two or more individuals as discussed below. Using the life of the survivor as the measuring life gives the estate or heirs of the deceased creator the opportunity to derive potential benefits from a work for a longer period of time than might otherwise be possible. A copyright owner's estate and/or heirs will benefit by the additional period of protection as the successor owner(s) of rights. Ownership of copyright passes on death by will or as personal property to an owner's estate or heirs. (A discussion of the ownership rights acquired by a creator's estate and/or heirs is found in Chapter 16.)

Protection may be prolonged for the benefit of the estate and/or heirs of an older individual if the individual collaborates in the creation of a work with a child. The resulting joint work will be protected for the life of the creator who lives longest. For instance, if an adult, who dies at age 70, creates a work at age 65 in collaboration with a 10-year-old child who lives to age 90, the joint work is entitled to protection for approximately 140 years. If this adult created the same work alone, protection would last for a period of only 55 years.

As a result of the collaboration, protection for the joint work in the example lasts 75 years longer than if the work was created only by the adult.

SEVENTY-FIVE YEARS FROM THE YEAR OF PUBLICATION

Circumstances when Applicable

There are four sets of circumstances where the maximum period of protection for a published work is 75 years. This maximum period begins on the date a work is first published and is applicable to that work under circumstances:

1. When a work has been created as a work made for hire

2. When the records of the U.S. Copyright Office do not reveal the identity of the creator of an anonymous work or a pseudonymous work

3. When a claim of copyright ownership for a published work was registered under the 1909 Act and the registration was in its renewal term at any time between September 19, 1962 and December 31, 1977

4. When a claim of copyright ownership was first registered under the 1909 Act between January 1, 1950 and December 31, 1978

It is important to note that the event of publication is a controlling factor insofar as this maximum time period is concerned. This period is not applicable to an unpublished work.

Congress adopted the 75-year period for a number of reasons. Article I, Section 8, Clause 8 gives Congress the power to grant exclusive rights to authors, but only for "limited times." Congress settled on the 75-year period because it reasonably concluded that, on the average, 75 years approximates the actual period of time protection would last for a published work entitled to the life plus 50 years term.

Works Made for Hire

In the case of a work made for hire, Congress elected to treat the employer or commissioning party as the creator and initial owner for copyright purposes. Apparently, Congress felt it would be inappropriate to use the life of an individual proprietor of a business or commissioning party as the measuring period for this kind of work because many employers and commissioning parties are business entities rather than individuals. Consequently, the 75-year term was selected.

Anonymous and Pseudonymous Works

Congress selected the 75-year period for anonymous and pseudonymous works in instances where there is no known life that can be referred to for purposes of ascertaining the maximum period of protection (life plus 50 years). However, if the identity of the creator is revealed in the records of the U.S. Copyright Office the maximum period of protection will be based on the span of the revealed creator's life. There are some exceptions.

That the identity of a creator is public information will not be sufficient to effect a change in the maximum period of protection from 75 years to life plus 50 years. The only way such a change can be made is by revealing the creator's identity in the records of the U.S. Copyright Office. Once this has occurred the change is automatic and nothing more is required.

The 1976 Act expressly provides for a number of ways to reveal the creator's identity in the records of the U.S. Copyright Office and a specific time by which this must be done. The creator's identity must be revealed prior to the expiration of the 75-year period and can be done by:

1. Registration of the copyright claim for the work, or
2. Recordation of a statement, with the Copyright Office, by any person having any interest in the copyright for an anonymous or pseudonymous work, which complies in form and content with the requirements prescribed by the U.S. Copyright Office and identifies:

   a. One or more of the creators
   b. The particular work affected
   c. The person recording the statement
   d. The nature of that person's interest
   e. The source of the information recorded

Disclosure of a creator's identity can actually shorten the period of protection for an anonymous or pseudonymous work if the creator dies soon after creating it. For instance, an anonymous or pseudonymous work is created by an individual (whose identity is not disclosed in the U.S. Copyright Office records) and first published in 1980. Protection will end in 2055, that is, 75 years from the year of first publication. On the other hand, if first publication occurs in 1980 and the identity of the creator (who died in 1985) is disclosed in the records of the U.S. Copyright Office in 2000 (prior to expiration of the 75-year period), protection will end in 2035, 50 years after the known creator's year of death.

Published Works Protected Under the 1909 Act

The 1976 Act extended protection for works protected under the 1909 Act by adding 19 years to the 28-year renewal term. The result of this change is a 75-year rather than a 56-year period of protection for published works that are in their renewal term prior to January 1, 1978. The 75-year period is measured from the date of first publication.

For example, a work was first published on March 5, 1921. If a renewal application for it were filed with the U.S. Copyright Office before March 15, 1949, the renewal term would have expired March 15, 1977. But by virtue of the 1976 Act, 19 years were added to the end of the renewal term, with protection now ending December 31, 1996. This new date is 75 years from 1921, the year of first publication.

The 75 year period of protection also applies to works protected under the 1909 Act, whose renewal term would have expired between September 19, 1962 and December 31, 1976. Beginning in 1962, Congress passed legislation which had the effect of preserving copyright protection for such works and extending it beyond 56 years. This legislation was in the form of nine separate laws.

The first law extended protection for all such registrations to December 31, 1965 and the ninth to December 31, 1976. The 1976 Act extended protection through December 31, 1982.

For example, a work first protected under federal copyright law on March 15, 1907, whose registration was timely renewed prior to March 15, 1935, would have expired on March 15, 1963. However, by virtue of each extension law and the 1975 Act, the registration did not expire until the end of 1982. Similarly, a work first protected under federal copyright law on October 10, 1912, whose registration was timely renewed, will expire on December 31, 1987.

Keeping the foregoing in mind, the passing of 56 years from the date a work was first published, or the date an unpublished work was registered, does not mean that copyright protection is not available for it now. A work first protected in 1917 may be protected until 1992.

Works First Registered between 1950 and 1978

In the process of establishing new and longer periods of protection for copyrightable works under the 1976 Act Congress did not disregard the 28-year initial period granted under the 1909 Act. All works in their initial 28-year period of protection on January 1, 1978 will continue to be protected for the balance of that period. This applies to works first protected under the 1909 Act between January 1, 1950 and December 31, 1977. The initial 28-year period of protection for them ends between December 31, 1978 and December 31, 2005.

The renewal requirement mandated for works registered under the 1909 Act was continued under the 1976 Act. Maintenance of this requirement means copyright owners must file renewal applications with the Copyright Office for all works due for renewal after January 1, 1978 (i.e., all works first protected between January 1, 1950 and January 31, 1977).

A renewal application must be filed prior to the end of the calendar year in which the initial 28-year period will expire. If this is done a renewal period of 47 years will be granted, thus affording such works a maximum protection period of 75 years (as opposed to 56 years under the 1909 Act).

A renewal application may be made with the U.S. Copyright Office by an eligible renewal claimant with respect to a particular work, but only if a copyright registration for that work for the first 28-year period was issued by the Copyright Office under the 1909 Act or under the 1976 Act.

In the event a work was first published prior to January 1, 1978 but has not been registered under either Act, it may still be possible to register it under the 1976 Act and thereby qualify for the new renewal period of 47 years. If the necessary applications, copies, and fees are all received in the U.S. Copyright Office prior to the expiration of 28 years from the date of first publication, the work to which they refer can be registered. In fact, it is possible to make simultaneous registration of a work for the initial period and renewal period of 47 years, if the required documents are timely filed.

In the case of any

1. Periodical, cyclopedic, or other composite work on which the copyright was originally secured by the proprietor thereof
2. Work copyrighted by a corporate body (otherwise than as assignee or licensee of the individual creator), or
3. Work made for hire copyrighted by an employer for whom such work was made,

an eligible renewal claimant is the copyright owner at the time of renewal.

In the case of a "posthumous work," an eligible renewal claimant is the copyright proprietor at the time the renewal application is due. A "posthumous work" is a work unpublished on the date of the death of the creator and with respect to which no copyright assignment or other contract for exploitation of the work occurred during the creator's lifetime.

It is not unusual that the estate or heirs of the creator of a work can be the copyright proprietor of a posthumous work at the time of a renewal application. It could be someone else, though, if the heirs transferred ownership to a third party or if the creator bequeathed copyright ownership to a third party.

If a contract for exploitation of a posthumous work, with no copyright assignment in it, has occurred during the creator's lifetime, an eligible renewal claimant for such work is:

1. The copyright proprietor at the time the renewal application is due
2. The following persons in descending order of eligibility:
   a. The widow, widower, or children of the creator
   b. The creator's executors, if there is a will and no widow, widower, or child of the creator is living

c. The creator's next of kin, in the absence of a will and if no widow, widower, or child of the creator is living

In case of any other work, including a "contribution by an individual creator to a periodical or to a cyclopedic or other composite work" an eligible renewal claimant is any of the following persons in descending order of eligibility:

1. The creator of the work if still living
2. The widow, widower, or children of the creator if the creator is not living
3. The creator's executors if there is a will and neither the creator nor any widow, widower, or child of the creator is living
4. The creator's next of kin in the absence of a will and if neither the creator nor any widow, widower, or child of the creator is living

As mentioned earlier, a renewal application must be filed within the last year of the initial 28-year period beginning December 31 of the twenty-seventh year and running through December 31 of the twenty-eighth year. The initial 28-year copyright period for a published work starts on the date of first publication of the work, or, if unpublished, on the date of registration in the U.S. Copyright Office. However, in any case where the year date in the notice, on copies of a work distributed by or under the authority of the copyright owner, is earlier than the year of first publication, a renewal application must be filed prior to the 28-year period measured from the year date in the notice.

An eligible renewal claimant should file an application for renewal using a preprinted form which is available free from the U.S. Copyright Office. This form is known as Form RE and a copy is included in Appendix C. As of July 1, 1986, the renewal fee is $6.00 per application.

ONE HUNDRED YEARS FROM THE YEAR OF CREATION

Circumstances when Applicable

There are two situations in which the maximum period of protection for an unpublished work is 100 years. This maximum period begins on the date a work is created and is applicable to that work under the following conditions:

1. Where a work has been created as a work made for hire
2. Where the records of the U.S. Copyright Office do not reveal the identity of the creator of an anonymous work or a pseudonymous work

This maximum period applies only to unpublished works. If a work is published and the previously mentioned two sets of circumstances exist, the 75-year period applies.

In addition, the year of creation marks the start of the 100-year maximum period in contrast to the year of first publication used as the starting date for the 75-year period.

The 100-year maximum period of protection satisfies the "limited times" provision of Clause 8 of the Constitution. It was settled on because, in the opinion of Congress, it too approximates the "actual" period of time that protection would last for an unpublished work if it were entitled to protection for the life plus 50-year term.

Work Made for Hire

The 1976 Act sets the maximum period of protection for a work made for hire at either:

1. Seventy-five years from the year of first publication
2. One hundred years from the year of creation

Whichever expires first.

Accordingly, under no circumstances can a work made for hire be protected for more than 100 years. This is the case, regardless of whether it is published or unpublished at any time within 100 years from the year of creation or whether the identity of the creator of an anonymous or pseudonymous work is revealed in the U.S. Copyright Office records. The minimum period of protection for such a work is 75 years, assuming nothing occurs to shorten this period, such as publication of copies or phonorecords without a copyright notice.

Anonymous and Pseudonymous Works

The same event that defeats the 100-year term of protection for a work made for hire defeats it for anonymous and pseudonymous works. That event is publication of a work. When it occurs, the 75-year term automatically applies.

The time limitation applicable to a work made for hire similarly applies here. Protection can last for either 75 years from the year of first publication, or 100 from the year of creation, whichever expires first.

Although protection for an anonymous or pseudonymous work cannot be extended beyond a period of 100 years through the act of delaying publication, it is possible to do so by disclosing a creator's identity in the records of the U.S. Copyright Office at any time during the 75-year period. The disclosure will automatically result in applicability of the life plus 50-year period.

This same act, occurring at any time within 100 years from the year of creation of an unpublished anonymous or pseudonymous work, has the same effect where the 100-year period applies.

Thus, by strategically timing disclosure of a creator's identity, it is possible to obtain protection for an anonymous or pseudonymous work beyond the 100-year term.

It is also possible that such disclosure will shorten the period of protection for such works.

For example, if such a work is created in 1980 by an individual who dies in 2035 (whose identity is not disclosed in the records of the U.S. Copyright Office), protection will end at two possible dates. Protection will end in 2080 if the work is not published (100 years from 1980, the year of creation). Or, it will end in 2060 if the work is published in 1985 (75 years from the year of publication), regardless of the year in which the creator dies.

However, if the identity of the creator is disclosed in the records of the Copyright Office in 2000 (prior to expiration of either the 75-year or 100-year term), protection will end in 2085, 50 years after the year of the creator's death. The act of disclosing the identity of the creator extends protection for a period of 25 years if the work is published and five years if it is unpublished.

On the other hand, it can be seen that the term of protection will be shortened if the identity of the creator is revealed in the U.S. Copyright Office records and the creator dies at any time prior to 2030. If this happens, the 100-year period is not available because it ends after the year of death of the creator. If death occurs prior to 2010, the 75-year period will not be reached because it would end after the creator's year of death.

NO DISCLOSURE OF CREATOR'S IDENTITY:

Year of creation	Year of first publication	Year of creator's death
1980 (factor)	1985 (factor)	any time between 2009 and 2029 (not a factor)

(continued)

NO DISCLOSURE OF CREATOR'S IDENTITY:

Year of creation	Year of first publication	Year of creator's death
	Protection ends 75 years after publication,	
	2060	
	or,	
	Protection ends 100 years after creation	
	2080	

DISCLOSURE OF CREATOR'S IDENTITY:

Year of disclosure of creator's identity	Protection ends 50 years after death
2000 (factor) (within 75-and 100-year term)	2059 and 2079

UNPUBLISHED WORKS NOT REGISTERED AS OF JANUARY 1, 1978

The 1976 Act changed the maximum period of protection available to all unpublished works not registered prior to January 1, 1978. As a consequence, it is no longer possible for such works to be protected for an indefinite period of time.

Specific language in the Act provides that the maximum period for such unpublished works is one of the following three periods:

1. The life of the creator plus 50 years
2. Seventy-five years from the date a copy or phonorecord embodying it is first published
3. One hundred years from the year of creation

However, by virtue of additional language in the Act, in no case will the period of protection for an unpublished work expire prior to December 31, 2002. This is the case even though protection for such a work would otherwise have ended prior to December 31, 2002, using one of the above periods as the applicable maximum period.

If an unpublished work is published on or before December 31, 2002, protection for it will last to December 31, 2027. Consequently, it is possible to protect an unpublished work for an additional 25 years simply by publishing it prior to December 31, 2002.

CHAPTER SUMMARY

- There are three maximum periods of protection for a work under the 1976 Act, namely, the life of the creator plus 50 years after death; 75 years from the date of publication; or 100 years from the year of creation.
- The applicable maximum period is dependent upon the employment status of the creator and whether the work is published as an anonymous or pseudonymous work.
- When two or more persons create a work, outside of an employment relationship, protection will last for the life of the creator who lives longest plus 50 years after that person's death.
- Failure to use a copyright notice on published copies or phonorecords may result in the loss of protection five years from the date of first publication.
- Works protected under the 1909 Act may now be protected for a maximum period of 75 years instead of 56 years.
- It is no longer possible to protect unpublished works for an indefinite period; the maximum period of protection for such works is one of the three periods provided by the 1976 Act.

10

Copyright Notice

The 1976 Act requires that a notice be used on copies or phonorecords whenever a work is published in the United States or elsewhere by authority of the copyright owner. Failure to place a notice on publicly distributed copies or phonorecords can make the difference between maintaining copyright protection for a work and losing all rights to it.

If a copyright notice does not timely appear on all publicly distributed copies or phonorecrods, or does not appear in the proper format, it is possible that some of the exclusive rights under the Act will be adversely affected. Or it is possible that ownership of all rights will be forfeited and the work will be in the public domain.

NOTICE REQUIREMENTS PRIOR TO JANUARY 1, 1978

The requirement to give notice of copyright ownership is not a new development. It was part of the first federal copyright statute enacted in 1790 and has been part of all federal copyright laws since then.

The use of a copyright notice serves four principal functions. They were set forth by Congress in the Report of the House of Representatives Committee on the Judiciary on Copyright Law Revision (House Report No. 19-1476). They are:

1. It has the effect of placing in the public domain a substantial body of published material that no one is interested in copyrighting

2. It informs the public whether a particular work is copyrighted

3. It identifies the copyright owner

4. It shows the date of publication

Under earlier copyright laws the consequences for failure to affix a proper copyright notice to publicly distributed copies or phonorecords were more severe than those under the 1976 Act. Forfeitures of rights through the unintentional failure to use a copyright notice were commonplace. In addition, trivial errors in the prescribed form of the notice also resulted in forfeitures.

For example, if notice was left off copies of a work at the time they were first made available to the public, or if it was put in the incorrect location on copies, protection for a work was automatically lost. It became part of the public domain and could not again be protected under copyright law. That this omission occurred through oversight or a lack of knowledge made no difference.

Congress recognized this inherent unfairness and corrected it under the 1976 Act. Errors in the notice, and even the failure to use one, can be cured and copyright protection saved as discussed in Chapter 11.

MISLEADING EFFECT OF THE COPYRIGHT NOTICE

As noted one of the functions a copyright notice is intended to serve is to inform the public that a particular work is protected by copyright. However, with the exception of works consisting preponderantly of U.S. government works, there is no requirement that the copyright notice specify what part of a work, if any, is not protected. As we have seen, many works contain copyrighted as well as public domain material.

Because there is no requirement to identify that portion of a work that may be public domain material, the copyright notice creates a misleading impression that everything included in a copy or phonorecord is protected.

For example, copyright notices that appear in different versions of the Bible do not contain any disclosure that only the editorial revisions, introductions, illustrations, or comments that have been added are protected by copyright. Nor do copyright notices found in books containing such classics as *Moby Dick*, Homer's *The Odyssey*, and the Shakespeare plays contain such disclosures. This is also the case with respect to copyright notices appearing on reproductions of pieces of fine art created centuries ago and even reproductions of sculptural pieces created in this century, which are in the public

domain. Sound recordings that feature performances of classical music originally created in the 1700s and 1800s do not indicate that only the arrangement and sounds of the performance may be protected, not the underlying
musical work.

The only way to know if everything included in a copy or phonorecord
featuring a copyright notice is protected is to file a lawsuit challenging or
asserting rights in the underlying work. The copyright claimant will then be
called upon to substantiate ownership rights.

An investigation of the U.S. Copyright Office records ordinarily will not
be of significant help in discovering what is protected for a given work and
what is not. Investigating whether a work is under copyright protection is
discussed in Chapter 12.

FORM OF THE COPYRIGHT NOTICE

Two Prescribed Versions

The 1976 Act prescribes two versions of the copyright notice, plus one special form of it for use on publicly distributed copies or phonorecords embodying a work. If a work has not been publicly distributed, it is not necessary to place either version of the notice on copies or phonorecords
embodying it. Therefore, the absence of a copyright notice on such copies
or phonorecords will have no adverse consequences on the copyright owner's rights to the work.

As discussed in Chapter 9, publicly displaying a copy or phonorecord of
a work that has not been previously published is not a public distribution of
the copy or phonorecord. That is, such public display will not be treated as
a public distribution if the copy or phonorecord is not offered for purposes
of further distribution, public performance, or public display.

For example, there would be no public distribution of a work where a
sculpture is displayed in a museum for purposes of viewing only and copies
of it have not been publicly distributed prior to that exhibition. Under such
circumstances, the copyright owner need not use either version of the notice
to protect his or her rights in the work. But, if copies of the work have been
published at any time prior to the public display, a notice must appear on
the piece displayed.

The appropriate version of the notice to use depends on whether a work
can be seen or heard. One form of the notice is for visually perceptible works
and the other is for sound recordings. The special form of the notice must be
used on material that incorporates a preponderant amount of U.S. government material.

Visually Perceptible Copies

If a work is of the type that can be visually perceived when it is embodied in a material object, either directly or with the aid of a machine or device, the version of the notice discussed below must be used. The following list exemplifies the kind of objects in which a work can be visually perceived: newspapers, books, magazines, and other publications; software program user materials; sheet music; motion pictures; photographs; fine and graphic art; toys; dolls; and sculpture. The kinds of objects in which a work cannot be visually perceived include phonograph records; cassette and reel-to-reel tapes; and audio disks. They embody works in the form of sounds, which can be heard but not seen.

The notice to use on visually perceptible copies of a work consists of three components, namely:

1. The encircled symbol © (a letter "C" in a circle), or the word "Copyright," or its abbreviation "Copr."

2. The year of first publication of the work, except in certain instances noted in Chapter 11

3. The name of the owner of copyright to the work, or an abbreviation by which the name of the owner can be recognized, or a generally known alternative designation of the owner

Statements like "This work is protected by copyright," or "No part of this work may be reproduced without permission," or "Copyrighted," or "All rights reserved" (which has a special meaning), among others, are frequently used by people who do not know the form of copyright notice required by the 1976 Act. Such statements are often used in an attempt to give notice of copyright ownership. But they are not equivalent to the prescribed form of copyright notice, nor are they acceptable alternatives. If they are featured on copies of a work, instead of the prescribed form, the work will be treated as published without copyright notice and protection for it may be forfeited or jeopardized.

The Symbol © or its Alternatives

The order of the aforementioned three components may vary as long as the symbol © or one of its alternatives appears first. When © but not its alternatives is used, copyright protection for the work applies outside the United States by virtue of the Universal Copyright Convention, a multilateral copyright treaty ratified by the United States in 1955. No less than 74 other countries have also ratified it, including the major countries of the world.

Under this treaty, use of the symbol © in combination with the two other components of the notice on copies of a published work is deemed to constitute compliance with any formalities a signatory country may require to obtain copyright protection in that country. In effect, use of this symbol exempts a copyright owner from having to fulfill any requirements a signatory country may set for its nationals in order to obtain copyright protection there. It also allows the owner to enjoy, in every signatory country, the same protection a country gives to works of its nationals who must meet such requirements.

The phrase "All rights reserved" has significance because it constitutes a copyright notice in certain Latin American countries. Under a treaty known as the Buenos Aires Convention, works owned by U.S. nationals may be protected in countries that are signatory to that treaty. Such protection may be obtained if the formalities for acquiring copyright protection in the United States are satisfied (i.e., use of a proper copyright notice on published works) and the equivalent of the Spanish phrase "Derechos Reservados" ("All rights reserved") is used on copies of the work.

Year of First Publication

The year of first publication is the year in which a copy of a work has been publicly distributed. (The public distribution of copies of a work is discussed in Chapter 6.) The calendar year in which this occurs is the year date that should be featured in the copyright notice.

The year of first publication may be the same year that a work has been created, or it may be years later. If first publication does not occur in the same year as the work is created, the year of creation is not the correct date to put in the notice.

It is not necessary or appropriate to use the month, day, and year, or the month and year alone, that first publication of a work occurs, as the date in a copyright notice. Roman numerals may be used to designate the year of first publication, or it may be spelled out.

Changing the Date in a Notice

Changing the date in a copyright notice may adversely affect the rights of the copyright owner. The use of an improper year date will be treated as an error in the notice and will affect a copyright owner's ability to obtain all of the remedies under the 1976 Act against an infringer. Or, it will negate the use of a notice, and copies of the work will be treated as publicly distributed without notice. (See Chapter 11 for a discussion of the effect of an error in the date on the rights of the copyright owner.)

The only time it may be appropriate to use a year date in a copyright notice different from the year of first publication is when a work is altered, added to, or otherwise modified to the extent that more than a trivial change has been made. If more than insubstantial changes are made to a work, the year of first publication of the new version may be used in the notice in lieu of the earlier year of first publication.

Permissible Omission of the Date

Under certain circumstances, the year of first publication can be omitted from the notice altogether. It does not have to be used when a pictorial, graphic, or sculptural work, with or without accompanying text, is reproduced in certain types of objects. These objects include greeting cards, post cards, stationery, jewelry, dolls, toys, or any useful articles. In all other cases, copies of this category of work must feature the full notice consisting of all three components.

The notice for this special group of objects consists of only the symbol ©, or one of its alternatives, plus the name of the copyright owner. For example, "ET" and "Star Wars" dolls may feature the symbol © followed by the name "Universal Studios" and the notice will be treated as a valid copyright notice.

Name of the Copyright Owner

The name that should be used in a copyright notice is the name of the individual or legal entity that owns all of the exclusive rights to the work which is embodied in the particular copy featuring the notice. Or it should be the name of the person who owns some of those rights as they relate to that copy.

It is possible for different individuals or entities to separately own the various exclusive rights to a work since these rights are divisible and can be possessed independently of each other. Transfers of copyright ownership are discussed in Chapter 15.

For example, the name of the owner of all rights to a literary work should be featured in the notice appearing on books, on printed material, on printouts of copies of computer software programs and on computer screens when those copies are displayed, and on other material objects where it can be visually perceived. If one individual or entity owns only the right to reproduce the literary work in book form and a second individual or entity owns only the right to reproduce this same work in a computer software program format, the name in the notice on books will be different from the name in the notice on copies of the software program.

If there is more than one owner of a work, the names of all owners should appear in the notice, regardless of their percentages of ownership. That one individual or entity may possess a larger percentage than another does not have any legal effect with respect to the ordering of the names, at least where the components of a copyright notice are concerned. There is no requirement that the percentage ownership be disclosed in the notice next to each owner's name.

In the event there are two or more owners and one transfers rights, the name of the new owner should thereafter appear in the notice along with the names of the others, but in lieu of the former owner.

The appearance in a notice of a name other than that of the copyright owner will result in a defective notice. As a consequence, certain rights of the owner will be adversely affected as noted in Chapter 11. However, a similar result will not occur where a name other than the owner's full or real name is used.

The use of an abbreviation by which the owner can be recognized, or a generally known alternative name, is acceptable. Likewise, it would be acceptable to use an owner's nickname, fictitious name, initials, last name alone, or other designation by which the owner is known. All of these variations are allowable as long as they accurately identify the owner or owners of the work.

Sound Recordings

Because sound recordings cannot be visually perceived, the version of notice featuring the symbol © or one of its alternatives is not the proper one to use for such works. The correct version of the notice differs only slightly from that version. It features the symbol ℗ rather than the symbol ©. The three components of the notice for sound recordings are:

1. The symbol ℗ (the letter "P" in a circle)
2. The year of first publication of the sound recording
3. The name of the owner of copyright in the sound recording, or an abbreviation by which the owner's name can be recognized, or a generally known alternative designation of the owner

As is the case with the version of the notice for visually perceptible copies of work, the version for sound recordings must be used on publicly distributed phonorecords embodying a sound recording. If phonorecords are not made available to the public, there is no need to use this version of the notice and there will be no adverse consequences if it is not used under such circumstances.

Symbol ℗

There is no acceptable alternative for the symbol ℗. If this symbol is not used, a notice will be defective. In addition, there are no substitute statements or abbreviations for this version of the notice. So, phrases like "Protected sound recording," or "This phonorecord may not be reproduced," and the like are not effective and the use of them instead of the prescribed version will be treated as no notice at all.

A different version of the copyright notice was selected by Congress for sound recordings so members of the public will be able to know the type of work for which a copyright claim is made. Congress felt that if the same notice applied to sound recordings and to works they may incorporate, there would be confusion.

The distinction between a sound recording and the underlying work that it aurally communicates is discussed in Chapter 3. As noted, a series of musical sounds, spoken sounds, or other sounds may be protected by copyright separate and apart from copyrightable words, numbers, or other verbal or numerical symbols communicated in the process of creating many sounds.

When and at the time original sounds are embodied in a material object, such as a record, tape, or disk, they become eligible for copyright protection. The symbol ℗ is used to give notice of the copyright claim made for those sounds.

When words or numbers are combined to form literary, dramatic, or musical works and embodied in a printed or visual format, they too are eligible for copyright protection. The symbol © or one of its alternatives is used to give notice that a copyright claim is similarly made for them. This version of the notice is used for visually perceptible forms.

Year of First Publication

The year of first publication of a sound recording is determined in the same way as this date is determined for a work reproduced in visually perceptible copies. It is the year phonorecords embodying a sound recording are first made available to the public.

Generally, the comments made earlier in this chapter in reference to the year of first publication for visually perceptible copies of a work apply equally to phonorecords. However, there is no exception allowing omission of the year date in the notice as is the case with copies of pictorial, graphic, and sculptural works.

Name of the Copyright Owner

The copyright for a sound recording is owned only by those persons who create the sounds embodied in it. Keep in mind that sounds are eligible for copyright protection separate and apart from other types of works as discussed in Chapter 3 and earlier in this chapter. As a result, it is possible that the owners of copyright for a sound recording will be different from the owners of copyright for material communicated by the sounds.

For example, in most instances the copyright owner of a musical composition embodied in a record is a different person from the copyright owner for the sounds communicating the performance of that composition. Ordinarily, songwriters or their music publishers own the copyright to the musical composition itself, while record companies own the copyright to the sound recordings.

In certain situations, only one name will be listed as the copyright owner of a sound recording in a notice for it although a number of people were involved in creating it. If everyone participating in creating a sound recording is an employee and does so as part of the employment relationship, only the name of the employer should appear in the copyright notice. And in the event everyone who is involved in creating a sound recording transfers ownership to one person, only the name of the transferee should appear in the notice.

For example, recording artists usually are either employees of record companies or sign work-made-for-hire agreements with them, or transfer copyright ownership to record companies so that the record company will be the owner of the copyright to the sound recording embodying their performances. This explains why the name of a record company appears in this version of the copyright notice and not the name of the recording artist.

COPIES OR PHONORECORDS INCORPORATING U.S. GOVERNMENT WORKS

A special form of the copyright notice must be used whenever copies or phonorecords published by an individual or legal entity consist preponderantly of one or more works of the U.S. government. The objective of mandating this form of notice is to have it indicate what portions of a work are protected so that the notice will not be misleading. As indicated in Chapter 4, works of the U.S. government are not protected by copyright.

Sometimes works of the U.S. government are republished on a commercial basis and, in connection with doing so, a small amount of new material is added. The use of a copyright notice may be justified because protection is available for the added material. However, to avoid giving the misleading impression that all of the material in the copy or phonorecord is protected by copyright, the notice must include a special statement.

The special form of copyright notice that must be used for such works must include a statement clearly indicating what has been added to U.S. government material and what is and is not protected.

Failure to include such a statement will be treated as an omission of notice as it applies to the added material entitled to copyright protection.

INCLUDING ADDITIONAL INFORMATION IN OR AROUND A NOTICE

There is no requirement under the 1976 Act to include a copyright registration number in the notice or to use any additional statements cautioning against the unauthorized use of a copyrighted work. If such data or warnings are used, they should be separated from the notice to the extent that they do not interfere with it.

The following statements represent the kind that may be used in addition to a copyright notice:

Unauthorized reproduction of this recording is prohibited by Federal law

This document may not, in whole or part, be copied, photocopied, reproduced, translated or reduced to any electronic medium or machine readable form without prior written consent, in writing.

This videotape has been licensed for institutional and private home use only. Any other use, reproduction, copying, or public performance is prohibited.

No part of this book may be reproduced in any form or by any means without permission in writing from the publisher.

CHAPTER SUMMARY

- A copyright notice, in a form prescribed by the 1976 Act, must be used on publicly distributed copies or phonorecords of a work to avoid invalidating protection.
- There are two versions of the copyright notice, each of which consists of three components; one version is used for publicly distributed copies of a work that can be visually perceived and it features the letter "C" inside a

circle or the word "Copyright" or its abbreviation "Copr."; the other version is used for a sound recording and it features the letter "P" inside a circle.

- Use of any form of notice other than the one required by the Act is not acceptable and may result in invalidation of protection.
- A copyright notice does not necessarily mean that everything included within a particular copy or phonorecord is protected.

11

What Happens if Copyright Notice Is Incorrect or not Used

The 1976 Act is more liberal than the 1909 Act with respect to the manner and location where a copyright notice should be placed on publicly distributed copies or phonorecords and with respect to the consequences of errors in the notice or the complete omission of it. The placement of a notice in a specific location is not required under the 1976 Act, and the use of a notice with errors in it or the failure to use a notice will not necessarily result in the immediate loss of copyright protection. However, if an infringement occurs and the copyright notice is not used or is not properly used on publicly distributed copies or phonorecords, a copyright owner may not be able to take advantage of all the remedies available under the Act. In addition, if a notice is not used, all rights to a work may be invalidated under certain circumstances.

LOCATION AND POSITION OF COPYRIGHT NOTICE

Reasonable Notice

The 1909 Act specified exact locations where a prescribed form of the copyright notice was required to be placed on copies of a work. If the notice was featured on a copy but was not placed in the location specified by that Act, protection for the work could be lost. Under such circumstances the notice was not considered to be effective because it was not in the right location.

For example, under the 1909 Act, a copyright notice for books and other printed publications was to be placed upon the title page or the page immediately following the title page. If it did not appear there but was placed elsewhere, such as on the last page, the third page, or in the middle, copyright protection could be lost.

The 1976 Act changed this requirement. Now, a notice can be located anywhere on a copy or phonorecord as long as it is affixed in such a manner and location to give reasonable notice of the copyright claim. Regulations promulgated under the Act specify examples of methods of affixation and positions of the notice on works published in book form, single-leaf works, contributions to collective works, works reproduced in machine-readable copies, motion pictures and other audiovisual works, and pictorial, graphic, and sculptural works.

If the notice is visually perceptible and is affixed to copies in such manner and position that, when affixed, it is not concealed from view upon reasonable examination it will satisfy this condition. For example, the placement of a copyright notice in the masthead of a periodical would be an acceptable location for giving the required reasonable notice, although the masthead does not appear on the title page or page immediately following it. Also, it would be acceptable to place a copyright notice on the base of a sculpture although to view it may require looking closely at the base. However, if a notice is placed on the back of a photograph or oil painting, which is then framed and the back covered in its entirety so that the notice is concealed, the notice would not be visible and, therefore, would not perform its function of giving notice.

Affixation of a copyright notice means that it must be physically attached to a copy or phonorecord and should be permanently legible to an ordinary user of the copy or phonorecord, under normal conditions of use. Accordingly, imprinting a notice directly on a copy or phonorecord, or in other ways attaching it directly to a copy or phonorecord, would satisfy this requirement. This would be the case even though the notice may be removed or concealed at a later time by someone other than the copyright owner.

For example, placing a notice on the margin, selvage, or reverse side of fabric would be proper, although the margin or selvage may be cut off and the reverse side of fabric hidden from view. But placing a notice on a tag or slip of paper loosely packaged with a copy or phonorecord which could be easily separated from the copy or phonorecord, would not be acceptable. On the other hand, placing a notice on a label or tag which is sewn, cemented, riveted, or otherwise attached durably so as to withstand normal use would be acceptable.

Size of the Notice

As long as a copyright notice is visually perceptible, the size or style used to display it can be of any dimension. However, the notice should not be blurred, or otherwise illegible. If it cannot be discerned or clearly seen without the use of special devices, such as a magnifying glass, it would not be an acceptable notice.

Dispersal of the Components

A notice may not perform its intended function if the three components are separated from each other to the extent that uncertainty is created as to their relationship with each other. For example, this may be the case where the copyright owner's name appears at the top of a page below the title of a book and the remaining components are placed at the bottom of the page. Another example is where an artist places his or her name and year of creation on the front of a painting and the symbol ©, or one of its alternatives, on the back of the painting.

If the components of the notice are dispersed to the extent that they are not viewed as performing the intended function, it is likely that the notice will be treated as omitted.

The one exception to this rule has to do with the use of a notice for sound recordings. If the producer's name appears on the record label, album sleeve, jacket, or other container, it will be considered part of the notice, though remote from the other components. However, this form of a notice is acceptable only if no other name appears in conjunction with the other components.

Frequency of Use

Where only one copy of a work appears on an article, such as the label design for COORS beer on the front of a t-shirt, only one copyright notice for that design need be placed on the shirt. However, where a copy of a work is repeated on an article resulting in the copy appearing numerous times on the article, such as designs on fabrics, a question arises whether a separate copyright notice is required for each appearance of the copyrighted design.

The 1976 Act requires placement of a notice on all publicly distributed copies. This means that literally every copy of a work must feature its own notice each time it appears on an article. This requirement often presents a practical problem. Placing a notice next to each copy of a work every time it appears on an article may adversely affect the market value of the article.

From an aesthetic standpoint, appearance of a large number of notices on the article may interfere with or detract from its overall appearance.

Keeping this in mind, the courts have generally accepted the use of only one notice on an article for a copyrighted design even though the design may appear on it many times. This exception is only available where the notice appears at least once on every commercial unit of the article. At a minimum, it must appear on the smallest commercial unit by which the article is normally sold.

For example, if a palm tree scene is featured over and over again on clothing or furniture upholstery fabric, one notice may be used for all of the copyrighted scenes featured on the fabric, subject to the minimum unit size requirement. Thus, if the smallest commercial unit by which the fabric is normally sold is by the bolt, at least one notice must appear somewhere on every bolt of fabric.

Pictorial, Graphic, and Sculptural Works

The general rule requires placement of copyright notice directly on copies of works. However, if it is impossible or extremely impracticable to place a notice directly on copies of pictorial, graphic, or sculptural works because of the size or physical characteristics of the material in which such a work is embodied, an acceptable alternative method of giving notice can be used. It can be placed on a tag made of a durable material attached to the copy of the work. This is acceptable as long as the tag will remain with the copy while it is passing through normal channels of commerce.

If a work falling within this category is embodied in two- or three-dimensional copies, a notice can be on a label glued, sewn, or otherwise firmly attached to the copies. It can be placed on the front or back, or to any mounting, matting, framing, backing or other material, or to any containers in which the copies of such works are permanently housed as long as the notice is visible.

Computer Software

For works embodied in machine-readable copies, such as computer software programs or video games, a copyright notice can be placed at any one of the following locations:

1. On visually perceptible print-outs
2. At the user's terminal at sign on

3. Continuously on terminal display
4. On a gummed or other label securely affixed to the container used as a permanent receptacle for the copies

Sound Recordings

The copyright notice for a sound recording may be placed on the surface of the phonorecord that embodies it, on the phonorecord label, sleeve, cover, or container for it. These locations are acceptable if they give reasonable notice of the copyright claim for the sound recording. And, as noted earlier, if the producer's name is placed in a location remote from the other components, the notice will nonetheless be acceptable although all three components are not adjacent to each other.

Contributions to Collective Works

The 1976 Act expressly provides that a single copyright notice applicable to a collective work as a whole is sufficient to satisfy the notice requirement with respect to the separate contributions it contains. In addition, it expressly provides that the validity and ownership of the exclusive rights to a contribution will not be affected if the name of the owner of rights in the collective work is used in the notice instead of the name of the contributor. However, if there is no separate copyright notice on the contribution (featuring the name of the contributor), the contributors' ability to obtain all applicable remedies for infringement of the contribution may be adversely affected.

The notice for the collective work will be treated as a notice for the contribution in accordance with the provisions of the Act referred to above, but it will be treated as a notice with an error in the name. When a notice contains an error in the name portion, an innocent infringer may have a complete defense to any action for infringement by the contributor.

The use of a notice with an error in the name portion usually occurs when an article by a writer is reproduced in a newspaper, magazine, periodical, anthology, encyclopedia, or other collective work. For example, this will occur when an article written by a freelance writer is included in a magazine and the article does not bear its own copyright notice, but there is one for the magazine as a whole in its masthead. While the freelancer will not lose copyright protection for his or her literary work, he or she may lose the ability to preclude others from copying it. Consequently, it is definitely to the advantage of a freelancer to place a separate copyright notice on contributed articles.

The owner of rights in an advertisement inserted in collective works is not in the same position as an owner of rights in other kinds of material included in a collective work. The 1976 Act expressly indicates that a copyright notice for the collective work does not satisfy the copyright notice requirement for inserted advertisements. Advertisements must bear a separate copyright notice, featuring the name of the owner of rights in it, to satisfy the notice requirement.

OMISSION OF COPYRIGHT NOTICE

Limitations on the Ability to Protect or Loss of Protection

If the copyright notice requirement of the 1976 Act is not satisfied, two things are possible. The rights of the copyright owner will be limited, or they will be wholly forfeited and the work will go into the public domain.

An error in the name and certain errors in the date are treated as a failure to meet the notice requirement. This can result in limitations on the right of the copyright owner but will not affect the validity and ownership of the work.

Omission of the symbol © (or one of its alternatives), copyright owner's name, date (except with respect to pictorial, graphic, or sculptural works), or the notice in its entirety are also treated as a failure to meet the notice requirement. However, when any one of these omissions occurs, the rights of a copyright owner will be lost, not merely limited.

Omission of Notice Prior to January 1, 1978

Generally, the 1909 Act was not forgiving where a copyright notice was omitted when its use was required. If it was not placed on copies or on phonorecords (after 1972) at the time they were first publicly distributed by or with the authority of the copyright owner, all rights to the work would be immediately and automatically lost.

As a rule, the failure to use a copyright notice was unexcused, except when the omission was by accident or mistake. But this exception was very narrowly interpreted and qualification for it was extremely difficult. Ignorance of the law, oversight, or mere negligence on the part of the creator of a work were not acceptable justification for not using a notice.

In addition to the failure to use a notice in its entirety, the omission of any necessary components, such as the symbol, name, and date, or the failure to use them as required by the 1909 Act ordinarily resulted in the permanent loss of all rights. Errors made with respect to these components had the same effect.

Keeping the foregoing in mind, if a physical inspection of a publicly distributed copy or phonorecord of a work published prior to January 1, 1978 fails to disclose a copyright notice, it is possible that the work may be in the public domain. If so, it can be utilized by everyone without liability for infringement.

However, if a copy or phonorecord of an unpublished work is inspected and a copyright notice is not found on it, the same conclusion should not be reached. The absence of a notice will not be any indicator of whether protection is available because, as is the case under the 1976 Act, there was no requirement to use a notice on unpublished works under the 1909 Act.

Omission of Notice After January 1, 1978

The 1976 Act made a major change in the law with regard to the failure to use a copyright notice and the consequences of using a notice with errors in it. Now, nonuse of a notice, or the use of one with errors in it, may be excused under certain circumstances and the exclusive rights of an owner maintained.

Under the 1976 Act, the loss of all rights in a work can occur if a copyright notice is not used or if one is used with errors in it. However, the loss of rights will not occur immediately at the time copies or phonorecords are first publicly distributed. That is, the loss of rights will not immediately happen unless the creator of a work deliberately intends this to happen.

When there is no intention on the part of a creator or subsequent owner of copyright to give up protection for a work, it is possible that the loss of all rights can be avoided. There are three sets of circumstances set forth in the 1976 Act when omission of the copyright notice is excused and protection for a work will not be invalidated.

Omission of Notice on a Relatively Small Number of Copies

When notice has been omitted, partially or totally, copyright protection will not be invalidated if the notice has been omitted from no more than a relatively small number of copies or phonorecords distributed to the public. The intent of the copyright owner in failing to use a notice is not considered, and it makes no difference whether the notice was omitted due to oversight, mistake, or lack of knowledge. In such a case, nothing need be done by the copyright owner to avoid losing protection.

Although protection for a work will not be completely lost in this kind of situation, the rights of a copyright owner may be adversely affected. In the event an innocent infringement occurs, because there is no notice on a copy or phonorecord, the owner's ability to obtain monetary relief from the infringer may be limited.

As of July 1986 there is no accepted standard for what constitutes a "relatively small number of copies or phonorecords." However, in one case a court concluded that omission of the notice on 400 dolls, out of approximately 40,000 of the same dolls distributed to the public, meets the relatively small number test and sustained the claim to copyright protection for the doll. Thus, in at least one instance the absence of notice on one percent of the total number of copies publicly distributed did not defeat copyright ownership.

Registration Before or Within Five Years After Publication Without Notice

In the event more than a relatively small number of copies or phonorecords has been publicly distributed without a copyright notice on them, all is not lost. The Act indicates that protection will not be immediately forfeited if:

1. Registration for the work has been made before, or is made within, five years after publication without notice

2. A reasonable effort is made to add notice to all copies or phonorecords that are distributed to the public in the United States after the omission has been discovered

As long as a copyright owner does not deliberately fail to affix a notice to publicly distributed copies or phonorecords, it is possible for protection to continue for a period of five years past the date of first publication of a work, in cases where the work has not been previously registered.

If registration is made before that five-year period elapses and the required reasonable effort is made, copyright protection for the work will not be invalidated. However, up to the time the omission is cured by registration, innocent infringements of the work may occur and the ability of the copyright owner to obtain monetary relief may be limited.

This safety mechanism has two parts: registration five years prior to or five years after publication without notice, and reasonable effort to put the notice on undistributed copies after the omission has been discovered. Both must be performed for it to be effective, but there is no requirement that they must be performed at the same time.

The critical and controlling factors in this mechanism are the date of publication without the notice and the date of registration. If registration takes place five years before or five years after this date, protection will not be invalidated. But if registration takes place outside of this time frame, it will not be effective for purposes of avoiding the loss of protection.

Assuming the registration requirement is timely satisfied, discovery of the omission can occur at almost any time and protection maintained, if the required notice affixation effort is made with respect to copies or phonorecords not yet publicly distributed.

For example, a book is published without the notice in 1988, registration of the copyright claim for this work anytime between 1983 and 1993 is treated as fulfilling one part of the mechanism. If discovery of the omission occurs at any time after 1988, protection can be saved if the copyright owner makes the required notice affixation effort upon such discovery. However, if registration is made in 1982 or in 1994, it will not be timely and protection will be lost even though a reasonable effort is made to add the notice in 1994.

As of July 1986 there appears to be no indication of what constitutes a "reasonable effort made to add notice." However, a number of court decisions have established the point in time at which the owner must add notice. If, upon discovery of the omission, copies without the notice are under the control of someone other than the copyright owner but are not distributed to the public, the notice must be added to those copies to qualify for the savings mechanism. That is, a reasonable effort must be made to affix a notice to all copies that are in the hands of distributors.

Omission of Notice When Copyright Owner Mandates Use

Under certain circumstances, protection will not be lost if the notice is not placed on publicly distributed copies or phonorecords. This is possible where they are distributed, with the copyright owner's permission, by someone other than the copyright owner. Protection will not be lost if the notice has been omitted in violation of an express written requirement by the copyright owner that, as a condition of the owner's authorization to distribute, copies or phonorecords bear the prescribed notice. However, the owner's ability to obtain monetary relief from an innocent infringer will be limited.

For example, protection for a pictorial work, such as an oil painting, will not be lost if an express written condition of reproducing it is to place the artist's copyright notice on copies of it. If this condition is imposed and copies are publicly distributed without the notice, the artist will not lose copyright protection for the work.

If copies of a work are publicly distributed without the authority of the copyright owner and they do not feature a copyright notice, there will be no loss of protection. Omission of notice invalidates protection only where copies are publicly distributed by authority of the copyright owner

OMISSION OF OWNER'S NAME OR YEAR OF PUBLICATION

If copies or phonorecords, which are publicly distributed by the authority of the copyright owner, contain no name or date that can be reasonably considered a part of the notice, the work is considered to have been published without notice. That is, if the name and date components of the notice are not present or are so dispersed, making it reasonable to conclude they are not related to each other or to the symbol © (or one of its alternatives), the copy or phonorecord will be treated as having no notice (except where the year is missing from the notice for copies of pictorial, graphic, and sculptural works).

Protection will be lost, under those circumstances, if more than a relatively small number of copies were publicly distributed with the notice dispersed or with a missing component. It will also be lost if registration of the copyright claim is not made before or within five years after copies or phonorecords have been published with an incomplete copyright notice and the reasonable effort requirement is not satisfied.

ERRORS IN THE NOTICE

Error in Name

Errors in the copyright notice, whether in the name or the date, may affect the owner's ability to obtain monetary relief from innocent infringers or be treated as an omission of notice.

When the name that appears in the notice on copies or phonorecords publicly distributed by authority of the copyright owner is not the name of the copyright owner, the validity and ownership of rights are not affected. For example, the rights of a copyright owner will not be affected where the name of a licensee or other person who is not an owner of rights appears in the notice. However, the owner will not be able to obtain an injunction against, or be paid actual or statutory damages by, any person who innocently begins an undertaking that infringes the work if such person proves:

1. That he or she was misled by the notice
2. Began the undertaking in good faith under a purported transfer or license from the person named in the notice

Any time an exclusive right is exercised without permission of the owner, an infringement of that right occurs. However, when acting under these two conditions, the copyright infringer is considered innocent and is given a complete defense to any action for infringement.

The 1976 Act expressly provides that if the person named in the notice gave permission and received payment from an innocent infringer, the person named in the notice must account to the copyright owner for all such receipts. For example, a magazine publisher would be required to account to the author of a contributed copyrighted article if:

1. The magazine was given permission by the author to publish and distribute the article
2. A separate copyright notice was not used on the article as it appeared in the magazine
3. The publisher's name appeared in a copyright notice in the masthead for the magazine
4. The publisher gave permission to another person to make copies of the article and charged that person a fee for doing so, or the publisher made copies of the article for that person and charged a fee for doing so

The complete defense to infringement as noted is not applicable if (before an innocent infringer began the undertaking):

1. Registration for the work had been made in the name of the copyright owner; or
2. A document executed by the person named in the notice and showing the ownership of the copyright had been recorded

An error in the name will not be a basis for a person to innocently infringe a work, if a search of the U.S. Copyright Office records would show that the owner is someone other than the person named in the notice.

In the event copies with an error in the name are distributed publicly but without the authority of the copyright owner, there can be no complete defense to an infringement even when an innocent infringer is involved. A complete defense is only available with respect to copies distributed by authority of the copyright owner.

Error in the Date

If the date in the notice is earlier than one year before the year of first publication, it will be treated as an error in the date. Protection will not be lost as a consequence of this error, but any period of protection available under the 1976 Act that is measured from the year of first publication will be computed from the incorrect year in the notice. The actual year of first publication will not be used for such calculations.

When the date in the notice is more than one year after the year of first publication, the notice is treated as being omitted. In such case, protection will be lost if more than a relatively small number of copies have been publicly distributed and registration is not made within the prescribed five-year period and the reasonable effort requirement is not satisfied.

EFFECT OF OMISSION OF NOTICE ON INNOCENT INFRINGERS

Any person who innocently infringes a work, in reliance on the omission of a notice from an authorized copy or phonorecord, will not be liable for actual or statutory damages for any infringing acts committed before receiving actual notice that the work has been registered. This is possible only if that person can prove that he or she was misled by the omission of notice.

It is incumbent on a copyright owner to advise the innocent infringer directly that the work has been registered. This can be done by giving the infringer written notice of the registration or by other means.

Although an innocent infringer may not be liable for damages under the above circumstances, it is possible that the infringer's profits attributable to the infringement may be recovered by the copyright owner in an infringement lawsuit. In addition, a court may issue an order prohibiting that person from continuing the infringing activity. Or, as a condition of permitting the continuation of the infringing activity, the court may require the infringer pay to the copyright owner a reasonable license fee. If a court permits the continuation of the infringing activity, the terms of the license can be set by the court.

REMOVAL OF NOTICE WITHOUT AUTHORIZATION

If a copyright notice is attached to copies or phonorecords of a work at the time they leave the control of the copyright owner, or the control of persons authorized to distribute publicly those copies or phonorecords, protection for the work will not be affected by the removal, destruction, or obliteration of it at a later time by someone else without the copyright owner's authorization to do so.

PENALTIES FOR REMOVAL OF COPYRIGHT NOTICE

As noted in the preceding section, the removal of a copyright notice without permission of the copyright owner will not affect the copyright owner's rights. However, the person who removes or alters it may be penalized. Any person who, with fraudulent intent, removes or alters any copyright notice is punishable by fine as a criminal offense.

FRAUDULENT USE OF COPYRIGHT NOTICE

Any person who places a copyright notice on a copy or phonorecord of a work with fraudulent intent is punishable by fine as a criminal offense. Also, any person who places words of similar import knowing them to be false, or who publicly distributes or imports for public distribution any copy or phonorecord bearing a copyright notice or words of similar import known to be false, is punishable by fine as a criminal offense.

CHAPTER SUMMARY

- A copyright notice must be affixed to publicly distributed copies and phonorecords in such manner and location as to give reasonable notice of the claim of copyright.
- If there is an error in the notice because the name in it is not the name of the copyright owner, the validity and ownership of the exclusive rights are not affected, but the owner may lose the ability to protect the work fully.
- If the date in the notice is later than the year of first publication the work will be treated as published without notice; if the date is earlier than the year of first publication the period of protection may be shortened.
- If no notice is used, copyright protection may be invalidated.

- A person who fraudulently uses a copyright notice is subject to a monetary fine, as is anyone who fraudulently removes a copyright notice appearing on a copy of a work.
- Copyright protection is not affected by the removal, destruction, or obliteration of a notice from publicly distributed copies or phonorecords without authorization of the copyright owner.

12

What Is Copyright Registration?

Registration of a copyright ownership claim in a work, commonly referred to as "registration of a work," is a relatively simple procedure that gives a copyright owner the ability to *enforce* the exclusive rights in a work, something the owner of rights in an unregistered work cannot do. However, a copyright owner does not have to register a copyright ownership claim with the U.S. Copyright Office to *acquire* the five exclusive rights associated with such ownership. Contrary to the belief of some people, placing copies of material in an envelope and mailing it to themselves by registered or certified mail is not equivalent to registration of a copyright ownership claim. Doing this may be of some value in establishing that a work existed as of the date of mailing, but it may not accomplish much more.

REGISTRATION OCCURS AFTER RIGHTS ARE ACQUIRED

The date registration occurs is not the date when the rights of a copyright owner come into existence or the date when protection associated with them begins. As indicated in Chapter 5, a creator acquires the exclusive rights of a copyright owner (together with the protection corresponding to them) by the simple act of creating a copyrightable work. The date this occurs is the date rights come into existence and protection begins.

Copyright registration is a legal formality. It is a procedure separate and distinct from the act of acquiring rights, but it is nonetheless dependent upon that act. A work must be created before registration of a copyright ownership claim in it can occur. Thus, registration takes place after the exclusive rights of a copyright owner have been acquired.

It is not necessary for a copyright owner to file any documents with the U.S. Copyright Office or to submit any material to it as a condition of acquiring rights. But this does not mean a copyright owner should forgo registration or conclude that there is no obligation whatsoever to submit material to the U.S. Copyright Office.

MANDATORY DEPOSIT OF COPIES

At any time prior to the date a registration is secured for a published work, it is possible that the copyright owner may be required to provide the U.S. Copyright Office with at least one copy of the work. If a published work is of the type subject to the "mandatory deposit" provisions of the 1976 Act, the copyright owner must deposit at least one copy of it with the U.S. Copyright Office.

The deposit requirement is separate and distinguishable from the copyright registration procedure yet it may be fulfilled by registering a copyright ownership claim in a work. In fact, many copyright owners satisfy this requirement in connection with the registration procedure. The process of registration is discussed in Chapter 13 and the mandatory deposit requirement is discussed in Chapter 14.

REGISTRATION MAY BE REQUIRED

Although copyright registration is not a procedure that must be undertaken to acquire rights, it is one that must be completed to avoid losing rights when a copyright notice is not placed on publicly distributed copies or phonorecords, or when the notice is treated as omitted because of certain errors made in it. In addition, it must be completed to enable a copyright owner to obtain certain benefits available only to registered works and to enforce rights as well as be eligible for certain remedies for copyright infringement provided by the 1976 Act.

WHEN REGISTRATION CAN OCCUR

If a copyright notice is placed on publicly distributed copies or phonorecords of a work and there are no errors in the notice, there is no requirement to register the copyright ownership claim. If a proper notice is placed on published copies or phonorecords, registration may take place at any time at the election of the copyright owner, or for the owner's benefit, at any time during the applicable maximum period of copyright protection for a particular work.

Similarly, if a work has not been published, registration can occur at any time at the election of the copyright owner or, for the owner's benefit, at any time during the applicable maximum period of protection.

Registration of a copyright ownership claim to works made for hire can take place at any time within 75 years from the date the work was first published, or within 100 years from the date it was created. As noted in Chapter 9, one or the other of these periods is the maximum period of protection depending on whether the work has been published or not.

When the five exclusive rights are initially owned by the creator or creators of a work (in those situations when the work-made-for-hire rule does not apply), registration can be made at any time during the life of the creator(s) or at any time within 50 years after the date of the creator's death or the death of the last surviving creator.

Although registration may take place at any time during the applicable period of protection, there are advantages to registering an ownership claim in a work within a relatively short period of time after the date of its creation. By doing so a copyright owner reduces the chances of losing some of the benefits and remedies available to the owner of a registered work because, in certain instances, their availability is dependent upon the date that registration occurs. This is discussed in more detail later in this chapter.

PERSONS ENTITLED TO REGISTER AN OWNERSHIP CLAIM

The 1976 Act provides that the owner of all the exclusive rights, or of any exclusive right, in any published or unpublished work may obtain registration of the claim of ownership to the exclusive rights in a work by filing an application for registration with the U.S. Copyright Office. This has been interpreted to mean that anyone who falls within the following groups is entitled to file an application to register a work:

1. The creator of the work (i.e., either the individual who actually created the work or, if it was created as a work made for hire, the employer or other person for whom it was created)

2. A person or organization that has obtained ownership of *all* the exclusive rights in the work which initially belonged to the creator (that is,

a person or organization who acquired ownership of those rights by means of the sale, gift, or bequest by will of them directly from the creator or through a chain of owners that started with the creator)

3. The owner of any exclusive right in the work (as noted in Chapter 6, the exclusive rights comprised in a work may be owned as a group by one person or any one of them may be owned separately by different persons even though such ownership may be limited in scope)

4. The authorized agent of the creator or other owner of the work

Regardless of the group within which the person who obtains a registration belongs, or in whose name a work is registered, all owners of rights in it may enjoy the applicable benefits and remedies for infringement associated with a registered work. Consequently, in most cases the importance of obtaining a registration outweighs the importance of the person or group of persons who obtained it.

Although anyone who falls within one of these groups is entitled to register a work, it is possible that a particular person who qualifies to do so may not be able to register a work for a number of reasons. These are discussed in the following section.

ONLY ONE BASIC REGISTRATION IS PERMITTED

As a general rule, the U.S. Copyright Office will permit only one basic copyright registration for the same version of a particular work. Consequently, the same version of a work cannot be registered more than once unless, as provided by the Copyright Office Regulations, one of the following exceptions applies:

1. If a registration has been obtained for the work as an unpublished work, another registration may be made for the first published edition of the work, even if it does not represent a new version

2. If an applicant for registration alleges that an earlier registration for the same version is unauthorized and legally invalid, a registration may be made by that applicant

3. If someone other than the creator is identified as the "copyright claimant" (defined below) in a registration, another registration may be made by the creator in his or her own name as copyright claimant

4. Supplementary registrations (discussed in Chapter 13) may be made to correct or amplify the information in a registration

For example, if a person acquires rights in a work (whether from the creator or from someone who acquired rights from the creator) and it has already been registered, that person cannot register it again if one of the foregoing exceptions is not applicable. But, if a person acquires rights in a work and it has not been previously registered by anyone else, that person would be able to register it. This is possible even though the person who registers the work may be the second, the third, or the fourth owner of all rights in a work (in a succession of such owners), or who may be an exclusive licensee of one or more but less than all rights to it. However, it is possible that the person who registers the work may not be able to obtain the registration in his or her name for the reasons discussed in the following section.

REGISTRATION IN THE NAME OF THE COPYRIGHT CLAIMANT

A person who is entitled to register a work may not necessarily be the copyright claimant, although the name under which the work is registered must be the copyright claimant's. As provided in the U.S. Copyright Office Regulations, "a copyright 'claimant' is either (i) The author of a work, or (ii) A person or organization that has obtained ownership of *all* rights initially belonging to the creator."

Referring to the rule permitting only one basic registration for each version of a work, it is possible that a person who is a copyright claimant will not be able to obtain a registration. This would be the case where a registration for the same version of the work has already been obtained in the name of a prior copyright claimant for the work. For example, if the creator registered the work as a copyright claimant, it would not be possible for any subsequent owner of all rights to register it in his or her name as copyright claimant.

COMPELLING REASONS TO REGISTER

Prerequisite to Enforcing Rights

Registration of a work is a prerequisite to any action by a copyright owner to enforce rights recognized under the 1976 Act and to take advantage of any benefits that the Act gives to copyright owners.

For example, until such time as a work has been registered, a statutory presumption that the copyright is valid is not available to the owner and neither is any of the remedies for infringement of the work. By delaying registration, the owner of rights assumes the risk of losing the right to be awarded statutory damages and attorney's fees in an infringement action. They can be obtained only if registration is made before the date of an infringement or it is made within three months from the date of first publication when an infringement occurs before the registration date.

When a copyright notice has been omitted from publicly distributed copies of a work, registration is required within a specific time period to avoid forfeiture of rights.

While the date of registration is not critical with regard to the availability of remedies for infringement other than those referred to above, they cannot be sought until registration is made. Accordingly, if a copyright owner wishes to enforce rights in an unregistered work, it will be necessary to register it first.

The benefits, remedies, and actions by a copyright owner set forth below are conditioned on registration of a work. Specific time periods are associated with the availability of the first three.

A Registration Certificate Is *Prima Facie* Evidence

If a work is *registered before its first publication or within five years after the date of its first publication*, the certificate of registration will constitute *prima facie* evidence of the validity of the rights in it as well as the facts stated in the registration certificate. By reason of this benefit, there is a rebuttable presumption that all of the facts set forth in the certificate are true. The effect of this is to relieve the copyright owner of the burden of proving those facts in a judicial proceeding involving the work—that is, unless an infringer effectively challenges them, at which time the burden shifts back to the copyright owner who must then prove them.

Statutory Damages and Attorney's Fees

The owner of rights in a published or unpublished work is entitled to be awarded reasonable attorney's fees, plus statutory damages, incurred by the owner in successfully claiming an infringement of rights in the work.

This remedy is not available if the infringement is commenced before the date the work is registered. However, two exceptions to the registration requirement apply here:

1. The first exception covers a published work which has not been registered prior to an infringement of rights in it:

The owner of such a work is entitled to this remedy but only if the work is registered within three months after the date of its first publication *and* the infringement is commenced within this grace period. (Congress indicated that this exception is necessary to cover newsworthy or suddenly popular works that may be infringed almost as soon as they are published and before the copyright owner has had a reasonable opportunity to register the work);

2. The second exception covers a work consisting of sounds, images, or both where they are first embodied in a physical object simultaneously with transmission of the work:

   By express language in the 1976 Act the owner of rights in such a work is not precluded from seeking this remedy even though an infringement occurs before the work is published or registered.

Avoids Invalidation of Copyright

If more than a relatively small number of copies of a work have been publicly distributed and those copies do not feature a copyright notice, or the notice on them is erroneous to the extent it is treated as being omitted, timely registration (see Chapter 11) of the work will have the effect of avoiding forfeiture of all rights in it. In addition to registration, the owner must make a reasonable effort to add the notice to all copies of the work not yet distributed to the public.

Prerequisite to an Infringement Lawsuit

The owner of rights in a work cannot enforce those rights until the work is registered. A literal reading of this requirement indicates that registration of the work must be made before a copyright infringement lawsuit can be instituted. However, there is considerable precedent allowing an owner to maintain a copyright infringement action where registration is made after institution of the lawsuit. However, this is subject to the requirement that a work is actually registered prior to the time the court considers the infringement claim. That is, registration must occur before trial or a hearing on any preliminary injunction motion. If registration does not occur prior to that time, the lawsuit can be dismissed by the court. There are two exceptions to this requirement:

1. The first exception covers circumstances where registration of a work is refused by the U.S. Copyright Office:

Where an application has been delivered to the Copyright Office in proper form and accompanied by the required fee and material but registration is refused, the owner of rights is entitled to institute a copyright infringement action if a notice of the action, along with a copy of the Complaint, is served on the Register of Copyrights.

2. The second exception covers a work consisting of sounds, images, or both where they are first embodied in a physical object simultaneously with transmission of the work:

The owner of rights in such a work may institute a copyright infringement action before registration of it is made if the owner (a) serves notice on the infringer not less than 10 or more than 30 days before the work is embodied in a physical object, identifying the work and the specific time and source of its first transmission, and declaring an intention to secure copyright in the work; and (b) registers the work within three months after its first transmission.

Prevents Reliance on an Error in the Notice as a Complete Defense

An error in the copyright notice does not affect the validity of the owner's rights in the work even when copies of it are publicly distributed by authority of the owner. However, it may prevent the owner from effectively enforcing those rights against an innocent infringer (see Chapter 11).

An innocent infringer is any person who infringes the rights of an owner but can prove that he or she was misled by the error in the notice, and show that the infringing activity was undertaken in good faith pursuant to a purported transfer of rights or license from the person named in the notice. If the infringer is able to satisfy both of these requirements, he or she is entitled to raise these facts as a "complete defense" to an infringement action by the author.

A complete defense bars the entry of an injunction against the infringer, which has the effect of permitting the infringing activity, and it bars the entry of any award against the infringer for damages and/or profits arising from the infringement.

In the absence of a complete defense, an infringer is fully liable for the infringement.

Registration of a work prior to an infringing activity (of the type noted here) will defeat an innocent infringer's complete defense. Also, this defense will be defeated if a search of the U.S. Copyright Office records would have shown that the owner was someone other than the person whose name appears in the notice.

A Condition of Constructive Notice of Facts in a Transfer Document

When rights in a work are transferred, it is in the best interest of the transferee to record the document evidencing the transaction in the U.S. Copyright Office. This will have the effect of giving all members of the public constructive notice of the facts stated in the recorded document (whether they are aware of them or not), but only if the work has been registered prior to recordation.

Until such time as a work has been registered there is no constructive notice of the facts in the transfer document even though it has been recorded. However, once registration of the work is made, constructive notice becomes effective, but only after the date of registration.

If there are conflicting transfers of rights in a work, constructive notice will affect the ability of one transferee to prevail over another with respect to acquiring those rights. Constructive notice of an ownership transfer is an important benefit. It is discussed in Chapter 16, along with the document recording requirement in general.

INVESTIGATING THE COPYRIGHT STATUS OF A WORK

In compliance with the Freedom of Information Act and the 1976 Act, the U.S. Copyright Office makes available for public inspection and copying its records of copyright registration and of final refusals to register claims to copyright. The 1976 Act provides that "copies may be made of any public records or indexes of the Copyright Office . . . and copies of any public records or indexes may be furnished upon request and payment of the fees specified. . . ."

The Catalog of Copyright Entries may be referred to for purposes of obtaining essential facts concerning a registration. It is not a complete source of information for data on registrations because it is not a verbatim transcript of the registration record and it does not include entries for assignments or other recorded documents. Accordingly, it cannot be relied on as a basis for obtaining all available information regarding the ownership of rights.

The Catalog of Copyright Entries is prepared by the Cataloging Division of the U.S. Copyright Office. That division prepares the bibliographic description of all copyrighted works registered in the Copyright Office, including the recording of legal facts of copyright pertaining to each work, and creates a data base from which catalog cards and the Catalog of Entries are produced.

The records of the U.S. Copyright Office are open to the public for inspection and searching. Records freely available to the public include an extensive card catalog, record books, and microfilm records of assignments and related documents. Correspondence files and copies of works on deposit with the U.S. Copyright Office are not open to the public. Furthermore, it is a general policy of the U.S. Copyright Office to deny direct public access to in-process files. Requests for information in the in-process and open unfinished business files should be made to:

Certifications and Documents Section, LM-402
U.S. Copyright Office
Library of Congress
Washington, DC 20557

Requests for copies of U.S. Copyright Office records can be made to the Certifications and Documents Section and should include, among other information, a clear identification of the type of records desired (e.g., registration certificates and correspondence), a specification of whether copies are to be certified or uncertified, and a clear identification of the specific records to be copied.

If there is a desire to have the Copyright Office make a search of its records for specific information, it will do so at the rate of $10.00 for each hour or fraction of an hour consumed (as of July 1, 1986). A request should be made to:

Reference and Bibliography Section, LM-450
Copyright Office
Library of Congress
Washington, DC 20559

If requests for information from the Copyright Office are made under the Freedom of Information Act, they should be submitted in writing to:

Supervisory Copyright Information Specialist
Information and Publications Section
Information and Reference Division
U.S. Copyright Office
Library of Congress
Washington, DC 20559

The U.S. Copyright Office will notify the requesting party whether or not the request will be granted. If it is denied, the basis for denial will be given and the names of all individuals who participated in the determination will be given. In addition, a description of procedures available to appeal the determination will be given. If a request has been approved, the records of the U.S. Copyright Office covered by it may be inspected and copied at the Copyright Office.

CHAPTER SUMMARY

• Registration of a copyright ownership claim is not a prerequisite to acquiring exclusive rights in a work.

• The registration procedure involves recordation of a copyright ownership claim through the filing of an application form and depositing copies or phonorecords of a work with the U.S. Copyright Office.

• Generally, registration may occur at any time during the maximum period of protection applicable to a particular work and is voluntary.

• If a work is published without a copyright notice or treated as published without a notice, registration must occur before or within five years of the date of publication without notice to avoid invalidation of copyright protection.

• Registration is required in all cases if a copyright owner desires to enforce the exclusive rights in a work.

13

How To Register a Work

Copyright registration is not a complicated procedure. Undertaking and completing it does not require a knowledge of the law and does not entail any significant effort or cost in terms of filing fees.

In effect, copyright registration is nothing more than the act of giving specific information about a copyrighted work to the U.S. Copyright Office in connection with submitting copies or phonorecords of the work to that agency, and paying a prescribed filing fee.

The forms supplied by the U.S. Copyright Office contain easy-to-follow line-by-line instructions for their use. They may be obtained, at no cost, by anyone desiring to register a work. Copies of the application forms are found in Appendix C and are discussed in the following sections of this chapter.

CHOOSING THE PROPER FORM TO USE

Application forms may be obtained directly from the Copyright Office by calling that agency in Washington, D.C., or by writing to:

Informations and Publications Section LM-455
U.S. Copyright Office
Library of Congress
Washington, D.C. 20559, or

from the U.S. Government Printing Office through its field offices located throughout the country.

Only officially printed application forms may be used to register a work and, in most instances, it will be possible to register only one work per form. Photocopies or other reproductions of the official forms will not be accepted by the U.S. Copyright Office. Since it may take several weeks to receive the requested forms, anyone interested in registering more than one work should request a number of copies so that a sufficient quantity will always be on hand.

When requesting an application form from the U.S. Copyright Office, it is important to specify the version appropriate for the work to be registered. There are four basic versions of the application form. Each version corresponds to a particular class of work.

Although all of the forms are substantially similar in appearance and call for substantially the same information regardless of the class of works covered, the use of each is limited to registering only works within the class it covers. They are not interchangeable and therefore cannot be used to register works that do not fall within their respective classes.

The four classes were established by the U.S. Copyright Office, pursuant to its authority to do so under the 1976 Act. This was done strictly for practical administrative purposes and only for purposes of the registration process. These classes do not limit or otherwise have any adverse effect on the exclusive rights of a copyright owner or the kind of material that can be protected under copyright law. Thus, that a work is registered in one class has no particular significance outside of the U.S. Copyright Office record-keeping system.

When seeking registration of a work, the application form to use should be the one most appropriate to the nature of the work sought to be registered. In some cases where a work contains elements that fall within two or more classes, use the form most appropriate to the kind of work that predominates in the work as a whole. For example, if a work is in the nature of a book consisting of predominantly visual illustrations with some text, Form VA (for visual works) should be used and not Form TX (for literary works). And if a work is in the nature of a musical composition embodied in a sound recording, and there is a desire to register the sound recording, Form SR (for sound recordings) should be used and not Form PA (for musical works).

COVERAGE OF EACH FORM

Alphabet Letters Differentiate Each Version

Each version of the application form is identified and distinguished from the others by means of a two-letter code appearing on the first page in the upper right corner. The letters, on three of the four applications, readily denote the nature of the works covered by the form.

Class PA: Works of the Performing Arts (Form PA)

This class includes all published and unpublished works prepared for the purpose of being performed directly before an audience or indirectly by means of a device or process. For example, musical works (including any accompanying words), dramatic works (including any accompanying music), pantomimes and choreographic works, and motion pictures and other audiovisual works can be registered using Form PA.

Class SR: Sound Recordings (Form SR)

This class includes all published and unpublished sound recordings embodied in a physical object after February 15, 1972. Prior to that date sound recordings were not protected under federal copyright law. Form SR should be used if the work to be registered is the sound recording itself as distinguished from the underlying material that has been expressed aurally. For example, this form should be used when there is an intent to register an individual's recorded aural performance of a work, such as a song on a phonograph record, rather than the musical work that may already be the subject of a registration.

This form may also be used to register the sound recording and the underlying material simultaneously as long as the copyright claimant is the same for both. For example, this form can be used to register a sound recording for a musical work when the person who created the sound recording also created the musical work communicated through the sounds embodied in the sound recording. However, if the claimants differ for each work this form should be used to register only the sound recording, and it should be filed by the copyright claimant for the sound recording.

If a work comprises the audio portion of an audiovisual work, such as the sound track of a motion picture, this form should not be used. As the definition of motion pictures indicates, sounds accompanying a motion picture or other audiovisual work are part of those works and should be registered using Form PA.

Class TX: Nondramatic Literary Works (Form TX)

This class includes all published and unpublished nondramatic literary works. For example, fiction, nonfiction, poetry, books, manuscripts, pamphlets, textbooks, reference works, directories, catalogs, advertising copy, periodicals and serials, compilations of information, and, computer programs and user's manuals can be registered using Form TX.

Class VA: Works of the Visual Arts (Form VA)

This class includes all published and unpublished pictorial, graphic, and sculptural works. For example, two- and three-dimensional works of the fine, graphic, and applied arts, as well as photographs, prints and art reproductions, maps, globes, charts, technical drawings, diagrams and models, and pictorial or graphic labels and advertisements can be registered using Form VA.

Form to Register Serials (Form SE)

An additional form available for use in registering work is not tied to a specific class of works although it appears to be more closely related to Class TX than the others.

Form SE is for use in registering each individual issue of a serial. For purposes of registration the word "serial" is defined as a work issued or intended to be issued in successive parts bearing numerical or other chronological designations and intended to be continued indefinitely. For example, the following material can be registered using this form: periodicals, newspapers, annuals, and the journals, proceedings, and transactions of societies.

Individual contributions to a work that falls within the definition of serial should be registered using Form TX rather than Form SE. For example, Form TX should be used to register a literary work in the nature of a column written by an author who contributes it to a newspaper but not under any work-made-for-hire relationship.

Forms Used To Provide Information in Reference to Existing Registrations

Two forms can be used to provide information to the Copyright Office in reference to existing registrations. They do not correspond to any of the administrative classes and therefore their use is not restricted to one particular group of works. Each is also coded by means of letters that designate the purpose for which they are intended to be used.

Application for Supplementary Copyright Registration To Correct or Amplify an Earlier Registration (Form CA)

This form can be filed by the creator of a work, by any other copyright claimant, by the owner of an exclusive right in the work, or by the duly authorized agent of the creator or other copyright claimant. It is used only for supplementary registration of the work to correct an error in an earlier registration of it, or to amplify the information given in the earlier registration.

The information in the Supplemental Registration augments but does not supersede that contained in the earlier registration nor does it result in the cancellation or expunging of the earlier registration.

A "correction" is appropriate if information in the basic registration was incorrect at the time the basic registration was made. For example, where a work was given a wrong date of publication, or where an author's name was incorrectly given, Form CA can be used to make a correction in this regard. If the information was incorrect at the time of the basic registration and the error is one that the U.S. Copyright Office itself should have recognized, the agency should take appropriate measures to rectify the error.

An "amplification" is appropriate to:

1. Reflect additional information that could have been given, but was omitted at the time basic registration was made. For example, Form CA can be used to add the name of a co-author where a co-author's name was omitted

2. Reflect changes in facts, other than those relating to transfer, license, or ownership of rights in the work, that have occurred since the basic registration was made. For example, Form CA can be used to change the title of a work where the title of the registered work has been changed since registration

3. To clarify information given in the basic information. For example, Form CA can be used to clarify a statement referring to new material added to a work or the identification of pre-existing material in a work

Use of this form is not appropriate to reflect the ownership, division, allocation, licensing, or other transfer of rights in a work. This can be done by recording transfer documents with the U.S. Copyright Office as described in Chapter 16. Similarly, it should not be used to correct errors in statements or notices on copies of a work, or to reflect changes in the content of a work. If a work has been changed substantially, resulting in a new work, a basic registration for the new work should be made, not a supplemental registration.

Adjunct Application for Registration for a Group of Contributions to Periodicals (Form GR/CP)

This form may be used to obtain a single registration for a group of works all created by the same individual instead of registering each one of them separately. In effect, this allows the creator the opportunity to save the time, effort, and filing fees associated with registering the works individually. However, not every group of works can be registered in this way. The 1976 Act provides that only those that satisfy the following conditions can be registered in this way:

1. The works must have been created by the same individual outside the context of a work-made-for-hire relationship

2. Each of the works was first published as a contribution to a periodical (including newspapers) within a 12-month period

3. Each of the contributions featured a separate copyright notice, and the name of the owner in it was the same (that is, the name of the creator)

4. The application is accompanied by one entire issue of the periodical, or of the entire section in the case of a newspaper, in which each contribution was first published

5. The application identifies each contribution separately, including the periodical containing it and the date of its first publication

6. An application for basic registration of the work is filed at the same time on Form TX, Form PA, or Form VA, whichever is appropriate for the group of contributions as a whole. For example, if the group of contributions consists of cartoons, Form VA would be used for the basic registration. And, if the group of contributions consists of a group of musical compositions, Form PA would be used for the basic registration

Application for Renewal Registration (Form RE)

This form is used to renew a registration issued by the Copyright Office prior to December 31, 1977. As noted in Chapter 9, prior to January 1, 1978 the first term of copyright protection lasted for a maximum period of 28 years from the date of first publication, or in the case of unpublished works, from the date such works were registered.

Protection for an additional 28 years was possible if a published work was registered prior to expiration of the first 28 years and a renewal application was likewise filed within that period. Protection for unpublished works registered under the 1909 Act could also be extended for another 28 years if a renewal application was filed for them prior to expiration of the first term.

As indicated in Chapter 9, the 1976 Act retained the renewal requirement for works registered under the 1909 Act but changed the renewal term to 47 years. To take advantage of this new period, a renewal application must be filed prior to the expiration of the applicable 28-year period for works registered as published or unpublished under the 1909 Act.

INFORMATION THAT MUST BE INCLUDED
IN THE COPYRIGHT APPLICATION

Specific information about a work sought to be registered must be furnished on an application form and submitted to the U.S. Copyright Office.

The information that must be provided is substantially the same in each application, regardless of the type of work to be registered. However, there are some variations due to the nature of the different works. Generally, each form requires that the following information be given:

Title of the Work. The title of the work is used by the U.S. Copyright Office for indexing and identification purposes. Every work must be given a title, at least for registration purposes.

Previous or Alternative Titles. This should be completed if there are additional titles under which someone searching for a registration might be likely to look.

Nature of the Work. (This is found only on Forms PA, SR, and VA.) A brief description of the general nature or character of the work should be inserted. For example, for Form VA this might be an "oil painting," "charcoal drawing," or "sculpture."

Publication as a Contribution. (This is found only on Forms TX and VA.) If the work is being registered as a contribution to a periodical, serial, or collection, information should be given about the publication in which the contribution appeared.

Name of Author. The fullest form of the name of the individual who created the work should be inserted, unless the work is a "work made for hire." If it is a "work made for hire," the name of the employer or other person for whom the work was created should be inserted. If there is more than one creator of the work additional spaces are included in the application forms to identify all of them.

Dates of Author's Birth and Death. The author's birthdate is optional. If the author is dead the date of death must be noted because the term of protection ends 50 years after that date.

Author's Nationality or Domicile. The author's nationality or domicile may affect the protectibility of the work in the United States if the author is not a citizen of or does not reside in the United States.

Was This Author's Contribution to the Work Anonymous or Pseudonymous? An author's contribution is "anonymous" where no natural person is identified as the owner in the copyright notice on copies or phonorecords of a work. An author's contribution is "pseudonymous" if the author is identified in the notice under a fictitious name.

Nature of Authorship. A brief general statement of the nature of the author's contribution to the work should be entered. For example, for a literary work it might be "entire text," or "coauthor of entire text," or "editorial revisions."

Year in which Creation of This Work Was Completed. This is the year in which the author completed the particular version of the work sought to be registered.

Date and Nation of First Publication of the Work. "Publication" is defined as the act of selling, giving away, renting, leasing, or loaning a copy of a work or the offering to distribute copies for further distribution, public performance, or public display. The month, day, and year this first occurs should be given. If the work sought to be registered has not been published, these spaces should be left blank. The country where first publication occurred must also be identified.

Copyright Claimant. Here the name and address of the person who claims ownership of all rights in the work should be inserted. If the author is the owner of all rights at the time of registration, the author's name should again appear here. Remember, an employer is considered to be the author of the work in work-made-for-hire situations. In instances where the author is not the owner of all rights at the time of registration, the name and address of the person who is the owner should be used.

Transfer. If the copyright claimant is not the author (the creator or employer), a brief statement of how the claimant obtained ownership should be inserted. For example, it may be "by assignment," or "by will."

Previous Registration. As discussed in Chapter 12, only one basic registration can be made for the same version of a work. Accordingly, the U.S. Copyright Office has an interest in knowing if the work sought to be registered has been registered before. If so, the Office must know if the work sought to be registered is a new version, or a published edition of a work previously registered in unpublished form, or is the first application submitted by the creator. As noted in Chapter 12, a creator is entitled to obtain a registration as copyright claimant where another person was named as a copyright claimant in an earlier registration.

Derivative Work or Compilation. If the work is a changed version, a compilation, or a derivative work, information identifying the preexisting material should be given, as well as a brief general statement of the added material for which copyright protection is claimed, for example, editorial revisions of a preexisting literary work, or arrangement of a preexisting musical work.

Certification. The capacity of the person who is signing the application must be indicated. If the space "Author" is checked it means the creator (employer, in the case of a work made for hire) is signing the application; if "Other Copyright Claimant" is checked it means the person signing is not the creator but someone who has acquired all of the rights of the creator; if "Owner of Exclusive Right(s)" is checked it means the person signing owns one or more of the rights in a work but less than all of them; if "Authorized agent of" is checked it means the person signing is doing so not as an owner of rights but on behalf of an owner of rights.

COPIES OR PHONORECORDS MUST ACCOMPANY THE APPLICATION

A Specific Number of Copies or Phonorecords Must Be Deposited

Registration of a work involves the deposit of at least one copy or phonorecord of a work, whether published or not, with the U.S. Copyright Office (in many instances two copies must be deposited). It must be accompanied by a properly completed application form and filing fee.

As a general rule, if the three elements are not received at the same time, they will not be processed for registration purposes but will be returned to the sender. An exception to this rule arises when copies of a published work are sent to the U.S. Copyright Office unaccompanied by an application form and fee but accompanied by a clear written request that they be held for connection with a separately forwarded application.

If copies of a published work are submitted by themselves they will not be returned but may be transferred to the Library of Congress for its collections. When this occurs those particular copies will no longer be available so that if registration of the work is desired, it will be necessary to submit additional copies.

In some cases quality standards have been set by the U.S. Copyright Office providing for the deposit of the "best edition" and for "complete copies." The required number of copies to deposit as well as the quality and nature of those copies are:

1. One "complete" copy or phonorecord if the work is unpublished.
2. Two "complete" copies or phonorecords of the "best edition" if the work is published.

3. One "complete" copy or phonorecord as so published if the work is first published outside of the United States.

4. One "complete" copy or phonorecord of the "best edition" of the collective work if the work is a contribution to a collective work.

The actual number of copies that must be deposited varies depending upon the kind of work to be registered and its publication status. Similarly, the nature and quality of copies to be deposited will vary for the same reasons. For example, in some cases only one copy is required to be deposited instead of two, and in other cases "identifying material" may be deposited instead of actual copies of a work. The U.S. Copyright Office has adopted regulations under the 1976 Act that prescribe rules pertaining to the deposit of "identifying material" as well as copies and phonorecords of works for the purpose of registration.

"Best Edition" and "Complete" Copies

For purposes of registration the "best edition" of a published work is the edition (in existence before the date of deposit) that the Library of Congress determines to be most suitable for its collections. A statement entitled "Best Edition of Published Copyrighted Works for the Collections of the Library of Congress" establishes the criteria used by the Library of Congress for determining the best edition of a work. This statement is available to the public and can be used as a guide in determining which copies are appropriate for deposit. It is reproduced in Appendix B. When there are two or more published editions of the same version of a work, the criteria generally provide for selecting the one of the highest quality.

Generally, a "complete" copy of an unpublished work is one representative of the entire copyrightable content of the work. A "complete" copy of a published work includes all elements comprising the applicable unit of publication of the work, including elements that, if considered separately, would not be copyrightable matter. For example, a complete copy of a literary work consists of all copyrightable text as well as public domain material within it such as photographs or illustrations.

In the case of phonorecords a "complete" copy includes the phonorecord and any printed or other visually perceptible material published with it, such as pictorial matter on sleeves, jackets, or album covers.

In the case of a published or unpublished motion picture a "complete" copy is defined in terms of the condition of the copy. A copy is "complete" if the reproduction of all the visual and aural elements comprising the copyrightable subject matter is clean, undamaged, undeteriorated, and free of splices. In addition, the copy itself and its physical housing should be free of any defects that would interfere with the performance of the work or that would cause mechanical, visual, or audible defects or distortions.

Number of Copies to Be Deposited

The following is a representative, but not exhaustive, list contained in the U.S. Copyright Office Regulations, of the kinds of works for which one (instead of two) complete copy or phonorecord may be deposited:

Published three-dimensional cartographic representations of areas, such as globes and relief models.

Published diagrams illustrating scientific or technical works or formulating scientific or technical information in linear or other two-dimensional form, such as an architectural or engineering blueprint or mechanical drawing.

Published greeting cards, picture postcards, and stationery.

Lectures, sermons, speeches, and addresses published individually and not as a collection of the works of one or more authors.

Published contributions to a collective work, such as articles contributed to a magazine.

Musical compositions published in copies only, or in copies and phonorecords, if the only publication of copies took place by rental, lease, or lending.

Published multimedia kits that are prepared for use in systematic instructional activities and that include literary works, audiovisual works, sound recordings, or any combination of such works.

Published and unpublished motion pictures accompanied by a separate description of its contents, such as a continuity, press-book, or synopsis. The Library of Congress may enter into an agreement permitting the return of copies of published motion pictures to the depositor under certain conditions. "Identifying material" may be deposited in the case of unpublished motion pictures in lieu of an actual copy.

Holograms accompanied by precise instructions for displaying the image fixed in the hologram, and photographs or other "identifying material" showing the displayed image.

Unpublished pictorial and graphic works and certain published pictorial and graphic works where an individual is the copyright owner and either (1) fewer than five copies of the work have been published; or (2) the work has been published and sold or offered for sale in a limited edition consisting of no more than 300 numbered copies. "Identifying material" may be deposited in lieu of one actual copy

Commercial prints, labels, and other advertising matter published in connection with the rental, lease, lending, licensing, or sale of articles of merchandise, works or authorship, or services. If a print or label is published in a larger work, such as a newspaper or other periodical, one copy of the entire page or pages upon which it appears may be submitted in lieu of the entire larger work. In the case of prints or labels physically inseparable from a three-dimensional object, "identifying material" may be deposited rather than an actual copy.

Tests and answer material for tests published separately from other literary works. In the case of a "secure" test the U.S. Copyright Office will return the copy promptly after examination subject to the right of the Office to retain sufficient portions, descriptions, or the like for archival purposes.

Machine-readable works in the form of unpublished or published literary works (e.g., computer programs, automated data bases, compilations, and statistical compendia) embodied in magnetic tape or disks, punched cards, or the like which cannot ordinarily be perceived except with the aid of a machine or device. "Identifying material" should be submitted for these kinds of works as noted:

Computer Programs. This material should consist of one copy of "identifying portions" of the program, reproduced in a form visually perceptible without the aid of a machine or device, either on paper or in microform. "Identifying portions" means either the first and last 25 pages or equivalent units of the program if reproduced on paper, or at least the first and last 25 pages or equivalent units of the program if reproduced in microform, together with the page or equivalent unit containing the copyright notice, if any.

Automated Data Bases, Compilations and Statistical Compendia, and Other Literary Works. One copy of "identifying portions" or, in the case of automated data bases comprising separate and distinct data files, representative portions of each separate "data file" consisting of either 50 complete data records from each "file" or the entire file, whichever is less. "Data file" and "file" mean a group of data records pertaining to a common subject matter, regardless of the physical size of the records or the number of data items included in them. In any case where the deposit comprises representative portions of each separate file of an automated data base it shall be accompanied by a typed or printed descriptive statement containing: (1) the title of the data base; (2) the name and address of the copyright claimant; (3) the name and content of each separate file within the data base, including the subject matter involved, the origin(s) of the data, and the approximate number of individual records within the file; and, (4) a description of the exact contents of any machine-readable copyright notice employed in or with the work and the manner and frequency with which it is displayed (e.g., at user's terminal only at sign-on, or continuously on terminal display, or on printouts, etc.) If a visually perceptible notice is placed on any copies of the work, such as on disks, reels, etc., or on their containers, a sample of such notice must also accompany the statement.

Published and unpublished works reproduced in or on two-dimensional sheetlike material such as textile and other fabrics, wallpaper and similar commercial wall coverings, carpeting, floor tile, and similar commercial floor coverings, and wrapping paper and similar packaging material. The copy should be in the form of an actual swatch or piece of such material sufficient to show all elements of the work in which rights are claimed and the notice appearing on the work, if any. If the work consists of a repeated pictorial or graphic design, the complete design and at least part of one repetition must be shown. If the sheetlike material in or on which a published work has been embodied in or attached to a three-dimensional object such as wearing apparel, furniture, or any other three-dimensional manufactured article, and the work has been published only in that form, "identifying material" must be deposited in lieu of an actual copy.

Three-dimensional sculptural works, including any illustration or formulation of artistic expression or information in three-dimensional form, such as statutes, carvings, ceramics, moldings, constructions, models, and maquettes, and any two-dimensional or three-dimensional work that has been embodied in or on jewelry, dolls, toys, games, or any three-dimensional useful article. "Identifying material" must be deposited for such works in lieu of actual copies.

Three-dimensional objects consisting of (1) works that are reproduced by intaglio or relief printing on two-dimensional materials such as paper or fabrics; (2) works embodied or published in or on a useful article that comprises one of the elements of the unit of publication of an educational or instructional kit which also includes a literary or audiovisual work, a sound recording, or any combination of such works; (3) published works exempt from the mandatory deposit requirements (see Chapter 14) where the "complete" copy consists of a reproduction of the work on two-dimensional materials such as paper or fabrics; (4) published works consisting of multiple parts that are packaged and published in a box or similar container with flat sides and with dimensions of no more than 12 × 24 × 6 inches, and that include among the copyrightable elements on the box or other container, three or more three-dimensional physically separable parts; and (5) works reproduced on three-dimensional containers or holders such as boxes, cases, and cartons, where the container or holder can be readily opened out, unfolded, slit at the corners, or in some other way made adaptable for flat storage, and the copy, when flattened, does not exceed 96 inches in any dimension. An actual copy of these types of works must be deposited and not "identifying material."

Sound tracks in the nature of unpublished works, or published as an integral part of a motion picture. "Identifying material" may be submitted in lieu of an actual copy or actual copies of the motion picture.

Works for which special relief has been granted by the U.S. Copyright Office in reference to the number or completeness of copies to be deposited, and/or allowing the deposit of "identifying material" in lieu of actual copies.

Identifying Material

Copies of particular works are often bulky, fragile, very valuable, limited in number, or for other reasons unsuitable for deposit with the U.S. Copyright Office. Accordingly, for certain kinds of works the U.S. Copyright Office Regulations either permit or require the deposit of "identifying material" rather than actual copies of such works. For example, where a copy exceeds 96 inches in any dimension, identifying material must be submitted.

The U.S. Copyright Office Regulations provide that identifying material must meet the following specifications:

Form. It may consist of photographic prints, transparencies, photostats, drawings, or similar two-dimensional reproductions or renderings of the work in a form visually perceptible without the aid of a machine or device.

Color. The actual colors employed in pictorial or graphic works must be reproduced. In all other cases black and white reproduction is acceptable as is reproduction of the actual colors.

Completeness. As many pieces as are necessary to show clearly the entire copyrightable content of the work for which deposit is being made.

Number of Sets. Only one set other than when being submitted for holograms which will be two sets if the hologram is a published work.

Size. All pieces (except separate drawings or similar reproductions of copyright notices) must be of uniform size. Photographic transparencies must be at least 35 mm in size and, if such transparencies are 3 × 3 inches or less, must be fixed in cardboard, plastic, or similar mounts to facilitate identification, handling, and storage. Transparencies larger than 3 × 3 inches should be mounted in a way that facilitates their handling and preservation. All types of identifying material other than photographic transparencies must be not less than 3 × 3 inches and not more than 9 × 12 inches, but preferably 8 × 10 inches. Except in the case of transparencies, the image of the work must be either lifesize or larger, or if less than lifesize it must be large enough to show clearly the entire copyrightable content of the work.

Title and Notation of Dimensions. At least one piece of identifying material must indicate the title of the work and an exact measurement of one or more dimensions. This notation must be on the front of the piece.

Copyright Notice. In the case of published works, the notice and its position on the work must be clearly shown on at least one piece of identifying material. Where necessary because of the size or position of the notice, a separate drawing or similar reproduction must be submitted. The reproduction must be no smaller than 3 × 3 inches and not larger than 9 × 12 inches. It must show the exact appearance and content of the notice, and its specific location on the work.

Sound Tracks. For separate registration of an unpublished work that is embodied, or of a published work that is published only as embodied in a sound track that is an integral part of a motion picture, the identifying material shall consist of:

1. A transcription of the entire work or a reproduction of the entire work on a phonorecord

2. Photographs or other reproductions from the motion picture showing the title of the motion picture, the sound track credits, and the copyright notice for the sound track, if any

3. The requirements as to completeness, size, title and notation of dimensions, and copyright notice for identifying material are not applicable.

Motion Pictures. For unpublished motion pictures the identifying material shall consist of:

1. An audiocassette or other phonorecord reproducing the entire sound track or other sound portion of the motion picture, and a description of the motion picture; or

2. A set consisting of one frame enlargement or similar visual reproduction from each 10-minute segment of the motion picture, and a description of the motion picture.

In either case the "description" may be a continuity, a pressbook, or a synopsis but in all cases it must include:

(a.) The title or continuing title of the work, and the episode title, if any

(b.) The nature and general content of the program

(c.) The date when the work was first embodied in a physical object and whether or not this occurred simultaneous with the first transmission of the work

(d.) The date of first transmission, if any

(e.) The running time

(f.) The credits appearing on the work, if any

3. The requirements as to completeness, size, title and notation of dimensions, and copyright notice for identifying material are not applicable.

RETURN AND DISPOSITION OF COPIES DEPOSITED

Copies of works deposited with the U.S. Copyright Office in accordance with the mandatory deposit requirement (see Chapter 14) and those deposited for purposes of registering a work become the property of the U.S. government. Copies of works for which registration has been refused also become the property of the government. Accordingly, once copies are deposited with the U.S. Copyright Office, they are not subject to return, unless all three elements of the filing package for an unpublished work are not received by the U.S. Copyright Office at the same time.

Upon becoming the owner of this property the government may retain or dispose of it as it determines appropriate, subject to any limitations on that right. With regard to published works, some of this property becomes part of the collections of the Library of Congress or is exchanged or transferred to any other library. And some is retained under the control of the U.S. Copyright Office for a specified period of time and then destroyed or otherwise disposed.

In the case of unpublished works the Library is entitled to select whichever copies it desires for its collections or for transfer to the National Archives of the United States or to a federal record center. Copies not selected by the Library, or identifying portions or reproductions of them, must be retained under the control of the U.S. Copyright Office for the longest period considered practicable and desirable by the U.S. Copyright Office and the Library. After that period, it is within their joint discretion to order the destruction or other disposition of such copies. However, no copy of an unpublished work should be knowingly or intentionally destroyed or disposed of during the applicable term of its protection unless a facsimile reproduction of the entire deposit has been made a part of the U.S. Copyright Office records.

As might be imagined, there are limitations on the storage space available for the retention of deposited copies of works. Accordingly, unless the U.S. Copyright Office decides to retain a copy of a published work for the full term of applicable copyright protection, it is possible it will be destroyed or disposed of either five or 10 years after the date of deposit. For storage purposes, full-term retention presently means a period of 75 years from the date of publication of a work.

If a copyright owner desires to have a copy of a published work retained for the full retention period and is willing to assume the cost of storage, he can request full-term retention. The procedure entails making a written request for retention to:

Chief
Records Management Division
U.S. Copyright Office
Washington, DC 20559

REPRODUCTIONS OF DEPOSITED COPIES AND PHONORECORDS CAN BE OBTAINED

The U.S. Copyright Office Regulations provide that requests for certified or uncertified reproductions of the copies, phonorecords, or identifying material deposited in connection with a work may be obtained if (1) the deposit material is under the control of the U.S. Copyright Office or the Library of Congress; (2) the person making the request can meet any one of three conditions to be noted; and (3) the applicable fee is paid.

To be entitled to receive a reproduction, any one of the following requirements must be satisfied:

1. Written authorization is received from the copyright claimant of record or his or her designated agent, or from the owner of any of the exclusive rights in the work as long as this ownership can be demonstrated by written documentation of the transfer of ownership.

2. A written request is received from an attorney on behalf of either the plaintiff or defendant in connection with litigation, actual or prospective, involving the copyrighted work. The following information must be included in such a request: (a) the names of all the parties involved and the nature of the controversy; (b) the name of the court in which the litigation is pending, or, in the case of a prospective proceeding, a full statement of the facts of the controversy in which the copyrighted work is involved; and (c) satisfactory assurance that the requested reproduction will be used only in connection with the specified litigation.

3. A court order for a reproduction of a deposited article, facsimile, or identifying portion of a work which is the subject of litigation in its jurisdiction. The order must be issued by a court having jurisdiction of a case in which the copy is to be submitted as evidence.

In responding to a proper request, the U.S. Copyright Office will supply a certified or uncertified reproduction of the actual deposit material, or a facsimile the U.S. Copyright Office has made if the deposited material has been disposed of or transferred. When a request is for reproduction of a phonorecord, such as an audiotape in which either a sound recording or underlying musical, dramatic, or literary work is embodied, a proximate reproduction will be provided. The form of reproduction for copies of other works will be photocopies of them where appropriate.

Information regarding the procedure to follow and the form a request should take may be obtained from:

Certification and Documents Section, LM-458
U.S. Copyright Office
Library of Congress
Washington, DC 20559

FILING FEES FOR REGISTRATION

As of July 1, 1986, a fee of $10.00 must be paid for each application for registration at the time it is filed with the U.S. Copyright Office.

If registration is not granted there is no refund of the fee since it is treated as a filing fee and not a registration fee. In the event it is not submitted at the same time the deposit material and the appropriate application form are submitted to the Copyright Office, that material will be returned. If the deposit material is a copy of a published work, that material will be transferred to the Library of Congress for its collections.

In the event there is a need for special handling of an application with objective of expediting registration of a work, as of July 1, 1986 a special handling fee of $120.00 is applicable. This amount is in addition to the $10.00 filing fee.

SPECIAL HANDLING TO EXPEDITE REGISTRATION

Ordinarily, a certificate of registration of a work will be issued within a period of 90 days or so from the date an application for registration is filed. This is not a significantly long period but, in some cases, it is desirable or necessary to shorten this time because of pending litigation, customs matters, contract deadlines, or for other reasons. They are representative of situations where the U.S. Copyright Office is most likely to act sooner on an application.

If the U.S. Copyright Office agrees that the request should be granted, it will expedite the registration process upon payment of the appropriate fees by special handling of the application so that a work may be registered within a few days after it is filed, or within a week or so after that date. It is within the discretion of the U.S. Copyright Office to grant such a request.

The request must include all of the reasons for special handling and contain a signed statement that the reasons are correct. If a request is made for reasons based on pending or prospective litigation the request must also include all of the details of the litigation.

EXAMINATION OF THE APPLICATION

Upon receipt of the application form, copies or phonorecords of a work (or identifying material), and the filing fee the examination process begins. Receipt of the application is not acknowledged by the U.S. Copyright Office.

If an applicant wishes to confirm receipt of these items, he or she may personally deliver them to the U.S. Copyright Office and obtain a receipt. Or they can be sent by registered or certified mail with a request for a return receipt. Or a self-addressed postpaid postcard can be enclosed with them along with a request to the Register of Copyrights that the postcard be date-stamped and returned on receipt of the materials. The back of the postcard may read as follows:

Receipt is hereby acknowledged for an Application Form ____ seeking registration of:
filed by:

The class of the form should be inserted as well as the applicant's name and a very brief description of the work sought to be registered.

After receipt of the application form and copies or other deposit material by the U.S. Copyright Office, an examination is made by that agency. The examination is made only to determine if the copies, phonorecords, or other deposit material constitute copyrightable material and to determine if all legal and formal requirements of the 1976 Act have been satisfied. An examination of deposit material to determine whether it constitutes copyrightable material consists of a review to see whether it represents enough original authorship to support a claim of rights.

Many people are under the impression that a work will not be registered by the U.S. Copyright Office if there is an existing registration for a work which is the same as or substantially similar to the work sought to be registered. This is not the case. It is possible for two separate works to be registered, if they have been independently created by different individuals, even though they are identical or closely resemble each other.

The examination process does not ordinarily include a comparison of a work sought to be registered with any previously deposited material or application forms submitted by others which refer to different works. Consequently, a decision by the U.S. Copyright Office to register a work is not based on whether a similar work has been registered by another party. However, it would be affected if there is already a basic registration for the same version of the work by a prior claimant or right holder.

If nothing in the information given in the application form appears to be inconsistent with the deposit material and that information is not otherwise questionable, the U.S. Copyright Office will issue a registration certificate. Information and material outside of that submitted for registration purposes ordinarily are not considered.

In the event the U.S. Copyright Office has a need for additional information regarding the work or for the deposit material, or otherwise requires a response from the applicant, the applicant will be contacted. Generally, a reasonable time will be allowed for submission of a response. If one is not made, the file will be closed and copies of published works will be made available to the Library of Congress while copies of unpublished works will be returned. The filing fee will not be refunded.

If the U.S. Copyright Office determines that the deposit material does not constitute copyrightable subject matter or that the claim of ownership is invalid for any other reason, registration of the work will be refused. In the event this occurs, a written notice of refusal will be mailed including the reasons for such action.

CERTIFICATE OF REGISTRATION

The registration process is completed by the issuance of a certificate of registration. The certificate is a photocopy of the application form submitted with the registration number, the effective date, and the seal of the U.S. Copyright Office in the upper left corner.

Registration numbers begin with the two letters of the registration class within which a work falls (i.e., PA, SR, TX, or VA), followed by a series of numbers — usually six of them. If the work is registered as an unpublished work, the small letter "u" will immediately follow the two class letters.

The effective date of registration is the day on which the application form, deposit material, and filing fee were received by the U.S. Copyright Office. This date can be relied upon regardless of the fact that a certificate of registration may not be issued for two or three months.

CHAPTER SUMMARY

- Registration of a copyright claim for a work is done by filing an application for registration with the U.S. Copyright Office using a prescribed form furnished by that agency.

- There are a number of versions of the application form; each version is designed for use with respect to registering a particular kind or category of work.

- The application should be accompanied by a filing fee and copies or phonorecords of the work sought to be registered.

- The application is examined by the U.S. Copyright Office only for purposes of determining if the requirements of the 1976 Act have been satisfied without regard to whether the work sought to be registered is the same as a work created and previously registered by another person.

- Registration is usually effective on the date a complete application is received by the U.S. Copyright Office although the certificate of registration is not issued for approximately one to two months after that date.

14

Depositing Copies with the Library of Congress

The 1976 Act contains a requirement that makes it mandatory to deposit copies or phonorecords of a work with the U.S. Copyright Office if they have been publicly distributed in the United States with a copyright notice. They must be deposited within a specific time period after the date of first publication.

Unpublished works are not subject to this requirement, except for unpublished transmission programs that have been transmitted to the public in the United States. The deposit requirement applicable to them is discussed below.

The mandatory deposit requirement is independent of but related to the copyright registration deposit requirement. The mandatory deposit requirement applies only to copies or phonorecords of published works. The registration deposit requirement applies to published as well as unpublished works. In addition to this distinction, the purposes for which the deposit is made are different.

Copies or phonorecords provided to the U.S. Copyright Office under the mandatory deposit requirement are primarily for the use and disposition of the Library of Congress, whose records are separate and apart from those of the U.S. Copyright Office. However, they can also be used in connection with registering a work to satisfy the registration deposit requirement if a completed application for registration and filing fee accompany them.

Copies or phonorecords given to the Library of Congress under the mandatory deposit requirement may be added to its collections, but there is no obligation on its part to use them for this purpose. The authority of Congress to use deposited copies in this manner existed under the 1909 Act, as well as earlier federal copyright laws. This authority was granted as a benefit, to give Congress the opportunity to build the collections of its library conveniently and economically.

Copies or phonorecords of a work that bears a copyright notice but is first published outside the United States are not subject to this requirement. However, at the time such a work is published in the United States, through the distribution of imported copies or phonorecords or the distribution of those produced here, the mandatory deposit requirement becomes applicable.

Certain categories of copies and phonorecords are exempt from this deposit requirement regardless of where the work embodied in them was first published.

NUMBER OF COPIES TO BE DEPOSITED AND BY WHOM

If the mandatory deposit requirement is applicable to a particular work, satisfying it entails providing the following deposit material to the U.S. Copyright Office within three months after the date of first publication:

1. Two complete copies of the best edition; or
2. If the work is a sound recording, two complete phonorecords of the best edition, together with any printed or other visually perceptible material published with such phonorecords

If the required deposit is not timely made, the U.S. Copyright Office may impose sanctions against the owner of all rights to a work or of the exclusive right of publication. But this cannot occur until after a prescribed series of acts have been taken.

In no event will copyright protection be forfeited due to failure to make a required deposit. Further, the 1976 Act expressly provides that compliance with this requirement is not a condition of protection.

To be in a position to impose sanctions, which are in the nature of monetary penalties, the U.S. Copyright Office must make a written demand for deposit to the owner of all rights in a work or the owner of the exclusive right of publication for it. If the deposit is not thereafter made within three months from the date the demand is received (not the date the notice is mailed), the person or persons upon whom the demand was made are liable:

1. To a fine of not more than $250 for each work
2. To pay into a specially designated fund in the Library of Congress the total retail price of the copies or phonorecords demanded, or, if no retail price has been fixed, the reasonable cost to the Library of Congress of acquiring them
3. To pay a fine of $2,500, in addition to any fine or liability imposed under the above two paragraphs, if the owner willfully or repeatedly fails or refuses to comply with the demand for deposit

DEPOSITED COPIES MAY BE USED FOR REGISTRATION

A person who deposits copies or phonorecords of a work to meet the mandatory deposit requirement will not obtain a registration for the work by doing that and nothing more. To obtain a registration, the copies or phonorecords should be accompanied by a completed application and the prescribed filing fee. If this is done, a single deposit will satisfy both the mandatory deposit and registration deposit requirement.

If copies or phonorecords are deposited without the application and fee, and later a registration of the work is desired, an additional deposit for registration will be required.

NO FORM TO FILE OR FEE TO PAY

There is no prescribed form that must be used in connection with depositing copies or phonorecords for purposes of complying with the mandatory deposit requirement. Furthermore, no fee must be paid. However, if there is a desire to obtain a certificate of receipt for copies deposited, a $2.00 fee is charged by the U.S. Copyright Office. This certificate is obtained by making a written request for it accompanied by the fee.

If there is no request for a certificate of receipt the person making the deposit will not receive confirmation that the copies or phonorecords have been received. If the deposit is made by certified or registered mail with a return receipt request, the receipt from the U.S. Postal Service will serve as unofficial confirmation that the U.S. Copyright Office has received the copies or phonorecords.

NATURE OF COPIES REQUIRED TO BE DEPOSITED

As with copies deposited for purposes of registering a work, not just any copy can be submitted under the mandatory deposit requirement. Copies must meet certain quality standards set by the Library of Congress.

The "best edition" standard applies here as it does with respect to copies deposited in connection with registering a work. The criteria used in determining what constitutes the "best edition" are referred to in Chapter 13.

"Complete" copies must also be deposited as is required with regard to registering a work. A complete copy of a musical composition published in copies only, or in both copies and phonorecords, consists of a full score if the only publication of copies in the United States took place by the rental, lease, or lending of a full score and parts. If publication took place by the rental, lease, or lending of a conductor's score and parts, a conductor's score is a complete copy.

In the case of published works that are not exempt from the mandatory deposit requirement, two copies must be deposited, except for those works noted in the following list in which case only one copy or identifying material can be submitted:

Three-dimensional cartographic representations of area, such as globes and relief models.

Motion pictures accompanied by a separate description of their contents, such as a continuity, pressbook, or synopsis. The Library of Congress may, at its sole discretion, enter into an agreement permitting the return of copies of motion pictures under certain conditions and establishing certain rights and obligations of the Library with respect to such copies.

Holograms accompanied by precise instructions for displaying the image fixed in the hologram, and photographs or other "identifying material" showing the displayed image.

Pictorial and graphic works, where an individual is the creator and first copyright owner and (1) fewer than five copies of the work have been published; or (2) the work has been published and sold or offered for sale in a limited edition consisting of no more than 300 numbered copies. "Identifying material" may be deposited in lieu of one actual copy.

Musical compositions published in copies only, or in copies and phonorecords, if the only publication of copies took place by rental, lease, or lending.

Published multimedia kits that are prepared for use in systematic instructional activities and that include literary works, audiovisual works, sound recordings, or any combination of such works.

Works for which special relief has been granted by the U.S. Copyright Office in reference to the number or completeness of copies to be deposited, and/or allowing the deposit of "identifying material" in lieu of actual copies.

EXEMPT CATEGORIES OF MATERIAL

The Library of Congress has elected to exclude certain categories of materials from the mandatory deposit requirement because it neither needs or wants them. At this time the U.S. Copyright Office Regulations indicate that the following categories of materials are exempt from deposit:

Diagrams and models illustrating scientific or technical works or formulating scientific or technical information in linear or three-dimensional form, such as an architectural or engineering blueprint, plan, or design, a mechanical drawing, or an anatomical model.

Greeting cards, picture postcards, and stationery.

Lectures, sermons, speeches, and addresses when published individually and not as a collection of the works of one or more authors.

Literary, dramatic, and musical works published only as embodied in phonorecords. This category does not exempt the owner of copyright or of the exclusive right of publication, in a sound recording resulting from the fixation of such works in a phonorecord, from the applicable deposit requirements for the sound recording.

Literary works, including computer programs and automated data bases, published in the United States only in the form of machine-readable copies (such as magnetic tape or disks, punched cards, or the like) from which the work cannot ordinarily be visually perceived except with the aid of a machine or device. Works published in a form requiring the use of a machine or device for purposes of optical enlargement (such as film, filmstrips, slide films, and works published in any variety of microform), and works published in visually perceivable form but used in connection with optical scanning devices, are not within this category and are subject to the applicable deposit requirements.

Three-dimensional sculptural works, and any works published only as reproduced in or on jewelry, dolls, toys, games, plaques, floor coverings, wallpaper and similar commercial wall coverings, textile and other fabrics, packaging material, or any useful article. Globes, relief models, and similar cartographic representations of area are not within this category and are subject to the applicable deposit requirement.

Prints, labels, and other advertising matter published in connection with the rental, lease, lending, licensing, or sale of articles of merchandise, works of authorship, or services.

Tests, and answer material for tests, when published separately from other literary works.

Works first published as individual contributions to collective works. This category does not exempt the owner of copyright or of the exclusive right of publication, in the collective work as a whole, from the applicable deposit requirements for the collective work.

Works first published outside the United States and later published in the United States without change in copyrightable content, if: (1) registration for the work was made before publication in the United States; or (2) registration of the work was made after publication in the United States but before a demand for deposit is made by the U.S. Copyright Office.

Works published only as embodied in a sound track that is an integral part of a motion picture. This category does not exempt the owner of copyright or of the exclusive right of publication, in the motion picture, from the applicable deposit requirements for the motion picture.

Motion pictures that consist of television transmission programs and that have been published, if at all, only by reason of a license or other grant to a nonprofit institution of the right to make a fixation of such programs directly from a transmission to the public, with or without the right to make further uses of such fixations.

UNPUBLISHED TRANSMISSION PROGRAMS

As a general rule, the mandatory deposit requirement applies only to published works. An exception applies to unpublished transmission programs. This type of program is subject to the deposit requirement, but, in lieu of a copyright owner or owner of the exclusive reproduction right, the 1976 Act permits the Library of Congress to make its own copy by taping an off-the-air transmission to the public.

The U.S. Copyright Office has adopted a regulation that prescribes rules pertaining to the acquisition of copies of such programs by the Library of Congress.

In addition to making a copy of a transmission program by noncommercial educational broadcast stations, the Library of Congress can make a copy of selected programming transmitted by commercial broadcast stations, both network and independent. But it must notify the transmitting organization or its agent that such activity is taking place.

The Register of Copyrights may make a written demand upon the owner of the right of transmission in the United States, for the deposit of a copy or phonorecord of a specific transmission program for the benefit of the Library of Congress. The demand must contain an explanation of the optional forms of compliance, including a transfer of ownership of a copy to the Library, lending a copy to the Library for reproduction, or selling a copy to the Library.

CHAPTER SUMMARY

- The mandatory deposit requirement provides for the submission of copies or phonorecords of certain types of published works to the U.S. Copyright Office for the use and disposition of the Library of Congress.

- This requirement does not apply to unpublished works, except unpublished transmission programs that have been transmitted to the public in the United States.

- Copies of works that are deposited must meet certain quality standards and must be deposited within three months after the date of first publication of the work in the United States.

- Failure to make a required deposit may result in liability in the nature of a monetary fine; deposit is not a condition of copyright protection.

- Registration of a work satisfies the mandatory deposit requirement.

15

Transferring Copyright Ownership

Ownership of all or some of the exclusive rights in a work can be transferred, just as ownership of other types of property can be transferred. However, where ownership of a work protected under copyright law is concerned, transfer of rights does not automatically occur when a copy or phonorecord of the work (e.g., a book, a painting, or a record) is sold or given away. Furthermore, a transfer of rights does not automatically occur when payment is made for the services of someone who creates a work as an independent contractor outside of a work-made-for-hire relationship (e.g., a photographer, a graphic artist, or a musician) or when payment is made for the materials used to create a work.

An exchange of copies or phonorecords of a work for money or other consideration, or simply giving away copies or phonorecords, is not enough to transfer ownership of all the exclusive rights in it, or any one or more of them.

As a general rule, a person who owns rights must sign a document evidencing an intent to transfer them. Until this takes place, ownership is not transferred. Exceptions to the general rule are transfers of rights by operation of the law, transfers that occur upon the death of a copyright owner, and involuntary transfers through bankruptcy proceedings. A transfer of rights under those circumstances can occur in the absence of a document signed by a copyright owner and providing for their transfer. However, the rights transferred in these situations do not necessarily go to a person or persons who acquire ownership of copies or phonorecords of the work.

OWNERSHIP OF RIGHTS DISTINCT FROM OWNERSHIP OF A COPY

When the owner of rights in a work sells or gives away a copy or phonorecord of it, the recipient becomes the new owner of that particular copy or phonorecord. And that owner, as well as others who follow, can also resell the copy or phonorecord or give it away free of any obligation to account to or obtain permission from the previous owner.

However, a person who acquires ownership of a copy or phonorecord of a work does not obtain all or any of the exclusive rights in it. In accordance with the provisions of the 1976 Act, ownership of the exclusive rights in a work, or of any one or more of them, is distinct from ownership of any material object in which the work is embodied.

For example, the transfer of ownership of a phonograph record album, which is a phonorecord embodying a sound recording and a copy of a musical composition, does not give the person acquiring it the right to reproduce the sound recording or musical composition. However, if ownership of this right is also expressly transferred in writing, the purchaser of the album can reproduce it without limitation.

If copyright ownership is not transferred, any exercise of an exclusive right by a person other than the copyright owner requires permission from that owner. Permission can be obtained in a variety of ways as discussed in later chapters. It can be obtained directly from the copyright owner on a negotiated basis, or possibly under a compulsory license.

Without permission, a person who acquires a phonograph record album has no right to play the musical composition embodied in it in public, or to make a copy of that musical composition on a cassette tape. Similarly, a person who purchases a videocassette embodying a motion picture needs permission from the copyright owner to do so. The purchaser of an oil painting embodying a work of fine art does not have permission to reproduce it in prints although he or she would have a right to publicly display it.

However, each one of these individuals does have the right to resell the particular copy as does every subsequent lawful owner of it. As discussed in Chapter 6, the 1976 Act expressly provides that the owner of a lawfully made copy has a right to publicly display it and the owner of a lawfully made copy or phonorecord has a right to publicly distribute it.

TRANSFER OF RIGHTS DISTINCT FROM TRANSFER OF COPIES OR PHONORECORDS

It is important to note that the transfer of ownership of rights in a work and the transfer of ownership to copies or phonorecords of a work are separate and independent transactions. However, they may occur at the same time with respect to a particular work and copies or phonorecords embodying it.

Keeping this in mind, a transfer of the exclusive rights in a work, or any one of them, does not by itself constitute a transfer of ownership of any material object in which the work is embodied. The ownership of particular copies or phonorecords of a work can be transferred to one person and the ownership of rights in the work embodied in them transferred to another person.

For example, a fine artist who transfers all rights in a work of art (e.g., an oil painting) to a printmaker, or the exclusive right to reproduce the work of art (e.g., to produce prints of it) does not by that transfer alone also pass ownership of the original painting itself. The artist may sell the original to someone else.

EACH RIGHT SEPARATELY TRANSFERABLE

All Rights Transfers Originate from Initial Owner

As discussed in Chapter 6, the five exclusive rights associated with a work constitute an integral unit or bundle of rights at the time a work is created although they are independent of each other and capable of being divided. Initially, this unit or bundle is owned as a whole by the creator of the work or, in the case of a work-made-for-hire relationship, they are initially owned by the creator's employer or the person who commissioned creation of the work.

If an initial owner of rights is so inclined, the bundle of rights can be divided and ownership of each one transferred by that person individually or together with one or more other rights. They can be subdivided in an infinite number of ways with ownership of any one or more subdivisions transferred as separate units or in groups. Similarly, these rights can be licensed as separate and independent rights or in groups of two or more. Subdivisions of these rights can be likewise licensed. The subject of voluntary licensing rights is discussed in Chapter 18.

Each subsequent owner of a right can transfer the ownership of it and license it the same as the initial owner. However, a licensee may not be able to grant a sublicense of it without permission from the licensor.

Transfer of Rights by Co-owners

As noted in Chapter 5, in the case of a joint work the 1976 Act provides that the creators of it are co-owners of the exclusive rights in it. Consequently, there is no division of those rights under the 1976 Act. Therefore, one creator will not initially own all rights to the exclusion of everyone else who participated in the creation of a work, or a higher percentage of ownership, even though he or she may have played a more substantial role in the creative process. When two or more persons create a work, each person who contributes to the creation of it will own the exclusive rights in common with the other contributors. The percentage of each creator's ownership interest will be in direct proportion to the number of persons involved in creating the work. However, this principle is applicable only in cases where a work is prepared by two or more persons with the intention that their contributions be merged into inseparable or interdependent parts of a unitary whole.

If one co-owner desires to transfer his or her ownership interest in the rights to a third party, this can be done and without the consent of the other co-owners. However, one co-owner cannot transfer the ownership interest of any other co-owner without that co-owner's consent. Furthermore, a co-owner can divide and subdivide his or her ownership interest and transfer divisions of it to third parties.

Each transferee of a co-owner's ownership interest takes the place of the co-owner to the extent of the ownership interest acquired. Accordingly, each transferee then becomes a co-owner with others who own the rights in common.

The ability and extent to which co-owners of rights can grant licenses are discussed in Chapter 18.

Examples of Rights Transfers

It is possible for the owner of a literary work, in the form of a novel, to transfer to another party the exclusive right to prepare a derivative work, such as a screenplay, based upon it. Similarly, the author can transfer to a publisher the exclusive right to reproduce the novel in book form retaining the right to perform it and all other rights publicly.

The owner of a musical work can transfer the exclusive right to perform that work publicly just as the owner of a motion picture can transfer the exclusive right to sell copies of the motion picture. Because each right can be separately owned there are many other variations of such transactions.

Some examples of how these rights can be subdivided are:

1. The owner of a literary work may transfer the exclusive right to reproduce it in hardcover to one publisher and in softcover to another, while retaining the exclusive right to reproduce it in magazines.

2. The owner of a motion picture may transfer the exclusive right to reproduce it in videocassette format to one company and in videodisk format to another. Also, at the same time, the owner of the motion picture may transfer the exclusive right to perform it publicly in a defined geographic area, such as Denver, Colorado, to one exhibitor and in a separate geographic area, such as Vail, Colorado, to another.

It is also possible to be more specific with regard to the scope of a right transferred. For example, ownership of it can be limited to a specific day or days of the week, or a given time during the day, or particular months, and on and on. Thus, it is possible to transfer ownership of the exclusive right to reproduce a literary work in the form of magazines only on Tuesdays in the city of Boulder, Colorado, during the time 10:00 A.M. to 12:00 P.M.

As noted earlier, licenses of these rights can be granted, and when they are, the grant can be along the same lines as those mentioned above. That is, one specific right can be exclusively or nonexclusively licensed to a particular person and/or that right may be subdivided and each of the subdivisions separately licensed.

An exclusive licensee assumes the position of the owner with respect to the right licensed, but for a limited time. More particularly, the exclusive licensee is in this position for the term of the license whether it be for one year, five years, or any other period. The right of a licensee is subject to being terminated as discussed in Chapter 18. This is contrary to acquiring ownership of a right ordinarily treated as an absolute transfer and not terminable.

Generally, the extent to which each of the exclusive rights in a work may be subdivided is dependent on the imagination and creativeness of the owner. Each right may be exercised in a multitude of ways.

WHAT CONSTITUTES A TRANSFER OF OWNERSHIP

Types of Ownership Transfers

The 1976 Act defines "transfer of copyright ownership" as:

> An assignment, mortgage, exclusive license, or any other conveyance, alienation, or hypothecation of a copyright or of any of the exclusive rights comprised in a copyright, whether or not it is limited in time or place of effect, but not including a nonexclusive license.

On the basis of this definition, anyone to whom all or some of the rights in a work are:

1. Transferred outright
2. Transferred as security for the payment of a debt
3. Pledged as security for a debt
4. Exclusively licensed

effectively becomes the owner of the rights transferred, pledged, or exclusively licensed. Thus, a mortgagee, a pledgee, and an exclusive licensee are deemed to be owners of rights on the same footing as persons who acquire ownership of rights through an absolute transfer. Reference to a "transfer" of ownership throughout this book, therefore, includes mortgages, pledges, and exclusive licenses.

Transfer of Ownership Upon Death

If an individual is the owner of rights in a work at the time of death, a bequest of those rights by will constitutes a transfer of ownership of them as personal property. When an individual dies without a will (intestate) and owns rights in a work at the time of death, a transfer of ownership occurs when those rights are distributed under laws of intestate succession.

Intestate succession may be loosely defined to be the distribution of an individual's property at death in accordance with a prescribed order of priority enumerated by applicable state statute. Usually property goes first to surviving members of the immediate family and then to other relatives.

Transfer of Ownership by Operation of Law

A transfer of ownership can also occur by operation of the law. That is, a court can order the transfer of rights in an appropriate judicial proceeding involving the owner of rights, if that person refuses to transfer them voluntarily.

For example, in the event an owner becomes bankrupt a bankruptcy court may order the transfer of all assets of the debtor, including all rights possessed in a work since they are treated as personal property. Similarly, the foreclosure of a mortgaged right can result in the transfer of that right by order of a court, and so can a court-ordered sale of a judgment debtor's property which includes rights in a work.

Involuntary Transfer of Ownership

A provision in the 1976 Act prohibits the involuntary transfer of rights in a work mandated by any governmental body or other official or organization purporting to seize, expropriate, transfer, or exercise rights of ownership with respect to all or any of those rights. This prohibition is applicable only if the owner of a right that is the subject of an involuntary transfer is the individual who created the work and only if the right has not been previously voluntarily transferred by that individual.

A transfer of rights which occurs as the result of a bankruptcy proceeding or mortgage foreclosure is an exception to the general rule. In such actions, Congress has expressed the view that an owner of rights who becomes involved in such a proceeding or who has pledged the rights has voluntarily done so and any resulting transfer is voluntary.

WHAT MUST BE DONE TO TRANSFER RIGHTS VALIDLY

No Transfer by Selling or Giving Away Copies

Selling or giving away a copy of a work does not transfer ownership of rights in it. Similarly, paying for the services and materials provided by a nonemployee and required to create a work will not effect an ownership transfer of it.

Transfer or License Must Be in Writing

A transfer of ownership of rights in a work, which by definition includes a mortgage, pledge, or exclusive license, must be in writing. The written instrument reflecting the transfer must be signed by the owner or licensor of the rights transferred, mortgaged, pledged, or exclusively licensed, or by that person's authorized agent. If this does not occur, the transfer is not valid and may be successfully challenged by another party depending on the circumstances surrounding the transfer.

There is one exception to this requirement. When there is a transfer by operation of law, such as by a court order in a judicial proceeding, the absence of a written instrument signed by the owner, licensor, or authorized agent will not affect the validity of the transfer.

In all other cases a written instrument is required but no special form is mandated although there are preferred formats. A representative assignment document is found in Appendix A. It may be used as a general assignment form by completing the blank spaces throughout with the appropriate information and using the schedule to clearly identify the work or right being transferred.

Writing Must Clearly Evidence Intent to Transfer

Whatever the format, it is critical that the written instrument used to transfer rights unquestionably manifest an intention to do so, whether the transfer is by mortgage, pledge, exclusive license, or otherwise. This can be accomplished by using such wording as:

A transfer of all right title, and interest in and to . . . . . . including the copyright therefor

A transfer of all rights to . . . . . .

A transfer of each and every right in and to . . . . . .

A transfer of copyright in . . . . . .

An exclusive license to . . . . . .

Mortage the . . . . . . right(s) for . . . . . .

Pledge the . . . . . . right(s) to secure the . . . . . .

Person Transferring Must Sign

The kind of language noted may be effective by appearing on the back of a check in the form of a restrictive endorsement. Or it may appear on the front of a check and accomplish the same results as long as the person transferring, mortgaging, pledging, or exclusively licensing rights signs it.

In addition, this kind of language may appear in written agreements to perform services and/or to provide materials, and on purchase order forms, receipts, invoices, or billing statements. It can also appear in a will. As long as the person who is transferring rights signs such a document it will accomplish the transfer or license.

If an instrument with such language on or in it is not signed by the owner or licensor of rights, there will be no valid transfer. The signature of that person, or his or her authorized representative, is critical. A signature of only one party to a transaction, namely that of the person who desires to acquire rights, or who desires to acquire an exclusive license for them, is not sufficient and will not accomplish the transfer or license.

Notarization Is not Required

It is not necessary to have the document transferring rights notarized. The transfer, mortgage, pledge, or exclusive license is effective without the notarization of signatures. However, there is a benefit to be gained if the document is signed in the presence of a notary public and it contains an acknowledgment paragraph. In some cases, a document whose signatures are acknowledged may have more significance from an evidentiary standpoint. An example of the kind of language that may be appropriate for such a paragraph is set forth below. It should be located after the signature line for the person transferring or exclusively licensing rights in a work:

State of . . . . . .
County of . . . . . .

Before me, a Notary Public in and for said county, personally appeared the above named . . . . . . who acknowledged that he/she did sign the foregoing instrument and that the same is his/her free act and deed.

In Testimony Whereof, I have hereunto affixed my name and official seal at . . . . . . , ... , this . . . . . . day of . . . . . ., 19_____.

_____
Notary Public

My Commission expires: _____

This format may be used for a document executed in the United States and elsewhere. However, if a document is executed outside of the United States, it can be acknowledged under the official seal of any diplomatic or consular officer of the United States or of a person who is authorized to administer oaths whose authority in this regard is proved by a certificate of a diplomatic or consular officer of the United States.

If an acknowledgment is used, the document reflecting a transfer or exclusive license will be accepted by a court of law and by the Copyright Office as prima facie evidence of the execution of the document. If the document attains this evidentiary status there is a rebuttable presumption that all of the facts set forth in it are true.

RIGHTS ACQUIRED BY TRANSFEREES AND LICENSEES

Transferee Entitled to All Protection and Remedies

A transferee of a specific right or of all rights in a work (including a mortgagee, pledgee, or exclusive licensee) assumes the position of the immediately previous owner (e.g., the previous mortgagor, pledgor, or licensor). The 1976 Act expressly provides that the owner of any particular exclusive right is entitled, to the extent of that right, to all of the protection and remedies accorded to the copyright owner. Under the Act a copyright owner is a person who owns *all* of the exclusive rights.

If a transferee acquires all of the rights in a work, the authority to exercise and protect them ordinarily will not be limited. However, if a transferee acquires less than all of the rights in a work, that person is only entitled to exercise the right(s) acquired as well as to protect and obtain the remedies available under the Act and applicable to them. Accordingly, a transferee of a particular right would not be entitled to exercise any rights in the work that are not owned by the transferee, or to exercise the transferee's right to the extent that it infringes a right in the same work owned by someone else.

For example, the owner of the exclusive right to reproduce a literary work is not entitled to any protection or remedies for the public performance of it by someone else even though the public performance of it is not authorized. Nor is the owner of the reproduction right entitled to publicly perform the work.

Right To Institute Infringement Actions

The right to protect a work under the 1976 Act gives an exclusive licensee and all other owners of rights in a work the authority to institute copyright infringement actions in their own names with respect to the particular right exclusively licensed or owned. This can be done independent of any cooperation, participation, or assistance from the owners or exclusive licensees of other rights. However, such an action must be limited only to the particular right violated. Ordinarily, if the right of someone else is infringed, the owner or exclusive licensee of that right is the only person who has authority to institute an action for violation of it.

For example, the exclusive licensee or owner of the right to reproduce a literary work in hardcover book form can institute a copyright infringement action against another party who reproduces the work in hardcover without permission. However, such an owner would have no authority to institute an action for public performance of the literary work or to institute one for reproduction of the literary work in the form of a magazine article.

Rights of a Nonexclusive Licensee

A person who obtains a nonexclusive license to exercise a right is not entitled to be treated the same as a transferee of rights. A nonexclusive licensee does not acquire ownership of the right but is granted permission only to exercise the right under specified terms and conditions. Consequently, a non-exclusive licensee must rely on his or her licensor for the protection as well as the remedies associated with the right licensed. A nonexclusive licensee has no authority to act independently of the licensor in this regard, unless the licensor expressly grants such authority.

On the other hand, an exclusive licensee of a right is considered to be an owner of it as noted earlier in this chapter. Therefore, an exclusive licensee has the ability and authority to act independently of the licensor just as any owner of a right in a work has the authority to act independently from the owners of other rights in the same work.

CHAPTER SUMMARY

- The exclusive rights of a copyright owner may be transferred to another party; it is possible to transfer each right separately, or to transfer them in groups, and to subdivide a right and transfer each subdivision.

- A transfer of ownership includes assigning, mortgaging, pledging, or exclusively licensing rights.

- Transfers can occur by death, involuntarily, and by operation of law.

- Ownership of rights is distinct from ownership of a particular copy or phonorecord; rights remain with the copyright owner until they are formally transferred regardless of who owns the object in which the work is embodied.

- A transfer of rights does not automatically occur by selling or giving away a material object in which a work is embodied.

- A transfer of rights is not valid if it is not evidenced by a written document signed by the copyright owner or the owner's authorized agent, or unless it happens by operation of law.

- Ordinarily, a transferee of less than all rights is entitled to all the protection and remedies afforded to an owner of all rights, but only with respect to the right acquired.

16

Recording Transfers of Copyright Ownership

It is very important for everyone who acquires rights in a work (whether by transfer, mortgage, pledge, or exclusive license) to record the document reflecting the transaction with the U.S. Copyright Office. A number of conditions are satisfied by recording this type of document and advantages are to be gained as a result of such action. Similarly, there can be some adverse legal consequences for failing to do so or failing to timely do so.

PREREQUISITE TO INSTITUTING AN INFRINGEMENT SUIT

The recordation of a transfer document in the U.S. Copyright Office is necessary if a person acquiring rights wishes to institute an infringement action based upon the violation of them. The 1976 Act expressly provides that no person claiming ownership of rights, or of any exclusive right, by virtue of a transfer is entitled to institute an infringement action until the applicable transfer document is recorded. However, recordation of a transfer document is not the only prerequisite that must be satisfied by an owner of rights. Registration of a work is also a prerequisite. Therefore, a transferee of rights may find it necessary to register a work as well as record the transfer of ownership to be in a position to take action in the event an infringement of the acquired rights occurs.

Once recordation of the ownership transfer is made, the transferee has a right to institute an infringement action even though the infringement has occurred prior to the date of recordation. However, this is the case only if the infringement occurred during the time the transferee owned the infringed right.

RECORDING IS A CONDITION OF GIVING CONSTRUCTIVE NOTICE

Often, only a few people have actual knowledge of all the facts contained in a document evidencing a transfer of rights in a particular work. This can be to the disadvantage of a party to such a transaction because in many instances those people who do not know what has transpired cannot generally be held accountable for action they take in reference to the work or rights covered by it.

For example, if the owner of rights in a work transfers ownership of rights to one person and transfers the same rights to another person, it is possible that the second transferee may be able to annul the first transfer and keep the transferred rights even though they were previously given to the first transferee. This can occur where the second transferee did not have actual knowledge that the rights acquired had already been transferred to someone else.

To avoid such situations, the 1976 Act provides that recording a document in the U.S. Copyright Office, which refers to a particular work, gives all persons constructive notice of the facts stated in the document. This will be the case only if:

1. The document, or material attached to it, specifically identifies the work to which it pertains so that, after the document is indexed by the Register of Copyrights, it would be revealed by a reasonable search under the title or registration of the work.

2. Registration has been made for the work.

Constructive notice is a presumption of the law making it impossible for a person to deny the matter concerning which notice is given even though the person has no actual knowledge of the matter.

RECORDATION MAY DEFEAT A COMPLETE DEFENSE TO INFRINGEMENT

By promptly recording the ownership transfer document, the transferee may be able to defeat the right of an innocent infringer to rely upon an error in the name in the copyright notice as a complete defense to an infringement.

As discussed in Chapter 11, it is possible that an innocent infringer's reliance on an error in the name in the copyright notice will give that person a complete defense to an infringement action. However, as noted in Chapter 11, this defense is not available if before the infringement was begun the work was registered in the name of the owner of rights or a document executed by the person named in the notice and showing the ownership of the rights had been recorded.

Ordinarily, there will be an error in the name portion of a copyright notice if the person whose name appears in it transferred ownership of rights to another party (a transferee). If this occurs and the person named in the notice thereafter gives permission to exercise a right to a third party who exercises it in good faith in reliance on such permission, the third party may have a complete defense to a claim of infringement of the right by the transferee. This defense will not be available if the transferee records the document evidencing the transfer in the U.S. Copyright Office before the infringement began.

For example, if the writer of a magazine article, which features the writer's name in a copyright notice below its title, transfers copyright ownership of it to a publisher after it has been published, the publisher should promptly record the transfer document. By doing so, the publisher can preclude an innocent infringer from raising an error in the copyright notice as a defense, if the writer later gives someone else permission to reproduce the article.

RECORDATION GIVES PRIORITY TO THE TRANSFER THAT OCCURS FIRST

Generally, a person who buys or is given property and takes possession of it can feel confident that he or she owns it and that the person from whom it was obtained will not be able to successfully sell it or give it away to someone else. Generally, the law is such that once ownership of a particular piece of property has been transferred, the transferor no longer has an ownership in it and therefore cannot make another conflicting transfer. Consequently, a later conflicting transfer of the same property ordinarily would not annul an earlier transfer of it and the later transferee would not get anything.

This is not necessarily the case when there are conflicting transfers of rights in a copyrightable work. An earlier transferee may not always prevail over a later transferee. If the later transfer prevails it will annul the earlier transfer.

The 1976 Act provides that, as between two conflicting transfers, the one executed first prevails. That is, the one executed first will be effective and negate a later conflicting transfer of the same rights, but only if the document is recorded in the U.S. Copyright Office in the manner required to give constructive notice:

1. Within one month after it has been executed within the United States.
2. Within two months after its execution outside the United States.
3. At any time before recordation of the document evidencing the later transfer.

For example, a conflicting transfer will occur if ownership of rights to reproduce and to publicly distribute copies of a literary work in all printed formats (e.g., book, magazine, newspapers) is sold by an author to a trade book publisher, and shortly thereafter those same rights are also sold by the author to a magazine publisher. Under these circumstances, both the trade book publisher and magazine publisher have been transferred the same rights, but only one is entitled to own them.

The 1976 Act gives the trade book publisher the opportunity to prevail, but it must take some action to do so. The purchase of the reproduction and distribution rights must be evidenced by a document signed by the author. If this document was executed within the United States, the trade book publisher has a period of one month after the document was executed to record it in the U.S. Copyright Office. If the literary work was not previously registered, the trade book publisher must register that work.

In the event the trade book publisher fulfills these conditions, or does so at any time prior to action by the magazine publisher, the trade book publisher will prevail with regard to the conflicting transfer. If the trade book publisher delays recording the assignment document past the one-month grace period, that publisher is assuming a risk of losing the rights acquired.

On the other hand, if the transfer which was executed first is not recorded within the applicable time period noted above, the later transfer will prevail if:

1. It is recorded, in the manner required to give constructive notice, before the earlier transfer is recorded.
2. The earlier document was not properly recorded within the one- or two-month grace period (whichever is applicable).

3. The person in whose favor the later document was executed acquired the right(s) in good faith.

4. A valuable consideration was given for it, or a binding promise to pay royalties was made in exchange for it.

5. The person who acquired rights by the later transfer had no notice of the earlier transfer or had no knowledge of facts that would make a reasonable person inquire as to an earlier transfer.

If the magazine publisher records its assignment document in the U.S. Copyright Office at any time prior to the date the trade book publisher records its assignment document (assuming the trade book publisher does not do this within the one-month grace period), it may be able to prevail over the trade book publisher with regard to ownership of the rights transferred. To do so, the magazine publisher must not have known of the earlier transfer to the trade book publisher. In addition, the magazine publisher must have taken the rights transferred in good faith and paid for those rights or promised to pay for them.

Oral transfers of rights are not valid. Therefore, oral transfers are not entitled to any priority or preference where a conflicting transfer of rights occurs.

AN EARLIER TRANSFER MAY DEFEAT A LATER ONE

The one- or two-month grace period for recording a transfer document makes acquiring ownership of rights in a work risky and uncertain. Until such time as two months have passed (measured from the date a person acquires ownership rights in a work) there can be no certainty on that person's part that ownership of the rights acquired is secure. It is possible that the transfer of them may be annulled at any time during this grace period because someone else may have previously acquired those rights through a conflicting transfer. If so, and if the document evidencing the earlier transfer is recorded during the grace period, the earlier transfer will prevail.

Again, referring back to the previous example, anyone who purchases rights from an author assumes a risk of losing those rights. In the example, the risk will be for a period of no more than one month after the date of a purchase because ownership of rights was transferred by a document executed in the United States. If it was executed outside of the United States the risk period would be for no more than two months from the date of execution.

The risk arises due to the transfer to the trade book publisher. During the one month grace period after it acquired ownership of the rights transferred, it is in a guaranteed position of being able to defeat any subsequent transfer of them.

A NONEXCLUSIVE LICENSE CAN PREVAIL OVER A CONFLICTING TRANSFER

A person who has a nonexclusive license to exercise a right in a work will not necessarily lose permission to do so merely because the licensor (the owner of the right) transfers ownership of it to someone else. This will be the case if the following conditions are met:

1. The nonexclusive license is in writing and the written instrument is signed by the owner of the right licensed or the owner's authorized agent
2. The nonexclusive license was granted before a transfer of ownership of rights in the licensed work by the licensor
3. The nonexclusive license was taken in good faith after the transfer of ownership rights but without notice of such transfer, and before a document evidencing the transfer is recorded in the U.S. Copyright Office.

For example, a person who obtains a nonexclusive license to reproduce a work of art from the artist (the owner of the reproduction right) will continue to have the right even though the artist sells the reproduction right to another person, as long as the enumerated conditions are met.

The nonexclusive licensee possesses the right to continue reproducing the work of art for the life of the license. The purchaser of the reproduction right acquires the reproduction right subject to the outstanding nonexclusive license.

WHAT SHOULD BE SUBMITTED TO THE COPYRIGHT OFFICE

An ownership transfer document must be recorded in the U.S. Copyright Office in a manner required to give constructive notice in order for that document to have priority over a subsequently recorded transfer document. In the event it does not meet the requirement for giving constructive notice, it is possible a subsequent transfer document will prevail.

As noted earlier, a document will satisfy this requirement if it, or the material attached to it, specifically identifies the work to which it pertains. This means that the work must be identified so that, after the document has been indexed by the U.S. Copyright Office, the document will be revealed by a reasonable search under the title or registration number of the work.

Forms for transferring ownership of rights in a work, or for use in connection with recording such a document, are not available from or provided by the U.S. Copyright Office. Therefore, it is necessary for the parties to prepare such a document based upon the facts of the transaction.

There are accepted formats which can be used, one of which is followed in the copy of the assignment document found in Appendix A. It is a somewhat generic, short-form version of a transfer document. This format is used when the parties to a transfer do not want all of the facts relating to it to be made part of the public record. In such cases, a more complete document setting forth all of the details of the transaction is also executed and is usually treated as the controlling document regarding the agreement of the parties.

If a short-form transfer document is not used, it will be necessary to record the document reciting all of the relevant and controlling facts. For example, this typically occurs where a transfer of rights is executed in the form of a mortgage or a will.

Whatever form of document is submitted for recordation, it must satisfy the following requirements as provided by the U.S. Copyright Office Regulations:

1. It must bear the actual signature or signatures of the person or persons who executed it. Alternatively, a copy of the original signed document may be submitted if it is a legible photocopy or other full-size facsimile reproduction of the signed document. But it must be accompanied by a sworn or official certification that the reproduction is a true copy of the signed document. Any sworn certification accompanying a reproduction must be signed by one of the persons who executed the document, or by his or her authorized agent.

2. The document must be complete by its own terms. Accordingly, if it contains any reference to a schedule, appendix, exhibit, addendum, or other material as being attached to it or made a part of it, such material must also be submitted for recordation with the document.

3. The document must be capable of being reproduced in legible microform copies.

A "sworn certification" is an affidavit under the official seal of any officer authorized to administer oaths within the United States. If the original is located outside of the United States, a sworn certification is an affidavit under the official seal of any diplomatic or consular officer of the United States or of a person authorized to administer oaths whose authority is proved by the certificate of such an officer.

An "official certification" is a certification, by the appropriate government official, that the original of the document is on file in a public office and that the reproduction is a true copy of the original.

Once a document has been recorded, it is returned by the U.S. Copyright Office to the person who submitted it along with a certificate of record bearing the date of recordation. In addition, the certificate indicates the volume and page number of the microfilm on which the document has been recorded by the U.S. Copyright Office.

The date of recordation is the date when a document meeting the aforementioned requirements and a proper filing fee are all received in the U.S. Copyright Office. Documents and the fee should be submitted to:

Renewals and Documents Section, LM-444
Examining Division
U.S. Copyright Office
Library of Congress
Washington, DC 20559

CHAPTER SUMMARY

- A transfer of rights in a work, which is in writing and signed by the owner of the rights conveyed, will be valid insofar as the parties and the 1976 Act are concerned.

- If a transfer document is not recorded in the U.S. Copyright Office the transferee will not be entitled to institute an infringement action until such time as it is recorded and may not be able to prevail in a dispute with another party who claims ownership of the same rights through a subsequent conflicting transfer.

- The 1976 Act gives priority to the first transferee of rights when there are conflicting transfers of them.

- Recordation of a transfer document offers a significant benefit to a transferee of rights; it gives all persons constructive notice of the facts stated in the recorded document, but only if the work to which it pertains is specifically identified and that work has been registered.

- Recordation of a transfer document may defeat an innocent infringer's right to rely on an error in the name or date in a copyright notice as a complete defense to an infringement action.

17

How to Recover Ownership of Transferred Rights

When the creator of a work sells or gives away a copy or phonorecord, that person usually permanently parts with ownership of the copy or phonorecord. However, this is not the case when the creator sells or gives away all or some of the rights in a work. Unlike the sale or gift of automobiles, jewelry, appliances, and other kinds of property (as well as copies or phonorecords), the creator does not necessarily part with those rights forever.

The creator, or certain members of his or her immediate family, can regain ownership of rights that have been transferred, but not until at least 35 years have passed from the date the creator first transferred ownership. This may be accomplished, at the appropriate time, if the creator or members of his or her family give a written request to the then-current owner to return them. Such a request is known as a "notice of termination" and must comply with requirements set by the U.S. Copyright Office.

Subject to a few exceptions, the 1976 Act gives the creator of a work the irrevocable right to recover ownership of all rights in it that have been exclusively or nonexclusively licensed, sold, or given away. It is not necessary that there be an agreement between the parties providing for the return of rights. The creator has no obligation to pay for their return.

This right is referred to as the "right of termination." The right to terminate is limited to the recovery of rights only. It does not give the creator any power to recover ownership of any physical object in which the work is embodied.

As discussed in Chapter 15, ownership of rights in a work is separate and distinguishable from ownership of any physical object in which the work is embodied. Consequently, the owner of a copyrighted oil painting cannot be required to return it to the creator, but the owner of the right to reproduce it may be required to do so.

To be effective, the right of termination must be exercised in accordance with requirements prescribed by the 1976 Act. For works first protected under the 1976 Act, it cannot be exercised until at least 35 years have elapsed from the date a creator made a transfer. For works initially protected under the 1909 Act, and the subject of a transfer covering the renewal term made by a creator before January 1, 1978, the right of termination cannot be exercised until 56 years have elapsed from the date copyright was first secured.

RIGHTS RECOVERY PRIOR TO 1976 ACT

The right to recover ownership of transferred or nonexclusively licensed rights under the 1976 Act is unique in comparison to the right of an owner of other kinds of property to regain ownership of it. But it is not a new development in the copyright law.

The creator of a work, or members of his or her family, could recover ownership of transferred rights under the 1909 Act, but the means by which this occurred was not referred to as a "right of termination." Moreover, the 1909 Act did not contain language that directly and expressly indicated that the creator of a work possessed a right to recover ownership of transferred rights.

On the other hand, the creator of a work that was not registered under the 1909 Act did not have any statutory basis to recover ownership of rights transferred to another person. Such works were protected under the common law and there was no specific mechanism to provide for the ability of a creator to recover ownership of transferred rights.

The renewal procedure was the means under the 1909 Act by which a creator could regain ownership of rights transferred for the initial 28-year period of protection. As noted in Chapter 9, it was possible to renew a copyright registration and gain an additional 28-year period of protection for the work covered by it. Accordingly, if a creator transferred rights for the initial period of protection, but not for the renewal term, the creator could recover ownership of those rights at the expiration of the initial period and retain them for the renewal period by filing a renewal application for his or her own benefit.

The right of a creator to recover ownership at the end of the initial period by renewing a registration for his or her own benefit was the result of Congress's desire to give creators of works a second chance to profit from their creative efforts. Congress believed, for a number of reasons, that the bargaining position of many creators is not strong at the time they first transfer rights. Among the reasons is the difficulty in knowing what value to place on those rights. At the time that most creators first transfer rights they have no way of determining the actual worth of them. Usually this cannot be measured until after most copies of most works are introduced into the marketplace and made available to the public or to the intended class of users.

By providing for the right to recover ownership at the end of the initial 28-year term of protection, Congress made it possible for the creator to commercially or otherwise exploit rights in the work directly for his or her own account during the renewal term. Or, Congress gave the creator the opportunity to negotiate a second transfer of them for this term to someone else on a more informed basis as to their value, if that is what the creator desired to do. With knowledge of the commercial success or failure of a work during the first 28-year term, it was Congress's belief that a creator would be in a much better position to value his or her rights in it.

RIGHT TO TERMINATE GRANTS MADE AFTER JANUARY 1, 1978

Most grants made by the creator of a work after January 1, 1978, are subject to being terminated under certain conditions. Many grants covering the renewal term, which were made by the creator of a work (or his or her executor, members of the family, or next of kin) before January 1, 1978, are also subject to being terminated.

The 1976 Act states that in the case of any work, other than a work made for hire, the exclusive or nonexclusive grant of a transfer or license of rights, or of any right, executed by the creator on or after January 1, 1978 (other than by will) is subject to termination by the creator or, if the creator is dead, by the creator's survivors.

The right of termination exists whether all or some rights have been covered by a grant, irrespective of the fact that ownership has passed by means of what is intended to be an absolute sale or gift of the rights with no provision for regaining ownership. Similarly, it exists without regard to the fact that rights are exclusively or nonexclusively licensed for the applicable term of protection covering the work. This right covers any "transfer of rights" whether they are mortgaged, pledged, exclusively licensed, or otherwise conveyed or alienated.

A mortgage or pledge of rights can be terminated contrary to any resistance on the part of a mortgagee or pledgee to give up a secured position with respect to rights in a work. Furthermore, it can be terminated notwithstanding any state laws that provide for the existence of security interests in property until released by the secured party.

All legal or equitable rights equivalent to any of the exclusive rights of a copyright owner are governed solely by the 1976 Act. Accordingly, since the 1976 Act gives the creator a right to terminate a mortgage or pledge of rights in a work, this can occur even though a state law covering such a secured interest provides otherwise.

The possible loss of rights is an inherent risk associated with acquiring rights in a work. However, most creators are not aware that this is possible and, therefore, may unknowingly forgo the opportunity to take advantage of the right of termination when it is time to exercise it.

EXCEPTIONS TO THE RIGHT OF TERMINATION

Certain works are not subject to the right of termination. Accordingly, a grant with respect to rights in them cannot be terminated by virtue of that right and will be effective for the entire period agreed upon by the parties (which may be for the full term of protection applicable to the work), unless it ends earlier for other reasons.

Works Made for Hire

The 1976 Act expressly states that a work made for hire is not subject to the right of termination. Accordingly, this right is not available to employers or anyone else who acquires ownership of rights by virtue of a work-made-for-hire relationship.

For example, in the absence of an agreement providing otherwise, when an advertising agency transfers ownership of all rights in a promotional piece (created by its employees) to a client, the agency has no right to recover ownership at a later time. In this situation the promotional piece was created under a work-made-for-hire relationship by the agency's employees.

Works Protected Under Foreign Copyright Laws

The 1976 Act expressly provides that the right of termination in no way affects rights arising under foreign laws. Accordingly, if a creator has made a grant covering rights in a work, which are recognized by a foreign country,

those rights may continue to be exercised in the foreign country by the ac-
quiror even though the same rights revert to the creator in the United States.

Grants Made by Any Person Other Than the Creator

The intention of Congress, as expressed in the 1976 Act, was to give the right
of termination only to the creator of a work (but not a creator of a work made
for hire) or to the creator's survivors if the creator dies before it can be exercised and the creator has not made a grant of rights by will. Consequently,
no person to whom the creator transferred or licensed rights, including any
subsequent owner or licensee, is entitled to execute the right of termination.

For example, a book publisher who acquires ownership of the exclusive
right to reproduce a literary work in hardcover and paperback versions from
an author cannot terminate its grant of the right to reproduce the work in
paperback. However, the author or the author's survivors (if the right of termination is possessed by them) can do so; they can also terminate the grant
to the book publisher. If this is done, all rights to reproduce the work in both
hardcover and paperback form return to the author or to the author's survivors.

If a creator does not make any grant of rights during his or her lifetime
and dies intestate (without a will), his or her survivors will not be entitled
to terminate any grants of rights they may make. If a creator did not make a
grant of rights during his or her lifetime there is nothing for the survivors to
terminate. A transfer of rights to the creator's survivors by the law of intestate
succession is not considered to be a grant of rights by the creator in any
event.

Grants Made in the Creator's Will

The 1976 Act provides that a grant executed by a creator on or after January
1, 1978, by means of a will is not subject to the right of termination. This
exception is premised on Congress's objective to make the right of termination available only to the creator of a work, to be exercised as he or she
deems appropriate. This exception prevents a creator's survivors from regaining ownership of rights he or she intended to remain with the person to
whom they were bequeathed.

PERSONS ENTITLED TO EXERCISE THE RIGHT

The right of termination belongs only to the creator of a work. Therefore, if
the creator is alive at the time this right can be exercised, that person is the
only one entitled to exercise it.

If the creator is not alive when this right can be exercised, or is alive at the time it can be exercised but dies before the time for exercising it expires, this right automatically passes by operation of the 1976 Act to specific members of the creator's family, not to his or her estate. Nor does it pass by his or her will because the right of termination cannot be transferred.

The widow or widower of a creator and his or her children or grandchildren are the specific family members who acquire and may exercise the right of termination. The 1976 Act specifies the ownership percentage each family member acquires and the percentage of owners required to effectively exercise it.

WORKS CREATED BY TWO OR MORE CREATORS

In the event a work has been created by two or more persons, each creator has an undivided ownership interest in the work as noted in Chapter 5. As discussed in Chapter 15, each joint owner has the authority to transfer his or her undivided ownership interest in the work to someone else, and to give a nonexclusive license to another party to exercise one or more rights in the work.

Consequently, each joint owner has a right of termination with respect to any such grant or nonexclusive license of rights in it he or she made and is the only person who may exercise that right. Other joint creators who did not participate in making the grant do not possess a right of termination with respect to it and therefore have no right to terminate it.

If a grant was made by two or more joint creators, they are the only persons entitled to exercise the right of termination with respect to it if they are alive at the time it can be exercised.

If a joint creator is alive at the time his or her right of termination can be exercised but dies before the time for exercising it expires, ownership of this right automatically passes by operation of the 1976 Act to specific members of his or her family. More particularly, it passes to the same family members and in the same percentages as happens when the right of termination of a single creator passes to his or her family members.

When a grant is made by two or more joint creators and they are alive at the time the right of termination can be exercised but one or more dies before the time for exercising it expires, the deceased joint creator's right of termination with respect to the grant passes as one unit to members of his or her family. More particularly, the percentage ownership of the deceased joint creator's right of termination passes to his or her family.

The percentage ownership of this right acquired by family members of a deceased joint creator is determined by the number of joint creators who participated in making the grant and is equal to 100 percent of the deceased joint creator's proportionate interest. For example, if two joint creators participated in making the grant, each joint creator owns an undivided 50 percent interest in the right of termination. Accordingly, the surviving family members of a deceased joint owner will own, as a group, all of the 50 percent interest.

If a joint creator is not alive when this right can be exercised, it passes by operation of the 1976 Act to specific members of the joint creator's family in the same way and in accordance with the same percentages as happens when the right of termination of a single creator passes to his or her family.

THE PROCEDURE TO FOLLOW TO EXERCISE THE RIGHT

It is not difficult to exercise the right of termination. All that is required is to serve a written notice of termination upon the owner or owners of rights in a work at the time this right can be exercised. There may be more than one owner because it is possible for each of the exclusive rights, as well as subdivisions of them, to be owned separately as discussed in Chapter 15.

The U.S. Copyright Office does not provide printed forms that give notice of termination, but it does prescribe what should be included in the notice for terminating grants made before January 1, 1978.

To be effective the notice must be signed by all individuals who participated in termination of a grant. When the right of termination is exercised by the creator, the notice must be signed by the creator or the creator's authorized agent; if it is exercised by a surviving member or members of the creator's family, the notice must be signed by all individuals who join together to exercise it, or by their authorized agents.

A notice served on behalf of joint creators who are alive and have the power to exercise the right of termination must be signed by each person who desires to terminate, or by his or her authorized agents. If the right is exercised by one or more joint creators and the surviving members of the family of a deceased joint creator, the notice must be signed by all individuals who join together to exercise the right or their authorized agents.

WHEN A NOTICE OF TERMINATION CAN BE SERVED

Once a notice of termination has been prepared and signed, it must be served on the person or persons who own rights at the time the notice can be served. It must be served within the time frame established by the 1976 Act. This time frame is measured from the date termination is to be effective and this date must be specified in the notice.

Using the date of termination as a reference point, the notice of termination will be valid if it is served at any time:

1. Not later than two years before this date; or
2. Not earlier than 10 years before this date

Once the notice has been served, a copy of it must be recorded in the U.S. Copyright Office and a recordation fee paid. Recordation of the notice can occur at any time after service, but it must be done prior to the effective date of termination specified in the notice. Recordation is a condition to termination taking effect. If the notice is not timely recorded, it will not be valid and termination of the transfer will not be possible.

WHEN A GRANT MAY BE TERMINATED

The applicable minimum period that must elapse before a grant can be terminated is determined on the basis of whether a work has been published prior to the date of a grant:

If the work has been published prior to the date of a grant, termination may be effected:

- At any time during a period of five years beginning at the end of 35 years from the date the grant was executed by the creator(s)

If the work has not been published prior to the date of a grant, termination may be effected:

- At any time during a period of five years beginning at the end of 35 years from the date of publication by the subsequent owner of the rights; or
- At any time during a period of five years beginning at the end of 40 years from the date the grant was executed by the creator(s).

whichever term ends earlier.

ACTUAL DATE OF TERMINATION

The actual date that termination will be effective within the relevant five-year period is the date selected by the creator or by the surviving members of his or her family. That date is specified in the notice of termination.

There is a distinction between the time when termination becomes effective and the time when the right of termination may be exercised. While termination cannot occur earlier than 35 years from the date of a grant, the notice of intent to exercise the right of termination may be served as early as 10 years before the date of termination specified in the notice. Although the notice may be served as early as 25 years after the date of the grant, the actual termination will not take effect until the thirty-fifth year, assuming that year is specified in the notice.

THE RIGHT OF TERMINATION CANNOT BE WAIVED OR CONTRACTED AWAY

The 1976 Act expressly provides this right cannot be waived or contracted away. A creator must wait until the *effective date of termination* (at least 35 years after the date of the grant) before making an agreement to grant the same rights to *another party*. For example, if rights were first granted in 1984, an agreement made prior to 2019 regarding a further grant covered by the 1984 grant will not be effective. The creator must wait until 2019 (35 years after 1984) to make a further grant of the same rights.

There is one exception to this rule. A creator must wait only to the *date a notice of termination can be served* (at least 25 years after the date of the grant) to agree to grant the same rights to *the person who then owns the rights*. For example, using the 1984 date as the date rights were first granted, an agreement made in 2009 regarding a further grant of those rights to the person who owns them at that time will be effective. The earliest date a creator can serve a notice of termination is 2009 (25 years afater the date of the initial grant).

The prohibition on waiving or contracting away the right of termination was made for the creator's benefit, to provide the creator a reasonable period of time to assess the value of his or her exclusive rights.

FAILURE TO GIVE A NOTICE OF TERMINATION

If a notice of termination is not given, or is not timely given, or is not timely recorded with the U.S. Copyright Office by the creator (or by his or her surviving family members), all rights covered by a grant will continue unchanged. That is, the person or persons who own rights in a work will have the right to continue exercising them for the balance of the period of protection without any ability of the creator or the creator's surviving family members to regain ownership.

However, if an agreement between the creator and a person who has acquired rights from the creator specifically provides for the recovery of rights by the creator at some date 35 or 40 years after the agreement, its terms will be effective. Accordingly, a failure by the creator, or surviving family members, to give a notice of termination will not preclude the recovery of rights as specifically provided in the agreement. The provisions of the agreement will take precedence over any limitation that may exist with respect to the recovery of rights under the 1976 Act's right of termination.

THE RIGHT TO RECOVER RIGHTS FOR THE ENTIRE RENEWAL TERM

If a grant of rights is made after January 1, 1978 (for a work protected under the 1909 Act) but covers only the initial 28-year term of protection, it is possible for the creator (or surviving family members) to recover ownership for the entire renewal term without relying on the right of termination. At the expiration of the initial 28-year term, the grant ends since it covers only that term. If the creator (or surviving family members) renews the registration of the work for his or her own benefit, the creator (or surviving family members) retains ownership for the renewal term under the 1976 Act.

THE RIGHT TO TERMINATE GRANTS MADE BEFORE JANUARY 1, 1978 COVERING THE EXTENDED RENEWAL TERMS

The 1976 Act provides that the right of termination is applicable to works protected under the 1909 Act, even though a grant covering the 47-year renewal term was made prior to January 1, 1978. However, the recovery of rights covered by such grants will be for the last 19 years of the 47-year renewal term, rather than for the entire renewal term.

Grants Subject to Termination

As is the case with respect to the right of termination as it applies to grants made after January 1, 1978, certain grants made before January 1, 1978, and certain works created before that date are not subject to the right of termination. More particularly, the right of termination is not applicable to:

1. Any grant of rights in a work which is a work made for hire
2. Any grant of rights in a work protected under foreign copyright laws
3. Any grant of rights in a work which is made in the will of the creator of the work and which becomes effective at the death of the creator.

With the exception of those grants and works referred to above, the 1976 Act provides that the right of termination is applicable to grants made prior to January 1, 1978 by:

1. The creator of a work
2. The widow, widower, or children of the creator or grants made by the creator's executors or, in the absence of a will, by the creator's next of kin.

As discussed in Chapter 9, under the 1909 Act, the widow, widower, or children of the creator were entitled to renew a registered work if the creator was dead at the time a renewal application was due. They were also entitled to make grants for the renewal term if the creator died prior to the time a renewal application was due.

In addition to the widow, widower, or children of the creator, a renewal application could be filed by the creator's executors or, in the absence of a will, his or her next of kin if the widow, widower, or children of the creator were not alive at the time the renewal application was due. Similarly, under such circumstances the creator's executors, and so on, were entitled to make grants for the renewal term.

Since Congress mandated the right of termination to give the creator of a work and his or her survivors a second chance to profit from the creator's creative efforts, those persons who possessed a right to make grants for the renewal term under the 1909 Act are entitled to terminate a grant covering that term. However, they are entitled to recover rights only for the last 19 years of that term as extended by the 1976 Act.

Persons Entitled to Exercise

The right of termination applicable to the renewal period extension belongs to the creator of a work. However, if the creator is dead at the time it can be exercised, this right passes to the same family members who acquire the right of termination for grants made after January 1, 1978, and in the same percentages.

Works Created by One Individual

Termination of rights in a work created by only one individual may or may not require unanimous consent on the part of all owners of the right to terminate. In some cases a grant covering the last 19 years of the renewal term can be terminated only by unanimous consent of everyone who participated in making the grant. In other cases, majority action by the owners of the right to terminate is enough. This will depend on who made the grant and is determined by rules set forth in the 1976 Act.

Works Created by Two or More Creators

Termination of rights in a work created by two or more individuals may be made by only one creator, by a majority of the owners who have the right to terminate, or by the unanimous consent of all of them.

If a grant was made by two or more creators of a work who are all alive at the time the right of termination can be exercised, each creator is entitled to terminate the grant but only with respect to his or her interest in those rights. Ordinarily, that interest is an undivided interest in all the rights.

For example, if a work was created by four individuals and all of them made a grant to a third party, each creator can terminate the grant, but only with respect to the percentage ownership of those rights possessed by the terminating creator. If each creator possesses a 25 percent ownership interest and one terminates the grant, the net result is that the terminating creator recovers a 25 percent undivided ownership interest in the rights covered by the grant and becomes a co-owner of them with the third party. The third party then owns a 75 percent undivided ownership interest instead of 100 percent.

Procedure To Follow To Exercise the Right of Termination

The procedure to terminate grants made prior to January 1, 1978, is the same as for those made after January 1, 1978.

When a Grant Can Be Terminated

Termination of rights in a work become effective as noted in the following list, without regard to whether a grant included the right to first publish the work:

At any time during a period of five years beginning at the end of 56 years from the date protection was first secured (the date an unpublished work was registered under the 1909 Act, or the date of first publication for a work which has been published and registered under that act)

At any time during a period of five years beginning on January 1, 1978; whichever date is later.

The actual date that termination will be effective within the five-year period is selected by the person or persons giving the notice of termination. This date must be set forth in that notice.

Right To Terminate Cannot Be Waived or Contracted Away

Similar to the right of termination for grants made after January 1, 1978, Congress included language in the 1976 Act providing for the exercise of this right in spite of any agreements by the creator, or other persons possessing the right to terminate, to the contrary. By virtue of such language, until the time arrives that the right can be exercised, no one can agree to waive the right to exercise it. And no one, with one exception, can agree to transfer the same rights to someone else after the date of termination. Once the notice of termination has been served, an agreement can be made to transfer rights to the person who then owns the rights.

Failure To Give a Notice of Termination

If a notice of termination is not given, or is not timely given, or is not timely recorded with the U.S. Copyright Office by the creator (or by his or her surviving family members), all rights covered by a grant for the last 19 years of the renewal term will remain where they are. That is, all rights will continue to be owned by the person or persons who acquired rights directly from the creator (or surviving family members), or from someone else who did. This is the same kind of result that occurs when there is a failure to terminate or properly terminate grants made after January 1, 1978.

WHAT HAPPENS WHEN RIGHTS ARE RECOVERED

The process of recovering rights covered by a grant begins on the date a notice of termination is served and is completed on the date specified in the notice. Nothing more must be done to complete the recovery than to record the notice prior to the effective date of termination set forth in the notice.

The release and recovery of rights covered by a grant occurs simultaneously and automatically on the date of termination. Unlike any other transfer of rights in a work (see Chapter 15), the person surrendering ownership is not required to execute any document or otherwise do anything to acknowledge relinquishment of them. And, unlike other transfers, the person surrendering rights has no authority to decide to whom they should be surrendered. The 1976 Act expressly sets forth who is entitled to recover rights.

Individuals Entitled to Recover Rights

The persons entitled to recover rights covered by a grant are the same as those persons entitled to exercise the right of termination on the date a notice of termination is given. The 1976 Act expressly provides that, subject to a few exceptions, persons who can recover rights include those persons who gave the notice of termination as well as persons who possessed the right of termination but who did not participate in exercising it by giving the required notice.

The identity of persons entitled to recover rights is known as early as the date the notice of termination is given. If those persons are alive on the effective date of termination, they can recover the creator's rights. However, if an eligible person dies prior to the date of termination, his or her estate may be the recipient of the recovered rights. This can occur because, at a minimum, before termination can take place, two years must elapse after a notice of termination has been given.

To determine who is entitled to recover rights for a particular work, the following information must be known:

1. The identity of all persons who are entitled to exercise the right of termination
2. The identity of all persons who gave the notice of termination

Individuals Who Recover Rights Can Exercise Them and Make Further Grants

If only one individual recovers rights in a work, that individual (whether the creator or a surviving family member) can exercise those rights as fully as possible and without any obligation to account to or obtain the consent of anyone else to do so. In addition, he or she can grant nonexclusive licenses or make an outright transfer of them with the same degree of independence, whether for all or a portion of the remaining period of protection for the work.

When rights are recovered by more than one individual (whether by joint creators or by surviving family members), the foregoing is not necessarily true. Each co-owner of recovered rights is entitled to exercise them to the same extent as a sole creator can. But, because of a requirement imposed by the 1976 Act, one co-owner may not be able to make an outright transfer of his or her ownership interest in the rights or grant a nonexclusive license of them without the consent of a majority of the other co-owners.

Who Must Join Together to Make a Valid Grant

A grant, or agreement to make a grant, of recovered rights will not be valid if the number of co-owners of such rights (who possess the requisite percentage ownership) do not join to make it. This number and the percentage ownership are determined by referring back to the number of individuals and the percentage ownership needed to terminate the grant which resulted in the recovery of rights in the first place.

The 1976 Act provides that the number and percentage ownership in the rights which are required to make a further grant of them are the same as the number and percentage ownership required to terminate the grant that resulted in the recovery of rights. However, it is not necessary that the exact same individuals who gave the notice also make the grant of recovered rights. It is only necessary that the same number and percentage ownership join together. Thus, it is possible for individuals who did not participate in terminating the earlier grant to join in making the later grant. And, if an individual who is an owner of recovered rights dies, it is possible for that individual's legal representatives, legatees, or heirs at law to represent his or her interest for purposes of making the further grant.

Who Is Bound by Further Grants

In the event the requisite number of co-owners of recovered rights (who possess the requisite percentage ownership interest) join to make a grant of those rights, that grant is binding on all co-owners including those who did not join to make it. Consequently, the rights of nonconsenting owners can be involuntarily transferred.

This cannot occur with respect to rights owned by a co-owner who did not acquire a co-ownership interest by reason of the right of termination. As noted in Chapter 5, an outright grant of rights cannot be made unless all owners agree to it. At the same time, a co-owner can make a grant of a nonexclusive license without any requirement to obtain the consent of the other co-owners. The only obligation imposed on such a co-owner is to share any money earned from the grant with all others. Each is entitled to a proportionate share, as determined by his or her percentage of ownership in the right.

When Recovered Rights Can Be Transferred

As noted earlier in this chapter, until such time as rights have been recovered, it is not possible to make a valid grant with respect to them. Any agreement to make a grant, executed before the date of termination and in anticipation of recovering ownership, will not be effective.

There is an exception to this rule. An enforceable agreement to make a grant can be executed before the date of termination, but not until after the notice of termination has been served. However, this agreement will be enforceable only if it is made by the individual or individuals entitled to recover rights and for the benefit of the person or persons who own them on the date the notice is served.

Use of a Derivative Work Created Under the Authority of a Grant

If a grant by the creator included a right to create a derivative work and such a work is created prior to the date of termination of the grant, the owner of the derivative work is entitled to continue using it after termination for the then-remaining term of protection. This is the case whether the grant was made before or after January 1, 1978. If the grant was made before that date, this holds true whether the grant was made by the creator or by the surviving members of his or her family who had authority to make it.

Thus, there is a limitation on the right of termination. This right does not always bring to an end the authority of someone, other than the creator, to exercise the rights in a work.

As long as the derivative work is used within the scope of the grant that has been terminated, the owner of the derivative work can exercise the applicable exclusive rights with respect to it. There is no requirement to obtain permission to do so from whoever recovers the rights in the underlying work. However, if the owner of the derivative work desires to create other derivative works based on the underlying work covered by the terminated grant, it is necessary to obtain permission from whoever recovers the rights.

A sound recording is one type of derivative work that may be created under the terms of a grant covering rights in a musical work. A motion picture is another kind of derivative work that might be created under the terms of a broad grant covering rights in a literary work.

If a sound recording is created prior to termination of a grant covering the underlying musical work, the owner of the sound recording can continue to reproduce it after the date of termination, if the grant expressly authorized use of the musical work to create sound recordings and to reproduce it in phonorecords. However, the owner of rights in the sound recording would not be entitled to create a different sound recording using the same musical work, without obtaining permission from the owner of rights in the musical work.

This same type of limitation on the right of termination (or, in other words, exception to the rights of those who recover ownership of rights) does not arise in those instances where a derivative work has not been created prior to termination of a grant. In such cases, after the date of termination, a person who relinquishes rights no longer has any authority to exercise them unless permission is obtained from whoever recovers them. This is the case, although ownership of all copies of the work prepared prior to termination stays with and belongs to the person who surrenders the rights.

For example, if a book publisher acquires the right to reproduce a literary work in book form by means of a grant from the author, the publisher can do so as long as the publisher possesses that right. However, if the author terminates that grant, the publisher loses all further right to reproduce the work. The publisher retains ownership of the plates (they are copies of the work) from which the book can be reproduced and all books printed by it prior to termination. But the publisher cannot use those plates to print additional copies of the book after the date of termination unless permission to do so is given by the author or members of his or her family who recover the rights.

The publisher does have a right to sell and distribute the inventory of books on hand on the date of termination because they were lawfully made. An exception to a copyright owner's exclusive right to sell and distribute copies of a work comes into play with respect to lawfully made copies of a work (see Chapter 6). The owner of a lawfully made copy of a work is entitled to dispose of possession of that copy without having to obtain permission from the owner of exclusive rights.

CHAPTER SUMMARY

- The 1976 Act expressly provides for a "right of termination" whereby the creator of a work can recover ownership of all rights that have been licensed, sold, or given away notwithstanding any agreement or understanding that the creator intended to part with ownership of them forever.

- The right of termination is available only to the creator of a work, subject to a few exceptions, and cannot be exercised earlier than 35 years from the date a creator transfers ownership of rights; it must be exercised in accordance with a prescribed procedure.

- Ownership of this right always remains with the creator and does not pass when the creator transfers the other rights in a work; ownership of this right cannot be transferred prior to the time it can be exercised.

- To regain ownership of rights all that is required is to give a written "notice of termination," which must comply in form, content, and manner of service prescribed by the U.S. Copyright Office. The notice must be given within a specified time frame and must state the effective date of termination.

- If the creator is not alive at the time the notice should be given, members of the creator's immediate family may do so and, if they give the notice, they will be entitled to recover ownership of rights.

- If a notice of termination is not given, or it is not timely given, the creator or members of the creator's family will not be able to recover ownership of any transferred rights.

- On the date of termination all rights in a work that are covered by a notice of termination automatically revert to the person or persons who give the notice; in many cases, they also revert to persons who had the right to give the notice but did not participate in doing so.

- The ownership percentage of the rights recovered by each person will be equal to that person's proportionate interest in the right to terminate.

- The person or persons who recover ownership of rights can exercise them to the fullest extent possible for the then-remaining period of protection and may make a grant of them to others to the same degree that the creator could do so.

- Although all rights are recovered by the creator or his or her surviving family members, in some cases, the person who relinquished those rights may nonetheless be entitled to continue utilizing a derivative work which was prepared while that person owned the rights.

18

Voluntary Copyright Licenses

In many cases an owner of rights in a work may not be in a position to utilize them as fully as possible. For example, the owner may not have the financial resources, the marketing know-how, or the necessary expertise to exercise them in a way that produces maximum benefits. However, if the owner finds someone who can do so, it is possible for the owner to enter into an agreement with that person. Under such an agreement, the owner retains ownership of rights, but gives permission to that person to exercise those rights in accordance with terms and conditions acceptable to both of them.

An agreement by one person giving another person permission to act is commonly referred to as a license. A license that covers rights protected under copyright law is generally referred to as a "copyright license." The owner of rights covered by a license, or the person who grants permission to exercise them, is referred to as the "licensor" and the person who obtains permission is known as a "licensee." The particular rights covered by a copyright license are frequently called "licensed rights" and the act of granting permission to exercise them is referred to as "licensing."

If permission is given to exercise a right on a nonexclusive basis, the license is referred to as a "nonexclusive license." Under the terms of a nonexclusive license, the same right can be licensed by a licensor to a number of different persons who are given permission to exercise it for the same time periods, throughout the same geographic areas, and for the same uses. A nonexclusive licensee may be faced with competition by other nonexclusive licensees with permission to exercise the same right.

If permission to exercise a right is given on an exclusive basis, the license is referred to as an "exclusive license." Under the terms of an exclusive license, there is only one licensee of the right. In effect that person has a monopoly on the right for the time period, place of effect, and use specified by the license. An exclusive license is treated as a "transfer" of ownership under the 1976 Act. Therefore, during the term of an exclusive license, the licensor cannot grant permission to another party to exercise the right in a way that conflicts with the terms of the exclusive license because, in effect, the licensor no longer owns the right.

An exclusive licensee is entitled to all of the protection and remedies accorded to an owner under the 1976 Act, but only for the term of the license. Both a nonexclusive license and an exclusive license are subject to termination.

There is a significant difference between a nonexclusive license of rights and a transfer of ownership of rights. A nonexclusive licensee's ability to exercise a right is subject to the control of the owner by means of the provisions of the license, and comes to an end at the expiration or termination of the license. A transferee becomes the owner of the right transferred and has the ability to freely exercise it for the maximum period of protection applicable to it or to make a further transfer of it without accountability to the transferor.

NEGOTIATED COPYRIGHT LICENSES

In some instances a person desiring to exercise a particular right may do so without contacting, negotiating with, or obtaining the express consent of the owner of the right, and without incurring liability for copyright infringement. This can be accomplished if there is an applicable compulsory license for the right under the 1976 Act. A compulsory license is one forced upon the owner of a right, and means he or she has no voice in deciding who may exercise the right.

Presently, the Act provides for compulsory licensing with respect to the making of phonorecords embodying nondramatic musical works, public performance of nondramatic musical works by means of jukeboxes, and public performance of works by cable systems and noncommercial educational broadcasting (see Chapter 19). By complying with the provisions of the applicable compulsory license, permission to exercise a right is automatically obtained, but only to the extent authorized by the compulsory license.

Most licenses, however, are voluntary, and their terms are negotiable. They need not comply with a particular format nor require royalty payments or reporting obligations by the licensee. To a certain extent, the imagination of the licensor and licensee are the only limiting factors on how and when rights may be exercised under the license, subject to the scope of the particular right licensed. The exercise of rights under a voluntary license may be without restriction or it may be limited to specific ways in which it can be exercised, such as during a particular time period or throughout a designated geographic location.

Each of the rights in a work may be separately licensed by the owner, independent of the other rights. In addition, each right can be subdivided and each subdivision licensed in much the same way that each of the rights in a work, or subdivisions of them, can be separately owned.

A LICENSE AGREEMENT SHOULD BE WRITTEN

It is in the interest of both the licensor and licensee to draw up a written licensing agreement although there is no requirement to do so. If there is a dispute regarding the terms of an oral agreement, the court will have nothing to refer to and it may be very difficult to determine who is entitled to what. For instance, if the licensor disavows or disputes the terms of the license, and the licensee is unable to establish that a license was granted and what its terms were, the licensee's exercise of rights may be found to constitute copyright infringement.

This may happen even if a licensee can establish the terms of an oral license. To be enforceable under the laws of most states, agreements that cannot be fully performed in less than one year, or which have a value in excess of $500.00, must be written. Such laws are generally referred to by the phrase "statute of frauds." Thus, a licensee may not be able to enforce the terms of the license if the agreement is not written.

If no written agreement for an exclusive license is recorded in the U.S. Copyright Office, the licensor could make a conflicting grant of an exclusive license to another party and, in a dispute between the two licensees, the later licensee would prevail (see Chapter 16). Similarly, if a nonexclusive license agreement is not written, it may not prevail over a conflicting ownership transfer of the right licensed.

A licensor can also be at risk if a license agreement is not reduced to a written form. If a "statute of frauds" type of law is applicable, the licensor may not be able to enforce the terms of the license. Furthermore, because an exclusive license is considered to be a transfer of ownership, the 1976 Act conditions the enforceability of an exclusive license agreement on the existence of a written document. A transfer of ownership (other than by operation of law) is not valid unless it is in writing and signed by the owner of the rights exclusively licensed.

It would appear that the only time an oral license may be sufficient is in cases where there are no misunderstandings between the licensor and licensee, or when licensor does not enter into any conflicting transfers of ownership of the right covered by the oral license. Unfortunately, this is usually not known until a license expires and then it may not make any difference whether it was orally granted. Prior to that time, there is no guarantee that there will be no disputes between a licensor and licensee nor conflicting transfers.

AN EXCLUSIVE LICENSE SHOULD BE RECORDED

Provides Constructive Notice

Once an exclusive license has been reduced to writing, it should be promptly recorded in the U.S. Copyright Office, and the work to which it refers should be registered (if this has not been previously done). By doing both of these things everyone throughout the United States is given constructive notice of the facts stated in the exclusive license (see Chapter 16). This is important and beneficial to the exclusive licensee because constructive notice of the license can defeat a claim of innocent infringement of the rights covered by the license.

Defeats Conflicting Transfers

Recordation of an exclusive license is important for many reasons. In the event of conflicting transfers of the rights covered by the exclusive license, the transfer executed first prevails, if it is recorded within a specified period of time or at any time before a later transfer is recorded. If the earlier transfer is not timely recorded, the later transfer prevails, if it is recorded first and certain other conditions are satisfied.

A later transfer, or even an earlier one, will not prevail over a nonexclusive license if the nonexclusive license is signed by the owner, or that person's duly authorized agent, and if the nonexclusive license was granted before the conflicting transfer, or if the nonexclusive license was taken in good faith before recordation of the ownership transfer and without notice of it. When these facts exist, a nonexclusive license, whether recorded or not, prevails over a conflicting transfer.

Prerequisite to Instituting an Infringement Action

The 1976 Act provides that a person who owns rights in a work is not entitled to institute an infringement action until the instrument of transfer has been recorded. Accordingly, since an exclusive license is considered to be a transfer of ownership, it must be recorded as a prerequisite to the institution of a copyright infringement lawsuit by the exclusive licensee.

EXCLUSIVE LICENSEE MAY BE ABLE TO REGISTER LICENSED WORK

An exclusive licensee is entitled to file an application to register a copyright ownership claim in the licensed work if the claim has not been previously registered by someone else (see Chapter 12). However, it cannot be registered in the name of the exclusive licensee. Registration must be made in the name of the creator or another party who is the copyright claimant.

A nonexclusive licensee is not entitled to file an application to register the work covered by the license unless the nonexclusive licensee is an authorized agent of the creator or other person who owns *all* of the rights in the work. Even if the nonexclusive licensee is an authorized agent, the work cannot be registered in the nonexclusive licensee's name. It can only be registered in the name of the creator or other person who owns *all* rights in the work.

LICENSEE'S NAME SHOULD NOT APPEAR IN THE COPYRIGHT NOTICE

The name of a nonexclusive licensee should not appear in the copyright notice featured on copies of a work produced and distributed by the nonexclusive licensee. The 1976 Act provides that the name of the owner of *all* rights must be included in the notice. Since a nonexclusive licensee is not an owner of any rights it would be inappropriate to use that person's name in the notice.

If the name of the nonexclusive licensee is used, the validity and ownership of rights in the work are not affected. However, since such use would be treated as an error in the name in the notice, the ability of the owner of rights (with respect to innocent infringers) may be adversely affected (see Chapter 11).

EXCLUSIVE LICENSEE CAN INSTITUTE AN INFRINGEMENT ACTION

Under the 1976 Act only the owner of a right is entitled to institute an action for infringement of that right. Since a nonexclusive licensee is not an owner of the right(s) covered by the license, such a licensee cannot bring an action for infringement of the licensed right(s). A nonexclusive licensee must rely on the owner of the licensed right to do this.

An exclusive licensee, on the other hand, is considered to be the owner of the rights(s) covered by the license. Accordingly, an exclusive licensee may institute an infringement action but only with respect to the right(s) covered by the license. An exclusive licensee is entitled to all of the protection and remedies accorded to an owner of rights.

LICENSES ARE SUBJECT TO THE RIGHT OF TERMINATION

The creator of a work (or the surviving members of his or her family) has the right to terminate an exclusive or nonexclusive grant of rights in the work (see Chapter 17). That is, an exclusive or nonexclusive grant can be terminated regardless of whether it was made directly by the creator or, under certain circumstances, by the surviving members of his or her family.

REPRESENTATIVE PROVISIONS FOR NEGOTIATED LICENSES

The extent to which the responsibilities and rights of the licensor and licensee are set forth and described in a copyright license agreement will depend upon the objectives of the parties and how comfortable each feels with respect to general versus detailed language.

Many kinds of provisions may be included in a negotiated license agreement, but even the lengthiest agreement may not cover every possible contingency. Reference to the license found in Appendix A should give a feeling for the format of a license as well as some of the commonly used terms and conditions. The following list highlights some basic provisions:

1. An indication of the term of the agreement by setting forth a beginning date and an expiration date (it is not uncommon for an agreement to last for the life of the copyright for the work covered by the agreement).

2. An indication of whether the license is exclusive or nonexclusive.

3. Representations and warranties by the licensor regarding ownership of all rights, title, and interest in and to the rights covered by the agreement as well as the fact that the work is an original work.

4. An indication as to whether the work is registered in the U.S. Copyright Office.

5. A description of the rights and work covered by the agreement.

6. An indication of any obligation on the part of the licensee to pay royalties or other fees based upon the exercise of rights covered by the agreement.

7. An indication of any obligations on the part of the licensee to keep and maintain accurate and complete books and records relating to the payment of royalties or other fees, and to make such payments at specific times and to be accompanied by written statements setting forth how the royalties or fees were calculated.

8. An indication of any right of the licensor to inspect and copy the licensee's books and records to verify the accuracy of payments.

9. An agreement on the part of the licensee to indemnify, hold harmless, and defend the licensor against any claims, lawsuits, etc., that may arise as a result of the licensee's exercise of the rights.

10. An agreement on the part of the licensor to indemnify, hold harmless, and defend the licensee against any claims or lawsuits that may arise as a result of the licensor's breach of any representations and warranties made by the licensor.

11. An agreement on the part of the licensee to carry insurance to protect the licensor in the event of any claims asserted against the licensor as a result of the licensee's acts.

12. An agreement on the part of the licensee to cooperate with the licensor in the event the rights are infringed by another party.

13. An agreement on the part of the licensor to protect and defend the rights licensed to the licensee.

14. A provision for termination in the event of default by either party.

15. A provision for the serving of notices and payment of royalties and where they may be served (paid) and how.

16. A prohibition on the right of one or both of the parties to assign any rights and/or obligations under the agreement to another party.

17. An indication of the state or jurisdiction where a lawsuit involving any controversies between the parties may be filed.

18. A representation that the persons who sign the agreement have the authority to do so.

19. A statement to the effect that the licensee will execute any and all documents that the licensor may reasonably require to effect a termination of the license.

20. A statement to the effect that the agreement constitutes the entire

agreement between the parties and that no other agreement, whether oral or written, is effective unless it is signed by the parties.

21. A statement to the effect that the agreement is binding not only on the parties but also upon their parent companies, subsidiaries, related companies, affiliates, legal representatives, heirs, assigns, and successors.

22. An obligation on the part of the licensee to use all copyright notices designated by the licensor, on all copies of the work produced and distributed under the license, and an acknowledgment on the part of the licensee that compliance with this obligation is a condition of the licensee having the authority to exercise the rights covered by the license. [This is an extremely important provision and should be in all copyright licenses. Failure to include it could result in the invalidation of copyright protection for the work, that is, if the licensee fails to place a copyright notice on copies that are distributed to the public and the work has not been registered (see Chapter 15).]

Generally, it is not necessary for the licensor and licensee to sign a license before a notary public or other official, or to have their signatures acknowledged. The agreement is usually valid and binding when it is signed. However, if a license is signed before a notary and the signatures of the licensor and licensee are acknowledged, an exclusive license will be accepted by a court of law and the U.S. Copyright Office as prima facie evidence of the execution of the license (see Chapter 15).

CHAPTER SUMMARY

- In most cases, to avoid liability for copyright infringement, a person who desires to reproduce or to publicly perform a work, or to exercise one of the other exclusive rights in it, must first obtain permission to do so.
- Permission to exercise rights is often granted by means of an agreement commonly referred to as a "copyright license."
- The person who grants permission may be referred to as the "licensor," the person who obtains permission may be referred to as the "licensee," and the rights covered by this kind of agreement are known as "licensed rights."
- A copyright license may be exclusive or nonexclusive; an exclusive license is considered to be a transfer of rights under the 1976 Act.
- All of the provisions of a license should be written to avoid later misunderstandings regarding the nature and extent of permission granted.

- Exclusive licenses should be recorded with the U.S. Copyright Office to take advantage of the constructive notice provisions of the 1976 Act, to avoid conflicting transfers, and to enable the exclusive licensee to institute an action for infringement of the licensed rights.
- Ordinarily, the name of the owner of a licensed right, not the name of the licensee, should appear in the copyright notice featured on copies or phonorecords produced by the licensee.

19

Compulsory Copyright Licenses

If the owner of rights and the person seeking permission to exercise them are unable to reach an agreement on the terms and conditions for a license, it may not be possible for that person to exercise those rights without incurring liability for copyright infringement. As a general rule, the owner of rights is the only one who has the authority to exercise them and, by virtue thereof, is in a position to prevent anyone else from exercising them, unless an exception to the rule exists.

All the limitations on an owner's rights are exceptions to this general rule. Hence, if one of them is applicable, such as fair use, an owner cannot prevent a person qualifying under it from exercising a right.

In addition to the limitations on an owner's rights, "compulsory" licenses are exceptions to this general rule. Compulsory licenses are expressly provided for in the 1976 Act and permit the exercise of rights belonging to an owner of a work without liability for infringement and without need to obtain permission to do so from the owner. However, they are applicable only to works published by or under the authority of the owner. Unpublished works are not subject to compulsory licensing.

A compulsory license is obtained by satisfying all applicable statutory requirements for it set forth in the 1976 Act. In effect, a compulsory license is one forced upon the copyright owner, without any voice on the owner's part in deciding who may exercise the rights or the terms and conditions under which they may be exercised. Anyone who qualifies for such a license can obtain one regardless of an owner's wishes. The terms are specified in the Act and are not subject to negotiation nor can they be varied.

Noninvolvement of the copyright owner in the compulsory licensing process does not prevent the owner from enforcing his or her rights against a compulsory licensee. A copyright owner is entitled to institute an infringement suit against a licensee who fails to comply with the terms of the compulsory license.

There are four separate compulsory licenses which permit:

Making and distributing phonorecords embodying musical works

Publicly performing music on jukeboxes

Making secondary transmissions by cable systems

Publicly performing works by noncommercial public broadcasters

With one exception, each of these compulsory licenses is obtained by dealing with the U.S. Copyright Office rather than the copyright owner. The compulsory license for making and distributing phonorecords provides for direct contact between a licensee and the owner of the musical work licensed, if that person can be located. If the owner cannot be located all dealings are with the U.S. Copyright Office.

BACKGROUND OF COMPULSORY LICENSING

Compulsory licensing in federal copyright law first arose when the 1909 Act was enacted. It was a response to the concerns of many player-piano manufacturers in the early 1900s who were fearful that proposed legislation covering recording and mechanical reproduction rights in musical compositions would give a monopoly on the pianola roll business to one company, namely the Aeolian Co. At that time, recording and mechanical reproduction rights were being considered by Congress for inclusion in pending legislation for a new federal copyright act.

Prior to enactment of the 1909 Act, the Aeolian Co. had received long-term license agreements from more than 80 leading music publishers in the United States covering all of the musical compositions in their catalogs. As a result, that company was the only one that possessed the right to reproduce almost all of the then popular music on pianola rolls for player pianos. The performance of musical compositions by this means was very significant at that time.

The exclusive right to record and mechanically reproduce musical compositions was included in the 1909 Act, but Congress made it subject to a compulsory license, to the delight of a large number of competitors of the Aeolian Co. However, a compulsory license could not be obtained by anyone until the owner of a musical work reproduced it in the form of "the parts of instruments serving to reproduce mechanically the musical work." Or, until the owner knowingly acquiesced in the reproduction of the musical work in such form by others.

The language quoted above is directly from the 1909 Act and referred to pianola rolls and phonograph records that were first being introduced to the public at the time the 1909 Act became effective. In the early 1900s, music was mechanically reproduced from pianola rolls and phonograph records as contrasted with electrical reproduction (a method now used to reproduce music embodied in records and tapes). Accordingly, this means of reproducing music was the basis for the phrase "mechanical license." It continues to be used today to denote licenses authorizing the reproduction of musical works in phonograph records and tapes.

The 1909 Act's compulsory license for making phonorecords prescribed a procedure for obtaining it. Among other things, the Act imposed an obligation on the compulsory licensee to pay a flat royalty on each phonorecord produced. That royalty was and continues to be called a "mechanical license fee." The royalty amount was set by the 1909 Act.

The compulsory license for coin-operated phonorecord players was adopted to provide for the payment of royalties to owners of nondramatic musical works for the performance of music on jukeboxes. There was no basis to require the operators of jukeboxes to make such payments under the 1909 Act because of an express exemption stating:

> The reproduction or rendition of musical compositions on coin-operated machines shall not be deemed a public performance for profit unless a fee is charged for admission to the place where such reproduction or rendition occurs.

At the time the 1976 Act was being considered by Congress, the general feeling was that whatever the justification for the 1909 Act's exemption, it no longer existed and copyright owners should not be deprived of revenues to which they are entitled for the commercial use of music.

The compulsory license for cable system transmissions was adopted to make it possible for cable systems to broadcast copyrighted works without contacting every owner of rights and to provide for the payment of royalties to such owners. A procedure for obtaining the license is provided for as well as for the payment of royalties to the U.S. Copyright Office for distribution to such owners.

The compulsory license for noncommercial educational broadcasting was adopted because Congress determined that public broadcasting warranted special treatment with regard to the use of nondramatic literary and musical works, as well as pictorial, graphic, and sculptural works, in noncommercial transmissions. It permits the use of such works in return for the payment of reasonable royalties directly to the owners of rights without an administratively cumbersome and costly clearance procedure.

COMPULSORY LICENSE FOR MAKING AND DISTRIBUTING PHONORECORDS EMBODYING NONDRAMATIC MUSICAL WORKS

This compulsory license is available for a particular nondramatic musical work after it has been embodied in phonorecords by or under the authority of the owner of it, and they have been distributed to the public in the United States under the owner's authority. Consequently, it will not be available if a musical work is embodied in phonorecords by the owner but they are not publicly distributed or are not publicly distributed in this country.

Reproduction of a musical work in any material object other than a phonorecord is not sufficient for purposes of making this license available for it. Consequently, reproduction of a musical work in such media as sheet music, videocassettes, videodisks, or as part of the sound track of a motion picture will not satisfy the statutory conditions for the availability of this license regardless of the media's public distribution.

Under a compulsory license, the owner of a musical work does not have the power to decide who can make phonorecords embodying it. However, the owner does have the power to decide if and when a compulsory license becomes available for that work. For example, if an owner elects not to reproduce a musical work in phonorecords or to authorize its reproduction, it will not be subject to a compulsory license. Or, if the work is reproduced in phonorecords but the owner does not distribute or authorize the distribution of them to the public in the United States, it will not be subject to a compulsory license.

The compulsory license provisions do not set forth a minimum number of phonorecords that must be distributed under the authority of the owner. Furthermore, they do not indicate what constitutes a "public" distribution for purposes of making the license available. Accordingly, it would appear that this license will be available for a particular musical work even though only a few phonorecords are publicly distributed whether such distribution is by sale, gift, or otherwise.

A person desiring to rely on this compulsory license is entitled to reproduce only nondramatic musical works, but only in the form of phonorecords, and to distribute the phonorecords to the public for sale, rental, lease, or lending (or by any acts or practices in the nature of rental, lease, or lending).

This compulsory license cannot be relied on to reproduce any other kind of musical work in a phonorecord or to reproduce a nondramatic musical work in material objects other than phonorecords. Therefore, it does not permit the reproduction of a popular song as the theme song on the sound track of a motion picture or as background music for a recorded television commercial. Permission to reproduce a musical work for such uses must be obtained directly from the copyright owner.

Although this compulsory license becomes available at the time a musical work is reproduced in phonorecords by the owner and they are publicly distributed in the United States, it may not be relied upon by anyone who desires to do so. This license does not permit the reproduction of a musical work unless a licensee's primary purpose in making the phonorecords under it is to distribute them to the public for private use.

However, if this is the licensee's primary purpose, the licensee can also distribute phonorecords made under this license to commercial users such as background music services, broadcasters, jukebox operators, and others. That distribution for private use is ultimately surpassed by distribution for commercial use does not appear to be a factor that would invalidate the license.

The 1976 Act does not indicate whether distribution by a licensee must be limited to the public in the United States or whether such distribution can be to the public anywhere in the world. However, since the jurisdiction of the Act covers only this country, the geographic coverage of the compulsory license is limited to the United States and a licensee would do well not to rely on it for distribution in other countries. Under the copyright laws of other countries, the owner of a musical work may not be compelled to allow the reproduction and distribution of phonorecords without the owner's express permission.

Permissible Ways to Reproduce

A musical work can be reproduced in phonorecords under this license using a number of different methods. One approach is to rerecord it, creating original sounds through the services of performers who may use "charts" of the musical work to perform from, which have been created specifically for purpose of recording it, or who can perform it simply by listening to an earlier recording of it by others.

In addition, a licensee may copy a sound recording of the work, which has been previously created under the authority of the owner of the work. However, this method of reproducing the work is not permissible unless:

1. The sound recording was lawfully made
2. The making of the phonorecords by the licensee is authorized by the owner of rights in the sound recording
3. If the sound recording was embodied in a phonorecord before February 15, 1972, the licensee can duplicate it if the licensee obtains permission from any person who created the sound recording and:
   a. Had the right to do so under an express license from the owner of the musical work, or
   b. Had the right to do so under a valid compulsory license for use of the musical work in a sound recording

Sound recordings were not subject to federal copyright protection prior to February 15, 1972. Accordingly, as long as the musical work that is reproduced by the sounds is not subject to copyright protection, a sound recording featuring that work and created before that date can be duplicated without constituting copyright infringement under federal law.

For example, the duplication of a sound recording, produced in 1960, of a musical work created by Beethoven, would not constitute copyright infringement under federal law because sound recordings were not protected under federal law at that time and Beethoven's works were not subject to copyright protection in 1972.

On the other hand, if the musical work in a sound recording produced before February 15, 1972 is protected by copyright, permission to duplicate the sound recording is required.

Keeping the two methods of reproducing a musical work in mind, a licensee can retain the services of an arranger, musicians, vocalists, and a recording engineer to record anew the song "Diana" written by Paul Anka. Or, the licensee can obtain permission to duplicate the master sound recording of "Diana" from the record company that first released this song under Paul Anka's authority.

New Arrangements Are Permitted

A compulsory licensee does not need to obtain permission from anyone to make an arrangement of the musical work to the extent an arrangement is necessary for the licensee to conform it to the style or manner of interpretation of the performance involved in recording the work. A licensee can make an arrangement of the work as long as the arrangement does not change the basic melody or fundamental character of it.

If a licensee desires to secure rights to the arrangement as a derivative work, the express consent of the owner of the musical work is required. In the event consent is given, the licensee will be the owner of all rights in the arrangement as a separate work and may deal with it the same as the owner of rights in any other work. On the other hand, if consent is not obtained, the licensee has no rights to the arrangement other than to use it as it is embodied in the phonorecord made under the license.

Compulsory License Does not Preclude Negotiating a License

It is often preferable to obtain a negotiated license directly from the owner rather than a compulsory license because of the obligations imposed upon a licensee under a compulsory license and the sanctions that may be imposed for failing to fulfill them. A "mechanical" license granted directly by or on behalf of an owner may not be more favorable than a compulsory license, in terms of the royalty rate to be paid, but it is usually more favorable than a compulsory license from the standpoint of accounting, serving of notices, and other obligations. However, regardless of which license is sought the first thing a licensee must do is identify the owner of the work.

The owner of a work may be identified by searching the records of the U.S. Copyright Office or, in many instances, by obtaining this information from one of the performing rights organizations in this country (ASCAP, BMI, or SESAC), or by obtaining it from a licensing agent of the owner of the work, such as the Harry Fox Agency in New York.

If a licensee desires to obtain a negotiated license, the owner of the musical work should be contacted with the objective of reaching an agreement in this regard. In the event a compulsory license is sought, the licensee should attempt to contact the owner for purposes of serving a notice on the owner.

Procedure To Obtain this Compulsory License

To obtain this compulsory license, a licensee must follow the procedure for doing so set forth in the 1976 Act and the U.S. Copyright Office Regulations. A monthly statement of account must be submitted and royalties paid to the copyright owner. The royalty is prescribed by the Act and referred to as a "statutory royalty." It is subject to periodic adjustment by the Copyright Royalty Tribunal.

As of July 1, 1986, the royalty payable for each musical work embodied in each phonorecord made and distributed under this compulsory license is either 5.0 cents, or 0.95 cent per minute of playing time or a fraction thereof, whichever amount is larger. Thus, the royalty for a musical work with a playing time of less than 5.2 minutes is 5.0 for each phonorecord embodying it. If the playing time is longer, the royalty will be an amount equal to the number of minutes of playing time multiplied by 0.95 cent.

If a licensee distributes phonorecords to the public for rental, lease, or lending, the licensee must also pay a royalty for every rental, lease, or loan of each phonorecord. At this time that royalty is a proportion of the revenue received by the licensee from every such rental, lease, or loan equal to the proportion of the revenue received from distribution for sale.

COMPULSORY LICENSE FOR THE PUBLIC PERFORMANCE OF NONDRAMATIC MUSICAL WORKS ON COIN-OPERATED PHONORECORD PLAYERS (JUKEBOXES)

This compulsory license is limited to the right to perform a nondramatic musical work publicly, only if it has been embodied in a phonorecord, and then only if it is performed on a "coin-operated phonorecord player" that meets the 1976 Act definition for such a device. Coin-operated phonorecord players are commonly referred to as "jukeboxes," but not all of them meet the 1976 Act definition for the type that qualifies for this particular license.

Anyone who is an "operator" of such a coin-operated phonorecord player can obtain this license by filing an application for one with the U.S. Copyright Office and by complying with requirements prescribed by the 1976 Act as well as regulations promulgated by the U.S. Copyright Office. Unlike the obligations imposed on a licensee with respect to the compulsory license to make and distribute phonorecords, there is no need for the operator to identify or contact the owner of the musical works sought to be performed. Furthermore, the operator does not pay royalties to such person, although royalties are payable as a condition of obtaining the license from the U.S. Copyright Office.

As is the case with respect to a compulsory license to make and distribute phonorecords, the owner of the musical work has no voice in who may publicly perform the work on a "coin-operated phonorecord player." But if a coin-operated phonorecord player does not meet the 1976 Act definition, it is not eligible for this license and the owner of the musical work has the right to determine whether the operator of it may publicly perform the work.

A jukebox is a coin-operated phonorecord player only if it meets all of the following conditions, as set forth in the 1976 Act:

1. It is employed solely for the performance of nondramatic music works by means of phonorecords upon being activated by insertion of coins, currency, tokens, or other monetary units or their equivalent.

2. It is located in an establishment that makes no direct charge for admission.

3. It is accompanied by a list of the titles of all the musical works available for performance on it, which list is affixed to the phonorecord player or posted in the establishment in a prominent position where it can be readily examined by the public.

4. It affords a choice of works available for performance and permits the choice to be made by the patrons of the establishment in which it is located.

These conditions exclude coin-operated radio and television sets as well as videocassette players. Similarly, they exclude devices that would otherwise qualify but for the fact that they also play literary works embodied in phonorecords. In addition, they exclude a device that meets the technical requirements for such a player but is in a location that charges an admission fee. For example, a coin-operated phonorecord player located in a restaurant open to the public, but that requires patrons to pay a fee to join its dining club, is not eligible for this license.

Furthermore, if music is played continuously on a qualifying device, but without the ability of patrons of the establishment to make selections, this license is not available.

If the jukebox meets all of the foregoing conditions, the "operator" of it should obtain this compulsory license rather than the proprietor of the establishment where it is located, unless the proprietor of the establishment is also the "operator" of the jukebox.

An "operator" of a coin-operated phonorecord player is any person who, alone or jointly with others:

1. Owns a coin-operated phonorecord player

2. Has the power to make a coin-operated phonorecord player available for placement in an establishment for purposes of public performance

3. Has the power to exercise primary control over the selection of the musical works made available for public performance on a coin-operated phonorecord player

Anyone within these categories must obtain a compulsory license to avoid liability for infringement for the public performance of a musical work on a qualifying jukebox. The licensing procedure is not complex.

Procedure to Obtain This Compulsory License

The acquisition of this compulsory license ordinarily requires that the licensee do three things:

1. File an application on a form provided free upon request to the Licensing Division, U.S. Copyright Office, Library of Congress, Washington, D.C. 20557 (Form JB, a copy of which is found in Appendix C) which identifies each jukebox to be covered by the license

2. Pay a royalty fee to the U.S. Copyright Office for each jukebox identified on the application form

3. Affix a certificate, issued by the U.S. Copyright Office, to each licensed jukebox

COMPULSORY LICENSE FOR SECONDARY TRANSMISSIONS BY CABLE SYSTEMS

This compulsory license is limited to the right to perform or display a work publicly by means of transmitting a broadcast of the performance or display from one place to another by television or radio signals. Under the 1976 Act, broadcasting the performance or display of a work as well as transmitting such a broadcast are themselves considered to be performances or displays.

Unlike the compulsory licenses for phonorecords and coin-operated phonorecord players, there are no category restrictions as to the kind of works subject to this license. Works in all categories may be publicly performed or displayed.

This compulsory license is not available to everyone who transmits a broadcast of television or radio signals, and it does not cover every television or radio broadcast signal that is transmitted. The 1976 Act provides that it can be obtained:

1. Only by cable television systems who meet the 1976 Act definition of "cable system."

2. Only for the further transmitting ("secondary transmission") to the public of television or radio signals broadcast to the public by certain broadcasters ("primary transmissions").

3. Only if the carriage of the signals comprising the "secondary transmission" by the cable system is permissible under the rules, regulations, or authorizations of the Federal Communications Commission.

If a cable system is eligible for this compulsory license it can obtain one by filing a required notice with the U.S. Copyright Office and paying a prescribed royalty fee. It is not necessary to serve notices on the owners of works covered by the license or to otherwise contact or deal with them. Rights owners only become involved, with respect to this license, when it is time for the Copyright Royalty Tribunal to distribute royalty fees collected under the license.

To be eligible for this license, a "cable system" must meet the following 1976 Act definition in all respects. It must be:

A facility,

   — located in any State, Territory, Trust Territory, or Possession,

   — that in whole or in part receives signals transmitted or programs broadcast by one or more television broadcast stations licensed by the Federal Communications Commission, and

   — makes secondary transmissions of such signals or programs by wires, cables, or other communications channels

   — to subscribing members of the public who pay for such service.

A closed circuit cable or wire system that *originates* programs, rather than transmits the television broadcast signals of others, does not meet this definition. Similarly, if a cable system does not have subscribing members who pay a fee for the right to receive the service it will not meet this definition.

In the event a cable system is not eligible for this license it must obtain permission to transmit a work from the owner of rights in it. A cable system must also do this for all programs it originates that embody the works of others.

This license permits an eligible cable system to transmit only performances or displays that satisfy the following two conditions:

1. The performance or display must be embodied in a signal the cable system is permitted to carry under the rules, regulations, or authorizations of the Federal Communications Commission
2. The signal must be part of a "primary transmission"

The 1976 Act defines a "primary transmission" as:

A transmission made to the public by the transmitting facility whose signals are being received and further transmitted by the secondary transmission service, regardless of where or when the performance or display was first transmitted.

Thus, a primary transmission consists of television and radio signals that are being picked up and further transmitted by a cable system. For example, a primary transmission consists of the broadcast signals of an over-the-air network television program, or the over-the-air signals of a locally originated television station broadcast.

The phrase "secondary transmission" refers to the further transmitting of a primary transmission. Secondary transmissions relay television and radio signals originated by a station other than the cable system. The 1976 Act defines a secondary transmission as:

> The further transmitting of a primary transmission simultaneously with the primary transmission, or nonsimultaneously with the primary transmission if by a "cable system" not located in whole or in part within the boundary of the forty-eight contiguous States, Hawaii, or Puerto Rico; Provided, however, That a nonsimultaneous further transmission by a cable system located in Hawaii of a primary transmission shall be deemed to be a secondary transmission if the carriage of the television broadcast signal comprising such further transmission is permissible under the rules, regulations, or authorizations of the Federal Communications Commission.

How To Obtain This Compulsory License

The 1976 Act conditions the acquisition of this compulsory license on the requirement that a cable system do the following three things:

1. An "Initital Notice of Identity and Signal Carriage Complement" must be filed with the Copyright Office no later than one month prior to the date of commencement of operations
2. A "Statement of Account" must be filed with the Copyright Office every six months
3. A royalty fee payment, for the period covered by each "Statement of Account," must be deposited with the U.S. Copyright Office

The amount of each royalty fee payment is computed on the basis of a specified percentage of a cable system's gross receipts. A fee, however minimal, must be paid regardless of whether a cable system makes a profit from its operations.

The royalty fee is paid to the U.S. Copyright Office every six months at the time the Statement of Account is due. The U.S. Copyright Office first deducts the reasonable costs incurred in collecting the fees and then deposits the balance in the U.S. Treasury. Thereafter, the fees are distributed by the Copyright Royalty Tribunal, on an annual basis, to owners of works who are entitled to share in them. In addition to acting as a royalty distribution agency, the Copyright Royalty Tribunal has the authority to review royalty rates periodically and make adjustments in them.

Persons who fall within any of the following groups are entitled to share in the royalty fees collected by the U.S. Copyright Office under this compulsory license:

1. Every owner of a work included in a secondary transmission of a non-network television program by a cable system if the program was transmitted in whole or in part beyond the local service area of the primary transmitter

2. Every owner of a work included in a secondary transmission that consisted of substituted programming

3. Every owner of a work included in nonnetwork programming consisting exclusively of aural signals carried by a cable system if the program was transmitted in whole or in part beyond the local service area of the primary transmitter.

Ownership of a work falling within any one of these groups is a prerequisite to sharing in the royalty fees paid by cable systems, but it does not necessarily mean that an owner will actually share in them. Every person entitled to share in these fees must file a claim with the Copyright Royalty Tribunal as a condition of being eligible to participate in the royalty distribution process. The claim should be filed in accordance with the requirements established by the Tribunal and must be done in July of each year.

Owners of works may agree among themselves as to the proportionate division of such royalties among them. They may lump their claims together and file them jointly as a single claim, or they may designate a common agent to receive payment on their behalf. If they agree among themselves regarding the division of royalties, their activities in doing so are immune from violation of the antitrust laws by virtue of language in the 1976 Act to this effect.

After the first day of August of each year, the Copyright Royalty Tribunal must determine whether any controversy exists regarding the distribution of the royalties. If there is none, they will be distributed. Otherwise, the Tribunal will conduct a proceeding to determine the appropriate distribution of them.

COMPULSORY LICENSE FOR NONCOMMERCIAL EDUCATIONAL BROADCASTING

This compulsory license was discussed to a certain extent in Chapter 8 as a limitation on the rights of an owner of a work. It is limited to the activities of public broadcasting entities (noncommercial educational broadcasters) with respect to published nondramatic musical works and published pictorial, graphic, and sculptural works. The performance or display of such works is permitted, but only by means of transmission programs.

The performance of nondramatic musical works in the nature of concerts can be broadcast under this license. In addition, the performance of nondramatic musical works can be broadcast as background or theme music in a transmission program.

Pictorial, graphic, and sculptural works may be displayed as featured displays (a full-screen display appearing on the screen for more than three seconds), or as background or montage displays (any display less than full-screen or substantially full-screen for three seconds or less). In addition, they may be displayed in the nature of thematic use (utilization of a work of one or more artists where the works constitute the central theme of the program or convey a story line).

This license does not permit the transmission of a performance of a dramatic work, choreography, a literary work, a motion picture, or an audiovisual work. Accordingly, the transmission of plays, operas, ballet and other stage presentations, motion pictures, television programs, documentary films, and audiovisual works cannot be done without obtaining permission to do so from the owners of such works. Similarly, this license does not permit the transmission of a performance of a literary work, such as the recital of a poem, short story, or portions of books, or the transmission of unpublished nondramatic literary, pictorial, graphic, or scupltural works.

This compulsory license is not available to everyone who makes transmissions or to everyone who reproduces such works in producing transmission programs. It can be obtained only by a "public broadcasting entity," by a governmental body, or a nonprofit institution.

The right to reproduce works subject to this license is permitted under it as long as such reproduction is in connection with the production and as part of a transmission program. This license also permits a licensee to distribute copies or phonorecords of such programs.

How To Obtain This Compulsory License

The procedure involved in obtaining this compulsory license differs significantly from the procedures followed to obtain the phonorecord, jukebox, and cable television system compulsory licenses. Here, there is no requirement to submit notices to the owners of works or with the Copyright Office.

A public broadcasting entity can obtain this license simply by:

1. Paying royalty fees directly to owners of works, or to their authorized representatives, at designated times of the year in accordance with a prescribed schedule of rates set by the Copyright Royalty Tribunal.

2. Maintaining records of use of works covered by this compulsory license, such as music use reports and music cue sheets or summaries of them for nondramatic musical works, and lists containing pictorial, graphic, and sculptural works displayed on programs.

3. Permitting owners of works, covered by this compulsory license, a reasonable opportunity to examine such records upon their request and, in certain instances, furnishing copies of such records to owners of the works and also to the Copyright Royalty Tribunal.

4. A public broadcasting entity that supplies a reproduction of a transmission program (made under this compulsory license) to a governmental body or nonprofit institution must satisfy one further condition: it must include a warning notice with each reproduced copy stating that the reproduction may be used for a period of no more than seven days from the date of the transmission and must be destroyed by the user before or at the end of such period, and that a failure to fully comply with these requirements will constitute copyright infringement by such governmental body or nonprofit institution.

COPYRIGHT ROYALTY TRIBUNAL

The Copyright Royalty Tribunal was created under the 1976 Act as an independent governmental agency in the legislative branch, separate and apart from the U.S. Copyright Office. It consists of five commissioners appointed by the president with the advice and consent of the Senate for a term of seven years each.

The Tribunal was established for the purpose of periodically reviewing and adjusting, when appropriate, the statutory royalty rates for the use of works covered by the four compulsory licenses under the 1976 Act. In determining the reasonableness of such rates the Tribunal is to consider, among other factors, the economic impact on owners of works as well as upon users of them.

Another function of the Tribunal is to distribute royalty fees received by the U.S. Copyright Office paid under compulsory licenses covering the performance of music on jukeboxes and secondary transmissions made by cable television systems. However, if the Tribunal determines that a controversy exists with respect to the distribution of such fees, it must conduct a preceeding to determine who is entitled to receive them and in what amounts.

Final decisions of the Tribunal regarding adjustments of royalty rates and distribution of royalties may be appealed to the U.S. Court of Appeals. This must be done within 30 days after publication of such a final decision in the *Federal Register*.

CHAPTER SUMMARY

- The 1976 Act provides for the acquisition of permission to exercise the exclusive rights in a work by forcing a license upon the owner in a limited number of situations; this type of license is referred to as a "compulsory" license.
- There are four separate compulsory licenses provided for by the 1976 Act, namely, a compulsory license for (1) making and distributing phonorecords embodying musical works, (2) publicly performing music on jukeboxes, (3) making "secondary transmissions" by cable systems, and (4) publicly performing works by noncommercial broadcasting.
- Each compulsory license may be obtained by satisfying all of the applicable requirements for it set forth in the 1976 Act.
- The terms and conditions of compulsory licenses are not negotiable and, in most instances, license fees payable under them are collected by the U.S. Copyright Office and distributed to the owners of rights licensed through the services of the Copyright Royalty Tribunal, an independent agency in the legislative branch of the federal government.
- The Copyright Royalty Tribunal has the authority to set royalty rates and to distribute royalties payable by cable systems.

20

What Constitutes Copyright Infringement?

Copyright infringement occurs frequently without most people being aware of it. For example, infringement is likely to occur each time a page from a textbook, newspaper, magazine, newsletter, or trade journal is photocopied, whether for business or personal use. Or it may occur when a computer software program, phonograph record, or video game is duplicated, or when music is played by a group in a nightclub or a videotaped motion picture is played in a department store.

If permission to copy or exercise one of the other exclusive rights of an owner is not obtained, and neither a compulsory license nor a limitation on an owner's right applies, there is a technical infringement of an owner's rights.

WHO IS LIABLE FOR INFRINGEMENT?

Everyone Is a Potential Infringer

Anyone who copies a protected work owned by someone else or exercises an exclusive right with respect to it without authorization is liable for infringement. In addition, anyone who imports copies or phonorecords into the United States without authority to do so may be an infringer.

Intent Is not a Factor

Lack of intent to infringe or ignorance of the law is not relevant in determining whether there has been an infringement. Intent is a factor considered only in connection with assessing the extent of the infringer's liability.

Anyone who violates an owner's rights is subject to an injunction. However, the liability of the person who did not intend to infringe, in terms of the other remedies available to the owner, ordinarily will not be as great as those that may be imposed on someone who intentionally infringes.

Both types of infringers may be ordered to pay to the owner all profits that are attributable to the infringement. In addition, both may be ordered to pay the owner's actual damages or, instead, statutory damages in an amount decided by the court. The amount of statutory damages assessed against the intentional infringer may be greater and criminal penalties may be applicable to that infringer.

Citing the Source of Material or Giving Credit

The unauthorized copying and/or public performance of a work belonging to someone else, whether credited or not, constitutes infringement. If giving credit to the owner of rights to a work were treated as sufficient to justify copying or public performance, it is likely most protected material would be routinely reproduced and/or publicly performed by anyone willing to acknowledge the source of it. The net effect would be to circumvent the owner's exclusive rights effectively and completely not only to control what happens to his or her work but also to profit from it.

Ownership of Copy or Phonorecord

As discussed in Chapter 15, the ownership of rights in a work is distinct from ownership of a particular copy or phonorecord. Consequently, in the absence of a transfer of rights, a person who acquires ownership of a particular copy or phonorecord does not obtain the right to reproduce, vary, publicly perform, or publicly display it. Accordingly, the unauthorized exercise of a right with respect to a particular copy or phonorecord will constitute copyright infringement even though the person who exercises the right is the owner of the copy or phonorecord.

For example, a musician who buys a piece of sheet music for a copyrighted musical work is not entitled to perform the work publicly, solely by virtue of owning the sheet music. Similarly, a person who rents or purchases a videotape of the motion picture *Star Wars* is not entitled to play it on a video player in a student lounge at a university, in a nightclub, or in a department store. A client of an advertising agency is not entitled to reproduce a copyrighted photograph created by an outside supplier of the agency if there was no transfer or license of the reproduction right to the agency or client.

However, as a general rule, a person who owns a lawfully made copy or phonorecord can sell it, give it away, or rent it without liability to the rights owner, notwithstanding the exclusive right to distribute publicly. An exception to this rule exists with regard to the owner of a lawfully made phonorecord embodying a musical work. That person is not permitted to rent, lease, or loan it for purposes of direct or indirect commercial advantage.

ABSENCE OF PROFIT MOTIVE, MAKING A SMALL NUMBER OF COPIES, OR COPYING SMALL PORTIONS

In the absence of authorization to do so, the making of one copy or a small number of copies of a work, or copying only a small portion of it, whether for profit or for private use constitutes an infringement. Similarly, the public performance of a work, whether all or part of it and whether for profit or not, constitutes infringement.

The number of copies, amount copied, and nature of a public performance are considered only in connection with assessing the extent of an infringer's liability, in the same way an infringer's intent is treated with regard to granting remedies to the owner of rights.

Similarly, that copies or public performances were made without any profit motive, or at a financial loss, does not bear on whether an infringement occurred. Again, such circumstances would be considered only in connection with determining the extent of an infringer's liability.

PERMITTING OR CAUSING SOMEONE ELSE TO INFRINGE

Liability for an infringing act may be imposed on someone other than the person who actually commits it. Generally, this is possible although not always the case where one person, without the requisite authority to do so, empowers or sanctions another person to exercise a right belonging to someone else, or assists in such an act. The owner of rights possesses the exclusive right to authorize others to exercise them.

While liability is possible in such situations, the person who enables, approves of, or aids another person's infringing act will not be held accountable for it in the absence of some additional elements. Ordinarily, liability is conditioned on the existence of one or more of the following facts. The person who empowered or approved the infringement must:

— Have the right and ability to supervise the activities of the person who actually commits the infringing act
— Be in a position to control the use of a protected work
— Have a financial interest in the infringing activities
— Have knowledge that the infringing act constitutes as infringement

Notwithstanding the existence of the above facts, in certain situations the 1976 Act expressly grants immunity from liability to persons who fall within the following specified groups:

1. A library or archives or its employees with respect to the unsupervised use of reproducing equipment located on its premises
2. A governmental body or nonprofit agricultural or horticultural organization, in the course of an annual agricultural or horticultural fair or exhibition conducted by such body or organization where it performs a nondramatic musical work
3. A television or radio signal carrier who has no direct or indirect control over the content or selection of a primary transmission it carries or over the particular recipients of the secondary transmission, and whose activities with respect to the secondary transmission consist solely of providing wires, cables, or other communications channels for the use of others
4. The proprietor of an establishment in which a nondramatic musical work is performed on a coin-operated phonorecord player (jukebox) unless the proprietor (a) is the owner of it, or (b) has the power to exercise primary control over the selection of music on it, or (c) has the power to make it available for placement in the establishment, or (d) the proprietor refuses or fails to make full disclosure of the identity of the owner of it

Employers and Owners of Places of Entertainment

An employer will be liable for the infringing act of an employee performed within the scope of employment. This is based on the general legal principle that an employer has the right to supervise and control the activities of employees and, as a consequence, is responsible for their wrongful acts.

In some cases, liability is imposed on the employer even though the infringing act was not requested by the employer or was done in spite of the employer's instructions not to do so. For example, an advertising agency would be liable for the unauthorized reproduction, by an agency employee, of protected artwork owned by a third party in promotional material for an agency client. Liability would be imposed regardless that the agency was unaware of the employee's infringement or expressly instructed the employee not to copy another party's material.

An employee, on the other hand, usually will not be held accountable for infringement where the employer commanded the employee to commit an infringing act. However, the employer would be liable.

The legal principle noted previously is also applicable to situations where the services of independent contractors are used. If the person contracting for such services has the right to supervise them and can gain financially from the performance of them, he or she may be liable for any infringing acts arising from the performance. For instance, the owner of a nightclub will be held accountable for the infringing acts of independent contractor musicians or other entertainers who perform there. Liability is not avoided on the basis that such independent contractors are not paid for their services or are given the unfettered right to select material they perform. Furthermore, liability will be imposed even where performers are instructed not to infringe the rights of others.

Officers of Corporations and Principals of Businesses

The president and other officers of a corporation may be individually and personally liable for infringing acts committed by the corporation in a number of situations. Acting on behalf of the corporation does not avoid individual liability if:

1. The officer is the sole employee of the corporation.
2. The officer directly causes the corporation to engage in the infringing activity and actually participates in such activity.
3. The officer directly benefits from the infringing activity by reason of owning a substantial number of shares in the corporation.

The principals of a business are likewise accountable for infringing activities of the business and by third parties when the principals participate in the infringement, directly benefit from it, or arrange for it.

Persons Who Aid Another's Infringing Act

For the same general reasons just noted, persons who know that a particular act constitutes an infringement, but nonetheless cause someone else to commit it, may be liable for infringement even though they do not actually perform the infringing act. Persons who aid another party in committing an infringement are equally liable, whether aware of the infringement or not.

For example, a stock photo company who requests a film processing laboratory to reproduce a protected image owned by a photographer is liable for the unauthorized copying regardless of the fact that the company did not make the copies. At the same time, the laboratory is liable for aiding in the infringement.

WHAT MUST BE SHOWN TO PROVE INFRINGEMENT

Ownership of Original Work and Unauthorized Exercise of Rights

To be successful in an infringement action, it is incumbent upon the owner of an infringed right to establish ownership of the right and originality of the work. This is rather easily done by using direct evidence.

Ordinarily, the certificate of registration can be relied on to show originality and ownership, since the 1976 Act provides that it shall constitute prima facie evidence of the validity of the facts stated in it and the originality of the registered work. A recorded ownership transfer document can be used to show ownership in cases where the person bringing the action acquired rights from someone else.

It is also incumbent on the owner of an infringed right to clearly establish, by a preponderance of the evidence, that there has been an unauthorized exercise of it. Depending on the particular right and work in question, this is accomplished by presenting evidence that shows that the work has been copied, varied, publicly performed, or publicly displayed, or that copies or phonorecords of it have been distributed to the public.

If direct evidence of an infringing act (for example, the testimony of witnesses to an unauthorized public performance) is available, it is usually the best type to rely upon. However, where direct evidence cannot be produced, indirect evidence can be used to prove infringement.

Typically, indirect evidence it used in actions for infringement claiming that a work has been copied or varied. For example, indirect evidence is used where there is a claim that one literary work has been copied from another. In such cases infringement is proven by showing that there was a reasonable opportunity for the infringer to copy the work by means of having access to it, and that there is substantial similarity between the work and the material claimed to be infringing.

Presenting evidence that an opportunity to copy existed, without showing substantial similarity, will not support a claim of infringement. Nor will a showing of substantial similarity, in the absence of some evidence or an inference of the opportunity to copy, support an infringement claim. On the other hand, that there may be evidence supporting both does not necessarily mean that there has been infringement. Proof of independent creation or copying from another source can be introduced to defeat a claim of infringement.

Opportunity To Copy

Evidence of an infringer's opportunity to copy a work is necessary to show that it was possible for one work to be the model, in whole or in part, for another. In some instances, the need to show an opportunity to copy may not be as great as in others. Such cases include those when the similarity between two works (which do not contain commonplace subject matter) is so striking and substantial that it would be unlikely for one to have been independently created and without any reference to the other, or to have been copied from a common source.

Two pieces of abstract art, for instance, closely resembling each other in specific and significant ways might suggest that one artist had the opportunity to copy from the other. Likewise, the opportunity to copy may be inferred when one literary work features the same error as found in another without reasonable explanation.

Generally, the opportunity to copy can be established by presenting evidence that copies of a work were distributed for sale or exhibited to the public, or were directly given to the infringer or to someone having contact with the infringer. Direct testimony that an infringer actually viewed or inspected an infringed work will clearly establish an opportunity to copy.

Substantial Similarity

A determination as to whether there is "substantial similarity" between two works sufficient to find infringement often involves more than a mere comparison of the material common to each work. Quantity is a factor to be considered, but a finding of "substantial similarity" is not necessarily based solely upon or limited to the amount of common material. In addition to quantity, equal consideration must be given to the nature of the common material as well the importance of that material to each work.

Similarity in Terms of Copying Large Amounts

In instances where one work literally reproduces a major or significant portion of another, "substantial similarity" exists and will support a claim of infringement. Paraphrasing will not avoid a finding of substantial similarity.

On the other hand, it is possible that the overall impression created by two separate works, each produced by a different person, may be substantially similar without one infringing the other. This is possible where the common material consists of:

1. *Facts*. There is no copyright protection for facts, per se, since they are in the public domain (see Chapter 4). However, there is protection for the manner in which they are expressed and if the manner of expression is copied, there will be infringement. Thus, if one person's expression of facts is copied verbatim by another, liability for infringement is a possibility. For example, historical facts about the German dirigible "Hindenburg" are not eligible for copyright protection although the manner in which they are put together and expressed can be protected. But if one person's account of that incident is literally copied by another, there would be infringement.

2. *Scènes à faire*. There is no copyright protection for incidents, characters, or settings that are as a practical matter indispensable, or at least standard, in the treatment of a given topic. It is virtually impossible to write about a particular historical era or fictional theme without employing certain "stock" or standard literary devices. For example, there would be no protection for descriptions in a book on black slavery of attempted escapes, flights through the woods pursued by baying dogs, the sorrowful or happy singing of slaves, and the atrocity of the buying and selling of human beings.

3. *Cliché Language*. There is no copyright protection for cliché language, or metaphors, or for phrases and expressions conveying an idea that can only be, or is typically, expressed in a limited number of stereotyped fashions.

4. *Ideas*. There is no copyright protection for ideas, per se, although the specific manner in which an idea is expressed is eligible for protection as is the case with facts (see Chapter 4). For example, there can be no protection for the idea of creating buff-colored plastic statues of children in various typical poses, or for the idea of painting three women in a cubist motif, or for the idea of creating a video arcade maze-chase game. But, there can be protection for the manner in which an idea is expressed, as distinguished

from the idea itself, and if that manner of expression is copied infringement will occur; provided, however, when an idea and its expression are inseparable, copying the expression of it will not be an infringement since protecting the expression under such circumstances would confer a monopoly on the idea free of the conditions and limitations imposed by the patent law. That would be contrary to public policy.

Similarity in Copying Small Amounts

That only a minimal amount of material is taken from one work and copied in another does not necessarily mean there can be no finding of substantial similarity between the two works. Copying one sentence, one line, one paragraph from a literary work, or four notes of a song or three bars from a musical composition can result in such a finding.

When only a small amount is copied, a determination with respect to the existence of substantial similarity involves a consideration of whether that amount is substantial in reference to the total number of words, or notes, for instance, in the work copied. If the amount copied, though small, is found to be a relatively substantial portion of the copied work the prospects for a finding of infringement are greater.

Substantial similarity may also be found when the amount copied, though small, constitutes a critical or valuable part of the work from which it is taken. Thus, copying a 7-to-12-second portion of a 28-minute film might support a finding of substantial similarity and so might copying three important sentences from a one-page newspaper advertisement.

Generally, an attempt to mask substantial similarity between two works by combining copied material with significant amounts of noncopied material will not be successful. An attempt to dilute or minimize the role or import of the copied material by emphasizing differences between two works will not avoid a finding of substantial similarity.

Similarity in Terms of the Pattern of a Work

Although copyright protection does not preclude the use of an idea disclosed in a work, it does provide a basis to prevent copying the means of expressing the idea. When there is a literal copying of words or pictures, for instance, and the idea as well as its expression are not inseparable, a finding that substantial similarity exists is easily made. However, when there is non-literal copying of bits and pieces of a work which results in the creation of another work conveying the same overall impression, a finding of substantial similarity may be harder to reach.

In instances where there is similarity between two works (such as story lines in literary works), but no significant literal copying of one is found in the other, the question is: was the idea disclosed in one work copied in another, or was the expression of that idea copied? For example, if two stories are written about the most beautiful woman in the world and both present the story line using an identical sequence of events but with different wording, has there been a copying of the story idea or its expression?

In determining whether more has been taken than the idea disclosed by a work, an "abstractions test" may be used. It Enunciated in a 1931 federal court case (*Nichols v. Universal Pictures Co.*) and generally followed since, it reads:

> Upon any work . . . a great number of patterns of increasing generality will fit equally well, as more and more of the incident is left out. . . . (T)here is a point in this series of abstractions where they are no longer protected, since otherwise the playwright could prevent the use of his "ideas," to which, apart from their expression, his property is never extended. Nobody has ever been able to fix that boundary, and nobody ever can. . . .

A further refinement of this test was offered by a legal commentator in 1945:

> No doubt the line does lie somewhere between the author's idea and the precise form in which he wrote it down. . . . (P)rotection covers the "pattern" of the work . . . the sequence of events, and the development of the interplay of characters.

In effect, a finding of substantial similarity, where there is no verbatim copying of an idea, is not based on the taking of the general theme of the idea but on the taking of its manner of expression through similarities of treatment, details, scenes, events, and characterizations.

Procedure Used To Determine Substantial Similarity

An evaluation of two works, for purposes of determining whether substantial similarity exists, is made using the foregoing points as guidelines and from the perspective of an "ordinary observer."

Usually, if an ordinary observer (who is not set out to detect differences between two works) would be disposed to overlook them and regard the two works or portions in question the same, a claim of substantial similarity will be supported. The observer's reaction to the two works should be spontaneous and immediate without dissection of them. Consequently, a determination of substantial similarity is often made on a subjective basis.

CRIMINAL OFFENSES

Under certain circumstances violating an exclusive right associated with a work, misusing a copyright notice, or making false representations in an application for registration will constitute a criminal offense, as distinguished from a civil wrong. When this occurs, penalties may be assessed against the offender in the nature of fines and possible imprisonment.

Commercial Advantage or Private Financial Gain

Any person who willfully violates an exclusive right associated with a work for purposes of commercial advantage or private financial gain is subject to prosecution as a criminal infringer. In addition, such person may be liable for civil liabilities to the owner of the right violated.

Fraudulent Use or Removal of Copyright Notice

It is a criminal offense for any person, with fraudulent intent and knowing that the notice is false, to place a copyright notice or words of the same purport on a copy of or phonorecord embodying a work. Similarly, it is a criminal offense for a person, with fraudulent intent, to publicly distribute or import for public distribution any copy of or phonorecord embodying a work that features a copyright notice that such person knows to be false. Finally, it is a criminal offense for any person, with fraudulent intent, to remove or alter any copyright notice appearing on a protected work.

False Representation in Application for Registration

Any person who knowingly makes a false representation of a material fact in an application for registration would be a criminal offender. And so would any person who knowingly makes a false representation of a material fact in any written statement filed in connection with the application.

DEFENSES TO INFRINGEMENT

A number of defenses may be available in response to a claim of copyright infringement. For example, the statute of limitations may be applicable if an infringement action is not commenced within three years after the cause of action accrued or arose; the legal principle of *res judicata* may apply if the claims of infringement have been previously decided in an earlier court action involving the same parties and same issues; or, the legal principles of "laches" or "estoppel" may be applicable if the owner of rights has inexcusably delayed in bringing an infringement suit and this has been prejudicial to the infringer.

In addition to defenses of the type noted above, a high percentage of defenses to infringement claims arise under the "fair use" limitation set forth in the 1976 Act. If the unauthorized exercise of a right associated with a work can be treated as falling within the guidelines set forth under that limitation, it is likely that there will be no finding of infringement. Representative of "fair use" defenses are parody, teacher photocopying, incidental use of a work, off-the-air videotaping of television broadcasts for private use, as well as educational and nonprofit uses of works under certain circumstances.

CHAPTER SUMMARY

- Copyright infringement occurs when an exclusive right associated with a particular work is exercised by someone other than the owner, unless permission has been granted by or on behalf of the owner or a compulsory license is applicable or one of the limitations on the rights of an owner is applicable.

- Absence of intent to infringe or lack of a profit motive does not avoid infringement and neither does ignorance of the law; furthermore, citing the source of copied material or giving the owner of rights credit does not avoid infringement.

- Liability for infringement is not limited to persons who actually perform an infringing act; persons who permit or cause someone else to infringe may be liable.

- To be successful in an infringement action the copyright owner must clearly establish two things: ownership of the right and, infringement of it.

- To prove infringement, it must be shown that the infringer had access to the work, and that the work has been copied, varied, publicly performed, publicly displayed, or publicly distributed without authorization by the owner.

- Proving infringement requires a showing that the infringing work is substantially similar to the protected work.

21

How To Institute an Infringement Action

As is the case with most other types of litigation, certain requirements must be satisfied and actions must be taken in connection with the filing of a copyright infringement lawsuit. The person in whose name the action is instituted must be the owner of the right violated and proof of such ownership should be presented. The proper court should be selected and the lawsuit filed within specific time periods set by the 1976 Act.

WHO HAS A RIGHT TO INSTITUTE AN ACTION

Copyright Office Does not Enforce Rights

The right to institute a copyright infringment lawsuit can be exercised only by those persons designated in the 1976 Act. The U.S. Copyright Office is not one of them. It is not the responsibility of the U.S. Copyright Office to enforce an owner's rights under the Act. If an infringement of rights occurs and the owner is not aware of it or does not elect to take any action, the U.S. Copyright Office will not assert a claim for or on behalf of the owner.

The U.S. Copyright Office has no authority under the Act to initiate an infringement action and, ordinarily, will not become involved in one as a party to it. An exception occurs where an application for registration of a claim of rights, in proper form, has been refused and the owner of them files an infringement action. Upon being notified of the action, as required by the Act, the U.S. Copyright Office may become a party to it but only with respect to the issue of registrability of the claim of rights.

Legal or Beneficial Owner of a Right May Enforce

The Act provides that the legal or beneficial owner of an exclusive right is entitled to institute an infringement action. However, that person can enforce it only with respect to the particular right owned and only for an infringement of it committed while that person is the owner of it.

For example, if a literary work is reproduced by a third party (who does not have permission to do so) at any time during the period a hardcover book publisher owns the exclusive reproduction right to publish only books, that publisher is entitled to institute an infringement action. However, if the act of infringement occurs after the hardcover book publisher has transferred that right to a paperback book publisher, it is the paperback publisher, not the hardcover publisher, who is entitled to file a lawsuit.

Along the same lines, the hardcover publisher would not have a right to institute an infringement action if the literary work were reproduced in the form of a motion picture. This is so even if this were done during the time the publisher owned the exclusive reproduction right. The book publisher is entitled to bring an action only with respect to infringements involving reproduction of the literary work in the form of books. The owner of the right to reproduce it in the form of motion pictures would be the proper owner to file a lawsuit for an infringement of that right.

Who Is a Legal Owner?

To be considered a legal owner of a right, a person must be one of the following:

1. The initial owner of the right (i.e., the creator of a work or the creator's employer) who has not transferred ownership or granted an exclusive license of it to someone else.
2. An assignee of the right.
3. An exclusive licensee of the right.
4. A television broadcast station owning a right or license to transmit or perform a work within its local service, but only in cases where (a) the same version of that work is imported into its area by a cable system (a secondary transmission) *and* (b) the cable system's carriage of that

transmission is not permissible under the rules, regulations, or authorizations of the Federal Communications or the cable system has not obtained or complied with the compulsory licensing requirements for secondary transmissions, *or* (c) if the secondary transmission consists of an unauthorized Canadian or Mexican primary transmission, *or* (d) if the cable system willfully alters, through changes, deletions, or additions, the content of the particular program in which the work is embodied or any commercial advertising or station announcements transmitted by the primary transmitter during, or immediately before or after the secondary transmission.

5. The primary transmitter of a transmission whose signal has been altered by a cable system as noted in (4)(c).

A nonexclusive licensee is not deemed to be a legal owner of a right. Consequently, a nonexclusive licensee cannot institute an infringement action.

Who Is a Beneficial Owner?

A beneficial owner of a right is someone entitled to derive a profit, advantage, or benefit from that right. For example, an author is a beneficial owner of rights in a literary work if he or she has transferred ownership of rights in it to a book publisher in return for the payment of royalties earned from sales of books embodying the work.

Unlike the legal owner who may exercise the right and has the power to deal with it in many ways including granting permission to others to do the same, a beneficial owner has no authority to exercise the right. However, a beneficial owner is entitled to enjoy benefits arising from the exercise of a right as is the case with a legal owner of it. Accordingly, the Act gives a beneficial owner the authority to enforce the right independent of and without having to rely upon the legal owner to take action. If a book publisher does not institute an infringement action against an unauthorized reproducer of an author's book, the author, as a beneficial owner of rights, is entitled to institute such an action.

INFRINGED WORK MUST BE REGISTERED

Ownership of a right is necessary to have a valid claim for infringement. But the owner is not entitled to enforce that right in the courts if an application for registration of the work has not been filed in the U.S. Copyright Office.

A registration should be obtained prior to the institution of an infringement suit unless one of the following exceptions to this requirement is applicable:

1. *Registration Has Been Refused by the U.S. Copyright Office.* If a properly filed application for registration has been refused by the U.S. Copyright Office, the owner can nonetheless institute an infringement action, but notice of the action and a copy of the Complaint is served on the Register of Copyrights.

2. *Certain Works That Are Transmitted Live and Simultaneously Recorded.* The owner of rights to a work consisting of sounds, images, or both, may institute an infringement action before it is registered if the work is being recorded for the first time at the same time it is being transmitted. However, the owner must:

   a. Serve notice on the infringer, not less than 10 or more than 30 days before it is so recorded, identifying the work and the specific time and source of its first transmission and declaring an intention to secure copyright protection for the work.

   b. Register the work within three months after its first transmission.

In addition to being a prerequisite to the institution of an infringement action, registration of a work is a prerequisite to obtaining certain benefits for the owner of rights.

For example, if registration of a work is made before or within five years after the date of first publication of the work, the registration certificate will be accepted by a court as rebuttable evidence of the originality of the work. That is, the registration certificate will be treated as *prima facie* evidence that the work was not copied from another work, and the person enforcing the infringed right will not be required to prove that the work is original unless the infringer introduces evidence that it was copied from another work.

Registration of a work also entitles the person enforcing the infringed right to an award of statutory damages and attorney's fees. However, in most cases this is possible only if registration occurred before infringement.

ALL OWNERSHIP TRANSFER DOCUMENTS MUST BE RECORDED

Ownership of a right and registration of the work with which it is associated may not be enough to entitle the owner to file an infringement action. In some instances a third condition must be met before a suit can be instituted.

If the owner desiring to enforce the right is not the initial copyright owner (i.e., the creator of the work or the owner of it by virtue of a "work made for hire"), the document evidencing that person's ownership must first be recorded in the U.S. Copyright Office. Similarly, when an exclusive licensee desires to enforce the right licensed, a copy of the exclusive license must be recorded.

FEDERAL DISTRICT COURTS HAVE EXCLUSIVE JURISDICTION

It is inappropriate to institute an action for infringement of a right in any court other than a federal court. The 1976 Act is a federal law and, by virtue of the preemption provision in the Act and another federal law, namely Title 28, U.S. Code, Section 1338(a)), the federal district courts:

> Shall have original jurisdiction of any civil action arising under any Act of Congress relating to . . . copyrights. . . . Such jurisdiction shall be exclusive of the courts of the states in . . . and copyright cases.

Federal courts are the only courts that have the authority to determine whether an infringement has occurred, and only they can grant injunctions to prevent or restrain infringements, and grant other kinds of relief to the owner of an infringed right.

Although state courts do not have the requisite power to entertain actions arising under the 1976 Act (such as claims of infringement or questions requiring an interpretation of the Act), they do have the authority to decide disputes involving matters that relate to rights arising under the 1976 Act. For example, a lawsuit can be filed in a state court by the owner of a right claiming there has been a failure on the part of a licensee to pay royalties under a license agreement. Also, a lawsuit can be filed in a state court involving an interpretation of the contractual obligations of the parties to an agreement dealing with subject matter that falls within the area of copyright protection.

If an action is improperly filed in a state court, it can be removed to a federal court on the basis of Section 1338(a) alone. Ordinarily, a federal court has no jurisdiction over a matter unless there is diversity of citizenship of the parties and the amount in question has a value over $10,000.00. However, this is not the case with actions involving copyright law.

Exception to Federal District Court Jurisdiction

There is one exception to exclusive jurisdiction over infringement actions by the federal district courts. This is provided for by a federal law, Title 28, U.S. Code, Section 1498(b).

If the infringer is the U.S. government or a corporation owned or controlled by the United States or a contractor, subcontractor, or any person, firm, or corporation acting for the United States and with the authorization or consent of the United States, the action must be filed in the U.S. Court of Claims.

The aforementioned federal law does not apply to infringement actions when a state government or agency is the infringer. To determine whether an action can be maintained against a state government or agency, refer to the statutes of the state. If there is no immunity, the action would be instituted in the federal district court for that state.

How To Determine the Proper Federal Court

To determine which federal district court is the proper one for filing an infringement action, it is necessary to determine the state where the infringer or his agent resides or may be found. If an infringer is doing business in a particular state, that is the state where the infringer may be found.

The state of residence of the owner of the infringed right is not a factor in deciding where the action should be instituted. For example, if the owner of the right resides in New York but the infringer or his agent resides or may be found in Colorado, it would be appropriate to file the action in the federal district court for Colorado, not in a federal district court in New York.

ACTION MUST BE COMMENCED WITHIN A SPECIFIC TIME PERIOD

An action for infringement of a right can be filed at any time within three years from the date the infringement occurs. This time period is set by the 1976 Act and is referred to as the "statute of limitations."

If the owner of the infringed right commences an action in court after this time period expires and attempts to enforce it, the infringer is entitled to raise the statute of limitations as a defense. If this is done successfully, the infringement action will be dismissed by the court and the owner will not be able to obtain any relief, but only with respect to the particular infringer and only with regard to the specific infringement in question. If the same person infringes again at a later time or someone else infringes the same right, and the owner timely commences an infringement action, the statute of limitations will not be applicable and the right may be enforced.

GIVING NOTICE OF AN INFRINGEMENT ACTION

The owner or exclusive licensee of the right infringed may be required (by the court where the action is filed) to give written notice of the lawsuit to persons who are in the following categories:

1. Any person shown, by the records of the U.S. Copyright Office or otherwise, to have or claim an interest in the right infringed.
2. Any person whose interest in the right is likely to be affected by a decision in the case.

For example, if an infringement lawsuit has been filed by a book publisher claiming violation of the reproduction right by a third party, it is within the court's discretion to require the publisher to serve a notice of the suit on the author, as an interested party in the reproduction right.

On the other hand, where the third party raises a question as to the validity of the reproduction right, the court must require that the author be notified. In such an action the author's interest in that right may be threatened.

Once notified of the action, a creator may become a party to it, depending on his or her interest in getting involved or a court's determination that he or she must get involved when the validity of a right is called into question.

CHAPTER SUMMARY

- It is up to the owner of an infringed right to take action; no one else has the authority to do so, not even the U.S. Copyright Office.
- An infringed work must be registered in the U.S. Copyright Office and if the person filing the lawsuit is not the creator, the document transferring ownership to that person must be recorded in the U.S. Copyright Office.
- An infringement action must be filed in a U.S. district court within a prescribed time period; state courts do not have jurisdiction over copyright matters.

22

Remedies for Infringement

$\mathbf{T}$he 1976 Act provides a variety of remedies to the owner of a right that has been infringed. The particular remedies available in a given case depend on the facts of that case. Although it is impossible for an owner to obtain all remedies in any one case, it is possible that a combination of less than all of them may be granted, if the appropriate facts exist. In some instances if one remedy is obtained others cannot be awarded. Under a different set of facts, the award of one will not preclude the granting of others.

Generally, available remedies may be separated into four groups: Injunctive relief can be obtained in the form of a court order prohibiting the further violation of the owner's right; impounding, destruction, or disposition of infringing copies or phonorecords can be mandated; money damages can be granted; the costs of the suit as well as attorney's fees may be awarded.

INJUNCTIVE RELIEF

Temporary and Permanent Injunctions

The Act expressly states that any court having jurisdiction under the Act may grant temporary and final injunctions to prevent or restrain an infringement. Accordingly, it is within the power of a federal court to enjoin an infringement since federal courts have jurisdiction under the Act.

Temporary Injunction

To restrain the infringer from continuing to violate the rights of the owner during the pendency of the lawsuit, a temporary injunction is ordinarily sought shortly after the institution of an infringement lawsuit. This type of injunction will usually last until a trial has been conducted and a decision is rendered by a court on the infringement claim and prohibits an alleged infringer from engaging in any activity covered by the injunction.

An owner of a right will seek this type of injunction in cases where it would be harmful to the owner if the infringer were allowed to continue engaging in the alleged infringing activities until a trial is conducted. In many instances, a period of one year or more can elapse between the time a lawsuit is filed and the time a trial is held.

Generally, to be entitled to the issuance of a temporary injunction, it is incumbent on the owner to convince the court that the owner will ultimately prevail after a trial. In many cases, the owner is not required to show that without a temporary injunction the owner will suffer immediate, irreparable damage and injury arising from the acts of the infringer. Such damage is commonly presumed in copyright infringement actions.

If a temporary injunction is entered, it is possible that the owner will be required to post a bond with the court. The amount of the bond will be determined by the court and will be sufficient to protect the interests of the alleged infringer, if the trial court ultimately decides that there was no infringement. If this occurs, the amount of the bond may be paid to the accused infringer as compensation for damage incurred during the period of the temporary injunction.

By virtue of the provisions of the 1976 Act, a temporary injunction will cover the entire United States, even though it has been issued by a federal court located in a particular state, and can be enforced by any federal court having jurisdiction over the person subject to such an injunction. Thus, a person will not be able to avoid the prohibitions in a temporary injunction by engaging in activities covered outside of the state where the court issuing it is located.

Permanent Injunction

A permanent injunction is one entered by a court after there has been a full evaluation and determination of the claims made in the infringement action. In many instances this will be after both the owner and the infringer have had the opportunity to present evidence in support of their respective positions.

A permanent injunction will remain in force unless it is overturned by an appellate court. And, similar to the effectiveness of a temporary injunction, it will be operative throughout the United States and enforceable everywhere in this country.

IMPOUNDING, DESTRUCTION, OR DISPOSITION OF INFRINGING COPIES OR PHONORECORDS

In addition to ordering injunctive relief in a given case, whether temporary or permanent, it is possible for a court to grant the owner another type of remedy. It involves a court order dealing with the infringing material itself and can be obtained to supplement the injunction remedy.

Impounding

The 1976 Act gives a court the authority to order the impounding of all copies or phonorecords claimed to have been made or used in violation of an owner's exclusive rights. This can be requested by an owner and ordered by the court any time an infringement action is pending, including immediately after it has been filed and before any injunction has been issued by the court. Thus it is not necessary for the owner to wait for this remedy until after a determination of the claims made in the infringement action.

A court can order the impounding on such terms as it may deem reasonable. And, in addition to the impounding of copies or phonorecords, a court may order the impounding of all plates, molds, matrices, masters, tapes, film negatives, or other articles by means of which such copies or phonorecords may be reproduced.

Copies or phonorecords that have been reproduced and acquired lawfully are subject to impounding the same as those reproduced or acquired without authorization. This is possible because a court is empowered to order the impounding of copies or phonorecords *used in violation* of an owner's exclusive rights, not only those *made in violation* of such rights.

Destruction or Disposition

Once it has been determined that infringement has occurred, as part of a final judgment or decree a court may order the destruction of all copies or phonorecords found to have been *made* or *used* in violation of the owner's exclusive rights. Similarly, a court may order the destruction of all plates, molds, matrices, masters, tapes, film negatives, or other articles by means of which such copies or phonorecords may be reproduced.

In lieu of ordering the destruction of such items, a court may order the reasonable disposition of them. Thus, it is possible that a court might order the infringer to deliver all infringing items to the owner of the right that has been violated. Or the court may order them to be disposed of in some other way that would avoid needless waste and yet serve the interests of the owner.

MONEY DAMAGE AWARDS

In addition to injunctive relief and an order for the destruction or other disposition of infringing copies or phonorecords, money can be awarded to the owner of rights. When it comes to the money damage remedy, as noted, two alternatives are available. They are: An award of the owner's actual damages and any additional profits of the infringer, or statutory damages. Since these remedies are exclusive of each other, if the owner elects to seek one, the other will not be available.

Actual Damages and Profits

An owner is entitled to receive the actual damages suffered as a result of the infringement. In addition, the owner is entitled to receive the profits of the infringer attributable to the infringement and not taken into account in computing the owner's actual damages.

The purpose of awarding damages and profits to the owner is to compensate for the losses the owner has incurred as a result of the infringement, and to prevent the infringer from unfairly benefiting from a wrongful act.

To establish actual damages, it is incumbent on the owner to introduce evidence that reasonably supports these damages. This is usually done by showing the affect of the infringement on the market value of the infringed work. This means the introduction of evidence showing the difference in market value of a work before and after infringement.

On the other hand, to establish the infringer's profits the owner is required to present proof only of the infringer's gross revenues arising from the infringement. Once this has been done, the burden shifts to the infringer who is then required to prove deductible expenses and the elements of profit attributable to factors other than the work that has been infringed. If the infringer can clearly show that some of the profits are due to the infringement and some due to noninfringing material or other factors, an apportionment will have to be made by the court.

Damages and Profits When There Is an Innocent Infringement

When there is an innocent infringement, in reliance upon an authorized copy or phonorecord that does not feature a copyright notice, the infringer will incur no liability for actual damages but only:

1. For any infringing acts committed before receiving actual notice that registration for the infringed work has been made, and where

2. The infringer proves that he or she was misled by the omission of the notice

Under these circumstances, it is within the discretion of a court to allow or disallow the recovery of the profits attributable to the infringement. Furthermore, it is within the discretion of a court to enjoin the continuation of the infringing act. The court may also elect to require, as a condition of permitting the continuation of the infringing act, that the infringer pay the owner a reasonable license fee in an amount and on terms fixed by the court.

Liability for statutory damages is likewise waived if there is an infringement under the above conditions.

Statutory Damages

Statutory damages are those expressly provided for in the 1976 Act (a "statute"). They are distinguishable from actual damages in a number of ways. Rather than reflecting the real damages suffered by an owner, they represent a somewhat arbitrary range of amounts that Congress determined applicable for infringements. Furthermore, unlike actual damages, it is not necessary for the owner to prove any losses to be entitled to them.

In the event the owner has not incurred any actual damages and/or finds that the infringer's profits are negligible, statutory damages may be sought. Regardless of the basis for seeking them, statutory damages can be obtained only if the owner is eligible to receive them and only if the election is made before the court renders final judgment.

An owner is not entitled to receive such damages if the infringement occurred prior to the date of registration. An exception to this limitation exists when the infringement occurred before registration but during a three-month period after the date of first publication of the infringed work and registration was made before the expiration of that period.

As a general rule, the range of statutory damages is between $250.00 and $10,000.00. The specific dollar amount awarded for each infringement in a given case is within the sole discretion of the court and can be at either end of this range or somewhere in the middle as the court considers just. The total dollar amount of statutory damages awarded in a case may be equal to the specific dollar amount set by the court, or equal to a multiple of that specific amount.

Factors Considered in Determining Amount

The controllng factor in making a total dollar amount award is the number of works that have been determined infringed in each lawsuit. Thus, if only one work is claimed to have been infringed, the specific dollar amount of damages awarded by the court will be multiplied by the number one. This is so no matter how many acts of infringement the lawsuit involves, and regardless of whether the acts were separate, isolated, or occurred in a related series. For example, the total statutory damages award in a lawsuit involving a single work may be $250.00, even though that work may have been reproduced or publicly performed 1,000 times without permission. On the other hand, if three works are involved (at a judgment of $250.00 each), the total will be $750.00, without regard to the number of infringing acts.

For purposes of determining the number of works involved in a lawsuit, all parts of a compilation or derivative work will be treated as constituting only one work. For example, the unauthorized reproduction of five different contributed copyrighted articles in the same issue of a magazine will be treated as an infringement of one work, rather than five, in an action filed by the publisher of the magazine.

Two or More Infringers

When the activities of two or more persons acting together constitute infringement of a work, they are liable for the infringement jointly (together) and severally (individually). This means that the owner of the infringed right has the option to sue one or more of the infringers alone or all of them together. However, it does not mean that the damages awarded will be increased. It remains the same, but is payable by more than one person.

Each infringer who is jointly and severally liable for an infringement with another person is potentially responsible for payment of the entire amount awarded. If the owner elects to sue only one infringer, that person must pay the entire amount and then seek reimbursement from the others who were not sued or who did not pay.

In situations where a single work is infringed by two or more persons acting independently of the other, each is separately liable for the amount awarded. For example, if two persons in two separate actions infringed the reproduction right to a literary work, and statutory damages in the amount of $250.00 are awarded to the owner, both infringers must pay $250.00 to the owner.

Minimum and Maximum Statutory Damages Award

There is an exception to the statutory damages minimum of $250.00 and maximum of $10,000.00. No statutory damages can be awarded where an infringer believed and had reasonable grounds for believing that his or her use of a work was a fair use. But this is possible only if the infringer was:

1. An employee or agent of a nonprofit educational institution, library, or archives acting within the scope of his or her employment who, or such institution, library or archives itself which, infringed by reproducing the work in copies or phonorecords; or
2. A public broadcasting entity which, or a person who, as a regular part of the nonprofit activity of a public broadcasting entity, infringed by performing a published nondramatic literary work or by reproducing a transmission program embodying a performance of such a work

The minimum can be reduced to a sum of not less than $100.00 where the infringer can prove that he or she was not aware and had no reason to believe that his or her acts constituted an infringement. If a court finds that the infringer was innocent, it has the discretion to reduce the award to the aforementioned amount, but is not compelled to do so.

The maximum can be increased when an owner can prove, and a court finds, that the infringement was committed willfully. When this occurs, the court has the discretion to increase the award to a sum of not more than $50,000.00

COSTS OF THE ACTION AND ATTORNEY'S FEES

As a matter of practice, it is expected that the losing party in a lawsuit may be required to pay the winning party's costs as determined by the court. The 1976 Act contains language that expressly gives the court the discretion to make such an award. However, it seems to go a bit further by providing that a court has the discretion to award the recovery of the full costs of an infringement action by or against any party. Therefore, it is possible that a winning party may be ordered to pay the costs of the losing party.

Usually the costs of an action include the filing fees paid by a party as well as the fees paid for the service of process and expert witness fees. Generally, in the absence of a contractual provision for the payment of attorney's fees, attorney's fees will not be awarded to a party unless there is an applicable statute providing for the awarding of attorney's fees. The 1976 Act is just such a statute. It expressly provides that a court may, but is not required to, award a reasonable attorney's fee to the prevailing party.

Notwithstanding such a provision, the owner of the right found to have been infringed may not be awarded attorney's fees simply because an order is entered in his or her favor. The Act specifically states that registration of a work is a prerequisite to the award of attorney's fees for infringement of it. Consequently, if infringement of an unpublished work commenced before the date the work is registered, the owner would not be eligible for an attorney's fee award. Similarly, if an infringement commences after a work is first published, but before it is registered, the owner is not eligible for an attorney's fee award, unless registration was made within three months after the date of first publication and the infringement was commenced within this period.

In instances where the prevailing party is the alleged infringer, that party is eligible to be awarded attorney's fees. This would be the case whether the work claimed to have been infringed was registered at the time of the claimed infringement, or not. Registration is not a condition for an award to an accused infringer.

The amount of attorney's fees awarded will not necessarily be the amount actually incurred by a party. A court has the discretion to base its award on the reasonable value of the services rendered.

CRIMINAL PENALTIES

Monetary as well as imprisonment penalties can be imposed where an infringement is found to constitute a criminal offense. The offenses and applicable penalties (as of July 1, 1986) are:

1. *Willful violation for commercial advantage or private financial gain.* A fine of not more than $250,000.00 may be imposed or imprisonment ordered for not more than five years, or both, when the infringement:

   • Involves the reproduction or distribution, during any 180-day period, of at least 1,000 phonorecords or copies infringing rights in one or more sound recordings

   • Involves the reproduction or distribution, during any 180-day period, of at least 65 copies infringing the rights in one or more motion pictures or other audiovisual works

- Is a second or subsequent offense involving the above activities where a prior offense involved a sound recording, or a motion picture, or other audiovisual work

A fine of not more than $250,000.00 may be imposed or imprisonment ordered for not more than two years, or both, where the infringement:

- Involves the reproduction or distribution, during any 180-day period, of more than 100 but less than 1,000 phonorecords or copies infringing the rights in one or more sound recordings

- Involves the reproduction or distribution, during any 180-day period, of more than seven but less than 65 copies infringing the rights in one or more motion pictures or other audiovisual works

A fine of not more than $250,000.00 may be imposed or imprisonment ordered for not more than one year, or both, in any other case.

In addition, all copies or phonorecords manufactured, reproduced, distributed, sold or otherwise used, intended for use, or possessed with intent to use may be seized and forfeited to the United States. This is also possible with respect to all plates, molds, matrices, masters, tapes, film negatives, or other articles by means of which such copies or phonorecords may be reproduced. And it is possible with respect to all electronic, mechanical, or other devices for manufacturing, reproducing, or assembling such copies or phonorecords.

2. *Fraudulent use or removal of copyright notice.* A fine of not more than $2,500.00 may be imposed where a copyright notice is fraudulently used or removed.

3. *False representation in application for copyright registration.* A fine of not more than $2,500.00 may likewise be imposed where there is a knowing false representation of a material fact in an application for copyright registration or when this is done in any written statement filed in connection with the application.

CHAPTER SUMMARY

- If infringement is proven, a copyright owner is entitled to certain remedies available under the 1976 Act, which include the right to the issuance of an injunction by a court to prevent or restrain the infringement; an order for the impounding and destruction of infringing copies; and an order for the payment of money to the owner.

- A monetary award may be based on the actual damages suffered by the owner as a result of the infringement plus any profits of the infringer that are attributable to the infringement.

- Instead of actual damages and the infringer's profits, a money award may be made in the nature of statutory damages, which range from $100 to $50,000.
- If a work is registered before infringement occurs the court may order the infringer to pay the copyright owner's attorney's fees.
- If a court finds that an infringement was willful and for purposes of commercial advantage or private financial gain it may be treated as a criminal offense subjecting the infringer to a fine and possible imprisonment.

23

Income Tax Considerations

Income tax consequences may occur in connection with creating licensing, and/or transferring rights as well as in connection with the sale, gift, lease, or renting of copies or phonorecords embodying a work. Whether this is the case or not depends upon the status of the owner of rights as either a person who exercises them in connection with a trade or business or holds them for the production of income; or exercises them on an amateur nonbusiness, nonincome-producing basis. Rights in a work are treated as a capital asset from an income tax standpoint and copies and phonorecord held for sale may be treated as the inventory of a business.

An in-depth discussion of tax law is beyond the scope of this book. However, some general information on this subject, below, directs attention to things that should be considered. It should be noted that this information is applicable as of July 1, 1986. The counsel of a tax advisor should be obtained for a thorough review of the tax consequences of a particular transaction based on tax law in effect at the time.

PROFIT-GENERATING ACTIVITIES

The profit motive of a person who creates a work and/or who licenses or transfers rights in it determines the tax consequences arising from such activities. A person who is engaged in activities for profit may be required to capitalize or may be entitled to deduct expenses incurred in connection with such activities.

Regulations under the Federal Internal Revenue Code, as of July 1, 1986, set forth a number of factors to be considered in evaluating whether there is a profit-making motive. They include:

(1) The manner in which the taxpayer carries on the activity. The fact that the taxpayer carries on the activity in a businesslike manner and maintains complete and accurate books and records may indicate that the activity is engaged in for profit. . . .

(2) The expertise of the taxpayer or his advisors. Preparation for the activity by extensive study of its accepted business, economic, and scientific practices, or consultation with those who are expert therein, may indicate that the taxpayer has a profit motive. . . .

(3) The time and effort expended by the taxpayer in carrying on the activity. The fact that the taxpayer devotes much of his personal time and effort to carrying on an activity, particularly if the activity does not have substantial personal or recreational aspects, may indicate an intention to derive a profit. . . .

(4) Expectation that assets used in activity may appreciate in value. The term "profit" encompasses appreciation in the value of assets, such as land, used in the activity. . . .

(5) The success of the taxpayer in carrying on other similar or dissimilar activities. The fact that the taxpayer has engaged in similar activities in the past and converted them from unprofitable to profitable enterprises may indicate that he is engaged in the present activity for profit, even though the activity is unprofitable.

(6) The taxpayer's history of income or losses with respect to the activity. A series of losses during the initial or start-up stage of an activity may not necessarily be an indication that the activity is not engaged in for profit. . . .

(7) The amount of occassional profits, if any, which are earned. The amount of profits in relation to the amount of losses incurred, and in relation to the amount of the taxpayer's investment and the value of the assets used in the activity, may provide useful criteria in determining the taxpayer's intent. . . .

(8) The financial status of the taxpayer. The fact that the taxpayer does not have substantial income or capital from sources other than the activity may indicate that an activity is engaged in for profit. . . .

(9) Elements of personal pleasure or recreation. The presence of personal motives in carrying on an activity may indicate that the activity is not engaged in for profit. . . .

A person not engaged in profit-making activities arising from the exercise of rights in a work may be required to capitalize expenses incurred in connection with creating it. However, such a person may not be entitled to deduct any expenses incurred in connection with exercising rights in the work.

CAPITALIZED EXPENSES

A taxpayer may be required to capitalize the following expenses, among others, and depreciate them over the useful life of the rights:

1. Amounts expended to create a work, excepting the cost of general supplies and materials not applicable to the creation of a specific work
2. Amounts expended to secure registration for a claim of ownership of rights
3. Amounts expended to acquire ownership of rights from someone else, including legal fees
4. Amounts expended for litigation to determine who owns rights in a work

DEDUCTIBLE EXPENSES

The following expenses, among others, deemed to be ordinary and necessary, may be currently deducted from taxable income:

1. General supplies and materials that are not normally charged to a capital account, such as paper, writing instruments, postage, telephone expense, office expense, subscriptions, and the like that are not incurred in connection with the creation of a specific work
2. Litigation costs to enforce rights in a work, including attorney's fees
3. License fees paid for the right to exercise rights
4. Amounts expended for the production or collection of income or for the management, conservation, or maintenance of income-producing property
5. Amounts paid as damages in an infringement suit

CAPITAL GAIN INCOME

A transfer of rights may result in capital gain income when the amount received by the seller exceeds his or her tax basis in the rights sold. When the rights have been owned by the person transferring them for the applicable long-term capital gain period, the gain will be taxed at the lower long-term capital gain rate. As of July 1, 1986, the long-term capital gain period is six months for rights acquired between June 23, 1984 and December 31, 1987. Reference should be made to the Federal Internal Revenue Code (Code) to confirm that this period continues to be applicable.

This type of tax treatment is not possible in cases when rights are held by a taxpayer primarily for sale to customers in the ordinary course of the taxpayer's trade or business. For example, this treatment would not be possible for a music publisher engaged in the business of buying and selling rights in songs.

Furthermore, this type of tax treatment is not possible for a transfer of rights by the creator of a work or by certain other persons. Capital gain treatment is barred in these cases by the Code because rights in a work owned by the creator and such persons are not considered to be capital assets for capital gain tax purposes. The Code provides:

> For purposes of this subtitle, the term "capital asset" means property held by the taxpayer (whether or not connected with his trade or business), but does not include. . . .
>
> (3) a copyright, a literary, musical, or artistic composition, a letter or memorandum, or similar property held by
>
>   (A) a taxpayer whose personal efforts created such property
>
>   (B) in the case of a letter, memorandum, or similar property, a taxpayer for whom such property was prepared or produced, or
>
>   (C) a taxpayer in whose hands the basis of such property is determined, for purposes of determining gain from a sale or exchange, in whole or part by reference to the basis of such property in the hands of a taxpayer described in subparagraph (A) or (B).

The phrase "similar property" is defined in the Internal Revenue Code Regulations to include:

> Such property as "a theatrical production, a radio program, a newspaper cartoon strip, or any other property eligible for copyright protection (whether under statute or common law). . . .

Individuals who acquire ownership of rights in a work by gift, transfer in trust, or bequest fall within (C) above and are not entitled to capital gain treatment on any transfer of rights to others.

ORDINARY INCOME

Income received by an owner of rights, of the kind noted below, may be treated as ordinary income in most cases:

1. Royalties arising from the licensing of rights (it should be noted that such royalties are treated as "passive" income and may affect a taxpayer's status as an S Corporation and the tax rate applicable to them).
2. Monies recovered as a result of an infringement lawsuit that are awarded as lost profits.
3. Moneys received from the sale of copies and phonorecords.
4. Moneys received by the creator (and those persons identified in 3(C) in the preceding subsection of this chapter), from the sale of rights in a work.

CHAPTER SUMMARY

- The income tax laws may impact the creation, licensing, and/or transfer of rights in a work; in many cases they are applied to the sale, gift, or lease of copies and/or phonorecords.
- The business status of a person who creates works and/or who sells or leases copies or phonorecords determines the affect of these laws on such events and transactions.
- Rights in a work are treated as intangible personal property and, from a tax standpoint, are viewed as depreciable capital assets.

A

Agreements

AGREEMENT FOR COMMISSIONED WORK

Schedule A

Date

Dear

    You are hereby commissioned by
(hereafter "Owner") to create illustrations as described in Schedule A, attached hereto and made a part hereof, (hereafter "Commissioned Work") for a book entitled " ". Both you and Owner agree the Commissioned Work shall be considered a work made for hire.

    You understand that all rights in the Commissioned Work, including but not limited to copyright, shall be the property of Owner. Owner shall not be required to publish the Commissioned Work, and whenever it does, Owner's editors may add to or delete from the Commissioned Work, and may or may not credit you as the illustrator. The editors of Owner, at their sole discretion, have the right to reject the Commissioned Work you submit within six weeks following delivery. The successors and assigns of Owner shall have the same rights in the Commissioned Work as Owner.

    You warrant that you will be the sole creator of the Commissioned Work you submit, that it will be original, unpublished and contain no plagiarized, defamatory, obscene or otherwise unlawful materials, and will not invade the privacy of any third party or otherwise violate any rights of a third party, including copyright.

The foregoing rights of Owner shall be exercisable throughout the world. If the likeness of an individual is included in the Commissioned Work you submit, you represent that all necessary permissions have been obtained and will be delivered to Owner at Owner's request. Such permissions will allow use by Owner, and those authorized by Owner, of said likeness(es) in advertising and for purposes of trade.

You agree to indemnify and save Owner harmless from any loss or liability including reasonable attorney's fees arising out of a breach or alleged breach of any of these warranties.

You shall be paid _____ within thirty days of acceptance of the Commissioned Work by Owner.

You shall be solely responsible for all costs, including but not limited to, travel expenses incurred in connection with producing the Commissioned Work, except when prior agreement has been made with Owner. Owner shall not be responsible for providing any services to you, including, but not limited to, desk or office space, office supplies, telephone services or stenographic services in connection with your creation of the Commissioned Work, except when prior written agreement has been made with Owner.

This agreement cannot be changed, modified, discharged or terminated except by an agreement in writing, signed by both parties.

Please indicate your acceptance of these terms by signing below and returning this letter to me.

Owner

By_____

Date:

Approved and Accepted:

_____

Date:

AGREEMENT FOR EMPLOYEE TO BE OWNER
OF RIGHTS IN A WORK

Date

Dear   :

This letter sets forth and confirms the agreement we have reached referring to your ownership of all exclusive rights, under copyright law, in the computer software program and user manual described on Schedule A, which you created within the scope of your employment by the undersigned company. More particularly, it is expressly understood and agreed that you shall be the owner of all rights in the program and manual, including copyright therefor, and to the extent necessary an authorized representative of company shall execute, on behalf of the company, any and all reasonably necessary documents to further effectuate the same.

I represent and warrant that I have the requisite authority to make this agreement and to sign this letter on behalf of the company.

Very truly yours,

ASSIGNMENT OF COPYRIGHT

WHEREAS, _____ ,
having a mailing address at _____ ,
(hereinafter "Assignor") is the owner of the entire right, title, and interest in and to the copyrighted work described in Schedule A attached hereto and made a part hereof (hereinafter "Work").

WHEREAS, _____ ,
having a mailing address at _____ ,
(hereinafter "Assignee") desires to acquire from Assignor the entire right, title, and interest in and to said Work including the copyright therefor and all the rights and privileges appertaining thereto including, without limitation, the exclusive right to reproduce, prepare derivative works based upon, distribute copies to the public by sale, and perform as well as display said Work.

NOW, THEREFORE, TO ALL WHOM IT MAY CONCERN, BE IT KNOWN that for good and valuable consideration, the receipt of which is hereby acknowledged, Assignor has sold, assigned, and transferred and by these presents does sell, assign, and transfer, to said Assignee, Assignee's successors, assigns, heirs, and legal representatives the said Work and copyright hereinabove designated, including the entire right, title, and interest in and to the same and all the rights and privileges appertaining thereto including, without limitation, the exclusive right to reproduce, prepare derivative works based upon, distribute copies to the public by sale, and perform as well as display said copyrighted Work, the same to be held and employed by Assignee, for Assignee's own benefit and use and for the benefit and use of Assignee's successors, assigns, heirs, and legal representatives forever.

IN WITNESS WHEREOF, Assignor has signed this document as of this _____ day of _____ , 19 _____ .

State of _____   )
County of _____   )

ACKNOWLEDGEMENT

Before me, a Notary Public in and for said county, personally appeared the above named _____ who acknowledged that he did sign the foregoing instrument and that the same is his free act and deed.

In Testimony Whereof, I have hereunto affixed my name and official seal at this _____ day of _____ , 19 _____ .

Notary Public

Address

My commission expires:

COLLABORATION AGREEMENT

Dear   :

This letter is to confirm and set forth our agreement referring to creation of a nonfiction book dealing with the subject of _____ tentatively entitled " _____ " (hereafter "Book"). More particularly, it is my desire to collaborate with you in the writing of the Book subject to the following terms and conditions:

1. I shall furnish you with all reasonably necessary material and information pertaining to _____
insofar as the subject matter of the Book is concerned, so that we will be able to co-author a comprehensive, well-rounded and thoroughly documented final manuscript of the Book.

2. Each of us shall proceed diligently towards the preparation, editing, and prompt completion of the final manuscript and we shall confer with each other as often as may be necessary to accomplish this objective.

3. On a regular basis, we shall submit drafts of successive portions of the manuscript to each other for review, comments, suggestions, and editing and agree to fully cooperate with each other so that the final manuscript will be satisfactory and suitable, in form and content, for submission to a book publisher.

4. We contemplate that we will complete the manuscript of the Book by _____ . If we fail to do so, we may by mutual written agreement extend the time for completion. In the absence of any such extension, we shall endeavor to fix by negotiation our respective rights in the material we have created under the terms of this agreement, and in the collaboration project itself. That is, whether one or the other of us shall have the right to complete the Book alone or in collaboration with someone else, and upon what terms. Our understanding as to these matters shall be embodied in a settlement agreement. If we are unable to agree, our respective rights and the terms pertaining thereto shall be fixed by arbitration, as referred to herein. In either event, this agreement shall cease when our rights have been fixed by agreement or otherwise. Thereafter, we shall have only such rights and obligations as will be set forth in the settlement agreement or the arbitration award, as the case may be.

5. If the manuscript of the Book is completed, we shall endeavor to secure a publisher. Each of us shall have the right to negotiate for this purpose, but we shall keep each other fully informed with reference thereto. No agreement for the publication of the Book or for the disposition and/or licensing of any rights relating thereto, including subsidiary rights among others, shall be valid without the signature of each of us. However, either of us may grant a written power of attorney to the other or another party specifically setting forth the conditions thereof and under which such power may be exercised.

6. As co-authors, we shall jointly own the copyright in the manuscript of the Book in equal shares and each of us shall receive equal authorship credit on the same line and in type of equal size, except that the name _____ shall precede that of _____ .

7. All receipts and returns arising, directly or indirectly, from publication of the Book and from the disposition and/or licensing of any rights relating thereto, including subsidiary rights among others, shall be divided equally between us. All agreements for publication and for the sale and/or licensing of rights relating thereto, including subsidiary rights among others, shall provide that our respective one-half shares shall be paid directly to each of us.

8. If we, by mutual agreement, select an agent to handle the publication rights in the Book and/or the disposition and/or licensing of any rights relating thereto, including subsidiary rights among others, and if the agent is author-

ized to make collection for our account, such agent shall remit our respective one-half shares direct to each of us.

9. After the completion of the manuscript of the Book, no change or alteration shall be made therein by either of us without the other's written consent. However, such consent shall not be unreasonably withheld. No written consent to make a particular revision shall be deemed authority for a general revision.

10. If either of us decides to transfer our respective one-half share in the Book or in any rights relating thereto, including subsidiary rights among others, to a third person, the party desiring to make such transfer shall give written notice, by certified mail return receipt requested, to the other of her intention to do so. The written notice shall include the terms and conditions of such transfer.

(a) In such case the nontransferring party shall have an option to acquire the transferring party's share at the same price and upon the same terms and conditions as may be offered to the party who desires to transfer, contained in a bona fide offer from a third party.

(b) If the nontransferring party fails to exercise her option to acquire the transferring party's share, the transferring party may transfer her rights to the third person at the price and upon the identical terms and conditions contained in such bona fide offer, and she shall forthwith send to the nontransferring party a copy of the contract of sale of such rights, with a statement that the transfer has been made.

(c) If the party desiring to transfer her rights, for any reason fails to make such transfer to a third person, and if she desires to make a subsequent transfer to someone else, the nontransferring party's option shall apply to such proposed subsequent transfer.

11. All expenses which may be reasonably incurred in connection with preparing, editing, and otherwise creating the manuscript of the Book shall be subject to mutual agreement in advance, and shall be shared equally by us. Each of us shall be required to keep and maintain accurate and complete records reflecting the costs and expenses we incur in connection with preparing, editing, and otherwise creating the manuscript. Said records shall include, where appropriate, copies of invoices and/or written statements containing itemizations and reasonable descriptions for such costs and expenses. We shall regularly account to each other for the costs and expenses we incur and make arrangements for the prompt payment and/or reimbursement thereof.

12. Nothing herein contained shall be construed to create a partnership between us. Our relationship shall be one of collaboration on a single work.

13. If the Book is published, this agreement shall continue for the life of the copyright therein. Otherwise, the duration of this agreement shall be governed by the provisions of paragraph 4.

14. If either one of us dies, or becomes incapacitated to the extent that the incapacitated party cannot make further contributions reasonably necessary for creation of a final manuscript of the Book, before completion of the final manuscript, the survivor or party who is not so incapacitated shall have the right to complete the same, to make changes in the text previously prepared, to nego-

tiate and contract for publication and for the disposition and/or licensing of any rights relating thereto, including subsidiary rights among others, and generally to act with regard thereto as though she were the sole author, except that (a) the name of the decedent or incapacitated party shall always appear as co-author; and (b) the survivor shall cause the decedent's share of the proceeds to be paid to her estate, and shall furnish to the estate true copies of all contracts made by the survivor pertaining to the Book; or (c) the party who is not incapacitated shall cause the incapacitated party's share of the proceeds to be paid to the incapacitated party or the incapacitated party's legal representative, and shall furnish to the incapacitated party true copies of all contracts made by the party who is not incapacitated pertaining to the Book. In the event either one of us dies or becomes incapacitated (to the extent noted earlier) before completion of the final manuscript of the Book, we (or our legal representatives) shall endeavor to fix by negotiation our respective shares in the material created up to the time of the death or incapacity. Our understanding (or that of our legal representatives) shall be embodied in a written agreement. If we (or our legal representatives) are unable to agree, our respective rights and shares as well as the terms pertaining thereto shall be fixed by arbitration, as referred to herein.

15. If either of us dies or is adjudicated mentally incompetent after completion of the manuscript, the survivor or mentally competent party shall have the right to manage and exercise every aspect of copyright ownership with regard to the Book and to negotiate and contract for publication (if not theretofore published) and for the disposition and/or licensing of any rights relating thereto, including subsidiary rights among others, to make revisions in any subsequent editions, and generally to act with regard thereto as if she were the sole author, subject only to the rights of the heirs of the deceased or adjudicated party to share in any income, royalties or other proceeds derived from such publication, disposition and/or licensing.

16. Upon death of the survivor, any and all copyrights owned by us shall thereafter be managed, administered, and/or disposed of by the literary executor appointed by the Will of the survivor. Such literary executor shall have the full power and authority to manage, administer, hold, and/or dispose of said copyrights, subject only to the rights of the heirs of both deceased authors of the Book to share in the income or proceeds derived from the management, administration, and/or disposition of such copyrights in accordance with the share allocation as set forth in paragraphs 6 or 14 hereunder, whichever may be applicable.

17. Any controversy or claim arising out of or relating to this agreement or any breach thereof shall be settled by arbitration in accordance with the Rules of the American Arbitration; and judgment upon the award rendered by the arbitrators may be entered in any court having jurisdiction thereof.

18. This agreement shall enure to the benefit of, and shall be binding upon, our executors, administrators, legal representatives, heirs, and assigns.

19. Whenever notice is required to be given hereunder, it shall be in writing and delivered to the party entitled thereto or mailed to the party entitled thereto by certified mail, return receipt requested. If delivered, said notice shall be effective and complete upon delivery. If mailed, said notice shall be effective

and complete upon mailing. Until changed by notice in writing, notice shall be given to each of us at the our addresses as set forth herein.

20. This document sets forth the entire agreement between us and no modification, amendment, waiver, or termination of this agreement or any provisions of this agreement shall be binding upon us unless confirmed in writing and signed by both of us.

21. Should any provision of this agreement be void or unenforceable, such provision shall be deemed severed and this agreement with such provision severed shall remain in full force and effect to the extent permitted by law.

If the foregoing accurately sets forth your understanding of our agreement and is acceptable to you, kindly sign and date the duplicate original of this letter, at the space provided below, and return it to me. This agreement shall become effective on the date it is signed by you and will last for the life of the copyright for the Book, unless otherwise terminated.

Sincerely,

Approved and accepted:

Date:

COPYRIGHT LICENSE

Date

Dear   :

This letter is to confirm our recent discussions referring to reproduction of an original piece of artwork by _____ , having an office at (hereafter "Company") and to set forth our agreement in this regard subject to the following terms and conditions:

1. You hereby represent and warrant that you created and are the exclusive owner of all right, title and interest in and to the artwork described and shown in Exhibit A attached hereto (hereafter "Work"), including the copyright therefor, and that you have the full power and requisite authority to enter into and execute this agreement.

2. You hereby grant to Company the sole and exclusive right and license to create derivative works based upon the Work by reproducing the Work, as set forth in Exhibit B attached hereto (hereafter "Reproduction" or, collectively, "Reproductions") and to distribute copies of the Reproduction to the public by sale or other transfer of ownership, or by rental, lease, or lending and to display said copies publicly.

3. (a) You agree to fully cooperate and work closely with Company in connection with its activities to reproduce the Work with regard to creating the Reproduction including, among other activities, delivering the original of the Work to Company to enable it to have the necessary action taken to reproduce it; making arrangements with a printer, approved by Company, to reproduce the Work; overseeing and, to the extent possible, controlling the actual reproduction of the Work; inspecting preliminary and final copies of the Reproduction, personally signing, numbering, and acknowledging your authorship of each copy of the Reproduction but only such copies as are specifically produced and expressly designated by Company, which shall be subject to your prior written approval, as limited editions of the Reproduction, as well as taking any and all action reasonably necessary to insure that final copies of the Reproduction are of a high quality, comparable to other works of fine art and merchandise reproduced in the same or similar manner; and, Company acknowledges and agrees that you shall have the sole and exclusive right to exercise all artistic control with regard to the aforementioned activities. Company shall be under no obligation to pay you for any services you perform hereunder or the license you have granted herein except as provided in Paragraphs 5 and 6 hereof.

(b) Company shall proceed promptly to have the Work reproduced hereunder and to return the original of the Work to you on or before _____ 19_____ . While the work is in the possession of Company, its employees, agents, representatives or contractors, Company will keep it insured against all risks in the sum of _____ & 00/100 Dollars ($ _____) with a loss payable clause to you such that in the event of loss or damage to the original of the Work you shall receive payment therefor directly from the insurance company.

4. You hereby represent and warrant that you shall not reproduce the Work in any medium whatsoever, prepare any derivative works based thereupon, and/or authorize any other party to reproduce or prepare variations of the Work during the Life of this Agreement without the prior written permission of Company. You reserve all rights in and to the Work not expressly granted to Company herein.

5. For and in consideration of the license granted to Company hereunder, Company agrees to exert its best efforts to sell copies of the Reproduction and to promote, advertise, publicize, and generally exploit copies of the Reproduction to the same extent as other sellers of art do with regard to artwork of a comparable nature. Company further agrees to pay you a royalty in an amount equal to _____percent (_____) of the gross receipts of Company as defined hereinafter. "Gross receipts" shall include all receipts, whether received in cash or other property, received by Company arising from the reproduction, marketing, sales, distribution rental, lease, or lending of copies of the Reproduction undiminished by any costs whatsoever. For purposes of this agreement, any transfer, gift, exchange, other disposition, rental, lease, or lending of copies of the Reproduction to any other party, whether such party be an individual, a subsidiary, parent company, partner or other related or affiliated party to Company, or whether such party be unrelated to Company, shall be considered a transfer for value and subject to payment of royalty by Company to you. Such value shall be considered to be the average "gross re-

ceipts" arising from the reproduction, marketing, sales, distribution, rental, lease, or lending of copies of the Reproduction received by Company over the ninety (90) days immediately preceding such transfer, gift, exchange, other disposition, rental, lease, or lending if less than the value actually received by Company, unless Company receives your prior written consent to make such transfer, gift, exchange, other disposition, rental, lease, or lending.

6. It is expressly agreed between the parties hereto that Company shall pay you a nonreturnable advance against royalties which shall be payable to you hereunder in an amount equal to _____00/100 Dollars per month, no later than the first day of each calendar for a period of _____ calendar months beginning on the first day of the calendar month after the calendar month in which this agreement is signed by you.

7. As between you and Company, Company shall be solely and fully responsible for and shall pay all costs and expenses for reproducing, manufacturing, distributing, marketing, advertising, promoting, selling, giving away, exchanging, otherwise disposing, rental, lease, or lending of the copies of the Reproduction and neither all or any part of such costs and expenses shall be assessable against or payable from your royalties hereunder or monies payable to you under any other written or oral agreement between you and Company.

8. Company agrees to keep accurate and complete books and records reflecting all sales, transfers, gifts, exchanges, other dispositions, rental, leases or lending of copies of the Reproduction as well as the date each occurs, "gross receipts," and date of payment directly or indirectly to or for the benefit of Company therefor. Company shall compute all amounts due and payable to you hereunder and shall prepare and submit written statements to you, no later than ten (10) days after the end of each calendar month setting forth the total number of copies of the Reproduction, sold transferred, given away, exchanged, otherwise disposed of, rented, leased, or loaned during the immediately preceding calendar month, or earlier ones, and for which Company has directly or indirectly received a portion of or full payment as well as the total "gross receipts" of Company for the period beginning on the date of this agreement to the date each calendar monthly statement is prepared. In addition, each statement shall set forth the total amount of royalties due and payable to you hereunder, for the period beginning on the date of this agreement to the date of such statement, as well as the total amount of advances paid to you by Company under the provisions of paragraph 6 hereof and the balance of such advances, if any, unrecouped by Company from royalties due and payable to you. Each and every statement to you shall be accompanied by all amounts, if any, due and payable to you less any unrecouped advances given to you by Company under the provisions of paragraph 6 hereof. You shall have a right to inspect and copy the books and records of Company relating to the sale, transfer, gift, exchange, other disposition, rental, lease or lending of copies of the Reproduction not more than once every six (6) month period during the life of this agreement and upon reasonable notice in writing to Company at Company's place of business during Company's usual business hours. All statements and payments shall be binding upon you and not subject to any objection by you for any reason unless you submit to Company a written statement of the specific objections to particulars of the statements and payments within twelve

(12) months of the dates submitted to you, and if Company denies the validity of such objections, unless suit is instituted by you within twelve (12) months after the date Company gives you such notice of such denial.

9. You shall take all reasonable and necessary steps to formalize your claim to copyright in and to the Work including the registration thereof and shall take all reasonable and necessary action against any infringements of the Work as you, in your sole discretion, deem to be appropriate. Company shall not institute any suit or take any action on account of any such infringements without first obtaining your written consent to do so.

10. You hereby agree to indemnify, and hold harmless Company against any and all claims, suits, and/or judgments including costs, expenses, and legal fees relating to the infringement of copyright owned by third parties and referring to the Work but not until such time as an adverse decision has been rendered against Company by a Court of record with no further right of appeal by Company.

11. It is the intention of the parties hereto to enter into a licensing agreement only and nothing herein contained shall be construed to regard the parties as being partners or joint venturers, or to constitute the arrangement herein provided for as a partnership or joint venture.

12. This agreement shall be effective on the date it is signed by you and shall end five (5) years from the date thereof. This agreement may be renewed for additional periods of time upon mutual written agreement of the parties hereto.

13. This agreement shall be binding upon and inure to the benefit of the legal representatives, heirs, parent companies, subsidiaries, affiliates, successors and assigns of the parties hereto. This agreement shall not be assigned by either party without the prior written consent of the other.

14. This agreement shall be construed and governed in accordance with the laws of the State of _____ .

15. Any notice or payment provided for in this agreement may be served by personal delivery or by certified mail, return receipt requested, addressed to the other party at its address as set forth herein, and, if served by personal delivery shall be effective on the date thereof, or if served by certified mail, return receipt requested, shall be effective seven (7) days after the date of mailing. Either party may, by written notice to the other, change its address for receiving notices and payments.

16. In the event Company shall, at any time fail to make payments, submit reports, or otherwise abide by the terms and conditions of this agreement, you shall have the right to notify Company of such default and your intention to terminate this agreement unless such default is corrected by Company within sixty (60) days from the date of mailing of such notice by you. If such default is not corrected within the aforementioned time period, you shall be entitled, without prejudice to any of your rights conferred by this agreement, to terminate this agreement at any time thereafter by sending a written notice of termination to Company to take effect immediately, Waiver by you of any specific default or breach shall not be deemed to be a Waiver of any other or subsequent default or breach. In the event that Company shall become insolvent, exercise

an assignment for the benefit of creditors, go into liquidation, a trustee is appointed for the benefit of creditors, whether any of the aforesaid events be the outcome of a voluntary act of Company or otherwise, you shall be entitled to terminate this agreement forthwith by giving written notice to such effect to Company. The termination of this agreement for any reason shall be without prejudice to any of your rights under this agreement. Notwithstanding the termination of this agreement, the parties shall be required to carry out any provisions hereof which contemplate performance by them subsequent to such termination and such termination shall not affect any liability or other obligation which shall have accrued prior to such termination.

17. The rights granted to Company hereunder are conditioned upon Company's use of your copyright notice on all copies of the Reproduction in the following format:

© 19 _____   _____

Company's failure to place the above notice on copies of the Reproduction shall be a basis for you to immediately terminate this agreement and all rights to Company hereunder, upon written notice to Company.

18. This agreement contains the entire understanding of the parties with respect to the subject matter herein contained. The parties may, from time to time during the continuance of this agreement, modify, vary, or alter any of the provisions of this agreement, but only by an instrument duly executed by both parties hereto. All provisions of this agreement shall be severable and no such provisions shall be affected by the invalidity of any other provisions. This agreement shall be interpreted and enforced as if all invalid provisions were not contained therein.

If the foregoing accurately sets forth your understanding of our agreement, kindly indicate your acceptance and approval thereof by dating and signing the duplicate original of this letter at the space provided below and return it to me.

Very truly yours,

Approved and Accepted:

B

Guidelines

GUIDELINES FOR CLASSROOM COPYING IN NOT-FOR-PROFIT EDUCATIONAL INSTITUTIONS WITH RESPECT TO BOOKS AND PERIODICALS

The purpose of the following guidelines is to state the minimum and not the maximum standards of educational fair use under Section 107 H.R. 2223. The parties agree the conditions determining the extent of permissible copying for educational purposes may change in the future; that certain types of copying permitted under these guidelines may not be permissible in the future; and, conversely, that in the future other types of copying not permitted under these guidelines may be permissible under revised guidelines.

Moreover, the following statement of guidelines is not intended to limit the types of copying permitted under the standards of fair use under judicial decision and which are stated in Section 107 of the Copyright Revision Bill. There may be instances in which copying which does not fall within the guidelines stated below may nonetheless be permitted under the criteria of fair use.

GUIDELINES

I.   Single Copying for Teachers

A single copy may be made of any of the following by or for a teacher at his or her individual request for his or her scholarly research or use in teaching or preparation to teach a class:

  A.   A chapter from a book;

  B.   An article from a periodical or newspaper;

C. A short story, short essay or short poem, whether or not from a collective work;

D. A chart, graph, diagram, drawing, cartoon or picture from a book, periodical, or newspaper;

II. Multiple Copies for Classroom Use

Multiple copies (not to exceed in any event more than one copy per pupil in a course) may be made by or for the teacher giving the course for classroom use or discussion; provided that:

A. The copying meets the tests of brevity and spontaneity as defined below; and

B. Meets the cumulative effect test as defined below; and,

C. Each copy includes a notice of copyright.

Definitions

Brevity

(i) Poetry: (a) A complete poem if less than 250 words and printed on not more than two pages or, (b) from a longer poem, an excerpt of not more than 250 words.

(ii) Prose: (a) Either a complete article, story, or essay of less than 2,500 words, or (b) an excerpt from any prose work of not more than 1,000 words or 10% of the work, whichever is less, but in any event a minimum of 500 words.

(Each of the numerical limits stated in "i" and "ii" above may be expanded to permit the completion of an unfinished line of a poem or of an unfinished prose paragraph.)

(iii) Illustration: One chart, graph, diagram, drawing, cartoon or picture per book or per periodical issue.

(iv) "Special" works: Certain works in poetry, prose, or in "poetic prose" which often combine language with illustrations and which are intended sometimes for children and at other times for a more general audience fall short of 2,500 words in their entirety. Paragraph "ii" above notwithstanding such "special works" may not be reproduced in their entirety; however, an excerpt comprising not more than two of the published pages of such special work and containing not more than 10% of the words found in the text thereof, may be reproduced.

Spontaneity

(i) The copying is at the instance and inspiration of the individual teacher, and

(ii) The inspiration and decision to use the work and the moment of its use for maximum teaching effectiveness are so close in time that it would be unreasonable to expect a timely reply to a request for permission.

Cumulative Effect

(i) The copy of the material is for only one course in the school in which the copies are made.

(ii) Not more than one short poem, article, story, essay or two excerpts may be copied from the same author, nor more than three from the same collective work or periodical volume during one class term.

(iii) There shall not be more than nine instances of such multiple copying for one course during one class term.

(The limitations stated in "ii" and "iii" above shall not apply to current news periodicals and newspapers and current news sections of other periodicals.)

III.   Prohibitions as to I and II above

Notwithstanding any of the above, the following shall be prohibited:

(A)   Copying shall not be used to create or to replace or substitute for anthologies, compilations, or collective works. Such replacement or substitution may occur whether copies of various works or excerpts therefrom are accumulated or reproduced and used separately.

(B)   There shall be no copying of or from works intended to be "consumable" in the course of study or of teaching. These include workbooks, exercises, standardized tests, and test booklets and answer sheets and like consumable material.

(C)   Copying shall not:

(a) substitute for the purchase of books, publishers' reprints or periodicals;

(b) be directed by higher authority;

(c) be repeated with respect to the same item by the same teacher from term to term.

(D)   No charge shall be made to the student beyond the actual cost of the photocopying.

Agreed March 19, 1976

GUIDELINES FOR EDUCATIONAL USES OF MUSIC

The purpose of the following guidelines is to state the minimum and not the maximum standards of educational fair use under Section 107 of HR 2223. The parties agree that the conditions determining the extent of permissible copying for educational purposes may change in the future; that certain types of copying permitted under these guidelines may not be permissible in the future, and conversely that in the future other types of copying not permitted under these guidelines may be permissible under revised guidelines.

Moreover, the following statement of guidelines is not intended to limit the types of copying permitted under the standards of fair use under judicial decision and which are stated in Section 107 of the Copyright Revision Bill. There may be instances in which copying which does not fall within the guidelines stated below may nonetheless be permitted under the criteria of fair use.

A. Permissible Uses

1. Emergency copying to replace purchased copies which for any reason are not available for an imminent performance provided purchased replacement copies shall be substituted in due course.

2. For academic purposes other than performance, single or multiple copies of excerpts of works may be made, provided that the excerpts do not comprise a part of the whole which would constitute a performable unit such as a section, movement, or aria, but in no case more than 10 percent of the whole work. The number of copies shall not exceed one copy per pupil.

3. Printed copies which have been purchased may be edited or simplified provided that the fundamental character of the work is not distorted or the lyrics, if any, altered or lyrics added if none exist.

4. A single copy of recordings of performances by students may be made for evaluation or rehearsal purposes and may be retained by the educational institution or individual teacher.

5. A single copy of a sound recording (such as a tape, disc, or cassette) of copyrighted music may be made from sound recordings owned by an educational institution or an individual teacher for the purpose of constructing aural exercises or examinations and may be retained by the educational institution or individual teacher. (This pertains only to the copyright of the music itself and not to any copyright which may exist in the sound recording.)

B. Prohibitions

1. Copying to create or replace or substitute for anthologies, compilations, or collective works.

2. Copying of or from works intended to be "consumable" in the course of study or of teaching such as workbooks, exercises, standardized tests and answer sheets and like material.

3. Copying for the purpose of performance, except as in A1. above.

4. Copying for the purpose of substituting for the purchase of music, except as in A1. and A2. above.

5. Copying without inclusion of the copyright notice which appears on the printed copy.

PHOTOCOPYING—INTERLIBRARY ARRANGEMENTS

Introduction

Subsection 108(g)(2) of the bill deals, among other things with limits on interlibrary arrangements for photocopying. It prohibits systematic photocopying of copyrighted materials but permits interlibrary arrangements "that do not have, as their purpose or effect, that the library or archives receiving such copies or phonorecords for distribution does so in such aggregate quantities as to substitute for a subscription to or purchase of such work."

The National Commission on New Technological Uses of Copyrighted Works offered its good offices to the House and Senate subcommittees in bringing the interested parties together to see if agreement could be reached on what a realistic definition would be of "such aggregate quantities." The Commission consulted with the parties and suggested the interpretation which follows, on which there has been substantial agreement by the principal library, publisher, and author organizations. The Commission considers the guidelines which follow to be a workable and fair interpretation of the intent of the proviso portion of subsection 108(g)(2).

These guidelines are intended to provide guidance in the application of section 108 to the most frequently encountered interlibrary case: a library's obtaining from another library, in lieu of interlibrary loan, copies of articles from relatively recent issues of periodicals—those published within five years prior to the date of the request. The guidelines do not specify what aggregate quantity of copies of an article or articles published in a periodical, the issue date of which more than five years prior to the date when the request for the copy thereof is made, constitutes a substitute for a subscription to such periodical. The meaning of the proviso to subsection 108(g)(2) in such case is left to future interpretation.

The point has been made that the present practice on interlibrary loans and use of photocopies in lieu of loans may be supplemented or even largely replaced by a system in which one or more agencies or institutions, public or private, exist for the specific purpose of providing a central source for photocopies. Of course, these guidelines would not apply to such a situation.

Guidelines for the Proviso of Subsection 108(g)(2)

1. As used in the proviso of subsection 108(g)(2), the words ". . . such aggregate quantities as to substitute for a subscription to or purchase of such work" shall mean:

(a) with respect to any given periodical (as opposed to any given issue of a periodical), filled requests of a library or archives (a "requesting entity") within any calendar year for a total of six or more copies of an article or articles published in such periodical within five years prior to the date of the request. These guidelines specifically shall not apply, directly or indirectly, to any request of a requesting entity for a copy or copies of an article or articles published in any issue of a periodical, the publication date of which is more than five years prior to the date when the request is made. These guidelines do not define the meaning, with respect to such a request, of ". . . such aggregate quantities as to substitute for a subscription to (such periodical)."

(b) With respect to any other material described in subsection 108(d), (including fiction and poetry), filled requests of a requesting entity within any calendar year for a total of six or more copies or phonorecords of or from any given work (including a collective work) during the entire period when such material shall be protected by copyright.

2. In the event that a requesting entity:

(a) shall have in force or shall have entered an order for a subscription to a periodical, or

(b) has within its collection, or shall have entered an order for, a copy or phonorecord of any other copyrighted work, material from either category of which it desires to obtain by copy from another library or archives (the "supplying entity"), because the material to be copied is not reasonably available for use by the requesting entity itself, then the fulfillment of such request shall be treated as though the requesting entity made such copy from its own collection. A library or archives may request a copy or phonorecord from a supplying entity only under those circumstances where the requesting entity would have been able, under the other provisions of section 108, to supply such copy from materials in its own collection.

3. No request for a copy or phonorecord of any material to which these guidelines apply may be fulfilled by the supplying entity unless such request is accompanied by a representation by the requesting entity that the request was made in conformity with these guidelines.

4. The requesting entity shall maintain records of all requests made by it for copies or phonorecords of any materials to which these guidelines apply and shall maintain records of the fulfillment of such request, which records shall be retained until the end of the third complete calendar year after the end of the calendar year in which the respective request shall have been made.

5. As part of the review provided for in subsection 108(i), these guidelines shall be reviewed no later than five years from the effective date of this bill.

"BEST EDITION" OF PUBLISHED COPYRIGHTED WORKS FOR THE COLLECTIONS OF THE LIBRARY OF CONGRESS

The Copyright Law (Title 17, United States Code) requires that copies or phonorecords deposited in the Copyright Office be of the "best edition" of the work. The law states that "the 'best edition' of a work is the edition, published in the United States at any time before the date of deposit, the Library of Congress determines to be most suitable for its purpose."

When two or more editions of the same version of a work have been published, the one of the highest quality is generally considered to be the best edition. In judging quality, the Library of Congress will adhere to the criteria set forth below in all but exceptional circumstances.

Appearing below are lists of criteria to be applied in determining the best edition of each of several types of material. The criteria are listed in descending order of importance. In deciding between two editions, a criterion-by-criterion comparison should be made. The edition which first fails to satisfy a criterion is to be considered of inferior quality and will not be an acceptable deposit. For example, if a comparison is made between two hardbound editions of a book, one a trade edition printed on acid-free paper and the other a specially bound edition printed on average paper, the former will be the best edition because the type of paper is a more important criterion than the binding.

Under regulations of the Copyright Office, potential depositors may request authorization to deposit copies or phonorecords of other than the best edition of a specific work (e.g., a microform rather than a printed edition of a serial).

I. PRINTED TEXTUAL MATTER
  A.   Paper, Binding, and Packaging:
     1.   Archival-quality rather than less-permanent paper.
     2.   Hard cover rather than soft cover.
     3.   Library binding rather than commercial binding.
     4.   Trade edition rather than book club edition.
     5.   Sewn rather than glue-only binding.
     6.   Sewn or glued rather than stapled or spiral-bound.
     7.   Stapled rather than spiral-bound or plastic-bound.
     8.   Bound rather than looseleaf, except when future looseleaf insertions are to be issued.
     9.   Slipcased rather than nonslipcased.
    10.   With protective folders rather than without (for broadsides).
    11.   Rolled rather than folded (for broadsides).
    12.   With protective coatings rather than without (except broadsides, which should not be coated).
  B.   Rarity:
     1.   Special limited edition having the greatest number of special features.
     2.   Other limited edition rather than trade edition.
     3.   Special binding rather than trade binding.
  C.   Illustrations:
     1.   Illustrated rather than unillustrated.
     2.   Illustrations in color rather than black and white.
  D.   Special Features:
     1.   With thumb notches or index tabs rather than without.
     2.   With aids to use such as overlays and magnifiers rather than without.
  E.   Size:
     1.   Larger rather than smaller sizes. (Except that largetype editions for the partially sighted are not required in place of editions employing type of more conventional size.)

II. PHOTOGRAPHS
    A.   Size and finish, in descending order of preference:
        1.   The most widely distributed edition.
        2.   8 × 10 = inch glossy print.
        3.   Other size or finish.
    B.   Unmounted rather than mounted.
    C.   Archival-quality rather than less-permanent paper stock or printing process.

III. MOTION PICTURES
    A.   Film rather than another medium. Film editions are listed below in descending order of preference.
        1.   Preprint material, by special arrangement.
        2.   Film gauge in which most widely distributed.
        3.   35 mm. rather than 16 mm.
        4.   16 mm. rather than 8 mm.
        5.   Special formats (e.g., 65 mm) only in exceptional cases.
        6.   Open reel rather than cartridge or cassette.
    B.   Videotape rather than videodisc. Videotape editions are listed in descending order of preference.
        1.   Tape gauge in which most widely distributed.
        2.   Two-inch tape.
        3.   One-inch tape.
        4.   Three-quarter inch tape cassette.
        5.   One-half inch tape cassette.

IV. OTHER GRAPHIC MATTER
    A.   Paper and Printing:
        1.   Archival-quality rather than less-permanent paper.
        2.   Color rather than black and white.
    B.   Size and Content:
        1.   Larger rather than smaller size.
        2.   In the case of cartographic works, editions with the greatest amount of information rather than those with less detail.
    C.   Rarity:
        1.   The most widely distributed edition rather than one of limited distribution.
        2.   In the case of a work published only in a limited, numbered edition, one copy outside the numbered series but otherwise identical.
        3.   A photographic reproduction of the original, by special arrangement only.

D. Text and Other Materials:
1. Works with annotations, accompanying tabular or textual matter, or other interpretative aids rather than those without them.

E. Binding and Packaging:
1. Bound rather than unbound.
2. If editions have different binding, apply the criteria in I.A.2—I.A.7, above.
3. (No number "3" is listed)
4. Rolled rather than folded.
5. With protective coatings rather than without.

V. PHONORECORDS
A. Disc rather than tape.
B. With special enclosures rather than without.
C. Open-reel rather than cartridge.
D. Cartridge rather than cassette.
E. Quadraphonic rather than stereophonic.
F. True stereophonic rather than monaural.
G. Monaural rather than electronically rechanneled stereo.

VI. MUSICAL COMPOSITIONS
A. Fullness of Score:
1. Vocal music:
a. With orchestral accompaniment
   i. Full score and parts, if any, rather than conductor's score and parts, if any. (In cases of compositions published only by rental, lease, or lending, this requirement is reduced to full score only.)

   ii. Conductor's score and parts, if any, rather than condensed score and parts, if any. (In cases of compositions published only by rental, lease, or lending, this requirement is reduced to conductor's score only.)
b. Unaccompanied: Open score (each part on separate staff) rather than closed score (all parts condensed to two staves.)
2. Instrumental music:
a. Full score and parts, if any, rather than conductor's score and parts, if any. (In cases of compositions published only by rental, lease, or lending, this requirement is reduced to full score only.)
b. Conductor's score and parts, if any, rather than condensed score and parts, if any. (In cases of compositions published only by rental, lease, or lending, this requirement is reduced to conductor's score only.)

Printing and Paper:
1. Archival-quality rather than less-permanent paper.

C. Binding and Packaging:
1. Special limited editions rather than trade editions.
2. Bound rather than unbound.

3. If editions have different binding, apply the criteria in I.A.2—I.A.12, above.

4. With protective folders rather than without.

VII. MICROFORMS

A. Related materials:

1. With indexes, study guides, or other printed matter rather than without.

B. Permanence and Appearance:

1. Silver halide rather than any other medium.

2. Positive rather than negative.

3. Color rather than black and white.

C. Format (Newspapers and newspaper-formatted serials):

1. Reel microfilm rather than any other microform.

D. Format (all other materials):

1. Microfiche rather than reel microfilm.

2. Reel microfilm rather than microform cassettes.

3. Microfilm cassettes rather than micro-opaque prints.

E. Size:

1. 35 mm rather than 16 mm.

VIII. WORKS EXISTING IN MORE THAN ONE MEDIUM

Editions are listed below in descending order of preference.

A. Newspapers, dissertations and theses, newspaper-formatted.

1. Microform.

2. Printed matter.

B. All other materials:

1. Printed matter.

2. Microform.

3. Phonorecord.

(Effective January 1, 1978)

C

Copyright Forms

APPLICATION FOR RECORDATION OF COIN-OPERATED PHONORECORD PLAYERS

FOR COPYRIGHT OFFICE USE ONLY	
AMOUNT	REMITTANCE NUMBER

FORM JB

COPYRIGHT OFFICE

APPLICATION RECEIVED:

CERTIFICATE(S) ISSUED:

CERTIFICATE(S) MAILED:

(A) Operator

NAME AND ADDRESS OF OPERATOR:

Name: . . . .

Address: . . . .
(Number and Street)

. . . .
(City or Town)   (State)   (Zip Code)

(B) Summary of Application

LICENSING YEAR: (Give the calendar year covered by this application.)

Year: 19 . . . .

ROYALTY FEE: Multiply the total number of players covered by this application (including continuation sheets) by $63.

. . . . × **$63.** =
No. of players   **Royalty Rate**

TOTAL ROYALTY FEE:

$

*Royalty fee must be paid by certified check, cashier's check or money order, payable to: Register of Copyrights before certificates can be issued.

(C) Certification

CERTIFICATION ✱ I, the undersigned, hereby certify that I am the: (Check one)

☐ operator   ☐ duly authorized agent of operator . . . .
(Name of operator)

of the phonorecord players identified in this application, and that the statements made by me are correct to the best of my knowledge.

Handwritten signature: (X) . . . .

Typed or printed name: . . . .

Title: . . . .
(Corporate officer or partner—See instructions)

Date: . . . .

(D) Contact

INDIVIDUAL TO BE CONTACTED IF FURTHER INFORMATION IS NEEDED:

Name . . . . Telephone (. . . . . .) . . . .
(Area Code)

Address . . . .
(Number, Street, Rural Route, Apt. No.)

. . . .
(City, Town, State, Zip Code)

(E) Identification

IDENTIFICATION OF COIN-OPERATED PHONORECORD PLAYERS: Full name or abbreviation of manufacturer *must* be given in all cases. Serial number must be given if available. Other information must be given if serial number is lacking. See instructions.

1

Manufacturer . . . .
Serial Number . . . .

Other identifying information:
Model No. . . . . Model Year . . . .
Type of Sound: ☐ Mono   ☐ Stereo ☐ Quadraphonic   ☐ Other
Record Capacity . . . . Charge per play . . . .
Model Name

2

Manufacturer . . . .
Serial Number . . . .

Other identifying information:
Model No. . . . . Model Year . . . .
Type of Sound: ☐ Mono   ☐ Stereo ☐ Quadraphonic   ☐ Other
Record Capacity . . . . Charge per play . . . .
Model Name

3

Manufacturer . . . .
Serial Number . . . .

Other identifying information:
Model No. . . . . Model Year . . . .
Type of Sound: ☐ Mono   ☐ Stereo ☐ Quadraphonic   ☐ Other
Record Capacity . . . . Charge per play . . . .
Model Name . . . .

E (Continued)

4
Manufacturer. . . . .
Serial Number . . . .
FOR COPYRIGHT OFFICE USE ONLY
Other identifying information:
Model No. . . . . Model Year. . . . .
Type of Sound: ☐ Mono ☐ Stereo ☐ Quadraphonic ☐ Other
Record Capacity . . . . Charge per play . . . .
Model Name . . . .

5
Manufacturer. . . . .
Serial Number . . . .
FOR COPYRIGHT OFFICE USE ONLY
Other identifying information:
Model No. . . . . Model Year. . . . .
Type of Sound: ☐ Mono ☐ Stereo ☐ Quadraphonic ☐ Other
Record Capacity . . . . Charge per play . . . .
Model Name . . . .

6
Manufacturer. . . . .
Serial Number . . . .
FOR COPYRIGHT OFFICE USE ONLY
Other identifying information:
Model No. . . . . Model Year. . . . .
Type of Sound: ☐ Mono ☐ Stereo ☐ Quadraphonic ☐ Other
Record Capacity . . . . Charge per play . . . .
Model Name . . . .

7
Manufacturer. . . . .
Serial Number . . . .
FOR COPYRIGHT OFFICE USE ONLY
Other identifying information:
Model No. . . . . Model Year. . . . .
Type of Sound: ☐ Mono ☐ Stereo ☐ Quadraphonic ☐ Other
Record Capacity . . . . Charge per play . . . .
Model Name . . . .

8
Manufacturer. . . . .
Serial Number . . . .
FOR COPYRIGHT OFFICE USE ONLY
Other identifying information:
Model No. . . . . Model Year. . . . .
Type of Sound: ☐ Mono ☐ Stereo ☐ Quadraphonic ☐ Other
Record Capacity . . . . Charge per play . . . .
Model Name . . . .

9
Manufacturer. . . . .
Serial Number . . . .
FOR COPYRIGHT OFFICE USE ONLY
Other identifying information:
Model No. . . . . Model Year. . . . .
Type of Sound: ☐ Mono ☐ Stereo ☐ Quadraphonic ☐ Other
Record Capacity . . . . Charge per play . . . .
Model Name . . . .

10
Manufacturer. . . . .
Serial Number . . . .
FOR COPYRIGHT OFFICE USE ONLY
Other identifying information:
Model No. . . . . Model Year. . . . .
Type of Sound: ☐ Mono ☐ Stereo ☐ Quadraphonic ☐ Other
Record Capacity . . . . Charge per play . . . .
Model Name . . . .

11
Manufacturer. . . . .
Serial Number . . . .
FOR COPYRIGHT OFFICE USE ONLY
Other identifying information:
Model No. . . . . Model Year. . . . .
Type of Sound: ☐ Mono ☐ Stereo ☐ Quadraphonic ☐ Other
Record Capacity . . . . Charge per play . . . .
Model Name . . . .

12
Manufacturer. . . . .
Serial Number . . . .
FOR COPYRIGHT OFFICE USE ONLY
Other identifying information:
Model No. . . . . Model Year. . . . .
Type of Sound: ☐ Mono ☐ Stereo ☐ Quadraphonic ☐ Other
Record Capacity . . . . Charge per play . . . .
Model Name . . . .

13
Manufacturer. . . . .
Serial Number . . . .
FOR COPYRIGHT OFFICE USE ONLY
Other identifying information:
Model No. . . . . Model Year. . . . .
Type of Sound: ☐ Mono ☐ Stereo ☐ Quadraphonic ☐ Other
Record Capacity . . . . Charge per play . . . .
Model Name . . . .

14
Manufacturer. . . . .
Serial Number . . . .
FOR COPYRIGHT OFFICE USE ONLY
Other identifying information:
Model No. . . . . Model Year. . . . .
Type of Sound: ☐ Mono ☐ Stereo ☐ Quadraphonic ☐ Other
Record Capacity . . . . Charge per play . . . .
Model Name . . . .

15
Manufacturer. . . . .
Serial Number . . . .
FOR COPYRIGHT OFFICE USE ONLY
Other identifying information:
Model No. . . . . Model Year. . . . .
Type of Sound: ☐ Mono ☐ Stereo ☐ Quadraphonic ☐ Other
Record Capacity . . . . Charge per play . . . .
Model Name . . . .

USE FORM JB/CON TO LIST ADDITIONAL PLAYERS

* 17 USC § 116 (d): CRIMINAL PENALTIES—Any person who knowingly makes a false representation of a material fact in an application filed under clause (1)(A) of subsection (b)[of § 116], or who knowingly alters a certificate issued under clause (1)(B) of subsection (b)[of § 116] or knowingly affixes such a certificate to a phonorecord player other than the one it covers shall be fined not more than $2,500.

RENEWAL APPLICATION
FOR RECORDATION OF COIN-OPERATED
PHONORECORD PLAYERS

USE THIS FORM: To renew the license(s) you obtained last year for your coin-operated phonorecord players.

ATTACH TO THIS FORM: (1) One copy of the computer printout listing your machines that were licensed last year, marked up to delete any machines that are not to be renewed; (2) one or more continuation sheets (Form JB/CON) listing any additional machines to be licensed, and (3) a certified check, cashier's check, or money order in the full amount for the royalty fee computed in Space 3, below.

BEFORE COMPLETING THIS FORM: Be sure to read the accompanying instructions and general information.

FOR COPYRIGHT OFFICE USE ONLY		
AMOUNT	REMITTANCE NUMBER	
APPLICATION RECEIVED:		
(Month)	(Day)	(Year)
CERTIFICATE(S) ISSUED:		
(Month)	(Day)	(Year)

---

① Operator

NAME AND ADDRESS OF OPERATOR: The information you give here must agree with Space A of the attached printout.

Name: ....

Address: ....
(Number and Street)

....
(City or Town)   (State)   (Zip Code)

BUSINESS NAME(S) OF OPERATOR (IF DIFFERENT):

---

② Contact

INDIVIDUAL TO BE CONTACTED IF FURTHER INFORMATION IS NEEDED:

Name: .... Telephone (..........) ....
(Area Code)

Address: ....
(Number, Street, Rural Route, Apt. No.)

....
(City, Town, State, Zip Code)

---

③ Number of Players and Royalty Fee

NUMBER OF PLAYERS:

(a) Total number of players listed on attached printout (excluding deletions) .... _____

(b) Total number of players listed on all attached continuation sheets .... _____

(c) Total number of players covered by this renewal application (add lines (a) and (b)) ....

ROYALTY FEE: Multiply the total number of players covered by this renewal application by $63.

Total from line (c) _____ × $63 = $ _____

IMPORTANT: The royalty fee must be in the form of a certified check, cashier's check, or money order, payable to: *Register of Copyrights* before certificates can be issued.

---

④ Certification

CERTIFICATION: * I, the undersigned, hereby certify that: (Check one, but only one, of the boxes)

☐ **(Operator other than corporation or partnership)** I am the operator as identified in Space 1;

☐ **(Agent of operator other than corporation or partnership)** I am the duly authorized agent of the operator as identified in Space 1, and that operator is not a corporation or partnership; or

☐ **(Officer or partner)** I am the officer (if a corporation) or a partner (if a partnership) of the legal entity identified as operator in Space 1.

I certify that the statements made by me in this application are correct to the best of my knowledge.

(Application is not acceptable unless certified and signed)

Handwritten signature: (X)...

Typed or printed name: ....

Title: ....
(Title of official position held in corporation or partnership)

Date: ....

REMEMBER: Be sure to sign and return this form with: one copy of the printout; one or more continuation sheets (Form JB/CON), if necessary; and a certified check, cashier's check, or money order in the full amount you gave in Space 3.

*17 USC §116(d): CRIMINAL PENALTIES—Any person who knowingly makes a false representation of a material fact in an application filed under clause (1)(A) of subsection (b) of §116, or who knowingly alters a certificate issued under clause (1)(B) of subsection (b) of §116] or knowingly affixes such a certificate to a phonorecord player other than the one it covers shall be fined not more than $2,500.

FORM PA

UNITED STATES COPYRIGHT OFFICE

REGISTRATION NUMBER

| PA | PAU |

EFFECTIVE DATE OF REGISTRATION

| Month | Day | Year |

DO NOT WRITE ABOVE THIS LINE. IF YOU NEED MORE SPACE, USE A SEPARATE CONTINUATION SHEET.

1

TITLE OF THIS WORK ▼

PREVIOUS OR ALTERNATIVE TITLES ▼

NATURE OF THIS WORK ▼ See instructions

2 a

NAME OF AUTHOR ▼

DATES OF BIRTH AND DEATH
Year Born ▼   Year Died ▼

Was this contribution to the work a "work made for hire"?
☐ Yes
☐ No

AUTHOR'S NATIONALITY OR DOMICILE
Name of Country
OR { Citizen of ▶
     Domiciled in ▶

WAS THIS AUTHOR'S CONTRIBUTION TO THE WORK
Anonymous? ☐ Yes ☐ No
Pseudonymous? ☐ Yes ☐ No
If the answer to either of these questions is "Yes," see detailed instructions.

NATURE OF AUTHORSHIP Briefly describe nature of the material created by this author in which copyright is claimed. ▼

NOTE

Under the law, the "author" of a "work made for hire" is generally the employer, not the employee (see instructions). For any part of this work that was "made for hire" check "Yes" in the space provided, give the employer (or other person for whom the work was prepared) as "Author" of that part, and leave the space for dates of birth and death blank.

b

NAME OF AUTHOR ▼

DATES OF BIRTH AND DEATH
Year Born ▼   Year Died ▼

Was this contribution to the work a "work made for hire"?
☐ Yes
☐ No

AUTHOR'S NATIONALITY OR DOMICILE
Name of Country
OR { Citizen of ▶
     Domiciled in ▶

WAS THIS AUTHOR'S CONTRIBUTION TO THE WORK
Anonymous? ☐ Yes ☐ No
Pseudonymous? ☐ Yes ☐ No
If the answer to either of these questions is "Yes," see detailed instructions.

NATURE OF AUTHORSHIP Briefly describe nature of the material created by this author in which copyright is claimed. ▼

c

NAME OF AUTHOR ▼

DATES OF BIRTH AND DEATH
Year Born ▼   Year Died ▼

Was this contribution to the work a "work made for hire"?
☐ Yes
☐ No

AUTHOR'S NATIONALITY OR DOMICILE
Name of Country
OR { Citizen of ▶
     Domiciled in ▶

WAS THIS AUTHOR'S CONTRIBUTION TO THE WORK
Anonymous? ☐ Yes ☐ No
Pseudonymous? ☐ Yes ☐ No
If the answer to either of these questions is "Yes," see detailed instructions.

NATURE OF AUTHORSHIP Briefly describe nature of the material created by this author in which copyright is claimed. ▼

3

YEAR IN WHICH CREATION OF THIS WORK WAS COMPLETED This information must be given in all cases.
◀ Year

DATE AND NATION OF FIRST PUBLICATION OF THIS PARTICULAR WORK
Complete this information ONLY if this work has been published.
Month ▶ _____ Day ▶ _____ Year ▶ _____
◀ Nation

4

COPYRIGHT CLAIMANT(S) Name and address must be given even if the claimant is the same as the author given in space 2.▼

See instructions before completing this space.

TRANSFER If the claimant(s) named here in space 4 are different from the author(s) named in space 2, give a brief statement of how the claimant(s) obtained ownership of the copyright.▼

APPLICATION RECEIVED

ONE DEPOSIT RECEIVED

TWO DEPOSITS RECEIVED

REMITTANCE NUMBER AND DATE

DO NOT WRITE HERE OFFICE USE ONLY

MORE ON BACK ▶ • Complete all applicable spaces (numbers 5-9) on the reverse side of this page.
• See detailed instructions.   • Sign the form at line 8.

DO NOT WRITE HERE

Page 1 of _____ pages

EXAMINED BY	FORM PA
CHECKED BY	
☐ CORRESPONDENCE Yes	FOR COPYRIGHT OFFICE
☐ DEPOSIT ACCOUNT FUNDS USED	USE ONLY

DO NOT WRITE ABOVE THIS LINE. IF YOU NEED MORE SPACE, USE A SEPARATE CONTINUATION SHEET.

PREVIOUS REGISTRATION Has registration for this work, or for an earlier version of this work, already been made in the Copyright Office?
☐ **Yes** ☐ **No** If your answer is "Yes," why is another registration being sought? (Check appropriate box) ▼

☐ This is the first published edition of a work previously registered in unpublished form.

☐ This is the first application submitted by this author as copyright claimant.

☐ This is a changed version of the work, as shown by space 6 on this application.

If your answer is "Yes," give: **Previous Registration Number** ▼   **Year of Registration** ▼

5

DERIVATIVE WORK OR COMPILATION Complete both space 6a & 6b for a derivative work; complete only 6b for a compilation.
a. Preexisting Material Identify any preexisting work or works that this work is based on or incorporates. ▼

6

See instructions before completing this space.

b. Material Added to This Work Give a brief, general statement of the material that has been added to this work and in which copyright is claimed. ▼

DEPOSIT ACCOUNT If the registration fee is to be charged to a Deposit Account established in the Copyright Office, give name and number of Account.
Name ▼   **Account Number** ▼

7

CORRESPONDENCE Give name and address to which correspondence about this application should be sent.   Name/Address/Apt/City/State/Zip ▼

Be sure to give your daytime phone number.

Area Code & Telephone Number ▶

CERTIFICATION* I, the undersigned, hereby certify that I am the
Check only one ▼

☐ author

☐ other copyright claimant

☐ owner of exclusive right(s)

☐ authorized agent of _____
Name of author or other copyright claimant, or owner of exclusive right(s) ▲

8

of the work identified in this application and that the statements made
by me in this application are correct to the best of my knowledge.

Typed or printed name and date ▼ If this is a published work, this date must be the same as or later than the date of publication given in space 3.

_____ date ▶ _____

☞ **Handwritten signature (X)** ▼

MAIL CERTIFI- CATE TO	Name ▼	**Have you:** • Completed all necessary spaces? • Signed your application in space 8?
	Number/Street/Apartment Number ▼	• Enclosed check or money order for $10 payable to Register of Copyrights? • Enclosed your deposit material with the application and fee?
Certificate will be mailed in window envelope	City/State/ZIP ▼	**MAIL TO:** Register of Copyrights, Library of Congress, Washington, D.C. 20559.

9

* 17 U.S.C. § 506(e): Any person who knowingly makes a false representation of a material fact in the application for copyright registration provided for by section 409, or in any written statement filed in connection with the application, shall be fined not more than $2,500.

☆U.S. GOVERNMENT PRINTING OFFICE: 1985: 461–584/20,003   July 1985—200,000

FORM SR
UNITED STATES COPYRIGHT OFFICE

REGISTRATION NUMBER

_____

SR   SRU

EFFECTIVE DATE OF REGISTRATION

_____

Month   Day   Year

DO NOT WRITE ABOVE THIS LINE. IF YOU NEED MORE SPACE, USE A SEPARATE CONTINUATION SHEET.

1

TITLE OF THIS WORK ▼

_____

PREVIOUS OR ALTERNATIVE TITLES ▼

_____

NATURE OF MATERIAL RECORDED ▼ See instructions.
☐ Musical   ☐ Musical-Dramatic
☐ Dramatic   ☐ Literary
☐ Other _____

2   a

NAME OF AUTHOR ▼

DATES OF BIRTH AND DEATH
Year Born ▼   Year Died ▼

Was this contribution to the work a "work made for hire"?	AUTHOR'S NATIONALITY OR DOMICILE Name of Country	WAS THIS AUTHOR'S CONTRIBUTION TO THE WORK	
☐ Yes	OR { Citizen of ▶ _____	Anonymous? ☐ Yes ☐ No	If the answer to either of these questions is "Yes," see detailed instructions.
☐ No	Domiciled in ▶ _____	Pseudonymous? ☐ Yes ☐ No	

NATURE OF AUTHORSHIP Briefly describe nature of the material created by this author in which copyright is claimed. ▼

NOTE

Under the law, the "author" of a "work made for hire" is generally the employer, not the employee (see instructions). For any part of this work that was "made for hire" check "Yes" in the space provided, give the employer (or other person for whom the work was prepared) as "Author" of that part, and leave the space for dates of birth and death blank.

b

NAME OF AUTHOR ▼

DATES OF BIRTH AND DEATH
Year Born ▼   Year Died ▼

Was this contribution to the work a "work made for hire"?	AUTHOR'S NATIONALITY OR DOMICILE Name of Country	WAS THIS AUTHOR'S CONTRIBUTION TO THE WORK	
☐ Yes	OR { Citizen of ▶ _____	Anonymous? ☐ Yes ☐ No	If the answer to either of these questions is "Yes," see detailed instructions.
☐ No	Domiciled in ▶ _____	Pseudonymous? ☐ Yes ☐ No	

NATURE OF AUTHORSHIP Briefly describe nature of the material created by this author in which copyright is claimed. ▼

c

NAME OF AUTHOR ▼

DATES OF BIRTH AND DEATH
Year Born ▼   Year Died ▼

Was this contribution to the work a "work made for hire"?	AUTHOR'S NATIONALITY OR DOMICILE Name of Country	WAS THIS AUTHOR'S CONTRIBUTION TO THE WORK	
☐ Yes	OR { Citizen of ▶ _____	Anonymous? ☐ Yes ☐ No	If the answer to either of these questions is "Yes," see detailed instructions.
☐ No	Domiciled in ▶ _____	Pseudonymous? ☐ Yes ☐ No	

NATURE OF AUTHORSHIP Briefly describe nature of the material created by this author in which copyright is claimed. ▼

3

YEAR IN WHICH CREATION OF THIS WORK WAS COMPLETED This information must be given in all cases.
◀ Year

DATE AND NATION OF FIRST PUBLICATION OF THIS PARTICULAR WORK
Complete this information Month ▶ _____ Day ▶ _____ Year ▶ _____
ONLY if this work has been published.
◀ Nation

4

See instructions before completing this space.

COPYRIGHT CLAIMANT(S) Name and address must be given even if the claimant is the same as the author given in space 2.▼

TRANSFER If the claimant(s) named here in space 4 are different from the author(s) named in space 2, give a brief statement of how the claimant(s) obtained ownership of the copyright.▼

DO NOT WRITE HERE
OFFICE USE ONLY

APPLICATION RECEIVED

ONE DEPOSIT RECEIVED

TWO DEPOSITS RECEIVED

REMITTANCE NUMBER AND DATE

MORE ON BACK ▶ • Complete all applicable spaces (numbers 5-9) on the reverse side of this page.
• See detailed instructions.   • Sign the form at line 8.

DO NOT WRITE HERE

Page 1 of_____pages

<table>
<tr><td>EXAMINED BY</td><td>FORM SR</td></tr>
<tr><td>CHECKED BY</td><td></td></tr>
<tr><td>☐ CORRESPONDENCE Yes</td><td rowspan="2">FOR COPYRIGHT OFFICE USE ONLY</td></tr>
<tr><td>☐ DEPOSIT ACCOUNT FUNDS USED</td></tr>
</table>

DO NOT WRITE ABOVE THIS LINE. IF YOU NEED MORE SPACE, USE A SEPARATE CONTINUATION SHEET.

PREVIOUS REGISTRATION Has registration for this work, or for an earlier version of this work, already been made in the Copyright Office?

☐ Yes ☐ No If your answer is "Yes," why is another registration being sought? (Check appropriate box) ▼

☐ This is the first published edition of a work previously registered in unpublished form.

☐ This is the first application submitted by this author as copyright claimant.

☐ This is a changed version of the work, as shown by space 6 on this application.

If your answer is "Yes," give: **Previous Registration Number ▼**   **Year of Registration ▼**

5

DERIVATIVE WORK OR COMPILATION Complete both space 6a & 6b for a derivative work; complete only 6b for a compilation.

a. Preexisting Material Identify any preexisting work or works that this work is based on or incorporates. ▼

b. Material Added to This Work Give a brief, general statement of the material that has been added to this work and in which copyright is claimed. ▼

6

See instructions before completing this space

DEPOSIT ACCOUNT If the registration fee is to be charged to a Deposit Account established in the Copyright Office, give name and number of Account.

Name ▼   **Account Number ▼**

7

CORRESPONDENCE Give name and address to which correspondence about this application should be sent.   Name Address Apt City State Zip ▼

Area Code & Telephone Number ►

Be sure to give your daytime phone ◄ number

CERTIFICATION* I, the undersigned, hereby certify that I am the

Check one ▼

☐ author

☐ other copyright claimant

☐ owner of exclusive right(s)

☐ authorized agent of _____
Name of author or other copyright claimant, or owner of exclusive right(s) ▲

of the work identified in this application and that the statements made by me in this application are correct to the best of my knowledge.

8

Typed or printed name and date ▼ If this is a published work, this date must be the same as or later than the date of publication given in space 3.

date ► _____

☞ **Handwritten signature (X) ▼**

MAIL CERTIFI-CATE TO	Name ▼	**Have you:** • Completed all necessary spaces? • Signed your application in space 8?
	Number/Street/Apartment Number ▼	• Enclosed check or money order for $10 payable to *Register of Copyrights*?
Certificate will be mailed in window envelope	City/State/ZIP ▼	• Enclosed your deposit material with the application and fee? **MAIL TO:** Register of Copyrights, Library of Congress, Washington, D.C. 20559

9

* 17 U.S.C. § 506(e) Any person who knowingly makes a false representation of a material fact in the application for copyright registration provided for by section 409, or in any written statement filed in connection with the application, shall be fined not more than $2,500.

☆ U.S. GOVERNMENT PRINTING OFFICE: 1984—461-584/10,011

November 1984 — 100,000

FORM TX

UNITED STATES COPYRIGHT OFFICE

REGISTRATION NUMBER

_____

TX   TXU

EFFECTIVE DATE OF REGISTRATION

Month   Day   Year

DO NOT WRITE ABOVE THIS LINE. IF YOU NEED MORE SPACE, USE A SEPARATE CONTINUATION SHEET.

1

TITLE OF THIS WORK ▼

PREVIOUS OR ALTERNATIVE TITLES ▼

PUBLICATION AS A CONTRIBUTION   If this work was published as a contribution to a periodical, serial, or collection, give information about the collective work in which the contribution appeared.   **Title of Collective Work ▼**

If published in a periodical or serial give: **Volume ▼**   **Number ▼**   **Issue Date ▼**   **On Pages ▼**

---

2   a

NAME OF AUTHOR ▼

DATES OF BIRTH AND DEATH
Year Born ▼   Year Died ▼

Was this contribution to the work a "work made for hire"?
☐ Yes
☐ No

AUTHOR'S NATIONALITY OR DOMICILE
Name of Country
OR { Citizen of ▶_____
Domiciled in ▶_____

WAS THIS AUTHOR'S CONTRIBUTION TO THE WORK
Anonymous?   ☐ Yes ☐ No
Pseudonymous?   ☐ Yes ☐ No
If the answer to either of these questions is "Yes," see detailed instructions.

NATURE OF AUTHORSHIP   Briefly describe nature of the material created by this author in which copyright is claimed. ▼

NOTE

Under the law, the "author" of a "work made for hire" is generally the employer, not the employee (see instructions). For any part of this work that was "made for hire" check "Yes" in the space provided, give the employer (or other person for whom the work was prepared) as "Author" of that part, and leave the space for dates of birth and death blank.

b

NAME OF AUTHOR ▼

DATES OF BIRTH AND DEATH
Year Born ▼   Year Died ▼

Was this contribution to the work a "work made for hire"?
☐ Yes
☐ No

AUTHOR'S NATIONALITY OR DOMICILE
Name of country
OR { Citizen of ▶_____
Domiciled in ▶_____

WAS THIS AUTHOR'S CONTRIBUTION TO THE WORK
Anonymous?   ☐ Yes ☐ No
Pseudonymous?   ☐ Yes ☐ No
If the answer to either of these questions is "Yes," see detailed instructions.

NATURE OF AUTHORSHIP   Briefly describe nature of the material created by this author in which copyright is claimed. ▼

c

NAME OF AUTHOR ▼

DATES OF BIRTH AND DEATH
Year Born ▼   Year Died ▼

Was this contribution to the work a "work made for hire"?
☐ Yes
☐ No

AUTHOR'S NATIONALITY OR DOMICILE
Name of Country
OR { Citizen of ▶_____
Domiciled in ▶_____

WAS THIS AUTHOR'S CONTRIBUTION TO THE WORK
Anonymous?   ☐ Yes ☐ No
Pseudonymous?   ☐ Yes ☐ No
If the answer to either of these questions is "Yes," see detailed instructions.

NATURE OF AUTHORSHIP   Briefly describe nature of the material created by this author in which copyright is claimed. ▼

3

YEAR IN WHICH CREATION OF THIS WORK WAS COMPLETED   This information must be given in all cases.
◀ Year

DATE AND NATION OF FIRST PUBLICATION OF THIS PARTICULAR WORK
Complete this information ONLY if this work has been published.
Month ▶_____ Day ▶_____ Year ▶_____
◀ Nation

4

See instructions before completing this space.

COPYRIGHT CLAIMANT(S) Name and address must be given even if the claimant is the same as the author given in space 2.▼

TRANSFER If the claimant(s) named here in space 4 are different from the author(s) named in space 2, give a brief statement of how the claimant(s) obtained ownership of the copyright.▼

APPLICATION RECEIVED

ONE DEPOSIT RECEIVED

TWO DEPOSITS RECEIVED

REMITTANCE NUMBER AND DATE

DO NOT WRITE HERE
OFFICE USE ONLY

MORE ON BACK ▶   • Complete all applicable spaces (numbers 5-11) on the reverse side of this page.
• See detailed instructions.   • Sign the form at line 10.

DO NOT WRITE HERE

Page 1 of_____pages

<table>
<tr><td></td><td>EXAMINED BY</td><td>FORM TX</td></tr>
<tr><td></td><td>CHECKED BY</td><td></td></tr>
<tr><td></td><td>☐ CORRESPONDENCE Yes</td><td rowspan="2">FOR COPYRIGHT OFFICE USE ONLY</td></tr>
<tr><td></td><td>☐ DEPOSIT ACCOUNT FUNDS USED</td></tr>
</table>

DO NOT WRITE ABOVE THIS LINE. IF YOU NEED MORE SPACE, USE A SEPARATE CONTINUATION SHEET.

PREVIOUS REGISTRATION Has registration for this work, or for an earlier version of this work, already been made in the Copyright Office?
☐ Yes ☐ No If your answer is "Yes," why is another registration being sought? (Check appropriate box) ▼

☐ This is the first published edition of a work previously registered in unpublished form.

☐ This is the first application submitted by this author as copyright claimant.

☐ This is a changed version of the work, as shown by space 6 on this application.

If your answer is "Yes," give: **Previous Registration Number** ▼   **Year of Registration** ▼

5

DERIVATIVE WORK OR COMPILATION Complete both space 6a & 6b for a derivative work; complete only 6b for a compilation.
a. Preexisting Material Identify any preexisting work or works that this work is based on or incorporates. ▼

b. Material Added to This Work Give a brief, general statement of the material that has been added to this work and in which copyright is claimed. ▼

See instructions before completing this space.

6

MANUFACTURERS AND LOCATIONS If this is a published work consisting preponderantly of nondramatic literary material in English, the law may require that the copies be manufactured in the United States or Canada for full protection. If so, the names of the manufacturers who performed certain processes, and the places where these processes were performed **must** be given. See instructions for details.
Names of Manufacturers ▼   **Places of Manufacture** ▼

7

REPRODUCTION FOR USE OF BLIND OR PHYSICALLY HANDICAPPED INDIVIDUALS   A signature on this form at space 10, and a check in one of the boxes here in space 8, constitutes a non-exclusive grant of permission to the Library of Congress to reproduce and distribute solely for the blind and physically handicapped and under the conditions and limitations prescribed by the regulations of the Copyright Office: (1) copies of the work identified in space 1 of this application in Braille (or similar tactile symbols); or (2) phonorecords embodying a fixation of a reading of that work; or (3) both.

a ☐ Copies and Phonorecords   b ☐ Copies Only   c ☐ Phonorecords Only   See instructions.

8

DEPOSIT ACCOUNT If the registration fee is to be charged to a Deposit Account established in the Copyright Office, give name and number of Account.
Name ▼   **Account Number** ▼

CORRESPONDENCE Give name and address to which correspondence about this application should be sent. Name/Address/Apt/City/State/Zip ▼

Be sure to give your daytime phone ◄ number.

Area Code & Telephone Number ►

9

CERTIFICATION* I, the undersigned, hereby certify that I am the

Check one ►

☐ author
☐ other copyright claimant
☐ owner of exclusive right(s)
☐ authorized agent of _____

of the work identified in this application and that the statements made by me in this application are correct to the best of my knowledge.

Name of author or other copyright claimant, or owner of exclusive right(s) ▲

Typed or printed name and date ▼ If this is a published work, this date must be the same as or later than the date of publication given in space 3.

_____ date ► _____

Handwritten signature (X) ▼

10

<table>
<tr><td rowspan="3">MAIL CERTIFI-CATE TO

Certificate will be mailed in window envelope</td><td>Name ▼</td><td rowspan="3">Have you:
• Completed all necessary spaces?
• Signed your application in space 10?
• Enclosed check or money order for $10 payable to Register of Copyrights?
• Enclosed your deposit material with the application and fee?
MAIL TO: Register of Copyrights, Library of Congress, Washington, D.C. 20559.</td></tr>
<tr><td>Number/Street/Apartment Number ▼</td></tr>
<tr><td>City/State/ZIP ▼</td></tr>
</table>

11

* 17 U.S.C. § 506(e): Any person who knowingly makes a false representation of a material fact in the application for copyright registration provided for by section 409, or in any written statement filed in connection with the application, shall be fined not more than $2,500.

☆ U.S. GOVERNMENT PRINTING OFFICE: 1985: 461-584/10,024   May 1985 — 200,000

FORM VA

UNITED STATES COPYRIGHT OFFICE

REGISTRATION NUMBER

VA   VAU

EFFECTIVE DATE OF REGISTRATION

Month   Day   Year

DO NOT WRITE ABOVE THIS LINE. IF YOU NEED MORE SPACE, USE A SEPARATE CONTINUATION SHEET.

1   **TITLE OF THIS WORK ▼**   **NATURE OF THIS WORK ▼** See instructions

PREVIOUS OR ALTERNATIVE TITLES ▼

PUBLICATION AS A CONTRIBUTION   If this work was published as a contribution to a periodical, serial, or collection, give information about the collective work in which the contribution appeared.   **Title of Collective Work ▼**

If published in a periodical or serial give: **Volume ▼**   **Number ▼**   **Issue Date ▼**   **On Pages ▼**

2   **a**   **NAME OF AUTHOR ▼**   **DATES OF BIRTH AND DEATH**
                                                        Year Born ▼   Year Died ▼

Was this contribution to the work a   **AUTHOR'S NATIONALITY OR DOMICILE**   **WAS THIS AUTHOR'S CONTRIBUTION TO**
         "work made for hire"?   Name of Country   **THE WORK**   If the answer to either
☐ Yes   { Citizen of ▶ ——————   Anonymous?   ☐ Yes ☐ No   of these questions is
☐ No   **OR** { Domiciled in ▶ ——————   Pseudonymous?   ☐ Yes ☐ No   "Yes," see detailed
                                                                           instructions.

NOTE   **NATURE OF AUTHORSHIP**   Briefly describe nature of the material created by this author in which copyright is claimed. ▼

Under the law, the "author" of a "work made for hire" is generally the employer, not the employee (see instructions). For any part of this work that was "made for hire" check "Yes" in the space provided, give the employer (or other person for whom the work was prepared) as "Author" of that part, and leave the space for dates of birth and death blank.

b   **NAME OF AUTHOR ▼**   **DATES OF BIRTH AND DEATH**
                                                        Year Born ▼   Year Died ▼

Was this contribution to the work a   **AUTHOR'S NATIONALITY OR DOMICILE**   **WAS THIS AUTHOR'S CONTRIBUTION TO**
         "work made for hire"?   Name of country   **THE WORK**   If the answer to either
☐ Yes   { Citizen of ▶ ——————   Anonymous?   ☐ Yes ☐ No   of these questions is
☐ No   **OR** { Domiciled in ▶ ——————   Pseudonymous?   ☐ Yes ☐ No   "Yes," see detailed
                                                                           instructions.

NATURE OF AUTHORSHIP   Briefly describe nature of the material created by this author in which copyright is claimed. ▼

c   **NAME OF AUTHOR ▼**   **DATES OF BIRTH AND DEATH**
                                                        Year Born ▼   Year Died ▼

Was this contribution to the work a   **AUTHOR'S NATIONALITY OR DOMICILE**   **WAS THIS AUTHOR'S CONTRIBUTION TO**
         "work made for hire"?   Name of Country   **THE WORK**   If the answer to either
☐ Yes   { Citizen of ▶ ——————   Anonymous?   ☐ Yes ☐ No   of these questions is
☐ No   **OR** { Domiciled in ▶ ——————   Pseudonymous?   ☐ Yes ☐ No   "Yes," see detailed
                                                                           instructions.

NATURE OF AUTHORSHIP   Briefly describe nature of the material created by this author in which copyright is claimed. ▼

3   **YEAR IN WHICH CREATION OF THIS**   **DATE AND NATION OF FIRST PUBLICATION OF THIS PARTICULAR WORK**
    WORK WAS COMPLETED This information   Complete this information Month ▶ ——————— Day ▶ ———— Year ▶ ————
                          must be given   ONLY if this work
             ◀ Year   in all cases.   has been published.   ◀ Nation

4   **COPYRIGHT CLAIMANT(S)** Name and address must be given even if the claimant is the same as the author given in space 2.▼

                                                              APPLICATION RECEIVED

See instructions before completing this space.

                                                              ONE DEPOSIT RECEIVED

                                                               TWO DEPOSITS RECEIVED

DO NOT WRITE HERE / OFFICE USE ONLY

TRANSFER If the claimant(s) named here in space 4 are different from the author(s) named in space 2, give a brief statement of how the claimant(s) obtained ownership of the copyright.▼   REMITTANCE NUMBER AND DATE

MORE ON BACK ▶   • Complete all applicable spaces (numbers 5-9) on the reverse side of this page.   **DO NOT WRITE HERE**
                 • See detailed instructions.   • Sign the form at line 8.   Page 1 of ———— pages

EXAMINED BY

CHECKED BY

FORM VA

☐ CORRESPONDENCE
  Yes

☐ DEPOSIT ACCOUNT
  FUNDS USED

FOR
COPYRIGHT
OFFICE
USE
ONLY

DO NOT WRITE ABOVE THIS LINE. IF YOU NEED MORE SPACE, USE A SEPARATE CONTINUATION SHEET.

PREVIOUS REGISTRATION   Has registration for this work, or for an earlier version of this work, already been made in the Copyright Office?
☐ Yes ☐ No   If your answer is "Yes," why is another registration being sought? (Check appropriate box) ▼

☐ This is the first published edition of a work previously registered in unpublished form.

☐ This is the first application submitted by this author as copyright claimant.

☐ This is a changed version of the work, as shown by space 6 on this application.

If your answer is "Yes," give: **Previous Registration Number** ▼   **Year of Registration** ▼

5

DERIVATIVE WORK OR COMPILATION   Complete both space 6a & 6b for a derivative work; complete only 6b for a compilation.
a.   Preexisting Material   Identify any preexisting work or works that this work is based on or incorporates. ▼

b.   Material Added to This Work   Give a brief, general statement of the material that has been added to this work and in which copyright is claimed.▼

6

See instructions
before completing
this space.

DEPOSIT ACCOUNT   If the registration fee is to be charged to a Deposit Account established in the Copyright Office, give name and number of Account.
Name ▼   **Account Number** ▼

7

CORRESPONDENCE   Give name and address to which correspondence about this application should be sent.   Name/Address/Apt/City/State/Zip ▼

Area Code & Telephone Number ▶

Be sure to
give your
daytime phone
◀ number.

CERTIFICATION*   I, the undersigned, hereby certify that I am the
Check only one ▼

☐ author
☐ other copyright claimant
☐ owner of exclusive right(s)
☐ authorized agent of_____
                      Name of author or other copyright claimant, or owner of exclusive right(s) ▲

8

of the work identified in this application and that the statements made
by me in this application are correct to the best of my knowledge.

Typed or printed name and date ▼ If this is a published work, this date must be the same as or later than the date of publication given in space 3.

                                                    date ▶

☞ **Handwritten signature (X)** ▼

**MAIL
CERTIFI-
CATE TO**

**Certificate
will be
mailed in
window
envelope**

Name ▼

Number/Street/Apartment Number ▼

City/State/ZIP ▼

Have you:
• Completed all necessary
  spaces?
• Signed your application in space
  8?
• Enclosed check or money order
  for $10 payable to Register of
  Copyrights?
• Enclosed your deposit material
  with the application and fee?
MAIL TO: Register of Copyrights,
Library of Congress, Washington,
D.C. 20559.

9

☆U.S. GOVERNMENT PRINTING OFFICE: 1986—491–560/20,016   February 1986—40,000

FORM SE
UNITED STATES COPYRIGHT OFFICE

REGISTRATION NUMBER

_____

U

EFFECTIVE DATE OF REGISTRATION

_____

Month   Day   Year

DO NOT WRITE ABOVE THIS LINE. IF YOU NEED MORE SPACE, USE A SEPARATE CONTINUATION SHEET.

1
TITLE OF THIS SERIAL ▼

Volume ▼   Number ▼   Date on Copies ▼   Frequency of Publication ▼

PREVIOUS OR ALTERNATIVE TITLES ▼

2
a

NAME OF AUTHOR ▼

DATES OF BIRTH AND DEATH
Year Born ▼   Year Died ▼

Was this contribution to the work a "work made for hire"?
☐ Yes
☐ No

AUTHOR'S NATIONALITY OR DOMICILE
Name of Country
OR { Citizen of ▶ _____
Domiciled in ▶ _____

WAS THIS AUTHOR'S CONTRIBUTION TO THE WORK
Anonymous? ☐ Yes ☐ No
Pseudonymous? ☐ Yes ☐ No
If the answer to either of these questions is "Yes," see detailed instructions.

NATURE OF AUTHORSHIP Briefly describe nature of the material created by this author in which copyright is claimed. ▼
☐ Collective Work   Other:

NOTE
Under the law, the "author" of a "work made for hire" is generally the employer, not the employee (see instructions). For any part of this work that was "made for hire" check "Yes" in the space provided, give the employer (or other person for whom the work was prepared) as "Author" of that part, and leave the space for dates of birth and death blank.

b

NAME OF AUTHOR ▼

DATES OF BIRTH AND DEATH
Year Born ▼   Year Died ▼

Was this contribution to the work a "work made for hire"?
☐ Yes
☐ No

AUTHOR'S NATIONALITY OR DOMICILE
Name of country
OR { Citizen of ▶ _____
Domiciled in ▶ _____

WAS THIS AUTHOR'S CONTRIBUTION TO THE WORK
Anonymous? ☐ Yes ☐ No
Pseudonymous? ☐ Yes ☐ No
If the answer to either of these questions is "Yes," see detailed instructions.

NATURE OF AUTHORSHIP Briefly describe nature of the material created by this author in which copyright is claimed. ▼
☐ Collective Work   Other:

c

NAME OF AUTHOR ▼

DATES OF BIRTH AND DEATH
Year Born ▼   Year Died ▼

Was this contribution to the work a "work made for hire"?
☐ Yes
☐ No

AUTHOR'S NATIONALITY OR DOMICILE
Name of Country
OR { Citizen of ▶ _____
Domiciled in ▶ _____

WAS THIS AUTHOR'S CONTRIBUTION TO THE WORK
Anonymous? ☐ Yes ☐ No
Pseudonymous? ☐ Yes ☐ No
If the answer to either of these questions is "Yes," see detailed instructions.

NATURE OF AUTHORSHIP Briefly describe nature of the material created by this author in which copyright is claimed. ▼
☐ Collective Work   Other:

3
YEAR IN WHICH CREATION OF THIS ISSUE WAS COMPLETED This information must be given in all cases. ◀ Year

DATE AND NATION OF FIRST PUBLICATION OF THIS PARTICULAR ISSUE
Complete this information ONLY if this work has been published. Month ▶ _____ Day ▶ _____ Year ▶ _____ ◀ Nation

4
COPYRIGHT CLAIMANT(S) Name and address must be given even if the claimant is the same as the author given in space 2.▼

See instructions before completing this space.

TRANSFER If the claimant(s) named here in space 4 are different from the author(s) named in space 2, give a brief statement of how the claimant(s) obtained ownership of the copyright.▼

APPLICATION RECEIVED

ONE DEPOSIT RECEIVED

TWO DEPOSITS RECEIVED

REMITTANCE NUMBER AND DATE

DO NOT WRITE HERE OFFICE USE ONLY

MORE ON BACK ▶
- Complete all applicable spaces (numbers 5-11) on the reverse side of this page.
- See detailed instructions.
- Sign the form at line 10.

DO NOT WRITE HERE

Page 1 of _____ pages

EXAMINED BY		FORM SE
CHECKED BY		
☐ CORRESPONDENCE Yes		FOR COPYRIGHT OFFICE USE ONLY
☐ DEPOSIT ACCOUNT FUNDS USED		

DO NOT WRITE ABOVE THIS LINE. IF YOU NEED MORE SPACE, USE A SEPARATE CONTINUATION SHEET.

PREVIOUS REGISTRATION   Has registration for this issue, or for an earlier version of this particular issue, already been made in the Copyright Office?

☐ **Yes** ☐ **No**   If your answer is "Yes," why is another registration being sought? (Check appropriate box) ▼

a. ☐ This is the first published version of an issue previously registered in unpublished form.

b. ☐ This is the first application submitted by this author as copyright claimant.

c. ☐ This is a changed version of this issue, as shown by space 6 on this application.

If your answer is "Yes," give: **Previous Registration Number** ▼   **Year of Registration** ▼

5

DERIVATIVE WORK OR COMPILATION   Complete both space 6a & 6b for a derivative work; complete only 6b for a compilation.

a.   **Preexisting Material**   Identify any preexisting work or works that this work is based on or incorporates. ▼

b.   **Material Added to This Work**   Give a brief, general statement of the material that has been added to this work and in which copyright is claimed.▼

6

See instructions
before completing
this space.

MANUFACTURERS AND LOCATIONS   If this is a published work consisting preponderantly of nondramatic literary material in English, the law may require that the copies be manufactured in the United States or Canada for full protection. If so, the names of the manufacturers who performed certain processes, and the places where these processes were performed **must** be given. See instructions for details.

Names of Manufacturers ▼   **Places of Manufacture** ▼

7

REPRODUCTION FOR USE OF BLIND OR PHYSICALLY HANDICAPPED INDIVIDUALS   A signature on this form at space 10, and a check in one of the boxes here in space 8, constitutes a non-exclusive grant of permission to the Library of Congress to reproduce and distribute solely for the blind and physically handicapped and under the conditions and limitations prescribed by the regulations of the Copyright Office: (1) copies of the work identified in space 1 of this application in Braille (or similar tactile symbols); or (2) phonorecords embodying a fixation of a reading of that work; or (3) both.

a ☐ Copies and Phonorecords   **b** ☐ Copies Only   **c** ☐ Phonorecords Only

8

See instructions.

DEPOSIT ACCOUNT   If the registration fee is to be charged to a Deposit Account established in the Copyright Office, give name and number of Account.

Name ▼   **Account Number** ▼

CORRESPONDENCE   Give name and address to which correspondence about this application should be sent.   Name/Address/Apt/City/State/Zip ▼

9

Area Code & Telephone Number ▶

Be sure to
give your
daytime phone
◀ number.

CERTIFICATION*   I, the undersigned, hereby certify that I am the

Check one ▶

☐ author
☐ other copyright claimant
☐ owner of exclusive right(s)
☐ authorized agent of _____

of the work identified in this application and that the statements made by me in this application are correct to the best of my knowledge.

Name of author or other copyright claimant, or owner of exclusive right(s) ▲

10

Typed or printed name and date ▼ If this is a published work, this date must be the same as or later than the date of publication given in space 3.

_____ **date** ▶ _____

☞ **Handwritten signature (X)** ▼

**MAIL
CERTIFI-
CATE TO**

Certificate
will be
mailed in
window
envelope

Name ▼

Number/Street/Apartment Number ▼

City/State/ZIP ▼

Have you:
• Completed all necessary spaces?
• Signed your application in space 10?
• Enclosed check or money order for $10 payable to *Register of Copyrights*?
• Enclosed your deposit material with the application and fee?
MAIL TO: Register of Copyrights, Library of Congress, Washington, D.C. 20559

11

☆U.S. GOVERNMENT PRINTING OFFICE: 1985—461–584—20,004   July 1985—50,000

FORM CA
UNITED STATES COPYRIGHT OFFICE

REGISTRATION NUMBER

TX	TXU	PA	PAU	VA	VAU	SR	SRU	RE

Effective Date of Supplementary Registration

. . . .
MONTH   DAY   YEAR

DO NOT WRITE ABOVE THIS LINE. FOR COPYRIGHT OFFICE USE ONLY

A — **Basic Instructions**

TITLE OF WORK:

REGISTRATION NUMBER OF BASIC REGISTRATION: YEAR OF BASIC REGISTRATION:

NAME(S) OF AUTHOR(S):   NAME(S) OF COPYRIGHT CLAIMANT(S):

B — **Correction**

LOCATION AND NATURE OF INCORRECT INFORMATION IN BASIC REGISTRATION:

Line Number . . . . Line Heading or Description . . . .

INCORRECT INFORMATION AS IT APPEARS IN BASIC REGISTRATION:

CORRECTED INFORMATION:

EXPLANATION OF CORRECTION: (Optional)

C — **Amplification**

LOCATION AND NATURE OF INFORMATION IN BASIC REGISTRATION TO BE AMPLIFIED:

Line Number . . . . Line Heading or Description . . . .

AMPLIFIED INFORMATION:

EXPLANATION OF AMPLIFIED INFORMATION: (Optional)

	EXAMINED BY: . . . . CHECKED BY:	FORM CA RECEIVED:	FOR COPYRIGHT OFFICE USE ONLY
	CORRESPONDENCE: ☐ YES	REMITTANCE NUMBER AND DATE:	
	REFERENCE TO THIS REGISTRATION ADDED TO BASIC REGISTRATION: ☐ YES ☐ NO	DEPOSIT ACCOUNT FUNDS USED: ☐	

DO NOT WRITE ABOVE THIS LINE. FOR COPYRIGHT OFFICE USE ONLY

CONTINUATION OF: (Check which) ☐ PART B OR ☐ PART C

D
Continuation

DEPOSIT ACCOUNT: If the registration fee is to be charged to a Deposit Account established in the Copyright Office, give name and number of
Account:

Name . . . . Account Number . . . .

E
Deposit
Account and
Mailing
Instructions

CORRESPONDENCE: Give name and address to which correspondence should be sent:

Name . . . . Apt. No. . . . .

Address . . . .
            (Number and Street)   (City)   (State)   (ZIP Code)

CERTIFICATION ✱ I, the undersigned, hereby certify that I am the: (Check one)

☐ author ☐ other copyright claimant ☐ owner of exclusive right(s) ☐ authorized agent of: . . . .
                                                       (Name of author or other copyright claimant, or owner of exclusive right(s))
of the work identified in this application and that the statements made by me in this application are correct to the best of my knowledge.

F
Certification
(Application
must be
signed)

Handwritten signature: (X) . . . .

Typed or printed name . . . .

Date: . . . .

✱ 17 USC §506(e) FALSE REPRESENTATION – Any person who knowingly makes a false representation of a material fact in the application for copyright registration provided for by
section 409, or in any written statement filed in connection with the application, shall be fined not more than $2,500.

. . . .
                                     (Name)

. . . .
                  (Number, Street and Apartment Number)

. . . .
        (City)   (State)   (ZIP code)

**MAIL
CERTIFICATE
TO**

(Certificate will
be mailed in
window envelope)

G
Address for
Return of
Certificate

ADJUNCT APPLICATION
for
Copyright Registration for a
Group of Contributions to Periodicals

- Use this adjunct form only if your are making a single registration for a group of contributions to periodicals, and you are also filing a basic application on Form TX, Form PA, or Form VA. Follow the instructions, attached.
- Number each line in Part B consecutively. Use additional Forms GR/CP if you need more space.
- Submit this adjunct form with the basic application form. Clip (do not tape or staple) and fold all sheets together before submitting them.

FORM GR/CP
UNITED STATES COPYRIGHT OFFICE

REGISTRATION NUMBER
TX   PA   VA

EFFECTIVE DATE OF REGISTRATION
. . . .
(Month)   (Day)   (Year)

FORM GR/CP RECEIVED

Page _____ of _____ pages

DO NOT WRITE ABOVE THIS LINE. FOR COPYRIGHT OFFICE USE ONLY

(A)
Identification of Application

IDENTIFICATION OF BASIC APPLICATION:
- This application for copyright registration for a group of contributions to periodicals is submitted as an adjunct to an application filed on: (Check which)

☐ Form TX   ☐ Form PA   ☐ Form VA

IDENTIFICATION OF AUTHOR AND CLAIMANT: (Give the name of the author and the name of the copyright claimant in all of the contributions listed in Part B of this form. The names should be the same as the names given in spaces 2 and 4 of the basic application.)

Name of Author: . . . .

Name of Copyright Claimant: . . . .

(B)
Registration For Group of Contributions

COPYRIGHT REGISTRATION FOR A GROUP OF CONTRIBUTIONS TO PERIODICALS: (To make a single registration for a group of works by the same individual author, all first published as contributions to periodicals within a 12-month period (see instructions), give full information about each contribution. If more space is needed, use additional Forms GR/CP.)

☐ Title of Contribution: . . . .
Title of Periodical: . . . . Vol. . . . . . No. . . . . . Issue Date . . . . Pages. . . . .
Date of First Publication:. . . . . Nation of First Publication . . . .
(Month)   (Day)   (Year)   (Country)

☐ Title of Contribution: . . . .
Title of Periodical: . . . . Vol. . . . . . No. . . . . . Issue Date . . . . Pages. . . . .
Date of First Publication:. . . . . Nation of First Publication . . . .
(Month)   (Day)   (Year)   (Country)

☐ Title of Contribution: . . . .
Title of Periodical: . . . . Vol. . . . . . No. . . . . . Issue Date . . . . Pages. . . . .
Date of First Publication:. . . . . Nation of First Publication . . . .
(Month)   (Day)   (Year)   (Country)

☐ Title of Contribution: . . . .
Title of Periodical: . . . . Vol. . . . . . No. . . . . . Issue Date . . . . Pages. . . . .
Date of First Publication:. . . . . Nation of First Publication . . . .
(Month)   (Day)   (Year)   (Country)

☐ Title of Contribution: . . . .
Title of Periodical: . . . . Vol. . . . . . No. . . . . . Issue Date . . . . Pages. . . . .
Date of First Publication:. . . . . Nation of First Publication . . . .
(Month)   (Day)   (Year)   (Country)

☐ Title of Contribution: . . . .
Title of Periodical: . . . . Vol. . . . . . No. . . . . . Issue Date . . . . Pages. . . . .
Date of First Publication:. . . . . Nation of First Publication . . . .
(Month)   (Day)   (Year)   (Country)

☐ Title of Contribution: . . . .
Title of Periodical: . . . . Vol. . . . . . No. . . . . . Issue Date . . . . Pages. . . . .
Date of First Publication:. . . . . Nation of First Publication . . . .
(Month)   (Day)   (Year)   (Country)

<table>
<tr><td>FOR COPYRIGHT OFFICE USE ONLY</td></tr>
</table>

DO NOT WRITE ABOVE THIS LINE. FOR COPYRIGHT OFFICE USE ONLY

☐ Title of Contribution: ....
Title of Periodical: .... Vol..... No..... Issue Date........... Pages..........
Date of First Publication:............................. Nation of First Publication................................
(Month)   (Day)   (Year)   (Country)

Ⓑ **Continued**

☐ Title of Contribution: ....
Title of Periodical: .... Vol..... No..... Issue Date........... Pages..........
Date of First Publication:............................. Nation of First Publication................................
(Month)   (Day)   (Year)   (Country)

☐ Title of Contribution: ....
Title of Periodical: .... Vol..... No..... Issue Date........... Pages..........
Date of First Publication:............................. Nation of First Publication................................
(Month)   (Day)   (Year)   (Country)

☐ Title of Contribution: ....
Title of Periodical: .... Vol..... No..... Issue Date........... Pages..........
Date of First Publication:............................. Nation of First Publication................................
(Month)   (Day)   (Year)   (Country)

☐ Title of Contribution: ....
Title of Periodical: .... Vol..... No..... Issue Date........... Pages..........
Date of First Publication:............................. Nation of First Publication................................
(Month)   (Day)   (Year)   (Country)

☐ Title of Contribution: ....
Title of Periodical: .... Vol..... No..... Issue Date........... Pages..........
Date of First Publication:............................. Nation of First Publication................................
(Month)   (Day)   (Year)   (Country)

☐ Title of Contribution: ....
Title of Periodical: .... Vol..... No..... Issue Date........... Pages..........
Date of First Publication:............................. Nation of First Publication................................
(Month)   (Day)   (Year)   (Country)

☐ Title of Contribution: ....
Title of Periodical: .... Vol..... No..... Issue Date........... Pages..........
Date of First Publication:............................. Nation of First Publication................................
(Month)   (Day)   (Year)   (Country)

☐ Title of Contribution: ....
Title of Periodical: .... Vol..... No..... Issue Date........... Pages..........
Date of First Publication:............................. Nation of First Publication................................
(Month)   (Day)   (Year)   (Country)

☐ Title of Contribution: ....
Title of Periodical: .... Vol..... No..... Issue Date........... Pages..........
Date of First Publication:............................. Nation of First Publication................................
(Month)   (Day)   (Year)   (Country)

☐ Title of Contribution: ....
Title of Periodical: .... Vol..... No..... Issue Date........... Pages..........
Date of First Publication:............................. Nation of First Publication................................
(Month)   (Day)   (Year)   (Country)

☐ Title of Contribution: ....
Title of Periodical: .... Vol..... No..... Issue Date........... Pages..........
Date of First Publication:............................. Nation of First Publication................................
(Month)   (Day)   (Year)   (Country)

☆ U.S. GOVERNMENT PRINTING OFFICE: 1978—261-022/12   Apr. 1978—300,000

FORM RE

UNITED STATES COPYRIGHT OFFICE

REGISTRATION NUMBER

EFFECTIVE DATE OF RENEWAL REGISTRATION

....
(Month)   (Day)   (Year)

DO NOT WRITE ABOVE THIS LINE.   FOR COPYRIGHT OFFICE USE ONLY

---

①

Renewal Claimant(s)

RENEWAL CLAIMANT(S), ADDRESS(ES), AND STATEMENT OF CLAIM: (See Instructions)

1
Name...
Address...
Claiming as...
(Use appropriate statement from instructions)

2
Name...
Address...
Claiming as...
(Use appropriate statement from instructions)

3
Name...
Address...
Claiming as...
(Use appropriate statement from instructions)

---

②

Work Renewed

TITLE OF WORK IN WHICH RENEWAL IS CLAIMED:

RENEWABLE MATTER:

CONTRIBUTION TO PERIODICAL OR COMPOSITE WORK:

Title of periodical or composite work: ....

If a periodical or other serial, give: Vol.................. No. .... Issue Date ....

---

③

Author(s)

AUTHOR(S) OF RENEWABLE MATTER:

---

④

Facts of Original Registration

ORIGINAL REGISTRATION NUMBER:

....

ORIGINAL COPYRIGHT CLAIMANT:

ORIGINAL DATE OF COPYRIGHT:

• If the original registration for this work was made in published form, give:

DATE OF PUBLICATION: ....
(Month)   (Day)   (Year)

} OR {

• If the original registration for this work was made in unpublished form, give:

DATE OF REGISTRATION: ....
(Month)   (Day)   (Year)

	EXAMINED BY: . . . . CHECKED BY: . . . . DEPOSIT ACCOUNT FUNDS USED: ☐	RENEWAL APPLICATION RECEIVED: REMITTANCE NUMBER AND DATE:	FOR COPYRIGHT OFFICE USE ONLY

DO NOT WRITE ABOVE THIS LINE. FOR COPYRIGHT OFFICE USE ONLY

RENEWAL FOR GROUP OF WORKS BY SAME AUTHOR: To make a single registration for a group of works by the same individual author published as contributions to periodicals (see instructions), give full information about each contribution. If more space is needed, request continuation sheet (Form RE/CON).

⑤ Renewal for Group of Works

1
Title of Contribution: . . . .
Title of Periodical: . . . . Vol . . . . . . No . . . . Issue Date . . . .
Date of Publication: . . . . Registration Number: . . . .
(Month)   (Day)   (Year)

2
Title of Contribution: . . . .
Title of Periodical: . . . . Vol . . . . . . No . . . . Issue Date . . . .
Date of Publication: . . . . Registration Number: . . . .
(Month)   (Day)   (Year)

3
Title of Contribution: . . . .
Title of Periodical: . . . . Vol . . . . . . No . . . . Issue Date . . . .
Date of Publication: . . . . Registration Number: . . . .
(Month)   (Day)   (Year)

4
Title of Contribution: . . . .
Title of Periodical: . . . . Vol . . . . . . No . . . . Issue Date . . . .
Date of Publication: . . . . Registration Number: . . . .
(Month)   (Day)   (Year)

5
Title of Contribution: . . . .
Title of Periodical: . . . . Vol . . . . . . No . . . . Issue Date . . . .
Date of Publication: . . . . Registration Number: . . . .
(Month)   (Day)   (Year)

6
Title of Contribution: . . . .
Title of Periodical: . . . . Vol . . . . . . No . . . . Issue Date . . . .
Date of Publication: . . . . Registration Number: . . . .
(Month)   (Day)   (Year)

7
Title of Contribution: . . . .
Title of Periodical: . . . . Vol . . . . . . No . . . . Issue Date . . . .
Date of Publication: . . . . Registration Number: . . . .
(Month)   (Day)   (Year)

DEPOSIT ACCOUNT: (If the registration fee is to be charged to a Deposit Account established in the Copyright Office, give name and number of Account.)

Name: . . . .
Account Number: . . . .

CORRESPONDENCE: (Give name and address to which correspondence about this application should be sent.)

Name: . . . .
Address: . . . . (Apt.)
(City)   (State)   (ZIP)

⑥ Fee and Correspondence

CERTIFICATION: I, the undersigned, hereby certify that I am the: (Check one)
☐ renewal claimant   ☐ duly authorized agent of: . . . .
(Name of renewal claimant)
of the work identified in this application, and that the statements made by me in this application are correct to the best of my knowledge.

Handwritten signature: (X) . . . .
Typed or printed name: . . . .
Date: . . . .

⑦ Certification (Application must be signed)

. . . .
(Name)
. . . .
(Number, Street and Apartment Number)
. . . .
(City)   (State)   (ZIP code)

MAIL CERTIFICATE TO
(Certificate will be mailed in window envelope)

⑧ Address for Return of Certificate

Apr. 1978—500,000

Glossary

Access: A reasonable opportunity to view copies or hear sounds on phonorecords

Actual damages: The damages actually incurred by a copyright owner

All Rights Reserved: A phrase used on published copies of works as a condition of copyright protection for U.S. citizens in signatory countries under the Buenos Aires Convention without the necessity of complying with any other formalities

Anonymous work: A work on the copies or phonorecords of which no natural person is identified as author

Applied art: Pictorial, graphic, and sculptural creations intended to be embodied in useful articles and capable of being identified separate and apart from such articles

ASCAP: American Society of Composers, Authors, and Publishers; a performing right licensing organization representing songwriters and music publishers

Assignment: A transfer of an ownership interest in property

Audiovisual work: Works that consist of a series of related images which are intrinsically intended to be shown by the use of machines or devices such as projectors, viewers, or electronic equipment, together with accompanying sounds, if any, regardless of the nature of the material objects, such as films or tapes in which the works are embodied

Author: A person who is the creator, by his or her own intellectual labor, of subject matter protected under the copyright law

Authorized agent: A person who is given the right or authority to act on behalf of or represents another person

Basic fee: The fee that a cable system must pay to the Copyright Office under the compulsory license for secondary transmissions by cable systems for the privilege of transmitting secondary transmissions of nonnetwork programming

Basic registration: The basic copyright registration for a specific version of a particular work

Beneficial owner: A person who does not have the authority to exercise a right in a work but who is entitled to derive a profit, advantage, or benefit from a particular work

Beneficiary: A person who receives benefits or an advantage

Best edition: The edition of a work published in the United States at any time before the date of deposit with the Library of Congress, that the Library of Congress determines to be most suitable for its purposes

Best Edition of Published Copyrighted Works for the Collections of the Library of Congress: A set of guidelines used by the Library of Congress to determine the best edition of a work for deposit purposes

BMI: Broadcast Music, Inc.; a performing right organization representing songwriters and music publishers

Brand name: A trademark

Broadcast: To make public by means of transmitting a radio or television signal

Buenos Aires Convention: A multilateral treaty under which citizens and domiciliaries of the United States and Latin American countries are entitled to copyright protection in signatory countries

Cable royalties: Royalties payable by a cable system to the Copyright Office under the compulsory license for secondary transmissions by cable systems

Cable system: A facility, located in any State, Territory, Trust Territory, or Possession, that in whole or in part receives signals transmitted or programs broadcast by one or more television broadcast stations licensed by the Federal Communications Commission, and makes secondary transmissions of such signals or programs by wires, cables, or other communications channels to subscribing members of the public who pay for such service

Categories of works: Groups of works that are classified together based upon their composition

Catalog of Entries: A bibliographic description of copyrighted works registered in the Copyright Office prepared by the Cataloging Division

Cause of action: A fact or state of facts to which law, sought to be enforced, applies

Certificate for licensed coin-operated phonorecord players: A certificate issued by the Copyright Office for affixation on a coin-operated phonorecord player indicating that a compulsory license for public performances of music on phonorecords has been obtained

Certificate of Recordation: A certificate issued by the Copyright Office certifying that a document has been recorded with the Copyright Office

Children: A person's immediate offspring, whether legitimate or not, and any children legally adopted by that person

Choreographic work: The recorded or notated movements of a dancer of the type presented to an audience

Claim of ownership: An assertion of rights in a work as an owner

Co-author: A person who joins with another to create a work

Coin-operated phonorecord player: A machine or device employed solely for the performance of nondramatic musical works by means of phonorecords upon being activated by insertion of coins, currency, tokens, or other monetary units or their equivalent; that is located in an establishment making no direct or indirect charge for admission; that is accompanied by a list of titles of all the musical works available for performance on it, which list is affixed to the phonorecord player or posted in the establishment in a prominent position where it can be readily examined by the public; and, affords a choice of works available for performance and permits the choice to be made by the patrons of the establishment in which it is located

Collaborate: To work jointly with others in the creation of a work

Collective work: A work, such as a periodical issue, anthology, or encyclopedia, in which a number of contributions, constituting separate and independent works in themselves, are assembled into a collective whole

Commissioned work: A work specially ordered or commissioned for use as a contribution to a collective work, as a part of a motion picture or other audiovisual work, as a translation, as a supplementary work, as a compilation, as an instructional text, as a test, as answer material for a test, or as an atlas, if the parties expressly agree in a written instrument signed by them that the work shall be a work made for hire

Common law: Law based upon court decisions and developed through precedent

Compilation: A work formed by the collection and assembling of preexisting materials or of data selected, coordinated, or arranged in such a way that the resulting work as a whole constitutes an original work of authorship; the term "compilation" includes collective works

Complete copy: A complete copy of an unpublished work is one which is representative of the entire copyrightable content of the work; a complete copy of a published work includes all elements comprising the applicable unit of publication of the work, including elements, if considered separately, would not be copyrightable matter

Complete defense: A defense to a copyright infringement action resulting in no liability for actual or statutory damages to a person who innocently infringes a copyright, before actual knowledge of registration, in reliance upon an authorized copy or phonorecord from which the copyright notice has been omitted

Compulsory license: A license available under the 1976 Act that gives permission to exercise a right covered by it, upon compliance with a license procedure set forth in the Act and payment of royalties, without liability to a copyright owner

Compulsory license for making and distributing phonorecords: A compulsory license that becomes available to anyone who has the primary purpose of making and distributing phonorecords embodying a nondramatic musical work to the public for private use, but not until phonorecords of such a work have been first distributed in the United States under the authority of the owner of the work

Compulsory license for noncommercial educational broadcasting: A compulsory license that permits noncommercial educational broadcasters (1) to perform or display published nondramatic musical works and published pictorial, graphic, and sculptural works by or in the course of a transmission program; (2) to produce a transmission program, reproduce copies or phonorecords of such a transmission program, and distribute such copies or phonorecords where such production, reproduction, or distribution is made by a nonprofit institution or organization solely for purposes of transmissions specified in (1); and (3) to make reproductions of a transmission program simultaneously with its transmission.

Compulsory license for public performances by means of coin-operated phonorecord players: A compulsory license for public performances of nondramatic musical works on phonorecords by means of coin-operated phonorecord players

Compulsory license for secondary transmissions by cable systems: A compulsory license for secondary transmissions by cable systems

Computer program: A set of statements or instructions to be used directly or indirectly in a computer to bring about a certain result

Conflicting transfer: A transfer of the same ownership rights in a work by one person to two or more different persons

Consent: Agreement as to an action

Constitution: The Constitution of the United States

Contribution to a collective work: A separate and independent work assembled with other separate and independent works to produce a collective work

Constructive notice: A presumption of the law, making it impossible for a person to deny the matter concerning which notice is given, even though the person has no actual knowledge of the matter

Co-owner: A person who, with one or more other persons, owns the same rights in a work

Copies: Material objects, other than phonorecords, in which a work is fixed by any method now known or later developed, and from which the work can be perceived, reproduced, or otherwise communicated, either directly or with the aid of a machine or device; the term "copies" includes the material object, other than a phonorecord, in which the work is first fixed

Copyright: The five exclusive rights in a work recognized by and enforceable under the 1976 Act, namely exclusive rights to reproduce, create variations of, publicly perform, and publicly display works and to distribute copies and phonorecords to the public

Copyright Act of 1976:   A federal statute that exclusively governs all legal or equitable rights that are equivalent to any of the exclusive rights within the general scope of copyright in works of authorship that are fixed in a tangible medium of expression whether published or unpublished; also referred to as the 1976 Act

Copyright claimant: A person who claims ownership of all the exclusive rights in a work and one who is entitled to register a work in his, her, or its name

Copyright Extension Acts: A series of Congressional enactments beginning in 1962 that had the effect of extending the second term of all renewed copyrights through December 31, 1976 scheduled to expire between September 19, 1962 and December 31, 1976

Copyright infringement: The unauthorized exercise of one or more exclusive rights in a work

Copyright notice: A notice, which must comply with a format prescribed by the 1976 Act and be affixed to published copies or phonorecords, indicating that the copy or phonorecord embodies a work protected under the 1976 Act; a copyright notice consists of three components; the notice to be used on visually perceptible copies of a work consists of the symbol

© (or the work "Copyright" or abbreviation "Copr.), the year of first publication, and the name of the copyright owner; the notice to be used on
phonorecords consists of the symbol ℗, the year of first publication, and
the name of the owner of copyright in the sound recording embodied in
the phonorecord

Copyright Office: A federal agency within the Library of Congress, with
offices in Washington, D.C., having jurisdiction over the administration
of the 1976 Act including the registration of claims of exclusive rights in
copyrightable works, the recordation of documents referring to the ownership and transfer of such rights, the issuance of compulsory license, and
the receipt of royalties under such licenses

Copyright owner: The owner of any one or more of the exclusive rights
comprised in a copyright

Copyright ownership: Ownership of any one or more of the exclusive rights
comprised in a copyright

Copyright protection: The legal protection available under the 1976 Act for
rights in a copyrightable work

Copyright Royalty Tribunal: An independent federal agency in the legislative branch with jurisdiction to make determinations concerning the adjustment of royalty rates under compulsory licenses and to distribute royalty fees deposited with the Copyright Office

Copyright warning notice: A prescribed form of warning notice that the
making of a copy may be subject to copyright law; a copyright warning
notice is to be displayed at the place where orders for copies or phonorecords are accepted by certain libraries and archives, and included on
printed forms supplied by certain libraries and archives and used by their
patrons for ordering copies or phonorecords

Copyrightable subject matter: Works that are eligible for copyright protection falling within any one or more of the categories of works established
under the 1976 Act

Copyrightable work: A work eligible for copyright protection

Created: A work is created when it is fixed in a copy or phonorecord for
the first time; where a work is prepared over a period of time, the portion
of it that has been fixed at any particular time constitutes the work as of
that time, and where the work has been prepared in different versions,
each version constitutes a separate work

Creator: A person who is an author as that term is used in the 1976 Act

Deposit copies: Copies of works deposited with the Copyright Office in
connection with registering ownership claims in a work or in compliance
with the mandatory deposit requirement under the 1976 Act

Derivative work: A work based upon one or more preexisting works, such as a translation, musical arrangement, dramatization, fictionalization, motion picture version, sound recording, art reproduction, abridgment, condensation, or any other form in which a work may be recast, transformed, or adapted; a work consisting of editorial revisions, annotations, elaborations, or other modifications which, as a whole, represent an original work of authorship, is a 'derivative work'

Device: A piece of equipment or a mechanism, which is now known or later developed, designed to serve a special purpose or perform a special function

Display: To display a work means to show a copy of it either directly or by means of a film, slide, television image, or any other device or process or, in the case of a motion picture or other audiovisual work, to show individual images nonsequentially

Distant signal: A signal that carries nonnetwork programming and which is transmitted outside the local service area of the primary transmitter of such programming

Distant signal equivalent: The value assigned to the secondary transmission of any nonnetwork television programming carried by a cable system in whole or in part beyond the local service area of the primary transmitter of such programming

Distant signal equivalent fee: A royalty fee paid by a cable system under the compulsory license for secondary transmissions, based upon a percentage of a cable system's gross receipts multiplied the number of distant signal equivalents attributable to the secondary transmissions carried by the cable system

Distribute: To make copies or phonorecords available by sale or other transfer of ownership, or by rental, lease, or lending

Divisibility: Capable of being divided

Dramatic work: A work that consists of literary compositions that tell a story through action with dialogue, with or without accompanying music

Embody: To make concrete and perceptible

Ephemeral recording: A copy or phonorecord of a transmission program that embodies the performance or display of a work and is made for purposes of later transmission of the program and then destroyed within a specified time period

Error in date: An incorrect date of first publication in the date portion of the copyright notice

Error in name: The name of a person, other than the person who is owner of rights in a work, in the name portion of the copyright notice

Executor: A person appointed by a testator to carry out the directions and requests in his will and to dispose of property according to his testamentary provisions after his decease

Exclusive: Limited or limiting to possession, control, or use by a single individual or group

Exclusive license: Permission given by one person to another to do a thing and agreement not to give anyone else permission to do the same thing

Exclusive licensee: A person given the exclusive right and license to do a thing

Exclusive ownership: Ownership free from any kind of legal or equitable interest in anyone else

Exclusive rights: A right that only the grantee thereof can exercise, and from which all other persons are prohibited

Extended renewal term: A renewal term of 47 years available for works registered under the 1909 Act and in their first 28-year period of protection on January 1, 1978 period and for such works in their second 28-year period of protection or registered for renewal before January 1, 1978

Fair use: A limitation on exclusive rights recognized by the 1976 Act, expressed in terms of guidelines, permitting the exercise of one or more rights without direct authorization from the owner; it may be applicable where a work is used for purposes such as criticism, comment, news reporting, teaching, scholarship, or research

Federal Patent Act: The federal statute that exclusively governs all rights in and to inventions as well as the protection of them

Filing fees: Fees payable for the filing of applications with the Copyright Office

First publication: The date copies or phonorecords of a work are first distributed to the public by sale or other transfer of ownership, or by rental, lease, or lending

First sale: The first transfer of ownership of a copy or phonorecord by or under the authority of the owner of rights in it

Fixation: The act, process, or result of embodying a work in a tangible medium of expression

Fixed: A work is fixed in a tangible medium of expression when its embodiment in a copy or phonorecord, by or under the authority of the creator, is sufficiently permanent or stable to permit it to be perceived, reproduced, or otherwise communicated for a period of more than transitory duration; a work consisting of sounds, images, or both, that are being transmitted, is fixed if a fixation of the work is being made simultaneously with its transmission

Forms: Forms, which when completed, provide information to the Copyright Office in connection with registering claims of rights in a work, renewing a registration, and paying royalties

Further grant: A grant of rights made after the effective date of termination under the right of termination

Grant of a transfer or license of rights: To make a transfer of ownership of rights in a work or to allow the exercise of them

Graphic work: A two-dimensional work of graphic art; see Pictorial, graphic and sculptural works

Gross receipts for the basic service of providing secondary transmissions of primary transmissions: The full amount of monthly (or other periodic) service fees for any and all services or tiers of services that include one or more secondary transmissions of television or radio broadcast signals, for additional set fees, and for converter fees

Guidelines for classroom copying in not-for-profit educational institutions: Nonstatutory guidelines voluntarily developed independently of Congress through the joint effort of representatives of educational institutions, author organizations, and publishers to provide guidance with respect to the minimum standards of educational fair use; they do not cover the educational use of audiovisual works

Guidelines for educational uses of music: Nonstatutory guidelines voluntarily developed independently of Congress through the joint effort of representatives of educational institutions, publishers, and music educators to provide guidance with respect to the minimum standards of educational fair use of music

Harry Fox Agency: The mechanical licensing agency for United States music publishers

Heir: One who inherits or is entitled to inherit property

Identifying material: Material submitted to the Copyright Office, in lieu of actual copies or phonorecords, that may consist of photographic prints, transparencies, photostats, drawings, or similar two-dimensional reproductions or renderings of the work, in a form visually perceptible without the aid of a machine or device

Independent contractor: One, who exercising an independent employment, contracts to do work according to his or her own methods and without being subject to control of his or her employer except as to the result of the work

Independent creation: Creation of a work that is recognizably the result of the creator's own efforts

Infringement: The exercise of an exclusive right without permission from the owner and without permission under a compulsory license

Initial Notice of Identity and Signal Carriage Complement: A notice required to be recorded with the Copyright Office at least one month before the date or commencement of operations of a cable system for any secondary transmission by the system to be subject to compulsory licensing; includes a statement of the identity and address of the person who owns or operates the cable system or has power to exercise primary control over it, together with the name and location of the primary transmitter whose signals are regularly carried

Injunction: An order by a court requiring a person to do or refrain from doing a specified act

Instructional broadcasting: The performance of a nondramatic literary or musical work or display of a work, by or in the course of a transmission, if it is a regular part of the systematic instructional activities of a governmental body or a nonprofit educational institution

Intestate: Having made no will; a person is said to die intestate when he or she dies without making a will

Invalidation of copyright: The loss of copyright protection through the failure to use a copyright notice on copies or phonorecords, or for other reasons

Invention: The act of devising something not previously known or existing; a new and useful process, machine, or composition of matter

Irrevocable right: A right that cannot be revoked

Joint ownership: Ownership of the same rights in a work by two or more persons

Joint work: A work prepared by two or more creators with the intention that their contributions be merged into inseparable or interdependent parts of a unitary whole

Jukebox: A coin-operated phonograph that automatically plays records selected from its list

Lawfully made copy or phonorecord: A copy or phonorecord made by or under the authority of the owner of the reproduction right

Legal owner: The inital owner of copyright, an assignee of a right, an exclusive licensee of a right, a television broadcast station owning a right or license to perform or transmit a work within its local service area, or the primary transmitter of a transmission whose signal has been altered

License: Authority or permission to do something which, without such authority or permission, would violate an exclusive right

Licensed right: A right that is the subject of a license

Licensee: A person who holds a license

Licensor: A person who grants a license

Limitation: A restriction on an exclusive right

Literary work: A work, other than an audiovisual work, expressed in words, numbers, or other verbal or numerical symbols or indicia, regardless of the nature of the material objects, such as books, periodicals, manuscripts, phonorecords, film, tapes, disks, or cards in which they are printed

Local service area of a primary transmitter of a radio station: The primary service area of a radio station, pursuant to the rules and regulations of the Federal Communications Commission

Local service area of a primary transmitter of a television broadcast station: The area in which a television broadcast station is entitled to insist upon its signal being retransmitted by a cable system pursuant to the rules, regulations, and authorizations of the Federal Communications Commission in effect on April 15, 1976; or in the case of a television broadcast station licensed by an appropriate governmental authority of Canada or Mexico, the area in which it would be entitled to insist upon its signal being retransmitted if it were a television broadcast station subject to such rules, regulations, and authorizations

Maximum period of protection: The maximum period of protection for a work

Mandatory deposit requirement: A 1976 Act requirement that copies or phonorecords, of a work published with a copyright notice in the United States be deposited with the Copyright Office

Mechanical license: A license permitting the reproduction of phonorecords embodying nondramatic musical works

Money damages: A pecuniary compensation, which may be recovered in the courts by any person who has suffered a loss, detriment, or injury

Monthly statement of account under compulsory license for making and distributing phonorecords: A monthly statement submitted to the Copyright Office which must include information on the number of phonorecords made during the month covered by the statement, number of phonorecords sold, name(s) of the recording artist, and configuration of each phonorecord made, among other information

Motion picture: Audiovisual works consisting of a series of related images which, when shown in succession, impart an impression of motion, together with accompanying sounds, if any

Musical work: A work consisting of a combination of varying melody, harmony, rhythm, and timbre regardless of the material object in which it is embodied

Negotiated license: A license voluntarily granted by a licensor on a negotiated basis

Network station: A television broadcast station owned or operated by, or affiliated with, one or more of the television networks in the United States providing nationwide transmissions, and that transmits a substantial part of the programming supplied by such networks for a substantial part of that station's typical broadcast day

Next of kin: A person nearest in relationship by birth or blood to a decedent

Noncommercial educational broadcaster: A television or radio broadcast station that (1) under the rules and regulations of the Federal Communications Commission in effect on November 7, 1967, is eligible to be licensed or is licensed by the Commission as a noncommercial educational radio or television broadcast station and which is owned and operated by a public agency or nonprofit private foundation, corporation, or association, or (2) one owned and operated by a municipality and which transmits only noncommercial programs for educational purposes

Nonexclusive license: A person given the right and license to do a thing which may be concurrently done by one or more other persons

Nonnetwork station: A commercial television broadcast station other than a network station

Nonsimultaneous transmission: A transmission of a videotaped secondary transmission

Notice of objection to performance: A written notice by a copyright owner objecting to a nonprofit public performance of a nondramatic literary work or a musical work, which must be served at least seven days before the date of the performance

Notice of termination: A written notice of termination of a transfer made by the creator of a work (or by the members of his/her surviving family), which may be given by the creator (or by the members of his/her surviving family) after a specified time period has elapsed, to recover ownership of rights in the work

Notice of intention to obtain a compulsory license: A written notice required to be served on the owner of rights in a nondramatic musical work to obtain a compulsory license to make and distribute phonorecords of nondramatic musical works

Original: Something that is created firsthand

Original work of ownership: A work that is recognizably the result of the creator's own effort

Over-the-air transmission: The transmission of television and radio signals over-the-air rather than by wires, cables, or other communications channels

Ownership claim: A claim of ownership

Operator of a coin-operated phonorecord player: Any person who, alone or jointly with others, owns a coin-operated phonorecord player; or has the power to make a coin-operated phonorecord player available for placement in an establishment for purposes of public performance; or has the power to exercise primary control over the selection of the musical works made available for public performance on a coin-operated phonorecord player

Opportunity to copy: Access

Pantomime: A drama presented by gestures and action without words

Patent: A monopoly given by the federal government giving a patent owner the right to exclude others from making, selling, or using an invention

Patent grant: A patent

Patented invention: An invention that is the subject of a patent

Patent notice: A form of notice used on patented inventions

Patent Office: The federal agency that determines whether a patent should be issued for an invention

Patent ownership: Owner of a patent

Patent protection: The legal protection available for a patent

Patent rights: The right to exclude others from making, using, or selling a patented invention

Permanent injunction: An injunction issued by a court after there has been a full evaluation and determination of a cause of action and the rights of the parties have been determined

Perform a work: To recite, render, play, dance, or act a work, either directly or by means of any device or process or, in the case of a motion picture or other audiovisual work, to show its images in any sequence or to make the sounds accompanying it audible; to perform a work publicly. See Publicly perform or display a work

Person: An individual and/or a legal entity, such as a partnership or corporation

Phonorecord: Material objects in which sounds, other than those accompanying a motion picture or other audiovisual work, are fixed by any method now known or later developed, and from which the sounds can be perceived, reproduced, or otherwise communicated, either directly or with the aid of a machine or device; the term "phonorecords" includes the material object in which the sounds are first fixed

Pictorial, graphic, and sculptural works: Include two-dimensional and three-dimensional works of fine, graphic, and applied art, photographs, prints and art reproductions, maps, globes, charts, technical drawings, diagrams, and models; such works shall include works of artistic craftsmanship insofar as their form but not their mechanical or utilitarian aspects are concerned; the design of a useful article shall be considered a pictorial, graphic, or sculptural work only if, and only to the extent that, such design incorporates pictorial, graphic, or sculptural features that can be identified separately from, and are capable of existing independently of, the utilitarian aspects of the article

Posthumous work: A work first published after the death of its creator

Preempt: To take precedence over

Preexisting material: Material in existence at the time a work is created

Prima facie: Legally sufficient to establish a fact or case unless disproved

Primary transmission: A transmission made to the public by the transmitting facility whose signals are being received and further transmitted by the secondary transmission service, regardless of where or when the performance or display was first transmitted

Pseudonymous: A work on the copies or phonorecords of which the creator is identified under a fictitious name

Publication: The distribution of copies or phonorecords to the public; the offering to distribute copies or phonorecords to a group of persons for purposes of further distribution, public performance, or public display, constitutes publication; a public performance or display of a work does not of itself constitute publication

Public broadcasting entity: A noncommercial educational broadcaster

Publicly perform or display a work: To perform or display a work at a place open to the public or at any place where a substantial number of persons outside of a normal circle of a family and its social acquaintences is gathered; or to transmit or otherwise communicate a performance or display of the work to a place of the kind just noted or to the public, by means of any device or process, whether the members of the public capable of receiving the performance or display receive it in the same place or in separate places and at the same time or at different times.

Public domain material: Material that belongs to the general public and cannot be appropriated by anyone; material that is not protected by copyright

Public performance: See Publicly perform or display a work

Published work: A work that has been distributed to the public

Recordation: The act or process of recording a document with the Copyright Office

Record Rental Amendment of 1984:   An amendment to the 1976 Act providing that, unless authorized by the owners of copyright in the sound recording and in the musical works embodied therein, the owners of a particular phonorecord may not, for purposes of direct or indirect commercial advantage, dispose of, or authorize the disposal of, the possession of that phonorecord by rental, lease, or lending, or by any other act or practice in the nature of rental, lease, or lending

Registered United States Patent and Trademark Office: A phrase used to indicate that a trademark or service mark has been federally registered by the United States Patent and Trademark Office

Registration of copyright: A phrase used to indicate that a claim of ownership of rights in a work has been registered by the United States Copyright Office

Renewal of copyright: Renewing the period of protection for a work registered under the 1909 Act; See Renewal period and Extended renewal period

Renewal period: A period of protection for rights in a work consecutively following an initial period of protection; for works registered under the 1909 Act the renewal period was 28 years; See Extended renewal term

Right of publicity: Legal protection available to an individual with respect to his or her name as well as his or her physical features and characteristics; the right of celebrities and well-known persons to preclude the commercial use of their names or picture without authorization

Right of termination: The right of a creator (or of surviving members of his or her family) to recover ownership of rights in a work transferred by the creator

Royalty: A payment made to the owner of rights in a work in return for permission to exercise them

Secondary transmission: "The further transmitting of a primary transmission simultaneously with the primary transmission, or nonsimultaneously with the primary transmission if by a cable system not located in whole or in part within the boundary of the 48 contiguous States, Hawaii, or Puerto Rico; provided, however, that a nonsimultaneous further transmission by a cable system located in Hawaii of a primary transmission shall be deemed to be a secondary transmission if the carriage of the television broadcast signal comprising such further transmission is permissible under the rules, regulations, or authorizations of the Federal Communications Commission."

SESAC: Society of European Stage Authors and Composers; a performing-right licensing organization representing songwriters and music publishers

Scope of employment: The duties of an employee as may be defined by a job description, by custom and practice in the industry or otherwise

Service mark: Any word, name, symbol, or device, or any combination of them used in the sale or advertising of services to identify the services of one person and distinguish them from the services of others; see Trademark

Sound recording: Works that result from the fixation of a series of musical, spoken, or other sounds, but not including the sounds accompanying a motion picture or other audiovisual work, regardless of the nature of the material objects, such as disks, tapes, or other phonorecords, in which they are embodied

Specially ordered work: See Commissioned work

Statement of Account for Secondary Transmissions by Cable Systems: A written statement required to be filed with the Copyright Office providing information pertaining to the calculation of royalty fees by and due from a cable system for the right to make secondary transmissions

Statute of Limitations: A statute prescribing limitations to the right of action on certain described causes of action; that is, declaring that no suit shall be maintained on such causes of action unless brought within a specified period after the right accrued

Statutory damages: Damages expressly provided for in the 1976 Act which may be awarded by a court as it considers just, instead of actual damages and an infringer's profits, in a sum not less than $100 and or more than $50,000

Statutory royalty: A royalty provided for by statute

Supplementary work: A work prepared for publication as a secondary adjunct to a work by another author for the purpose of introducing, concluding, illustrating, explaining, revising, commenting upon, or assisting in the use of the other work, such as forewords, afterwords, pictorial illustrations, maps, charts, tables, editorial notes, musical arrangements, answer material for tests, bibliographies, appendixes, and indexes

Tangible medium of expression: A physical object

Temporary injunction: A preliminary or provisional injunction

Termination date: The date specified in a notice of termination when rights in a work transferred by a creator (or by his or her surviving family members) will revert to the creator (or his or her surviving family members)

Testamentary: Pertaining to a will

Testator: A person who makes or has made a will

Trademark: Any word, name, symbol, or device, or any combination of them used by a manufacturer or merchant to identify his or her products and distinguish them from those manufactured or sold by others; a brand name

Trademark notice: A notice used adjacent to or in association with a word, name, symbol, or device, or any combination of them to indicate that it is federally registered (®), or that common law rights are claimed in it (™)

Transfer of copyright ownership: An assignment, mortgage, exclusive license, or any other conveyance, alienation, or hypothecation of a copyright or of any of the exclusive rights comprised in a copyright, whether or not it is limited in time or place of effect, but not including a nonexclusive license

Transmission program: A body of material that, as an aggregate, has been produced for the sole purpose of transmission to the public in sequence and as a unit

Transmit: To transmit a performance or display is to communicate it by any device or process whereby images or sounds are received beyond the place from which they are sent

Universal Copyright Convention: A multilateral treaty under which citizens and domiciliaries of the United States are entitled to copyright protection in signatory countries for their works, wherever published, to the same extent copyright protection is granted to their citizens

United States Copyright Office: The federal agency, within the Library of Congress, that has jurisdiction over the registration of ownership claims in works under copyright law, issuance of compulsory licenses, collection of royalty fees, and receipt of deposited copies

United States Government work: A work prepared by an officer or employee of the United States Government as part of that person's official duties

United States Patent and Trademark Office: The Federal agency which has jurisdiction over the issuance of patent grants and federal registration of trademarks; See Patent Office

Useful article: An article having an intrinsic utilitarian function that is not merely to portray the appearance of the article or to convey information; an article that is normally part of a useful article is considered a 'useful article'

Visually perceptible copies: Copies of a work that can be visually perceived

Voluntary license: See Negotiated license

Widow or Widower: An author's surviving spouse under the law of the author's domicile at the time of his or her death, whether or not the spouse has later remarried

Work: The product of an individual's creative effort that is manifested in a material object by means of sounds and/or images

Work made for hire: A work prepared by an employee within the scope of his or her employment; or a work specially ordered or commissioned; See Commissioned work

Writings: For purposes of copyright, writings means and includes any pictorial rendering of the fruits of creative intellectual or aesthetic labor

Year of first publication: The year in which a work is first published

Index

"All rights reserved," see Copyright notice
Amplification:
  defined, 156
  see also Registration, forms, application,
    correct and amplify
Anonymous works:
  definition, 103, 159
  see also Period of protection
Applied art:
  definition, 21
  registration, 155
Attorney's fees:
  infringement, 267
  registration, 146
Audiovisual works:
  definition, 22
  registration, 154
Author, 11

Beneficial owner, 256
"Best edition":
  defined, 161
  see also Mandatory deposit; Registration
Brand name, see Trademark

Cable system:
  compulsory licensing, see Compulsory
    licensing
  definition, 93, 236
  see also Secondary transmissions
Catalog of Copyright Entries, see Copyright,
    status of
Choreographic works:
  defined, 19

registration, 154
Coin-operated phonorecord players:
  definition, 233
  see also License, compulsory
Collaborative creations, 37
  co-ownership, 37
  intention to create, 37
  joint works, 37
  ownership interest in, 38
  tenant in common, 38
Collective work:
  copyright notice, 131
  definition, 43
Commissioned works:
  defined, 42
  see also Works made for hire
Compilation:
  definition, 24
  preexisting material, 27
  work made for hire, 44
Complete defense, 148
Compulsory licensing:
  defined, 218, 226
  see also License
Computer programs:
  copyright notice, see Copyright notice
  definition, 97
  registration, 154
  see also Limitations on rights
Constructive notice:
  defined, 192
  recording documents, 192
  registration, 149
  transfer document, of facts in, 149

Contributions to periodicals:
  copyright notice, 131
  registration, 156
Coownership, *see* Collaborative creations
Copies:
  "best edition," *see* Mandatory deposit;
    Registration
  complete copies, *see* Mandatory deposit;
    Registration
  definition, 15
Copyright:
  defined, 5, 46, 47
  categories of material, 14
  claimant, 145, 159
  conditions of protection:
    country of first publication, 18
    creator's nationality, 18
  exclusive rights, 5, 46, 48
  invalidation, 132, 147
  notice, 5
    components, 6
    see also Copyright notice
  original work of authorship, 16
  owner, 5, 46
  ownership, 5, 46
  protection, 5, 46
  status of:
    Catalog of Copyright Entries, 149
    investigating, 149
  works, copyrightable, 5, 46
Copyright Act of 1976, 10
Copyright notice:
  additional information, in or around, 125
  advertisements, 132
  "all rights reserved," 119
  collective works, contributions to, 131
    errors in name, 131
  computer programs, 130
  date in, 120
    changing date, 120
    omission, 121
  dispersal of components, 129, 136
  errors in:
    date, 136, 138
    name, 131, 136
    infringement defense, 136
  form, 118
    pictorial, graphic and sculptural works,
      121
    prescribed versions, 118
    visually perceptible copies, 119
      components, 6, 119
    sound recordings, 122

    components, 122
    name of owner, 124
    United States Government works, 124
  infringement, affect on, 138, 265
  location and position, 127
  misleading effect, 117
  name in, 121
  omission, 132
    after January 1, 1979, 133
    innocent infringers, affect on, 138
    name or year, 136, 138
    owner mandated use, when, 135
    prior to January 1, 1978, 132
    registration, affect on, 134
    small number of copies, 133
  pictorial, graphic and sculptural works,
    130
  removal, 138, 252
    penalties for, 139
  requirements prior to January 1, 1978, 116
  size, 129
  sound recordings, 131
  use:
    fraudulent, 139, 252
    frequency, 129
Copyright Royalty Tribunal, 237, 238, 240
Creator, 11

Derivative work:
  definition, 24
  preexisting material, 25
  rights in:
    ownership of, 53
    recovering ownership, 214
Display works publicly, *see* Exclusive rights
Distribute copies or phonorecords publicly,
    see Exclusive rights
Dramatic works:
  defined, 19
  registration, 154

Educational copying and uses of music, *see*
    Fair use
Employee-employer relationship:
  definition, 39
  see also Works made for hire
Ephemeral recordings:
  definition, 94
  transmission program, 94
  see also Limitations on rights
Exclusive licensee:
  defined, 218
  rights acquired, 184, 218

see also License
Exclusive rights:
  authority to exercise, 47, 50
  defined, 5, 46, 48
  derivative works, creation of, 53
    all mediums, 53
    ownership of rights in, 53
    vary, alter, modify, or adapt, 53
  divisibility, 48, 219
  ownership, 47
    distinct from object, 47
  display publicly, 62
    copies, infringing and stolen, 64
    display:
      transmitting, repeating, or making to
        recur, 62, 63
      what constitutes, 62
    phonorecords, 64
      applicability to, 62
      "first sale" limitation, 63
      "lawfully made" copy, 63
      "public display," defined, 63
    rented, leased or loaned copies, display
      of, 64
    semipublic places, 63
  distribute publicly, 54
    copies or phonorecords:
      infringing, 57
      stolen, 57
    "first sale" limitation, 54
      rental, lease, or loan as, 56
    importation, 58
    "lawfully made copy or phonorecord,"
      55
    phonorecords embodying musical works,
      rental of, 57, 243
    sale, gift, rental, lease, control over, 54
    unauthorized importation, 58
  perform publicly, 59
    live and by broadcasting, 59
    performance, what constitutes, 59
    "public performance":
      defined, 60
      reciting, rendering, presenting,
        transmitting, 59
    semipublic places, 61
    sound recordings, pictorial, graphic, and
      sculptural works, 61
  right to reproduce, 50
    all mediums, 51
    control over reproducing only, 52
    purposes, private or commercial, 52
    reproduction, when it occurs, 50

source, from same, 50
scope of protection, 49

Fair use:
  copies for blind, 71
  definition, 67
  educational copying and uses of music, 70
  examples, 76
  factors to consider, 68
    amount and substantiality, 73
    effect of use, 74
    nature of work, 72
      entertaining, 73
      informational, 72
      limited circulation, unpublished,
        consumable, 72
    purpose and character, 68
  giving credit, 73
  guidelines for, 67
  incidental use, 70
  parody, 70
  taping, off-the-air audio and video, 70
Federal Patent Office, 6
"First sale," 54
"Fixed in tangible medium of expression,"
  16

Ideas, procedures, systems, 33
Identifying material, see Registration
Importation, unauthorized, 58
Independent contractor, see Works made for
  hire
Infringement:
  copyright notice, affect on, 138, 265
  courts, federal, 258
    proper court, determining, 259
    exception, 258
  defense to, 148, 252
    error in copyright notice, 136, 138
    giving credit as, 243
    ownership of copy or phonorecord as,
      243
    profit motive, copying small portions,
      244
  examples, 242
  exclusive licensee, enforcement of rights,
    221
  innocent infringers, 148
  intent as factor, 243
  notice, giving, 260
  offenses, criminal, 252
  penalties, criminal, 268
  persons entitled to institute action:

Infringement (*Continued*)
    Copyright Office, 254
    legal or beneficial owner, 255
        beneficial owner, 256
        legal owner, definition, 255
    nonexclusive licensee, 256
    persons immune from liability, 245
    persons liable for, 242
        employers and owners of places of
            entertainment, 245
        infringement by another party, causing,
            244
        officers of corporations, 246
        persons who aid others, 247
        principals of businesses, 246
        two or more infringers, 266
    recording documents, *see* Recording
            documents, required for
    remedies for:
        attorney's fees and costs of action, 267
        destruction or disposition of copies, 263
        impounding copies, 263
        injunctive relief, 261
            permanent injunction, 262
            temporary injunction, 262
        money damages:
            actual damages and profits, 264
            statutory damages, 265
                factors in determining, 266
                minimum and maximum amounts,
                    267
    requirements:
        to establish:
            abstractions test, 251
            certificate of registration, 247
            opportunity to copy, showing of, 248
            ownership of work/unauthorized
                exercise, 247
            substantial similarity, 248
                amount of, 249, 250
                pattern, 250
                procedure used to determine, 251
        to institute action for:
            recordation, transfer documents, 257
            registration, 145, 256
            exceptions, 257
    time for instituting action, limitation on,
            259
Initial copyright owner, 36
Injunctive relief, *see* Infringement, remedies
        for
Investigating copyright status of work, 149

Joint works:
    defined, 37
    see also Collaborative creations
Jukebox, *see* Coin-operated phonorecord
        players

Lanham Act, *see* Trademark Act of 1946
"Lawfully made copy or phonorecord," 63
Legal owner, definition, 255
Libraries and archives, *see* Limitations on
        rights
License:
    compulsory, 218, 227
        background, 227
        types, 227
            jukeboxes, public performance of
                music on, 233
            coin-operated phonorecord players,
                233
            operator, 234
            procedure to obtain, 234
        noncommercial educational
                broadcasting, 238
            procedure to obtain, 239
        nondramatic musical works,
                phonorecords embodying, 229
            arrangements, permissible, 231
            monthly statement of account, 232
            procedure to obtain, 232
            reproduction, permissible ways, 230
            statutory royalty, 232
        secondary transmissions, cable
                systems, 235
            cable system, 236
            definition, 237
            Initial Notice of Identity and Signal
                Carriage Complement, 237
            performances or displays,
                permissible, 236
            primary transmissions, 236
            procedure to obtain, 237
            requirements, for obtaining, 235
            royalty, 237
            royalty recipients, 237
            Statement of Account, 237
    defined, 217
    exclusive licensee, 218, 255
        authority to register, 221
        infringement action, entitled to enforce
            rights, 221
        recording of, 220
        right of termination, subject to, 222

licensed rights, 217
licensee, 217
licensing, 217
licensor, 217
  mechanical license, 228, 232
  nonexclusive licensee, 217, 256
  performing rights organizations, 232
  provisions of, 222
  writing, should be in, 219
    Statute of Frauds, 219
Limitations on rights:
  commercial rental, leasing, or lending
       phonorecords, 57
  defined, 78
  fair use, see Fair use
  libraries and archives, 90
    "warning of copyright," 91
  pictorial, graphic, and sculptural works,
       89
  secondary transmissions, 92
  sound recordings, 88, 89
  statutory limitations, 79
    broadcasting:
      instructional, 81
      noncommercial educational, 95
    broadcasts:
      noncommercial to blind or deaf, 86, 87
      reception, 84
    computer programs, 97
    ephemeral recordings, 94
    fairs, agricultural and horticultural, 85
    performances:
      and displays, certain kinds, 80
      nonprofit, 83
      religious services, 82
      records, retail sale of, 85
      teaching, face to face, 80
      veterans'/fraternal organizations,
           nonprofit, 87
Literary work:
  definition, 20
  registration, 154

Mandatory deposit:
  copies:
    nature of, 176
    number required, 174
  defined, 173
  exempt material, 177
  forms and fees, 175
  registration:
    independent of, 142, 173

  relationship to, 175
  sanctions, failure to comply, 174
  transmission programs, unpublished, 178
  works affected, 174
Mechanical license:
  defined, 228, 232
  see also License
Monthly statement of account, 232
Motion picture:
  definition, 22
  registration, 154
Musical works:
  defined, 19
  registration, 154
  see also Works

Noncommercial educational broadcasting:
  definition, 96
  licensing, 238
  public broadcasting entity, defined, 96
  see also Limitations on rights
Nonexclusive licensee, see License
Notice of termination, see Recovery of rights

Obscene material, 28
Official certification, see Recording
       documents, requirements
Original, 17, 18
"Original work of authorship," 16

Pantomimes:
  defined, 9
  registration, 154
Patent:
  exclusive rights, 7
  grant, 6
  owner, 6
  ownership, 6
  "patent applied for," 7
  patented invention, 6
  "patent pending," 7
  protection, 6, 7
Performing rights organization, 232
Perform works publicly, see Exclusive rights,
       perform publicly
Period of protection:
  anonymous work, 103
  maximum periods, 100
    factors affecting, 101
    life of creator, 103
      statement of death, 105
    one hundred years, 111

Period of protection (Continued)
  anonymous and pseudonymous works, 112
  work made for hire, 112
  seventy-five years, 106
  anonymous and pseudonymous works, 107
  contribution to periodical, 111
  posthumous work, 110
  renewal requirement, 109
  works:
    made for hire, 107
    protected under 1909 Act, 108
    registered between 1950 and 1978, 109
  pseudonymous work, 103
  publication, effect on, 102
Phonorecords, definition, 15
Pictorial, graphic and sculptural works:
  copyright notice, 121
  definition, 20
  limitations on rights, see Limitations on rights
  perform publicly, right to, 61
  registration, 155
Plots, thematic concepts, characters, 34
Posthumous work:
  definition, 110
  see also Renewal
Primary transmission, definition, 92, 236
Procedures, processes, systems, methods of operation, 33
  defined, 102

Recording documents:
  exclusive license, 220
  failure to timely record, 194
  nonexclusive licensee, effect on, 196
  ownership transfers, 191
  required, for:
    constructive notice, 192
    infringement defense, to defeat, 193
    rights, enforcement of, 191, 257
    transfer, priority of first, 193, 195
  requirements:
    complete document, 197
    identification of work, 196
    official certification, 198
    signature of transferor, 197
    sworn certification, 197
  time periods for, 194
Recovery of rights:
  defined, 199

derivative works, affected by, 214
grants subject to, 208
notice of termination, 199, 205
  failure to give, or timely give, 207, 211
  when served, 205
right of termination, 199
  coverage, 201
  exceptions to, 202
  grants:
    by persons other than creator, 203
    by will, 203
  works:
    made for hire, 202
    protected under foreign laws, 202
  exclusive licenses, subject to, 222
  persons entitled to, 203, 209
    creators, two or more, 204
    creator's family, 204
  procedure to exercise, 205, 210
  renewal term, 208
  waiver or contracting away, 207, 211
recovery:
  exercise of rights after, 212
  further grants, ability to make after, 212
    when effective, 213
    who can make, 213
    who is bound by, 213
  individuals entitled to, 212
termination:
  date, 206, 210
  after January 1, 1976, 201
  prior to 1976 Act, 200
  time of, 211
"Registered United States Patent & Trademark Office", 8
Registration:
  application, examination of, 170
  basic registration, 144
  certificate, 172
  copyright claimant, 145
  defined, 141
  deposit material:
    "best edition," 161
    complete copy, 161
    number required, 160, 162
    reproductions, obtaining, 168
    return and disposition, 167
  exclusive licensee, authority to register, 221
  filing fees, 169
  forms, application:
    how to obtain, 152
    information required, 158

versions:
  contributions to periodicals, 156
  correct and amplify, 155
    amplification, defined, 156
    correction, defined, 156
  nondramatic literary, 154
  performing arts, 154
  renewal, 157
  serials, 155
  sound recordings, 154
  visual arts, 155
  identifying material:
    defined, 165
    specifications, 165
omission of notice, see Copyright notice
owner's election, 6
persons entitled to, 143
reasons for:
  certificate, prima facie evidence, 146,
    247
  constructive notice, 149
  error in notice, 148
  invalidation of rights, avoids, 147
  rights enforcement, prerequisite, 145,
    147
  statutory damages and attorneys fees,
    146
renewal, 157
required, when, 142
special handling, 170
time for, 142
Renewal:
  application, 109
  claimant, 109
  contribution to periodical, 111
  posthumous work, 110
  registration, 157
  rights, recovering ownership of, 199
  see also Period of protection
Reproduction of works, see Exclusive rights,
    right to reproduce
Right of publicity, 9
Right of termination, see Recovery of rights
Royalty, 237

Secondary transmissions:
  broadcast signal common carriers, 93
  cable systems, 92, 93
  compulsory licensing, 93. See also
    Compulsory licensing
  definition, 92, 237
  governmental bodies and nonprofit
    organizations, 93

hotels and apartment houses, 93
limitations, see Limitations on rights
Serial, 155
Service mark, 8
Sound recordings:
  copyright notice, 131
  definition, 23
  limitations on rights, see Limitation on
    rights
  perform publicly, right to, 61
  registration, 154
  Sound Recording Amendment of 1971, 23
Specially ordered works, see Works made for
    hire
Statement of account, 237
Statement of death:
  certified report, 105
  see also Period of protection
Statute of limitations, see Infringement,
    time for instituting action
Statutory damages:
  defined, 265
  registration, 146
  see also Infringement, remedies for
Statutory royalty, see License, compulsory
Substantial similarity, see Infringement,
    requirements to establish
Supplementary work, see Works made for
    hire
Sworn certification, see Recording
    documents, requirements

Tax considerations, rights, creating,
    licensing, and transferring, 271
  capital gain, 274
  expenses:
    capitalized, 273
    deductible, 273
  ordinary income, 275
  profit-generating activities, 271
Teachers and professors, see Works made for
    hire
Trademark:
  brand name, 8
  definition, 8
  exclusive rights, 8
  owner, 7
  ownership, 7
  protection, 7
  "Registered United States Patent &
    Trademark Office", 8
  service mark, 8
  symbol R, 8

Trademark (Continued)
  "TM," 8
Trademark Act of 1946, 9
Transfer of rights:
  coowners, transfers by, 183
  copies and phonorecords, transfer of
        distinguished from, 182
  death, upon:
    bequest by will, 185
    intestate succession, 185
  definition, 184
  examples, 183
  exclusive licensee, rights acquired, 184,
        218
  exclusive rights, separately transferable,
        182
  general rule, 180
  involuntary, prohibitions on, 186
  operation of law by, 185
  requirements:
    intent to transfer, 187
    notarization, 187
    signature by owner, 187
    writing, 186
  rights acquired, 188, 189
    nonexclusive licensee, 189
  types of:
    exclusive license, 185
    mortgage, 185
    pledge, 185
    security interest, 185
Transmission, defined, 92
Transmission program:
  defined, 94
  mandatory deposit, 178
Transmit performance, 59
Transmitting organization, 94

United States Copyright Office, 6
United States Government works, 32
  copyright notice, 124
  defined, 32
Useful article, 21

Varying, altering, or modifying works, 53

"Warning of copyright," see Limitations on
        rights, libraries and archives
Works, 11, 15
  anonymous, see Anonymous works
  applied art, 21
  audiovisual, 22
  compilation, 24
  choreographic, 19
  derivative, 24
  dramatic, 19
  literary, 20
  motion pictures, 22
  musical, 19
  1909 Act, protected under, 108, 109
  pantomimes, 9
  pictorial, graphic and sculptural, 20
  posthumous, 10
  pseudonymous, see Pseudonymous work
  published, 102
  registered between 1970 and 1978, 108,
        109
  sound recordings, 23
  United States Government works, 32
Works made for hire:
  commissioned works, 42
    atlas, 44
    collective works, 43
    compilation, 44
    independent contractor, 42
    instructional texts, 44
    requirements for, 43
    tests, 44
      answer material for, 44
  defined, 39
  employee-employer relationship, 39
    employee's rights, 40, 41
    scope of employment, 41
  factors determining, 40
  general rule of ownership, exception to,
        39
  independent contractor, 39, 40, 42
  period of protection, 107, 112
  specially ordered works, 43
  supplementary works, 44
  teachers and professors, 42